The Changing
Mental Health Scene

The Changing
Mental Health Scene

Edited by RALPH G. HIRSCHOWITZ, M.D.
and BERNARD LEVY, M.D.,
both of Harvard University School of Medicine

S P Books Division of
SPECTRUM PUBLICATIONS, INC.
New York

Distributed by Halsted Press
A Division of John Wiley & Sons

New York   Toronto   London   Sydney

SPECTRUM PUBLICATIONS, INC.
86-19 Sancho Street, Holliswood, N.Y. 11423

Distributed solely by the Halsted Press division of John Wiley & Sons, Inc., New York

Library of Congress Cataloging in Publication Data

Main entry under title:

The changing mental health scene.

    Includes bibliographical references.
    1. Mental health services--United States.
2. Psychiatry–Philosophy. I. Hirschowitz, Ralph G.
II. Levy, Bernard, 1936- [DNLM: 1. Mental health
services–U. S. WM30 C456]
RA790.6.C4   362.2'0973   75-42398
ISBN 0-470-14981-7

Contributors

PAUL R. AHR
Mental Health and Mental Retardation
Commonwealth of Virginia

JUNE JACKSON CHRISTMAS
Department of Mental Health
    and Mental Retardation Services
New York City

ALFRED W. CLARK
Tavistock Institute of Human Relations
London

HORRIS HANSELL
Department of Psychiatry
Northwestern University
Chicago

RALPH G. HIRSCHOWITZ
Department of Psychiatry
Harvard Medical School

SHARON HUNT
West Virginia University

MAXWELL JONES
Fort Logan Mental Health Center
Denver, Colorado

GERALD L. KLERMAN
Harvard Medical School

A. LEFEBVRE
Department of Psychiatry
University of Toronto

MORTON A. LIBERMAN
University of Chicago

ROGER F. MALEY
West Virginia University

FRANCIS DE MARNEFFE
McLean Hospital
Belmont, Massachusetts

WERNER M. MENDEL
Department of Psychiatry
University of Southern California
    School of Medicine

E. MANSELL PATTISON
Department of Psychiatry
    and Human Behavior
University of California, Irvine

NORMAN P. PETERSON
Northwestern Hospital Service
Thief River Falls, Minnesota

VIVIAN M. RAKOFF
Department of Psychiatry
University of Toronto

SANDRA RASMUSSEN
Department of Mental Health
Boston, Massachusetts

PHYLLIS R. SILVERMAN
Laboratory of Community Psychiatry
Harvard Medical School

MAURICE VANDERPOL
McLean Hospital
Belmont, Massachusetts

ROLAND L. WARREN
Brandeis University
Waltham, Massachusetts

STEPHEN L. WASHBURN
McLean Hospital
Belmont, Massachusetts

BOB WILLIAMS
Orange County Mental Health Department
California

RONALD C. YOUNG
Commissioner's Office
Department of Public Welfare
Minnesota

CONTENTS

Part I

Introduction

The mental health scene has changed significantly in the past two decades and continues to do so. Polemical debates, punctuated by the impassioned advocacy of consumer interests, sometimes obscure the reality of the quiet revolution that has already occurred. The reality of this revolution is evidenced by the fact that the behavior of the mentally ill no longer arouses the automatic extrusive community responses of yesteryear. Behavior is better understood and a more sophisticated public now sees extrusion as only one of many possible regulatory responses. At the same time, the future is uncertain. The specter of national health insurance haunts the human service scene, and the only present certainty is the certainty of continuing change.

There have been changes in *social* definition of mental illness, reflected in the widening of the boundaries of accepted behavior, and more tightly circumscribed *legal* definitions of mental illness. The "right to treatment" has been asserted in dramatic redefinitions of individual rights. This has included the right to information, the exercise of informed consent, and the right to refuse treatment. (The past few years have seen precedent-creating adjudication on behalf of patient plantiffs in states as separate as Alabama and Michigan.)

New laws regulating involuntary commitment to mental health facilities have produced dramatic changes. In the first twelve months of the operation of Chapter 123 of the 1970 Mental Health Reform Act of Massachusetts, involuntary admissions to state mental hospital declined from 76 percent to 27 percent.

Changes have been multiple and interdependent, involving such dimensions as: the site of care, the content of care, the delivery, the deliverers and the models which inform the thought and action of providers, consumers and the general public. Changes in attitude have occurred within the still larger context of ideological change in the entire society. This ideological drift has been persuasively discussed in a recent paper by Lodge (Lodge, 1974). Of particular interest to human services is a movement in the society from the supremacy of rights of property to rights of social membership.

In the years immediately following the Second World War, services in the United States were starkly dichotomized: private market services (to those able and willing to pay) and public mental health services. In disproportionately large numbers, the consumers of public mental health services were poor, uneducated, unmarried or separated. They often lacked external resources and attachments, and/or suffered from the internal resource deficit occasioned by psychological damage, disease or defect. The particular implications of class position were analyzed in studies by Hollingshead and Redlich (1958) with subsequent follow-up by Myers and Roberts (1968). Many other studies corroborate a continuing relationship between low social class and poor treatment outcome. Social position influences professionals' diagnostic and prognostic behavior, decisions about treatment and, ultimately, both short and long-term outcome. The poor especially those bereft of attachments, stay longer in institutions and return more frequently. It is apparent that two service systems, "private market" and "public," provide parallel (but unequal) services. Troubled persons with adequate financial and social resources are treated in service systems endowed with disproportionately rich psychiatric resources, while the poor are serviced in "total institutions" where professional expertise is at a premium.

Following the Second World War, this service dichotomy became more visible to an enlightened citizenry. The change advocacy of mental health associations was strengthened by the development of new approaches in Britain and Europe. With this awareness, both citizen and professional advocates mobilized to improve public mental health services here. The influence of the "open hospital" movement rapidly spread to this side of the Atlantic.

A reference group of psychiatric "young Turks" mobilized as the Group for Advancement of Psychiatry. This had a salutary influence on psychiatric training programs. The creation of the National Institute of Mental Health provided a further spur. The experience of psychiatrists returning from military theaters brought an appreciation for the importance of social support in the management of mental illness. The principles of military psychiatry, first enunciated by Salmon as proximity, immediacy and expectancy, were refined in World War II and Korea and seen to be equally relevant for civilian service. However, while these principles were taught in residency training programs that attempted to place a priority upon the management of *major* mental illness, it became apparent that some elite mental health professional schools continued to produce professionals whose socialization and training exposure destined them to deal with problems of *minor*, not major, morbidity. Since training programs in mental health have received strong infusions of federal money, training schools have been called to account for their failure to produce professionals able and willing to serve our most severely disabled psychiatric casualties.

In the wake of European changes in institutional practice, some mental hospitals became more "open." Programs attacked institutionalization and attempted to develop alternatives to the total institution. This "social psychiatry"* movement,

---

*Imported from England as "social psychiatry," these practices became incorporated here as "community psychiatry" or "community mental health"; "social psychiatry" came to connote research rather than action endeavors.

with its melioristic approach to the mentally ill, gained impetus from (but was chronologically followed by) the advent of psychotropic medication. These simultaneous developments renewed the confidence of citizens and professionals in psychiatry's redemptive potential.

In 1955, Congress responded to the postwar pressures for improvement of services by appointing a Joint Commission on Mental Illness and Health to study the care of the mentally ill and to recommend changes. The commission's report was submitted to Congress in 1960 (and published as *Action for Mental Health* in 1961). Recommendations included: decentralization of institutions; the provision of services by smaller (noninstitutional) facilities; the upgrading of existing services and the determined development of alternatives to institutional care. The report was sympathetically received. President Kennedy heralded "a wholly new emphasis and approach to care for the mentally ill" in the recommendations to Congress which culminated in the Community Mental Health Centers Act of 1963. The Act provided financial support for community mental health centers; community mental health rapidly became the public mental health watchword of the sixties. While these centers remain inadequate in number (and, sometimes, quality) in discharging their mandate to provide comprehensive community mental health services to the *total* population, they have nonetheless ushered in a new era in psychiatric services. Enduring changes have occurred in the ideology and practice of many professionals and in the attitudes and expectations of citizens. Evidence for this shift is available from recent ideological studies. In some areas of the nation, the community mental health ideology has received more support from enlightened citizens than from professionals reared in the "two culture" tradition.

PSYCHIATRY'S RESPONSE TO THE CHALLENGE OF CHANGE

The past three decades have thus challenged psychiatry's service, training and research systems on multiple fronts. Consumers, once placid and predictable, ever "patient," have mobilized to influence public mental health policy through many channels, including formal citizen participation. They have voiced expectations and preferences which have often been alien and perplexing to professionals. Professionals—and professionalism—have been called into question as never before. In addition to challenging the theoretical assumptions and practices of professionals there has been criticism of the paternalistic posture of those professionals who habitually make decisions *for*, not *with*, their clients. (This posture has been simultaneously questioned in all people who carry socially ascribed authority in this society. Harris has reported declining confidence in business and political leaders as well as physicians and psychiatrists in polls conducted over the past decade.)

Guild-protected professionalism has come under severe assault, particularly when the allocation of public monies has been encumbered by mandatory "citizen participation." Citizen pressures have produced changes in the funding environments for service, training and research and in the ordering of public policy priorities for NIMH. Punctuated by internal strain and dissonance, the mental health professions' elitism is gradually yielding to acceptance of the participation of its relevant publics. A new pluralism and interactive engagement with public constituencies is developing as organized constituencies and protest groups push for services *they* define as relevant to their needs. From within professional ranks, the workers closest to these constituencies are attempting to respond to these newly declared (or heard) needs by the development of innovative services. However, many of these "cutting edge" adaptive innovations have yet to be incorporated into the mainstream of psychiatric service delivery. Often, professionals who have limited interaction with community or consumer groups are strongly resistant to any significant change in their practice or posture. This conservatism has been discussed by Vickers: "They [human beings] have extraordinary and growing powers on the one hand to predict the future course of events and on the other hand to alter it. The first is the gift of science, the second of technology." He points out that these may have opposite effects: "The first [science] with its capacity for prediction and mastery should make men the most adaptable of creatures; the second makes them the least ready to adapt, for when they encounter limitation, their tendency is not to adapt to it but to alter the limitation. For other creatures the natural environment is almost wholly constant or independently variable. Not so for man. He can effect it, as much as it can effect him. Clearly a system containing creatures which deal with limitations in this way cannot attain stabilities which other systems attain. Other creatures work out their dynamic balance within a framework of limitations; 'western' men change the framework to suit themselves and they are proud of it. They believe that they have escaped from a stable into an expanding world. *They need not adapt to their environment, so long as they can adapt the environment to themselves.* This statement explains the behavior of those health and mental health professionals who have attempted to control their consumer environments, rather than develop new responses to the adaptive challenges thrust at them since the Second World War. From a strong base of power and influence, some psychiatrists and allied professionals have united to fight change. In so doing, they have at times rationalized the protection of their vested interests as synonymous with the "best interests" of the public. When confronted with demands for "citizen participation," with its expectations of citizen involvement in policy, accountability and quality control, the professionals have often closed their ranks to resist the threat of such public scrutiny. Within professional ranks, between the professionals and their citizen consumers and amongst these consumers, there are many differences and little common ground. Interaction and integrative leadership are sorely needed to pursue the orchestration of these many differences.

While the service environments and public sanctioning bases for mental health are multiplying, the demands that emanate from them remain perplexing, contradictory and confusing. Some professionals have attempted, as Vickers suggests, to "adapt the environment to themselves," by attempts at control. These have been met by efforts at countercontrol. Other professionals have withdrawn from the emotional minefield of community involvement to the shelter of ivory towers or office practice. More prescient leaders have demonstrated that man *can* be "the most adaptable of creatures." They have engaged their public, referring and consumer constituencies in reciprocal and reciprocating commerce. In a spirit of constructive adaptation, agreements have been made and appropriate roles for citizens and professionals negotiated so that mutual advantages accrue and "ownership" of programs is shared. Leaders who have developed programs of this kind have been proactive and interactive. Unlike the "Hamlets," satirized by Warren, they have accepted the necessity for political involvement and equity development in "doing business" with their relevant environments.

On the changing mental health scene, therefore, there are ample case studies of emerging patterns of adaptation to the challenges of the seventies. There is abundant new knowledge and skill, clinical and sociotechnical, evident in these adaptive programs. These adaptive patterns emerge at a pace so rapid that dissemination lags behind their development. In addition, it is difficult for the concerned professional to keep abreast of what is published and to separate what is relevant and significant from the humdrum. It is even more difficult to discriminate between the written rhetoric and the actual reality of some programs. It is also necessary to discriminate between a program heavily dependent upon extraordinary resource allocations and rare, often charismatic leadership and the more useful program that can be replicated with "average, expectable" resources.

Given the professional interest in new knowledge and the difficulty with which program descriptions can be unearthed in the professional literature, or programs explored by field visits, we bring together in this volume descriptions of recent advances in service delivery. Chapters have been commissioned to avoid the duplication of previously published papers, to reduce redundancy or overlap and to pursue coherence. This book is addressed to all mental health professionals, being of equal relevance to workers giving direct service to individuals and families or to administrators responsible for service programs to large populations.

We have particularly sought contributors who exemplify the leadership demanded by our times: tolerance for ambiguity; proactive vision; flexible adaptation and readiness for interaction. We have also selected contributors who are scientists capable of objective analysis of their own operations and flexible enough to acknowledge and learn from error, and who are more concerned with framing relevant questions than prescribing answers for questions of little or diminished relevance.

As Vickers implies, there is "no way" by which we can control our environments so that *we* need not change. The demand for adaptive change is unequivocally upon us. Our volume therefore offers paradigms of *adaptation* to these inescapable change demands. In our coping, we need to be particularly concerned about the stresses upon the leaders who regulate the interfaces between

6

our organizations and their changing political, financial, sociotechnical and competitive environments. A new breed of leader is evolving, able and willing to take the stands that are required in these perplexing times. We will need more such leaders, in touch with the times, with the future and with us. Such a leader is not a paternocrat, abdicrat or oscillocrat; he invites—and we, perforce, must learn interactive engagement with him so that decisions involve our participation and the leader functions in genuine "representative" fashion. Both he, and we, will need to repair past failures to engage decisively and forthrightly in the business and politics of our profession. Our past posture still threatens us with obsolescence and impotence in the public domain.

Our volume therefore concludes with a section on the clinician-executive and the unique demands upon him. In consequence, we hope that the "executive role" of leaders will be better appreciated, supported and practiced. Without adaptive leaders, the professions are doomed to lag, not lead. We may well surrender our rights of governance to the publics whose confidence we have eroded and whose pleas for the renewal of credibility we run the risk of ignoring.

BIBLIOGRAPHY

Hollingshead, A.B., and Redlich, F.C. *Social Class and Mental Illness*. New York: Wiley, 1958.
Lodge, G.C. Business and the changing society. *Harvard Business Review*, 1974, 52-2, 59-72.
Myers, J.K., and Bean, L.L. *A Decade Later*. New York: Wiley, 1968.
Vickers, G. *Value Systems and Social Process*. London: Pelican, 1970, p. 40

Part II

Mental Health Programs: Changing Perspectives and Emerging Alternatives

In this section, we explore changing patterns of service delivery in public mental health practice. New programs and priorities have been influenced by citizens and mandated by legislatures. (A salient example is California's recent legislation on ECT regulations.) Innovation has also originated within the mental health professions, reflecting new technologies and ideologies. Against this background, we focus in this section upon two dynamic trends: the waning of the total institution and the growth of multiple modalities of alternative care.

In the "bandwagon" response to changing public mandates, some attempts to "go community" have floundered; we analyze the causes for such failure. These include the fact that hospitals have at times been closed—or their patients precipitously discharged—with little regard for the sentiments of community groups or care-giving agencies. The planning of change has often occurred without appreciation for the participative engagement demanded by today's communities. When hospital change has been introduced coercively, patients and professionals, denied the opportunity to voice their opposition actively, have sabotaged change efforts in passive, indirect ways. We have included here an evaluation of the impact of impulsively conceived discharge upon mental hospital patients, along with a consideration of a countervailing, systematic, planned approach to deinstitutionalization.

Many aspects of strategy and planning are discussed. These include the encouragement of voluntary participation and collaborative planning in the trapeze jump of patients from one service context to another. These processes are captured in this section's final chapter on the development of a comprehensive mental health center. The authors describe an interactive planning *process* in which alliances were built with community groups and professional agencies to forge a support base for the growth of innovative services.

Hirschowitz defines and discusses the institutional condition, emphasizing its multifactorial complexity. While addressing the issue of individual susceptibility, he focuses his attention upon those aspects of the institutionalizing field of forces where corrective leverage can be applied: the organization's structure and culture.

He outlines a conceptual model that details the process by which the institutional condition becomes grafted on to the mental hospital patient's presenting problems.

8

This model can guide the planning of the program administrator who attempts to reverse institutionalizing patterns or to prevent their occurrence. Because of the constraints upon institutional resources, he offers detailed suggestions for optimizing the deployment of institutional staff. Given the scarcity of seasoned professionals, he describes an echelon level structure in which nonprofessionals play direct service roles with the back-up support and supervision of professionals. He emphasizes the need for individualization with graduated stepladders designed for each patient's rehabilitation. He warns that carefully planned programs and strategies, with realistic goals, realistically monitored, are the only effective antidotes to community restoration programs based on the shifting sands of idealistic rhetoric. He also emphasizes the continuity vehicles and bridges required to sustain the impetus of movement as, and after, the patient returns to the community.

Our next chapter, by Rose, presents data illustrative of some of the pitfalls discussed by Hirschowitz. Tracking the fate of a cohort of patients recently discharged from a mental hospital, he describes the differing perceptions of their needs and condition by the hospital staff, the research staff and the patients themselves. Their high recidivism rate and "benign neglect" in the community can be partly attributed to failure on the part of this hospital's professionals to apply a community mental health technology. They appeared to have moved with fashionable impetuosity from long-established patterns of benign custodialism to newly mandated "revolving door" policies.

Rose highlights the apparent naïveté of the hospital's decision makers whose "dispositions" for patients appeared to ignore two significant realities: preparation and remotivation for the patients; and the building of enough resource capacity and commitment in the community to provide continuing care. They appear to have been selectively inattentive to what the "community," actualized through its nursing homes, boarding homes and foster homes, was actually able and willing to provide.

Many of Rose's subjects pined for the "country club" features of their mental hospital, which was apparently well endowed with recreational amenities. This raises questions of crucial public policy relevance. When does a legitimate need for asylum, recuperation and sanctuary become illegitimate exploitation—of patient by hospital or of hospital by patient? By what criteria, and with whose authority, should patients be denied the gratification of "shelter" care, which, by Rose's description, may become a more appealing reality to him than any "community" alternative? What "asylum" alternatives should continue to be available to those chronically ill mental patients who can only function in protected settings? In our zeal to dismantle the bureau-pathologized mental hospital, have we failed to confront this moral and ethical dilemma?

Washburn's chapter describes both a *program* and its systematic evaluation. He has evaluated the impact of his partial hospital program on its consumers and has compared outcomes and cost-effectiveness with a control group of inpatient subjects. He has followed many patients for more than four years. This long-term data-based perspective has facilitated successive refinement of criteria to determine what populations are best served by what type of partial-care program. Washburn compares his findings with those of other contemporary contributors to knowledge of the day hospital's potential.

In commenting on professional resistance to program innovation, he reports that many established professionals in his own hospital, when apprised of the potential of the day hospital program, declined to refer appropriate patients. Similarly, he points out that patients may needlessly enter an inpatient service, because professionals abet patient's relatives in their impulsive "wanting out" of situations temporarily contaminated by the contagious crisis behavior of over-whelmed patients. He recognizes the clear implication that workers in alternative programs must be willing to engage and guide the patient's "significant others" so that they support—and do not sabotage—therapeutic endeavors.

The data from Washburn's careful evaluation have relevance for the fiscal policies of health insurers and the allocation policies of citizen boards and legislators in the public mental health field.

In Mendel's chapter on a nonhospital patient care program, he elaborates the position he has maintained resolutely in recent years: that it is possible to serve the mentally ill without recourse to 24-hour "hospitalization." He presents his rationale for a "flexible and responsive nonhospital patient care program."

He deals with the reimbursement difficulties that presently impede innovative programming. He notes, with Washburn, that the reinbursement policies of third-party payers do not reward innovation and serve to maintain the existing unsatisfactory, costly, hospital-based pattern of service delivery. In attacking this sociotechnical "lag," he emphasizes the need for public education and political lobbying. In informing the general public of quality alternatives to the inpatient model, he presses for the demythologizing of existing service operations. He suggests that commonsense evaluation with instruments like Kiresuk's Goal Attainment Scale could contribute to this. In a final emphasis, he notes the significant potential for all forms of prevention, including primary, in population oriented programs that are supported by capitation fees.

Rakoff's chapter is a careful essay on the needs of patients with severe degrees of biopsychosocial deficit. He maintains that "community discharge" from the institutions may be a hollow statistical legerdemain concealing the fact that "community care" has often degenerated into mini-institutionalization. He dis-cusses evidence to support this position from a study of Canadian foster homes.

In advocating the "rights of patienthood" for these sufferers in need of semipermanent shelter care, Rakoff takes issue with Mendel. In fact, he has debated Mendel on more than one public platform in both Canada and the United States. The debate is an important one, and we have considered their antithetical views to be of sufficient importance to include in this volume. We deem it important for the debate to be kept open in the hope that data-based inquiry will curb whatever excesses may inhere in either position, so that considered public policy may follow.

Young, Williams and Peterson describe the development of a community mental health program into which a day-night general hospital unit was subsequently incorporated. The move from conception through gestation to delivery is detailed in steps that began with some failed insemination by consultants who spurted ideas of heady irrelevance into the "ionosphere." More realistic development occurred when they visited programs that appeared more relevant to their unique rural needs. They learned from others' mistakes and ultimately carefully fashioned a program tailored to local felt need. From early inception, there was involvement of community influentials, agencies and caregivers.

The authors document the careful integration of the day-night psychiatric unit into two overlapping suprasystems: the general hospital which housed the unit and the community mental health program of which it was a federally supported component. They provide many illustrations of the "boundary spanning" needed between program subsystems, overarching supraordinate systems and the coordinate community agencies, care givers and influentials from which sanction and support are drawn.

Their program is distinguished for the quality of its operational research; multiple feedback loops alerted them promptly to needed changes in tack, tactic or policy. Their pragmatic correction for error—enlarging and developing direct and indirect service constituencies as they went—is illuminating. They also planned for the future, proactively assuring programmatic self-sufficiency in anticipation of waning federal funds. Their leadership was strengthened by involving board members in the development of widely sanctioned criteria for evaluation and accountability.

1

The Attack on the Institutional Condition

RALPH G. HIRSCHOWITZ

BACKGROUND

In this chapter, we discuss factors that contribute to the institutional condition and strategies to combat it. The institutional condition is multidetermined: biological and psychological factors determine individual susceptibility; the social context and culture define positions, rules and roles in the institution. Approaches to the institutional condition thus require an appreciation of the interplay between its biopsychological and sociocultural determinants. Our term, "institutionalism" (1955) and the American Public Health Association's "social breakdown syndrome" (1962).

Some of the features of the institutional condition were described by Barton (1966) as: apathy, lack of initiative, loss of interest, submissiveness, inability to plan for the future, lack of individuality, and "sometimes, atypical posture and gait." While Barton's choice of the label "institutional neurosis" implied a condition *internal* to the psychological skin, his intervention addressed the *external* institutionalizing pressures which, in his view, generated institutional neurosis. This view was buttressed by his valuable observation that the institutional condition was not confined to the mental hospital and occured also in prisons, sanatoria, leprosaria, nunneries and monasteries. In his work as a hospital superintendent, Barton demonstrated that institutional neurosis could be remedied by radical modification of institutional procedures and staff behavior. The effectiveness of his approach to de-institutionalization was independently confirmed by the research studies of Wing and Brown (1970).

Goffman in his work on "asylums" described how the institution's socializing norms influenced "patient" role behavior. His writings attested to the adaptive resilience of those institution-resistant inmates who retain some sense of self while "playing the system" to fulfill the role demands of the institution. Kesey described a fictional struggle between such an inmate and the "system's" socializing agents (1962).

After the Second World War, Martin made an important contribution to our knowledge of the institutional condition in a paper on "institutionalism" (1955). He emphasized that infantilizing, overprotective, overcontrolling authoritarianism of hospital staff made dependent submission by patients inevitable. This had the further malignant effect of extinguishing existing, or nascent, individuality and initiative. In his analysis, he attributed considerable significance to the hospital's traditional overvaluation of tidiness, cleanliness and orderliness. He concluded that institutionalism could be combated by the selective recruitment of "men and women sufficiently independent and integrated to replace an authoritarian system by real human relationships."

Independently of his work together with Brown, Wing (1962) distinguished the behavior characteristic of chronic schizophrenia in pure culture from that of the institutional condition with which it often coexisted. He succeeded in demonstrating that the two conditions could occur quite independently of one another. (Wing's data are presented with descriptive clarity. By contrast, the boundaries between paranoid schizophrenia and the institutional condition are insufficiently delineated in American work on the "social breakdown syndrome.") Wing clarified the interplay of three critical variables in the institutional condition: individual vulnerability or susceptibility; the duration of institutionalization and the institutionalizing forces of the social system. Factors influencing individual susceptibility were also analyzed in a paper by Scheflen (1965).

In papers based on their Weyburn Hospital experience, Sommer and Ross (1962) discussed "chronicity." They described the movement from the front to the back wards of the mental hospital as forging links in a "chain of chronicity." This chain was seen to bind the patient into an ever-tightening, self-fulfilling prophecy of "back wards patient" deterioration. This concept of a chain or "code" of chronicity has been incorporated in the chain-breaking strategies of Ludwig and his colleagues (1971). Gruenberg, Suzman and a committee of the American Public Health Association (1962) elaborated the concept of the "social breakdown syndrome." They emphasized two contributing sets of factors: induction into a dependent, compliant inmate role with the simultaneous "disuse atrophy" of preexistent work and social skills. The syndrome was described as characterized by extremely withdrawn or hostile behavior; sometimes oscillations or admixtures occurred.

Wing and Brown's Seminal Research

Soon after the Second World War, the pioneering opening of the doors of Dingleton Mental Hospital in Scotland stimulated study of the custodial patterns then prevalent in many English institutions. Wing and Brown (1970) mounted a significant research study in three English mental hospitals. They compared wards in the three hospitals whose staff resources and patient populations were similar, but whose ideologies and practices were not. All of the patients were women. The patients' behavior and symptoms were correlated with such institutional variables as ward structure, culture and staff expectations.

Findings in their "Hospital B" were intermediate between those of "Hospital A" and "Hospital C"; our discussion will therefore confine itself to the two latter hospitals. Their work is of particular relevance in understanding—and modifying—current practices on the wards of public mental hospitals in the United

States and is therefore presented here in some detail. In Hospital A, 60 percent of patients whose length of stay was between two and ten years expressed some desire to leave the hospital. In Hospital C, the figure was 50 percent. For patients with a length of stay from eleven to twenty years, a wish to leave was expressed by 42 percent in Hospital A but only 25 percent in Hospital C.

Study of the use of time on a typical weekday showed that the average patient in Hospital A spent 8 hours 41 minutes on the ward and 4 hours 21 minutes off the ward. In her time on the ward, 2 hours 40 minutes was spent doing nothing; off the ward, she spent 3 hours 32 minutes at work, 41 minutes at O.T. or leisure and 8 minutes doing nothing. In Hospital C, the typical patient spent 11 hours 53 minutes on the ward of which 5 hours 36 minutes was spent doing nothing. She spent 1 hour 10 minutes off the ward. This comprised 20 minutes of O.T. or leisure, 47 minutes of work and 3 minutes doing nothing.

Significant differences were noted in the percentage of patients with personal possessions. Ninety percent of the patients in Hospital A had their own dresses or suits, compared with 49 percent in Hospital C; 80 percent in Hospital A had overcoats or raincoats compared with 30 percent in Hospital C; 80 percent of Hospital A's patients had cosmetics, combs or hairbrushes, while in Hospital C, the figure was 35 percent. Differences were striking in regard to "potentially dangerous" possessions. In Hospital A, 55 percent of patients had scissors or nail files, while in Hospital C the figure was 8 percent. In Hospital A, 48 percent of the patients had their own mirrors, compared with 4 percent in Hospital C.

These findings were correlated with the attitudes of "ward sisters" (charge nurses) and profiles of the wards' procedural norms. Attitudes were explored by asking the nurses to judge which patients were capable of doing useful work. In Hospital A, the percentage was 74, while Hospital C's percentage was 26. The nurses of Hospital A thought 75 percent of patients "could bathe without permission"; in Hospital C, 37 percent thought so. In Hospital A, 79 percent were allowed to have matches, compared with 21 percent in Hospital C. To the question, "Appreciates money?" the answer in Hospital A was 84 percent; in Hospital C it was 29 percent. "Who could be allowed out with a male patient?" elicited a response of 72 percent in Hospital A and 20 percent in Hospital C.

On the basis of these and related data, Wing and Brown constructed a "ward restrictiveness scale" on which Hospital C scored considerably higher than Hospital A.

They then correlated their findings with such patient symptomatology as mutism, apathy and social withdrawal, all of which were more evident in Hospital C than in Hospital A. The efflorescence of clinical symptoms thus correlated with:

—more "enforced idleness"
—fewer personal possessions
—more negative attitudes and expectations by nurses
—greater restrictiveness

—fewer opportunities for the exercise of autonomy or initiative
These findings are similar to Barton's dissection of the forces disposing towards institutional neurosis.* He emphasizes:
    —Loss of contact with the outside world
    —enforced idleness and loss of responsibility
    —"bossiness" of nursing and medical staff
    —loss of personal friends, possessions and events
    —stultifying ward atmosphere
    —loss of prospects outside the institution

A MODEL

A model, depicted in Figure 1, is now proposed which schematizes our approach to the cause, modification and prevention of the institutional condition.

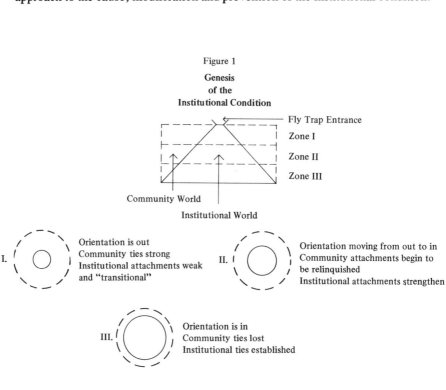

Figure 1

**Genesis
of the
Institutional Condition**

Fly Trap Entrance
Zone I
Zone II
Zone III

Community World
Institutional World

I. Orientation is out
Community ties strong
Institutional attachments weak
and "transitional"

II. Orientation moving from out to in
Community attachments begin to
be relinquished
Institutional attachments strengthen

III. Orientation is in
Community ties lost
Institutional ties established

---

*The hospital of which Barton was then the new superintendent was the Hospital C of this study. During his tenure, dramatic changes occurred in hospital culture and patient behavior. This is described in both Wing and Brown's follow-up study and Barton's monograph.

Figure 1 describes the change in a patient's orientation and relationships as he moves "backwards" towards the "back wards." Movement occurs in space and time, and the typical drift for a "long stay" patient is from Zones I to III. In Zone I, the patient's orientation is "outwards"; his family and community attachments are usually maintained intact because he is "in touch." They remain "attached" to him and he to them. During the early weeks of a typical patient's stay, communication with family and friends is frequent and can be measured by the number and length of letters, visits and telephone calls. While the patient is on "short stay," community attitudes support—and sanction—the occupancy of a "sick" role. This permits a moratorium on customary role responsibilities.* While the hospital stay is assumed to be brief the patient's place in the family, workplace and community is kept open for him. Since interaction continues with some intensity, there is little "disuse atrophy" of social role skills, and a continuing identity as member of a kin, kith and work network is maintained. In consequence, the institutional condition does not usually manifest itself while the patient is in Zone I. On the other hand, the vulnerable patient with few or no such network attachments is "at risk" within a few hours or days of institutionalization.

At what point, then, does the institutional condition become grafted on to the patient's original predicament? Signs of the institutional condition usually appear after three to six weeks of institutionalization. The patient's migration towards Zone II gathers momentum as institutionalizing processes become insidiously operative during this time. The tendency to attach "inside" accompanies a weakening of the patient's "outside" attachments. As his "back home" functions and roles are discharged by others, they learn "to get along without him." Bereft of habitual attachments and need satisfactions, he seeks emotional sustenance from dependency upon the staff. In so doing, he becomes insensibly socialized into a "chronic" sick role. A vicious circle follows. the assumption of a chronic sick role now arouses negative "back home" responses: networks which were previously open begin to "close ranks." Consequently, the patient must "prove himself" to achieve reentry. Reentry is by no means as smooth as in "acute" illness.

In Zone II, the attitudes and behavior of friends, neighbors, employers, workmates and kinfolk therefore show growing impatience with the apparent chronicity of his condition. They become "out of sympathy" with his continuing absence from family and social positions; mutual alienation occurs. Resentment and withdrawal are then demonstrated by a decline in visits and other communications. As mutual disengagement accelerates, the loss—or feared loss—of outside object relationships increases the tendency of dependent persons to "attach" to people in the institution. For those patients who characteristically defend against dependency by distancing and counterdependent avoidance of attachments, withdrawal and paranoid behavior are more typically observed.

---

*For a discussion of this view of the acute sick role, see Parsons (1951).

Without his external anchorages and reference points, the patient "loses touch" with the outside world's dominant values of autonomy, initiative and independence; his needs for attachment compel identification with the very different norms of the inside world. As he retreats into institutional shelter, his customary social roles begin to atrophy from the disuse described by Gruenberg (1967).

Since patients typically cluster as compliant-dependent or noncompliant-counterdependent, migration in Zone II assumes two typical forms. Patients who are disposed to be passive, submissive, obedient and dependent—or are successful in seductive manipulation of the system—are culled into "open" wards. Those overindependent (counterdependent, institution-resistant) patients who actively fight institutionalizing pressures with greater defiance and less political finesse than more charming manipulators are placed on "closed" wards.

Those who remain role-resistant on closed wards are eventually moved to "maximum security" wards. In the informal structure of the mental hospital such wards are, with some accuracy, called "punishment" wards. On such wards the "stripping" and "mortification" processes described by Goffman (1961) and caricatured by Kesey (1962) are starkly evident. These coercive pressures are applied to compel acceptance of the institution's ascribed role for the patient.

The final common pathway of these varied socializing routes is Zone III. Zone III contains the "back wards" where patienthood is in fullest bloom. Here the patient displays all or most of the features of the institutional condition. By the time he is in Zone III, his extrainstitutional attachments have weakened to such an extent that token Christmas cards and holiday visits cannot conceal the growing impoverishment of external emotional bonds.

With the reduction of attachments to external-reference persons, groups, values and ideas, aspirations for a renewed extrainstitutional identity begin to wither. This situation intensifies when the institution fails to maintain external relatedness by providing local newspapers or opportunities for continuing exchange. As the studies of Wing and Brown testify, few patients in Zone III conceive of a life outside the hospital for themselves; this expectation declines with each year of institutionalization. Emotional attachments and object relationships, however limited, become increasingly confined within the institution. Institutional practices thus have the insidious effect of " linking" the patient to institutional attachments while exerting little effort to ensure that original attachments are not "relinquished."

The "Sludge Back-up Road"

In Zone III, patients have often been institutionalized for ten or more years during which they have passed along the "sludge back-up road" described by Vail (1964).* Many of these Zone III patients suffer from chronic psychosis admixed

---

*For this population, it is naïve in the extreme to assume that community life is likely to be easily achieved—or maintained. Most "scandals" about ex-hospital patients in the community focus upon patients who have, in truth, been "dumped" rather than restored in the community. This chapter describes an orderly approach to responsible restoration.

with features of the institutional condition. The American Public Health Association's report on the social breakdown syndrome describes three characteristic patterns of such admixture. The first is "the standard picture of the deteriorated, dilapidated, unresponsive, soiling, helpless, vegetative creature who in former times (sic) inhabited our mental hospitals' "back wards." These is also a "pattern of anger and hostility" which is "manifested by expressions of resentfulness, quarrelsomeness and hostility." The report also describes a state of patterned ambivalence in which "there is a way of withdrawing aggressively by distortions of the usual responsiveness to other people, for example by stubbornly echoing whatever anyone else says, by assuming bizarre poses of body position or speech patterns, by odd gesticulations and so forth. These modes of response avoid the nonresponsiveness of pure withdrawal and the overt expressions of resentment such as cursing and striking out while effectively preventing real personal contact and indirectly expressing resentment or enmity." In their analysis they emphasize that "depersonalized institutionalization is considered to be capable of producing this syndrome."

Application of This Model to Management and Prevention

If migration to Zones II and III is to be prevented, the risks of institutionalization must be soberly appreciated. Vigilant efforts must be exercised to maintain the vitality of preexisting attachments and to discourage both "depersonalized institutionalization" and the development of *permanent* institutional attachments. These efforts should be based upon the realization that institutional attachment reflects both the "object hunger" of overdependent patients and the infantilizing proclivities of many staff persons.

On open wards, stable dominant-submissive, active-passive role complementarities are struck between staff and patients in the interest of mutual need gratification. On "closed" wards, such stability is rarer because there is commonly symmetry in the counterdependent behavior patterns of both staff *and* patients. In the absence of mutually satisfying psychological tradeoffs, control becomes the order of the day.

In some related publications (1967, 1969, 1971, 1973) we have drawn attention to the need for vigilant efforts at quarternary prevention, the prevention of institutional and iatrogenic artifact. Institutions can do harm. Every effort should consequently be exercised to prevent *needless* institutionalization—and to combat proneness to the institutional condition and institutionalizing forces during *needed* institutionalization. Institutionalization, when resorted to, should be precisely time-delineated and the "contract" between all parties should be crystal clear. The institution should discharge its responsibilities in a structure involving *continuity* of relationship, philosophy and treatment between patient, referring care-giver and family.

Within the institution, it is imperative that staff resources be deployed so that realistic, responsible demands are made upon the patient and retreat into the shelter of chronic dependent care is avoided. In order to achieve this necessary level of response demand, changed expectations of the mental health worker and his working environment are needed. Deployment of mental health workers with primary responsibility for the direct management of patients' lives is a crucial component of such change, and can usually be managed without having to recruit new or additional resources. Strategies can invariably be devised for the more productive use of existing resources. More effective resource utilization can be achieved by the delegation of greater management responsibility to "firing line" workers, with programs of training and consultation to "professionalize" these nonprofessionals. The training, consultation and integrative functions are assigned to the mental health professionals, who become less involved in direct management but multiply their contributions through *indirect* support and supervision of the newly created primary mental health worker. The worker's approach should be firmly grounded in reality; he attempts to form an alliance with the patient's autonomous ego, using the leverage of his relationship to promote the mastery of realistic tasks and the practice of socially appropriate interactional skills. He functions as the patient's guide and mentor; when a patient is relinked to the community, the worker remains in an expediting counselor-consultant role to the patient, community care-givers and family members until relationships are rebuilt and responsibility transferred.

Programs which incorporate these principles have been described by many writers, including Sullivan (1930), Freeman, Cameron and McGhee (1958), Appleby, Ellis and Smith (1965) and Hirschowitz (1969). The most effective role for psychiatrists within such a service delivery system may include "direct" medication prescription but, more importantly, involves the training, leadership and supervision of such a cadre of "firing line" mental health workers.

The primary mental health worker designs a rehabilitation stepladder for the patient. He helps the patient ascend this ladder with the assistance of the patient's family and all strategically placed care-givers. He is given the authority to contact and convene these significant other persons so that they are involved in planning for the patient. "Ownership" of the plan is thus shared—and so is responsibility for its implementation. When he is able to compete on the open job market, the worker helps the patient rehearse appropriate role behavior. If he is ill-prepared for the job market, plans are made for sheltered employment and vocational rehabilitation in his home community. While hospitalized, any continuing or potential bonds to kin, friends, neighbors and community groups are actively explored. When few or no adequate bonds exist, membership of transitional groups or residences in the community is sought. When the institutional condition has impaired the vitality or viability of attachments, every effort is made to resurrect them. The staff is constantly reminded of the need to practice a relinking, not a relinquishing, technology. Such relinking involves active engagement with the community by the worker—and often by the entire staff team. This is best done by face-to-face contact with family members, employers, community care-givers, friends or neighbors (instead of the labored, one-way, written communications of the traditional institution). Assisted by decisive guidance and rehearsal, the patient may be helped to exercise some initiative in reestablishing his own links. However, reentry and relinking are fraught with anxiety for the patient, and the mental health worker is usually wise to provide the "contact comfort" of his presence. He "lends ego" and provides supportive guidance in the early stages of rebuilding relationships.

Moving Out: Extending the Net

As a program for community restoration gains momentum, patients begin to recall, and practice, atrophied psychosocial role skills. The effective restoration program attempts to reverse the process that was depicted in Figure I by declining "in here" talk and by focusing attention upon what is "out there" for the patient: his family and interest groups in his community of origin and the role foreshadowed for him within these networks. If no such networks exist, attention is directed to the community alternative for which he is destined. Attachments to objects "inside" the institution are gradually loosened as the patient becomes mindful of renewable or possible attachments "outside." He is reoriented by discussion of information from local newspapers and by frequent home visits. He receives anticipatory guidance for such visits, and the family may be counseled on ways to re-include him.

As complete return approaches, the concerned involvement of family members, friends and community care-givers is enlisted. Families that have "closed ranks" will often be resistant to the patient's return. These resistances should not be ignored, and are best addressed by frequent interaction and negotiation with the family; attempts to ride roughshod over resistances are likely to be countered by sabotage of restitutive efforts. For many families multiple crises are precipitated by the patient's imminent resurrection. After years of a member's absence in the institution, they not only get along without him but psychologically "bury" him. These families need "demourning" help to open their ranks for reacceptance. The understanding painstakingly acquired by staff of any particular patient should be made freely available. Others can then be appropriately supportive through the critical transition of community reentry. During this phase, some continuity of relationship with the primary worker is important. This staff person must avoid the hazard of premature disruption of his relationship with the patient while maintaining sufficient distance so that "clinging" does not impede the bonding of relationships to the family. He takes care to function as a *transitional* object. Where the institutionalized inmate no longer has viable family or community ties, he is at high recidivist risk, and prior surrogate supports should be forged within the community. These can be provided in the context of transitional living facilities such as half-way houses, communities or foster homes. Sheltered employment or jobs should be available.*

---

*The failure to plan adequately for transitional bridges, objects and roles (and the absence of sufficient transitional structures in the community) has often been the cause of the irresponsible "dumping" that state hospitals have been accused of. While the goal of community return may be appropriate, program planning and "follow through" has often been technically inadequate.

An abiding concern for public mental health practice is the allocation of resources to these needed community "alternatives. " Alternative facilities are a sine qua non for the successful restoration of patients long institutionalized. However, most public mental health dollars are invested in institutional bricks and mortar and the consequent maintenance of ailing plants and obsolete staff. Strong local constituencies usually fight to maintain the institutions and oppose diversion of resources to alternative facilities. The need for resources to be rechanneled from institution to community was eloquently demonstrated in a study of Texas mental hospital inmates by Bettis and Roberts (1969). This showed that the majority of patients would have been better cared for in alternative, partial-care facilities—if these community alternatives had been available. The investigators also studied patients referred to a community screening center for institutional referral and concluded that two-thirds could be better served in alternative care facilities. A vicious circle patently exists in the public mental health arena: patients enter—or remain—in the institution and their presence then provides the rationale for institutional continuance.

ASSUMPTIONS AND STRATEGIES

Most programs designed to combat the malignancy of the institutional condition share assumptions and approaches which run counter to those of the traditional institution. In approaching de-institutionalization, the strategy of any change-agent should therefore be sensitive to the institution's values and assumptions, its ideology, its power distribution, organizational structure and division of labor. Without change in all these interdependent sectors, much dissonance and little improvement are likely. In breaking the chain of institutionalizing chronicity, a necessary condition therefore is the continuing reeducation of staff so that their basic assumptions and behavior are scrutinized and new commitments and contractual understandings are established. As we have previously discussed (1970), the remotivation of patients requires the prior remotivation of staff.

The ideology of staff is, in our experience, usually best inferred from observed behavior, rather than from verbal statements or questionnaire responses. In a recent visit to the ward of a state hospital claiming to be "innovative," we discovered a not uncommon pattern: the human "zoo," with its typical keeper-inmate reciprocals and structure of "feeding times" and "visiting times." The ward had barred windows and a "pacing" area. The role instructions to patients were thus embedded in the behavior setting. In the ward meeting we attended, it was not surprising to hear a patient suddenly snarl "I'm a wolf." A staff person responded with an animal-like growl, which was followed by reinforcing laughter from the ward physician. Later, a demonstration reality-oriented "town meeting" was held on this ward. At this meeting, staff became visibly tense as "normal" responses were elicited from patients who habitually displayed "crazy" behavior. Nervous gigglings and frequent interruptions by staff signaled their expectations of more "patient-like" behavior. Staff was particularly upset when a charge nurse and patient were asked to reverse roles. The patient "took the role of the other" perfectly, the nurse not at all.

Strategies to combat the staff attitudes and behavior described here are discussed in previous publications (1969, 1971, 1973).

What Is an Appropriate Therapeutic Milieu?

In analyzing programs that have successfully attacked the institutional condition, it should be apparent that the "therapeutic community" popularized by Jones is not the appropriate structure to facilitate the rehabilitation of patients with the institutional condition and/or the major psychoses that often accompany it. The early phases of successful restoration programs require that staff members exercise firm control and place unequivocal demands upon patients; this forceful intrusion upon the lives of patients runs counter to the permissiveness and democratic communalism of the classic therapeutic community. Chronic schizophrenic patients hang on tenaciously to habitual patterns of autistic insulation. Their avoidance patterns are not relinquished without determined "pushing."

The milieu is therefore structured to maintain an appropriate level of stimulation and interaction. In addition, regressed patients require reality-oriented responsible adults to identify with and against whom they can test and differentiate themselves.

In planning for patients, goals should be clarified and time limits set for their achievement. Outcomes can then be evaluated by the use of a goal attainment scale, such as that of Kiresuk (1968). Such planning delineates orderly steps for movement from institutional status to eventual community restoration. Final steps on such a ladder involve rehearsal for reentry into the community. These final steps should be taken in an environment in which the web of expectations and social cues corresponds to that of an "average, expectable" community. For this reason, the hospital environment should be as "real world" as possible, with ready reinforcement—and constant modeling—of socially appropriate behavior. A definition of the social context as "community" or "residence" is at this stage more appropriate than that of "hospital" or "ward." "Citizen" participation in a climate of healthy pluralism is now encouraged by accenting individual rights and ensuring active contribution of all patients to their own governance. Appleby, Ellis and Smith (1965) have reported on their experience with such a structure: "The accent on individuality results in group participation in decision making; a free exchange of ideas is encouraged. At some point, depending on the degree of their personal organization, patients are also brought into this process so that they too share in the obligation for maintaining the system."

The Management of Change: Resistances to Overcome

Inevitable resistance is encountered when attempts are made to modify the expectations, attitudes, behavior and culture of the staff. The need for change is often denied or distorted; token consent is accompanied by tendencies to hold on to familiar roles and behavior patterns. Since change involves the experience of loss, hostility is often expressed by overt or covert protest behavior. Objections to change may be projected as "the patients are unable (or unwilling) to change." This type of message often signals staff's needs to maintain the traditional role boundaries separating "staff" and "patients." (Technically, it is best approached through indirect mental health consultation techniques.)

The goal in programs that accent rehabilitation, restoration, resocialization, requalification and reentry is unremittingly focused upon *change* in the patient; such change injects uncertainty and reduces predictability. Understandably, staff struggles to reduce the consequent ambiguity and fights changed role expectations which call existing competencies and images of self into question. The introduction of change is difficult, and is best approached with a guide map that encompasses understanding of the psychological experience of change and an appreciation of strategies for its management.

Even when staff members have made some genuine commitment to innovative missions and roles, they often display "role clinging" when change produces too much ambiguity and violation of "law and order" norms. Psychological equilibrium becomes lost, and contagious disruption may be triggered. Staff may then respond in habitual ways to this contagious emotion because of simple failure to appreciate the dimensions of crisis behavior induced by change. When patients are compelled to respond to demands for adaptive change, their habitual patterns are disrupted; in the flurry of apparent "symptomatic" behavior that ensues, staff often falls into the occupational hazard of labeling developmental crisis behavior as "regressive" or "disturbed." Out of their own needs for control they may then impulsively dispense heroic "treatment ." Restoration of homeostasis by these automated means is likely to sanction true regression to the patient role. Staff behavior then becomes self-defeating and, sometimes unconsciously, self-fulfilling. Technically, a delicate balance must always be struck between stability and change. While older systems often maintain too much stability, the opposite "too much, too fast, too soon" error is often committed by young, impetuous staff. Their zealous overstimulation of previously understimulated patients causes excessive arousal with consequent flooding of the mental apparatus and the disruption of precarious ego boundaries. This unanticipated emotional backwash is then stemmed by "chemical restraint," or high dosage medication of the patients, rather than by "stimulus restraint," or reduction of the environment's arousal level.

The Institutional Condition and Chronic Illness

The philosophy underlying our approach neither ingores nor depreciates the "medical model." Since we have been emphasizing the institutional condition, we have deemphasized the multifaceted complexity of the chronic schizophrenia that often accompanies it. In focusing upon the repair of coping and psychosocial role deficits, we do recognize the need simultaneously to moderate perceptual, cognitive and behavioral schizophrenic processes with psychotropic medication. At the same time, we do not confuse the *rehabilitation* of the chronic schizophrenic with his *care*. We seek to apply a model which mitigates the severity and reduces the residual disabilities and institutional artifacts associated with chronic mental illness—in much the same way as we might approach the problems of a patient with chronic diabetes or epilepsy. Our view of chronic schizophrenia shares the pluralistic approach of Cumming and Cumming (1962):

> Our theory is in some ways a traditional biosocial theory embracing assumed neurophysiological substrata, congenital temperament, emerging biological stages, developmental crises, and the interactional aspects of personality. For schizophrenia, this seems roughly satisfactory, although we have not dealt with the issue of whether or not milieu therapy is thought of as curing schizophrenia. At this stage, it is not. Rather, it is thought of as arming the schizophrenic with skills that make his deficits less catastrophic. We do not feel, for example, that milieu therapy can alter an extreme reactor temperament in a patient, but it may provide him with instrumental and social skills sufficient to render his basic temperament less painful to himself and to others.

Approaches to Prevention

Early intervention when signals of distress are evident, can avert needless hospitalization. When hospitalization is indicated, inpatient beds are best used for purposes of *brief* sanctuary. External attachments can be effectively maintained by the energetic involvement of "significant others" in decisions with, for and about the prospective patient. Ideally, all people who are actually or potentially involved in a patient's predicament are convened to help with the problem definition (or diagnosis) and to play agreed roles in its resolution. A structure to achieve this has been described by Hansell (1967) as the "screening-linking-planning" conference. The appropriate use of such a convening structure enhances information exchange, spurs problem-solving and increases the likelihood that a patient's needs will be met as close to family, community and workplace as possible. In the overheated emotional climate of a patient "crisis," problem-solving is often impulsive, with automatic recourse to "wanting out." By "cooler" deliberation, it is often possible to relieve the patient of some of his responsibilities in the family, community or workplace without premature closure on the alternative of "shipping out."

When multiple alternatives are carefully weighed, it is sometimes appropriate to provide the patient or members of his network with the temporary relief of hospitalization. In such a case, the involvement of a local physician in screening-linking-planning may make it possible to use a local community hospital rather than a distant institution for precisely delineated hospitalization goals, such as stabilization with psychotrophic medication.

When personal or family resources are grossly inadequate or emotional reserves gravely depleted, the respite of temporary hospitalization can be used to help the troubled person and family replenish their supplies and link them to needed additional resources. If affectional attachments are impoverished, efforts are directed at linking the person to a surrogate support system in his community. When this is not available, the institution can provide temporary attachments and teach attachment behavior. However, the staff may require rigorous help in applying "*transitional* object relating" (Hansell, 1968). By using these techniques, relationships with staff become bridges to the formation of interdependent relationships *outside* the institution. Excessive dependency upon staff is prevented, and the institution can discharge its agreed responsibility as one of several agencies under an interagency umbrella in which goals and responsibilities are shared, intermediate steps clarified and goal achievement monitored. Such monitoring ensures that frequent signals are transmitted to remind the patient, family and involved care-givers of his imminent return and their—and his— continuing responsibilities. "Discharge" planning thus occurs along a defined, shared corridor of responsibility.

SUMMARY

In summary, it is possible to reverse the malignant features of the institutional condition and to improve the behavior of even the most regressed inmates. In attacking the institutional condition, a supportive organizational structure is required in which realistic demands are made of patients. These should be individualized; specific goals should be set and clear plans for attainment designed. Outcomes should be monitored and plans periodically reassessed. Design and implementation of plans are best achieved by delegation of the rehabilitation task to a primary mental health worker, who need not be a professional. This worker teaches coping skills. These skills are learned and practiced within a hospital environment redesigned as a "learning-living" behavior setting. As social skills develop they are enhanced in transitional facilities to the point where the patient can work and/or live in the community. As he ascends each step of a planned restoration ladder, the patient receives anticipatory guidance and rehearses the behavior that will be required of him at the next level. When any step involves new potential rehabilitative allies such as a foster parent or work supervisor, the worker recruits them to membership of an informal management team. In return, they receive consultation and recognition.

As restoration moves towards ultimate community return, the family and all concerned caregivers participate in planning. Together, they man a continuity bridge to support the patient while he is in transit.

The institutional condition emerges most rapidly when patients are institution-prone and when *institutionalizing* pressures are strong. The institutional career is learned in response to cues, some covert, from staff. We have emphasized the experience of those of us who have attempted to manage and prevent the institutional condition by managing and preventing the institutionalizing behavior of staff.

BIBLIOGRAPHY

American Public Health Association. A guide to control methods. Program Area Committee on Mental Health, Amer. Pub. Health Assn., New York, 1962

Appleby, L., Ellis, N.C., and R.J. Smith. Toward a definition of the therapeutic milieu. *Psychiat. Digest*, 1965, 26,31-35.

Barton, R. *Institutional Neurosis*, Bristol, England: John Wright & Sons, 1966.

Bettis, M.C., and R.E. Roberts. The mental health manpower dilemma. *Ment. Hyg.*, 1969, 59:2, 163-175.

Cummings, J., and E. Cumming. *Ego and Milieu.* New York: Atherton Press, 1962, 269.

Freeman, T., Cameron, J.L., and A. McGhie. *Chronic Schizophrenia.* New York: International Universities Press, 1958, 104-129.

Goffman, E. Assylums. New York: Anchor-Doubleday, 1961.

Gruenberg, E.M. The social breakdown syndrome—some origins. *Am. J. Psychiat.*, 1967, 12, 1481-1489.

Hansell, N. Patient predicament and clinical service: a system. *Arch. Gen. Psychiat.*, 1967, 17, 204-210.

———Casualty management method. Arch. Gen. Psychiat., 1968, 19, 288.

Hirschowitz, R.G., From chronic wards to therapeutic communities: Preparing and developing staff *Hosp. and Commun. Psychiat.*, 1967, 18, 304, 310.

———. Remotivating the remotivators. *Staff*, 4, 1967, 7-8.

———. Changing human behavior in the state hospital organization. *Psychiat. Quart.*, 1969, 43:4, 591-611.

———. Promotion of change in the state mental hospital—the "organic consultation" strategy. *Psychiat. Quart.*, 1971 45:3, 317-332.

———. A model for effective staff deployment in the revitalized mental hospital. *Psychiat. Quart.*, 1973, 47, 1-15.

Kesey, K. *One Flew Over the Cuckoo's Nest.* New York: Viking Press, 1962.

Kiresuk, T., and R. Sherman. Goal attainment scaling: a general method of evaluating comprehensive community mental health programs. *Commun. Ment. Health Journ.*,1968, 4:6, 443-453.

Ludwig, A.M. *Treating the Treatment Failures.* New York: Grune and Stratton, 1971.

Martin, D.V. Institutionalization, *Lancet*, 1955, 2, 1188-1190.

Parsons, T. *The Social System.* Glencoe, Ill.: The Free Press, 1951, 287-88.

Scheflen, A.E. The institutionalized, the institution-prone and the institution. *Psychiat. Quart.*, 1965, 39, 203-219.

Sommer, R., and H. Ross. Social interaction on a geriatric ward. *Int. Jour. Soc. Psychol.*, 1958, 4, 128-133.

Vail, D. J. Personal communication.

Wing, J. K. Institutionalism in mental hospitals. *Brit. Journ. Soc. Clin. Psychol.*, 1962, 1, 38.

———. and G. W. Brown. *Institutionalism and Schizophrenia.* Cambridge: Cambridge University Press, 1970.

2 | Partial Hospitalization—Day, Evening, And Night—in the Changing Mental Health Scene

STEPHEN L. WASHBURN

Americans are discovering the partial hospital. The Russians [1] wrote about the day hospital in the 1930's. In the next decade, the English established a unit, and the Canadians created—at the Allan Memorial Institute—the first formal day hospital in the Western Hemisphere. In 1962, Kramer[2] reviewed the development of these units and described the recent evolvement of a day hospital at the Massachusetts Mental Health Center. These new organizational structures held great emotional appeal to mental health professionals, who faced the limited benefits—not to mention the infringements on freedom—of the large mental hospital centers of the prior one hundred years. That the federal lawmakers also felt the appeal was reflected in the Community Mental Health Centers Act of 1963, which required a day hospital, as well as other partial hospital programs—evenings, nights, weekends—to be present for the center to be supported by federal funds. Yet by 1968 there were still more than forty psychiatric inpatients in the United States for every one in partial hospitalization (Glasscote).[3] Only a small portion of the mental hospital population had moved to partial hospital units. Then, as now, most medical insurance carriers did not finance partial hospital stays, although the proportion of inpatient charges receiving insurance coverage was steadily increasing. Federal employee insurance plans have been the refreshing exception to this unimaginative underwriting policy.

Today, across the country, the state governments are adopting the philosophy of closing out the large inpatient psychiatric institutions, and everyone is asking—sometimes before and sometimes after the fact—"Where will they go?" This problem was dramatically described in a *Medical World News*[4] article lead line: "Long Beach, N.Y. . . . 34,000 Residents, 31 Hotels, and 712 'Walkers,' " the latter referring to ex-mental patients who aimlessly stroll the boardwalk. To deal with this problem, at least one state* welfare department has developed criteria for day treatment programs for which it will pay, using Medicaid funds. Others are awaiting federal guidelines and will probably plan to finance them similarly. Private plans—e.g., the plan at the Massachusetts Institute of Technology—and some projected national health plans, include coverage in terms of two days of

---

*Massachusetts.

day hospitalization for one day of inpatient care. In some quarters, there is a crescendo of federal and state, as well as local community, involvement in the movement. In Massachusetts, for example, there are now day treatment units in approximately half of the state's thirty-nine mental health areas, and the Department of Mental Health is actively supporting plans for a unit in every area. The new patient-family-community consumer will expect a lot from his community-based programs, but fortunately the partial hospital movement is on firmer ground than was its now-aging parent, the Inpatient Hospital, in knowing what it can realistically provide. Thus, the new consumer can be more realistically informed.

WHAT IS A PARTIAL HOSPITAL PROGRAM
AND WHOM DOES IT SERVE?

A psychiatric partial hospital is an organization designed to produce a therapeutic program more complex than that of traditional outpatient services, yet without the 24-hour residency requirements, locked doors, quiet rooms, privileges or sanctions used by inpatient units. It may be based in a hospital, a mental health center, or a free-standing location in the community. Because the setting is less important than the program, it requires personnel trained and organized to deliver interventive, supportive and rehabilitative services in an open system. The people—patients, clients, consumers—who use the partial hospital program are too stressed or psychosocially disabled to be served by individual office visits or group therapy alone. They may be suffering from acute psychosis, serious chronic illness and/or the social breakdown which accompanies it. They may come from the community in need of crisis intervention, prevention of major illness or relapse, long-term habilitation or rehabilitation. They may seek these services for a limited period of transition from an inpatient hospital or as a continuing alternative to chronic institutionalization. In any case, they require multiple treatment modalities coordinated in a milieu which is both emotionally supportive and flexibly responsive to changing individual needs.

Such a milieu has its limitations, and, therefore, clinical parameters must be established which define the breadth of patient disability with which a partial hospital program can cope. These are fairly simple: the person cannot be actively suicidal or actively destructive; he must have some place to live in the community which is within commuting distance of the center and necessary traveling time of at the most an hour or two. In addition, he must have some minimal capacity to ally with the staff—he cannot be so impulsive or disorganized that he is unable to engage in the program to some degree. He must also be able to pay for services, either personally or through some form of third-party insurance.

Another, sometimes optional but often critical, criterion is the presence of a "significant other" in the community who can be involved in the intake procedure, who can ally with the treatment team and who is available to support the patient when he becomes disorganized, suicidal or unable to cope. This becomes essential if the program aspires to treat patients with a wide spectrum of psychopathology and a paucity of social skills. A husband, wife, parent or grown child is often thought to be a suitable "significant other," but a good friend, a roommate, a fellow commune dweller or anyone who is seriously concerned about the patient's welfare will do, assuming he or she has some capacity to act constructively in the patient's behalf.

For persons who fall within these criteria, any one of a coordinated network of programs may be appropriate. For example, a day program located in a community residence or rehabilitation building or former inpatient hall may be open from 8 A.M. to 5 P.M. for continuous service, or it may offer distinct three-hour modules to include specific treatment needs—group therapy, rehabilitation, and social and vocational skill development. The day program staff and patients may leave at 5 P.M., and by 6:30 an evening program can begin in the same physical setting with fresh staffing and different patients, many of whom have been attending work or school during the day. A small number of these evening patients, or others referred for just the night, may be too depressed or disorganized to manage the night at home, and they will require a night program minimally staffed from 10 P.M. to 7 A.M., at which time they are expected to leave for their usual community activity.

Some patients are organized during the working week, but cannot cope with their unstructured free time and come into the same day-evening center for a weekend program. This may be staffed for unscheduled crisis prevention and support, as well as periods of more intensive programming for rehabilitation and personality growth.

Some patients from hospital inpatient wards have been used to dealing with a particular nurse or a particular staff-patient group for discussion, or separation/transition support. If it is valuable for a person to have this special contact while living in the community, that aftercare service by the ward staff can be continued. In some settings, all or one of the above-mentioned partial hospital programs may be developed as an extension of an inpatient unit. Such programs have the potential disadvantage of being dominated by the inpatient philosophy unless staff for the partial hospital program is clearly demarcated and respective clinical missions and responsibilities are clearly defined. The rehabilitative advantage for the patient in working through the stresses of transfer to an autonomous partial hospital unit is also lost.

Specialized after-care opportunities can similarly be made available in relation to inpatient programs for alcoholism, geriatrics or other special populations. A specialized adolescent day program can be designed to deliver group therapy for students and families as well as therapeutic social activity group functions in hours after a high school program. This may complement a therapeutic school on hospital grounds or may be open to disturbed students from community high schools.

STAFFING

A staff-patient ratio of one qualified staff person to four or five patients seems to represent a staffing pattern of sufficient intensity to provide programs in a partial hospital or day care center ranging from acute intervention to long-term treatment. Some day hospitals choose not to offer crisis intervention and may be essentially staffed for long-term care or one of the other functions mentioned, and the staff density can decrease accordingly. Similarly, staffing requirements may also be related to the type of attendance expected of patients. Some day programs have required that all patients attend every day, five days a week, until discharged. It is simpler to plan staff requirements for stable attendance, but this does not fit the patients' needs when they are ready to taper off their supportive contacts. For evening and night care, a staff/patient ratio of one to five or six is workable, as most of these patients have enough effective ego functions to manage in the community during the day and require a less intensively staffed program.

RANGE OF PATIENTS TO BE TREATED

Now let us consider the spectrum of patients whom these programs can serve. In 1964, Zwerling and Wilder[5] reported the results of the landmark study in which they rigorously answered the question, "For whom is the day care program feasible?" People who came to the emergency room of the Bronx Municipal Hospital for psychiatric hospitalization were randomly referred either to the inpatient service or to the day hospital, which was a few miles away. Approximately two-thirds of the people referred to the day hospital could be managed there; 60 percent of these same patients could make it in a day hospital without the few nights of inpatient "boarding" which the other 40 percent required. Of the one-third of patients "rejected" by the day hospital, half had organic brain syndromes; their confusion and physical impairments made transportation particularly difficult. Later studies done at the Washington Heights Community Mental Health Center[6] in New York and McLean Hospital[7] arrived at similar figures: 31 percent and 25 percent, respectively, were too psychiatrically ill for the day care option. This figure was particularly validated by the McLean study in which people came to the admission ward by usual referral criteria. During the two-to five-week period of initial evaluation, every effort was made to offer them treatment through the day program. Workup staff was strongly supported to extend the option to anyone who could possible manage at the day center; nevertheless, using the basic criteria for partial hospitalization mentioned earlier, 25 percent of all admission hall patients were considered too sick or disturbed to possibly manage outside the hospital. Conceivably, this percentage might have been decreased through special nursing or some other extreme expenditure of staff time and energy. The proportion of patients requiring inpatient care appears to be the same for middle, upper and lower socio-economic groups.

Hogarty,[8] in his work at the Baltimore City Psychiatric Day Center, was interested to see if there really was a difference between the people who attended the day hospital and those who went to other kinds of outpatient or inpatient facilities. He found, in a systematic appraisal of the day hospital which attempted to treat people with a broad diversity of illness, that the psychopathology of day patients fell in between the people who were in outpatient clinics and those in inpatient settings. In the schizophrenic population, which comprised a large part of the day center clientele, there were fewer people with serious thought disorders than in the inpatient samples and more people who had a fairly large affective component to their psychopathology. This is consistent with a general clinical impression that people with a strong affective component are healthier, more tractable and have a better prognosis.

In spite of the broad range of feasibility demonstrated, the above reports contradict the claims of Winston and Crowley [9] from their experience at the Potomac Foundation, that nearly 96 percent of referred patients can be managed in a day hospital or a less complex facility. There continues to be a significant number, varied somewhat by the characteristics of the catchment area and the treatment center involved, that require intensive treatment around the clock. This residual group remains in spite of Mendel's [10] important demonstration that the decision for psychiatric hospitalization of seriously ill patients in Los Angeles County was not based on severity of symptoms or magnitude of the patient's distress, but "rather on social and attitudinal factors, some of which influenced the decision makers even though they were unaware of such influence." Similarly, our own observations revealed that the doctor's failure to support a decision for day care, when he had no rational evidence that the latter would be more beneficial to the patient, was often due to his unfamiliarity with that mode of service and to his anxiety regarding the use of an alternative to continuing inpatient hospitalization.

PATIENT OUTCOME IN PARTIAL HOSPITAL PROGRAMS

Having said something about who can manage or be tolerated in partial hospital system, let us consider its effectiveness as reflected in a long-term *follow-up study of the "natural history" type* with the first hundred people who came to the McLean Hospital Day Center, most of whom had previous hospitalization as inpatients. It was carried out by Grob, a research social worker, and the writer,[11] who founded the Center in 1962 and who did not want to keep churning out psychiatric care for psychotic and borderline psychotic patients without answering the question, "Where, and how, are the first one hundred patients four to seven years after attending our day hospital?" It turned out, on follow-up investigation, that 22 percent were still at the Day Center, some of them continuously. These were mostly people who had formerly been "custodial" patients inside a hospital and were now receiving more enriching continuing care based in the community.

Two were in a foster home, and one was in a nursing home. Only 6 percent were living in a psychiatric hospital, although 35 percent did use an inpatient facility at some point after they had come to the day hospital, a figure similar to that noted by Wilder[12] in his two-year follow-up of day patients. Four percent had died of natural causes. Five percent died of suicide: one death occurred while the person was at the Day Center and the others occurred after referral to an inpatient service.

What was the condition of these one hundred people at the time of the follow-up? We designed a global rating labeled "Current Adjustment," which is a combination of mental status, interpersonal functioning and social role effectiveness. An interviewer obtained this data, and then a research assistant combined them to give a global rating. We found that 79 percent of all the people were improved, 8 percent unchanged and 12 percent worse. The current adjustment rating referred to the change since the person left the Day Center after a median of fifteen months' experience there, or, for the few people who had never left it, since he or she came into the Day Center. At long-term follow-up by diagnostic group, chronic schizophrenics were 81 percent improved; residual schizophrenics (includes all people who had acute schizophrenic breakdowns which remitted, but who continued their basic schizophrenic character problems) were 85 percent improved; personality disorders, 70 percent improved; and affective disorders, 76 percent improved. It is important to notice that 12 percent of the personality disorders and 23 percent of the affective disorders were worse in this long-term follow-up.

This natural history follow-up reminds us, even though our improvement figures are quite reassuring, that there is clearly further work to be done.

In the assessment of "Change While at the Day Center," 54 percent of persons with personality disorders were considered unchanged, and many of them had left against advice. The interesting finding of the four- to seven-year current adjustment with this same group of people was that only 17 percent were unchanged and 70 percent had improved. This added a note of optimism to our previous discouragement in working with people with personality disorders. Perhaps it was just the natural course of the disease, but we like to think that the shift to improvement had something to do with our earlier interventions such as our efforts to block impulsive behavior and our struggles with patients and families to dissuade them from leaving prematurely. Perhaps the patient's self-esteem and sense of control had been heightened by the staff investment and his ego strengthened by some incorporation of the staff's limit-setting position.

It is interesting to compare this long-term outcome study of the day hospital with similar surveys of inpatient programs. Schulz's[13] follow-up study of Chestnut Lodge's inpatients three to thirteen years after admission categorized 58 percent of the patients as functioning (i.e., working, going to school or running a house) or making a marginal adjustment (i.e., living outside a hospital but unable to assume the responsibilities of the functioning group). Levinstein[14] and associates' study of former Hillside Hospital patients revealed that during the second year after discharge, 29 percent had good outcomes (i.e., they were functioning adequately), and 29 percent were equivocally functioning. These somewhat less favorable outcome percentages for Chestnut Lodge and Hillside studies may in part be due to different patient populations selected by day and inpatient admission procedures, as documented by Hogarty,[8] or to the differential effects of domicile during treatment.

The "natural history" type of follow-up gives us a picture of what happens to a cohort of patients in a particular treatment setting, but we must turn to the *controlled outcome study* to show "hard" conclusions about the comparative effects of the different treatment settings. In the process of randomization, people agree to be in the study, and then are randomized by a flip of the coin to different treatment settings, i.e., to be an inpatient or a day patient or, in some cases, to be a day patient or an outpatient. This kind of study is very hard to do because when people come to a psychiatric facility, they and their doctors think they are going to receive a certain kind of treatment in a particular location and they often want just that treatment. When the researcher comes along and says, "How would you like to try something else?" it can be very upsetting, especially to the clinician who sincerely believes he already knows the proper decision. A second complexity of controlled studies is encompassed in the question of who will be the reliable and valid observer of the outcome. Are we going to use the patient's story? The relatives'? The so-called neutral observer's? The observations of the service's own staff? It is naturally much simple and must less expensive if it can be shown that the unit's own staff members' results are as meaningful as those achieved with a full-scale scientific team. That one should also think of "significant others" as an untapped resource is supported by Ellsworth's conclusions that the observations by relatives may be as reliable and as valid as those done by a professional socialworker whose role is to carry out follow-up clinical observations. The question of control, the question of the observer, and the question of whether to use interviewing instruments or written questionnaires are matters of scientific method that clinical administrators interested in follow-up have to think about. Forethought on these issues can save the evaluator much time afterward.

Fortunately, there have been a number of controlled studies in the partial hospital movement. Perhaps because it was relatively new and was in some sense a challenge to a large and long-existing inpatient hospital delivery system, it had to prove what it could do.

The first convincing study was done by Kris[16] at the Manhattan State Hospital in the 1960's. Patients who had been discharged from New York state mental hospitals to the community and then began to relapse returned to the Manhattan State Hospital at the time of relapse. In the study, by randomization, half of them went into that state hospital, and the other half came to its day hospital. There were seventy people in each of the conditions, and the striking finding was that the people in the day hospital had an average stay of seven weeks, whereas those who went inside the state hospital remained an average stay of nine months. The social adjustment at follow-up was about the same, but twice as many day hospital patients as inpatients were able to return to work in the one-year follow-up.

Wilder's[12] controlled randomized study employed structured interviews by a research assistant who obtained data from patients and families about behavior and living patterns. However, the actual measure of change was done by a ten-point scale, really a global ten-point rating, in which such things as psychiatric status and family adjustment were rated in a global way. He found that there was no difference between the outcomes at two years on these global ratings that were given the inpatient and the day patient. He also concluded that the day hospital seemed to be superior for schizophrenic women, which was in line with our natural history findings. This is contradicted only by Michaux's[17] conclusion that schizophrenic inpatients obtain more symptom relief and fare better on some other measures than their counterparts in the day hospital. These differences are most apparent at the time of discharge and are no longer present at one-year follow-up. Although her two patient groups were demonstrated to be demographically similar, they were not truly randomized to the two conditions.

The Herz[6] study done at the Washington Heights Community Mental Health Center was more elaborate. Structured interview instruments were used: the Spitzer and Endicott Psychiatric Status Scale[18] and Psychiatric Evaluation Form.[19] Whereas in the Wilder study people came into a city emergency ward and were then randomized to a geographically separate day hospital, the Washington Heights people were randomized to the day program in the same setting as the inpatients. All patients were exposed to the same kind of treatment experience except that, of course, the day hospital patients were living at home. Herz found that the day patients remained in the program on an average of seven weeks, as compared to nineteen for inpatients, and the day patients were able to remain out of setting longer before any relapse. At the four-week mark, the day patients were better on measures of mental status and social role functioning. The differences at the one-year mark were less extreme between these groups, although the day patients still had an advantage on daily routine, leisure time and housekeeper functions.

Our more recent controlled study at McLean Hospital[20] was designed to evaluate outcome on enough levels of behavior so that it wouldn't be subject to the criticism that if we had looked at other kinds of levels, we would have seen different kinds of results. Thus, we used both the Psychiatric Evaluation Forms and Psychiatric Status Schedules of Spitzer and Endicott and an adapted Rating Scale for Family and Community Adjustment from Meltzoff and Blumenthal[21]. We designed our own scales for Burden on Family and tabulated Social Roles Attempted, Costs, Days of Attachment to Hospital, etc. Data analysis confirms the Wilder and Herz findings that for the range of seriously ill patients studied, all of whom had a brief initial inpatient stay, day treatment is equal to inpatient treatment in seven distinct areas and superior in five others.

All these studies emphasize positive findings, but include a number of comparisons which show that inpatients and day patients do more or less the same. Statistically speaking, everybody improves, but the fact that on certain measures the day patients improve more than the inpatients is vital information. However, it in turn leads us to ask how similar patients fare in (1) outpatient clinic settings less intensive than day care, or (2) in milieu settings which are a marked variation from partial hospitalization. There are some firm answers here, too.

Meltzoff and Blumenthal[21] did a careful study of chronic schizophrenic patients to compare day hospital effects with those of an outpatient clinic. They used their own eleven-point rating scales on community and family adjustment and found that low-adjusted patients were significantly improved as compared with those randomized to outpatient in such matters as interpersonal adjustment, family adjustment, self-concept and affect control. On the other hand, schizophrenic people who seem to be in fairly good shape when they entered didn't necessarily fare better than they would have in the outpatient setting. Guy, Cross and Hogarty[22] in a similar study at Baltimore City Psychiatric Day Care Center found that on a global basis, sicker patients did better in the day hospital, Schizophrenic patients improved specifically in terms of increased accessibility, whereas a more neurotic group did not particularly benefit from the day hospital.

Because home treatment relies on family members as a source of emotional support, it has much in common with a partial hospital setting. In Pasamanick's[23] study, patients were randomly assigned to home treatment or the regular inpatient care at a state hospital in Kentucky. Ratings were done by the project interviewer initially, at six-month intervals, then at twenty-four months, using a psychiatric inventory. Home treatment was given by a public health nurse, and patients could call the staff of the hospital when they felt it necessary. Seventy-seven percent of the home care patients whose treatment included psychotropic drugs remained at home during all six to twenty-four months of the study, but this figure dropped to 60 percent for those followed up for the full two-year period. Fifty percent of the hospital controls also required inpatient rehospitalization after their initial discharge. (A thirty-five to fifty percent rehospitalization rate is a very constant figure in all the studies mentioned, whether the patient received in-hospital, day or home treatment.) Pasamanick concluded that for the schizophrenic patients who had families who were willing to have them live at home, there was no reason for them to remain in the hospital unless they were grossly disturbed.

Although home-care, drug-treated patients functioned as well as, or better than, hospital control cases during the study, this advantage was not sustained in five-year follow-up after the home care had been discontinued and routine state hospital clinic treatment became the mode of treatment for patients of either group seeking further help. Domestic performance and social participation deteriorated to levels lower than when the study began in 1962.[24]

Another home treatment study in Finland[25] is interesting because it gives us comparative information from another culture. One hundred and two patients had home treatment by visits with mental health workers every one to two weeks.

There was a matched control comprised of patients admitted to the clinical hospital wards. Of the 44 percent of the study patients in home treatment and in a four-year follow-up, 63 percent were recovered at the end of the four years, and eleven patients were in the hospital. Of the control patients, 30 percent were recovered at the end of four years, and twenty-six patients were in the hospital. Fifty percent of the study group and 24 percent of the control patients were outside of the hospital throughout the four years. The study patients had twenty months of average employment, control patients fifteen months. However, the author makes a comment that neither group of these schizophrenics improved socially during that time.

RECENT INNOVATIONS

The clinical research reviewed solidly indicates that for a wide range of seriously ill patients who traditionally have been referred only to an inpatient mental hospital, the day hospital immediately or after a very brief inpatient stay is equally or more effective than the inpatient experience. This conclusion is drawn about treatment units which are staffed with professionals usually associated with urban psychiatric settings—psychiatrists, social workers, clinical psychologists, nurses, mental health workers, rehabilitation specialists and occupational therapists. Many variations from these staffing patterns are being implemented in communities far from the population centers where professionals are in great supply. For instance, a mental health unit in a small New England town of ten thousand persons may have a day program headed by a psychiatric nurse and staffed by a mental health worker and one or two volunteers. In some areas a nonprofessional administrator may be in charge. The second floor of the community residence may house a night care unit. In far-flung systems, psychiatrists and other professionals may supplement the program on one or two days a week as they arrive by helicopter from the regional mental health center.

A striking alternative to partial hospitalization is the nonmedical rehabilitation of recently discharged psychiatric patients in a culturally deprived neighborhood described by Bauman.[26] The former patient takes on a student role and attends a "school for living," which is run as a school. The content of the sessions includes high school equivalency preparation, vocational activities, sheltered real-life work and homemaking-skill training. The school's staff includes both professionals and indigenous paraprofessionals. He reports improvement at the six-month follow-up in vocational functioning, social participation, psychological functioning and rehospitalization rate. This interesting innovation, as well as the after-care vocational workshop instituted at the Throg's Neck Sound View Center, are examples of some of the successful efforts used to facilitate patient transition from acute care facilities, based primarily on the medical model of treatment, to those based on a rehabilitative model, which more closely approximates the pattern of community life to which the psychosis-vulnerable patient must return.

Another treatment model, "Training in Community Living," has been developed at the Mendota Mental Health Institute.[27] This model assumes that the lack of coping skills, vulnerability and lifelong dependency problems are responsible for high mental hospital admission rates and development of the chronic patient role. Former mental hospital employees have been retrained to work with patients in their homes and at their jobs. By daily or even hourly contact with patients in the community, they assist patients to develop a full schedule of daily living activities and guide them in developing coping skills for job, social situations and leisure time. It is an alternative to mental hospital treatment which may have powerful potential for reducing the chronic patient role in hospital and community.

A further development of the home treatment model is reported by Polak of the Southwest Denver Community Mental Health Services, Inc. He describes an "inpatient alternative program" in which patients are treated in private homes as a replacement for acute hospitalization.[28] Each family selected accepts up to two patients and is assigned a staff coordinator who assumes responsibility for family supervision and support. A nurse and a psychiatrist are available around the clock to provide appropriate back-up coverage. An apartment in the community where intensive observation can be maintained is also used for rapid tranquilization. As in the case of the Mendota model, controlled evaluation indicates that this system is more effective than inpatient hospitalization for a large portion of the patients for whom twenty-four hour psychiatric hospitalization would formerly have been used.

FUTURE DEVELOPMENTS

Just as the partial hospitalization movement with its day, evening, night and weekend programs represents a successful effort to tailor portions of the 24-hour inpatient facility to specific clinical needs of the patient and family, partial hospital programs will be further refined to offer modules or packages of treatment of which the patient may avail himself during different portions of the week. For instance, rather than whole or half days of general treatment milieu, the patient may take part in a morning-group therapy session, a prevocational discussion group, and a luncheon group two days a week. Or he might come in for an evening program which consists of an hour of informal supportive socializing, a group meeting on how to plan for the other six evenings of the week, followed by group psychotherapy. The days of the vagaries of the therapeutic milieu seem to be passing, as both the patient consumer and the third-party payer insist on a clearer picture of what they are purchasing for what problem and with what goal in mind.

Although the costs of staff and housing of day treatment units is considerably less than inpatient services which offer comparable intensity of treatment, day hospitals and the partial hospitalization movement generally continue to be plagued by problems of financing. The patient paying his own fee is much more able to handle the $30-$70 charge for a private hospital's day program than he is to the $120 plus fee charged for inpatient services. The vital point, however, is that most people cannot afford either of these charges for any sustained period and that most private health plans cover inpatient services only. Exceptions are the Federal Employee Blue Cross/Blue Shield Health Plan, which covers 80 percent of day hospital costs, CHAMPUS, and such enlightened innovations as the M.I.T. Health Plan, which gives the employee the option of using two days of day care for one of inpatient. Fortunately, some of the major national health proposals being considered by the United States Congress in 1974 also employed the two-for-one plan, but it is impossible to say whether this principle will be maintained in the final version of national health insurance when—and if—it is passed.

Some efforts to actively collaborate with and educate the insurance companies have been successful. Winston, Crowley et al.,[9] in their development of the Potomac Foundation, an independent day hospital in the Bethesda, Maryland, area, achieved an agreement with local insurance providers to finance care at that day hospital before it opened. Longabaugh et al. [28] in collaboration with Blue Cross of Rhode Island established an agreement in which Blue Cross would pay for forty-five days of day or inpatient care per calendar year on an experimental basis. This included conditions that service be jointly evaluated to determine "whether partial hospitalization is a viable alternative treatment modality to inpatient care and whether there is a reduction in the cost per spell of illness." In a comparison of matched cases, the authors concluded that when the day hospital is used as the only form of treatment, the cost to the patient is considerably less than if he had been an inpatient. If it is used as a continuing after-care site, the cost to the patient for each episode of illness is equal to what he would have accumulated had he remained an inpatient. Both forms of utilization were as effective in treatment as the inpatient service when measured at discharge.

In spite of this bleak picture of partial hospitalization financing, the development of viable organizations and interested workers across the United States continues to grow. According to a recent unofficial estimate from the Mental Health Services Division of the NIMH of all psychiatric facilities which claim to offer partial hospital programs, there were some 941 adult units in the country in 1974. This appears to be an increase of roughly 700 since Glasscote's generous estimate of 265 in 1968.

The Federation of Partial Hospitalization Study Groups, Inc., which had its beginning in the late 1960's with representatives from a small number of units associated with East Coast university settings, has expanded to include over two hundred members from some twenty-five Eastern states. It has biannual meetings in which papers and cross-disciplinary workshops are regularly provided by, and for, its members and their colleagues. In the past several years the Southwestern Partial Hospitalization Association has organized in a similar way with representatives from Texas, Oklahoma, New Mexico, Arkansas, Louisiana and Kansas. There is organizational and clinical exchange between these two organizations, and they are both receiving indications of interest from workers in other regions not yet represented. This seems to augur a national partial hospital organization to represent individuals of all professional backgrounds within the next year.

On another front, criteria for accreditation have been developed and are being refined. The Accreditation Council for Psychiatric Facilities of the American Psychiatric Association is now reported to be working out more specific standards and procedures that are required for community mental health centers, psychiatric partial hospitalization facilities and psychiatric facilities serving children. This would be in line with the direction of the Joint Commission on Accreditation of Hospitals, whose Accreditation Council for Psychiatric Facilities developed standards for partial hospitalization services several years ago, which are now being applied regularly in their surveys of mental hospitals.

In 1965, there were about 558,000 inpatients in mental hospitals in the United States. In 1973, there were 248,000. [29] To service previously overinstitutionalized people, the 1963 federal legislation called for two thousand partial hospital programs to be included in the similar number of proposed community mental health centers. Four hundred such centers have become operational and are included in the estimate of 941 existing partial hospital centers mentioned earlier.

With all the philosophical appeal and the enthusiasm engendered by the prospect of people being treated without the use of the inpatient mental hospital, one has to ask why this partial hospitalization movement is not moving even more swiftly. One obvious answer is the limitations of third-party insurance funding, which I have mentioned above. A second cause is the traditional thinking of the medical profession and others that somehow the occurrence of major illness calls for the use of a round-the-clock hospital facility with removal of the disturbing influence from the family or community. Third, and I believe most important, is the issue of the social support systems—whether it is family, community, private doctor or day hospital staff—which are taxed by the unique stresses the more seriously ill patients thrust upon them. The unpredictability of the patient's behavior, his unrelenting pressure for self-validation and support, life-and-death hints of suicide or destruction of others and aversion to implementing a self-propelled life course may all threaten those around the patient. It is factors such as these which limit the number of patients with which significant other persons, partial care and outpatient staffs can cope. The intensive effort to involve the community in mental health programs is, in a sense, an effort to expand patient-support systems, spreading the load so that a larger proportion of the mentally ill can be managed in the community. With a highly motivated support system, almost any patient can be managed in the community for brief periods. For longer periods the proportion for whom this is possible begins to decrease. The resolution of current disputes about distribution of mental health resources may well determine the proportion of mentally ill people who will receive treatment in partial hospitalization.

REFERENCES

1. Dzhagarov, M. A. Experience in organizing a day hospital for mental patients. *Nevropathol i Psyikhiat.*, 6:137-147, 1937.
2. Kramer, Bernard M. *Day Hospital: A Study of Partial Hospitalization in Psychiatry.* New York: Grune and Stratton, 1962.
3. Glasscote, Raymond; Kraft, Alan M.; Glassman, Sidney; and Jepson, William. *Partial Hospitalization for the Mentally Ill.* American Psychiatric Association, 1969.
4. The discharged chronic mental patient. *Medical World News*, Vol. 15, No. 15, April 12, 1974, pp. 47-58. New York: McGraw-Hill.
5. Zwerling, I., and Wilder, J.F. An evaluation of the applicability of the day hospital in treatment of acutely disturbed patients. *The Israel Annals of Psychiatry and Related Disciplines*, 2:162-185, 1964.
6. Herz, M. I.; Endicott, J.; Spitzer, R. L.; et al. Day vs. inpatient hospitalization: a controlled study. *American Journal of Psychiatry*, 127:1371-1381, 1971.
7. Washburn, Stephen L.; Vannicelli, Marsha; and Scheff, Betty-Jane. Irrational determinants of the place of psychiatric treatment. *Hospital & Community Psychiatry*. In press.
8. Hogarty, G. E., et al. "Who Goes There?" A critical evaluation of admissions to a psychiatric day hospital. *American Journal of Psychiatry*, 124:934-944, January 1968.
9. Winston, Herbert; Crowley, Brian; et al. Ariadne's spool: the independent day hospital. Scientific Proceedings of the 123rd Annual Meeting of the American Psychiatric Association, California, May 1970, p. 246.
10. Mendel, Werner M., and Rapport, Samuel. Determinants of the decision for psychiatric hospitalization. *Archives of General Psychiatry*, 20:321-328, 1969.
11. Washburn, Stephen L., and Grob, Mollie. Psychiatric day care patients—four- to seven-year outcome. *Massachusetts Journal of Mental Health*, V. IV, no. 1, Fall 1973.
12. Wilder, Jack F.; Levin, Gilbert; and Zwerling, Israel. A two-year follow-up evaluation of acute psychotic patients treated in a day hospital. *American Journal of Psychiatry*, 122:10, 1095-1101, April 1966.
13. Schulz, C.G. A follow-up report on admissions to Chestnut Lodge 1948-1958. *International Journal of Social Psychiatry*, 2:292-298, 1957.
14. Levenstein, S.; Klein, D. F.; and Pollack, M. Follow-up study of formerly hospitalized voluntary psychiatric patients: the first two years. *American Journal of Psychiatry*, 122:1102-1109, 1966.
15. Ellsworth, Robert B.; Foster, Leslie; Childers, Barry; Arthur, Gilbert; and Kroeker, Duane Hospital and community adjustment as perceived by psychiatric patients, their families, and staff. Monograph. *Journal of Consulting and Clinical Psychology*, Vol. 32, No. 5:II, October 1968.
16. Kris, E. Prevention of rehospitalization through relapse control in a day hospital. In Greenblatt, m., et al., *Mental Patients in Transition*. Springfield, Illinois: Charles C. Thomas, 1961; 155-162.
17. Michaux, Mary Helen; Chelst, Marvin R.; Foster, Shirley A.; Pruim, Robert J.; and Dasinger, Elizabeth M. Postrelease adjustment of day and full-time psychiatric patients. *Archives of General Psychiatry*, 29:647-651, 1973.
18. Spitzer, Robert L.; Endicott, Jean; and Cohen, George M. Psychiatric status schedule, informant form. Biometrics Research, New Yort State Department of Mental Hygiene, 1966.
19. Spitzer, Robert L.; Endicott, Jean; Mesnikoff, Alvin M.; and Cohen, George M. Psychiatric evaluation form, form R2. Biometrics Research, New York State Department of Mental Hygiene, 1966.

20. Washburn, Stephen L.; Longabaugh, Richard; and Vannicelli, Marsha. A controlled study of psychiatric day care. NIMH Grants MH17464 and MH17464-03A1, 1969-1974.
21. Meltzoff, Julian, and Blumenthal, Richard L. *The Day Treatment Center: Principles, Application, and Evaluation.* Springfield, Illinois: Charles C. Thomas, 1966.
22. Guy, William; Gross, Martin; Hogarty, Gerard E.; and Dennis, Helen. A controlled evaluation of day hospital effectiveness. *Archives of General Psychiatry,* 20:329-338, March 1969.
23. Pasamanick, Benjamin: Scarpette, Frank; and Dinitz, Simon. *Schizophrenics in the Community an Experimental Study in the Prevention of Hospitalization.* Sociology Series, Appleton-Century-Crofts, 1967.
24. Davis, Ann E.; Dinitz, Simon; and Pasamanick, Benjamin. *Schizophrenics in the New Custodial Community.* Ohio State University Press, 1974.
25. Niskanen, P.; and Pihkanen, T. A. A comparative study of home treatment and hospital care in the treatment of schizophrenic and paranoid psychotic patients. *Acta Psychiatric Scandinavica,* April 7, 1971, pp. 271-277.
26. Bauman, Gerald; and Grunes, Ruth., *Psychiatric Rehabilitation in the Ghetto.* Lexington Books, D. C. Health and Co.; 1974.
27. Stein, Leonard I., and Test, Mary Ann. Training in community living: one year evaluation. Scientific Proceedings of the 128th Annual Meeting of the American Psychiatric Association, May 1975, p. 18.
28. Polak, Paul R., and Kirby, Michael W. Follow-up evaluation of an inpatient alternative program. Scientific Proceedings of the 128th Annual Meeting of the American Psychiatric Association, May 1975, p. 16.
29. Longabaugh, Richard; McAuley, Thomas; Imerman, Laurence; and Westlake, Robert. The acute day hospital as an alternative and/or addition to inpatient psychiatric treatment. Butler Hospital Treatment Evaluation Series, July 1974.
30. Statistical Note 106, U.S. Department of Health, Education, and Welfare: Provisional Patient Movement and Administrative Data—State and County Mental Hospital Inpatient Services, July 1, 1972-June 20, 1973. DHEW Publication No. (ADM) 74-6, 1973, Monograph.

3

A Flexible and Responsive Non-Hospital Patient Care Program

WERNER M. MENDEL

Psychiatry has not fulfilled the promise it made over a generation ago. At the close of World War II there was to be a leap forward in health care and health maintenance as well as in political, social and economic well-being for all.[1] In spite of the expenditure of huge sums of public money and tremendous emphasis on training and innovation, psychiatry has not generated a major breakthrough in understanding the cause of illness or in delivery of treatment. Mental health remains as elusive a concept as ever, open to heated philosophical discussions and severely limited by the absence of facts. There is no evidence that the mental health of the citizens of the United States has significantly improved since the promises of a generation ago.

The mystery of human behavior, thought, feeling or interpersonal transactions has not yielded its secrets. To attribute this failure to the complexity of the subject is not justified. Problems and issues which seem every bit as complex, have been solved by competent research. Man can travel to the moon, transplant hearts, and just about create life. Yet we have failed to unlock the secrets of love and aggression, of altruism and predatory behavior, of schizophrenia and depression.

How can we understand this significant failure of our science? First, we do not have the tools with which to observe and describe the phenomena which need to be studied and altered. Second, we have only recently asked questions which are answerable. Third, we have looked for a singular model in which to work out the issues of psychiatry. Several models have been proposed and have competed with each other. No one of these seems to give us a satisfactory platform from which to approach research, understanding and intervention.

Now the question has been changed and that is a beginning. We no longer ask what causes mental illness. We now ask what conditions taken together in this individual at this time bring about what we observe? We can ask, How can we alter each of these conditions to bring about changes?[2] New questions open new doors and give us new tools of observation. These in turn lead to new models of behavior and mental health. It is quite possible today to approach intra- and inter-personal affairs in the medical model, in the educational model and in the legal model. Each of these adds to our understanding. There need not be conflict between these models. Hopefully we are getting to the point where no one will insist on the all-or-none approach. Although it has been troublesome to the concept of parsimony, physics has learned to live with both the wave theory and the particle theory of light. At this stage of knowledge in psychiatry, it appears that we need to live with an educational as well as a medical model of treatment.

Brain and behavior are related but they are not the same. Brain influences behavior and behavior influences brain. The simplistic approach of demanding primacy of one or the other is counterproductive.

In spite of the limitations of our knowledge and the problems we have in our understanding, all of us in the mental health field are engaged in the business of intervening in human behavior. We have promised, and the public expects from us, help with problems in living. In our interventions we have leaned primarily on the medical model so that our professions are those of therapists who treat sick people. We follow the customs of these models, including defining people as patients and places of treatment as hospitals and clinics. We use procedures which have been devised for the care of human beings with physiological and anatomical illnesses. We put patients to bed in hospitals because they hold the erroneous thought that they are Jesus Christ or Napoleon or because they are not motivated to go to work. We have them lie on the couch or sit in groups to discuss how they felt about their parents, or a sister, or a friend, because they have perceptual disorders which are manifested by hearing accusatory voices. Because a man murders his wife instead of loving her, because he rapes a woman instead of seducing her, because a woman kills her children instead of feeding them, or because she steals money instead of borrowing it, we study brain waves and biochemistry. It is, as Szasz has remarked, as though we call the TV repairman to change the tubes because we don't like the violence in the programming on the 8:30 show.

In spite of the failure of our science, we have tools and approaches with which to be helpful. Yet, in looking at our treatment behavior and treatment outcome we see that there is relatively little relationship between what we know and what we do.[3] The field of psychiatric treatment is buffeted by fads and fashions. It is laced with religious fanaticism, trade unionism and the repetition compulsion. Anything anyone does is as good as anything anyone else does. Even when adequate outcome studies are beginning to appear, their impact on the practice of the helping professions in the field of mental health is slow. For a generation we have wasted our resources, misapplied our talents and exhausted the patience of the public.

Even though the gaps in the science of psychiatry are great and there is much confusion, we do know a great deal more than we have used. One of the major crises which confronts our profession is the issue of comprehensive mental health care delivery. For many years American psychiatry has delivered expensive psychiatric care by frequently utilizing systems which are proven ineffective. Generally, psychiatric care has not been available to the people who most need it.[4]

The issue of controlling costs and, even more important, the thought that one should get as much as possible for each treatment dollar, has not been a legitimate concern for the psychiatric profession until recently. In part, this is because the data have not been available. In large part, however, it is the tradition of liberal humanists in the field of psychiatry who take the stand that all treatment is good, that all people should have all services, and that cost is a problem with which politicians and tax assessors and insurance companies must deal by providing the money the profession wants. The tradition is beginning to change. It has finally become acceptable for serious clinicians and program planners who are liberal and humanistic to also begin to think how best to spend the dollars, rather than simply how to get the largest possible budget. Some of our senior colleagues continue to see our concern with cost effectiveness as the unhealthy influence of accountants and politicians in the field of medicine. The disaster caused in human services by the carefully planned benign neglect of the present federal administration, which has set human services in this country back at least thirty years, is used as an example of what happens when the profession becomes concerned with costs. Yet it is precisely the failure of our profession to concern itself with outcome and costs which allowed the federal attitude to develop. To now return to mushy liberalism, which takes the stand that no cost is too much for human services, would be to return to a position which the overtaxed public and the skeptical allied professions are hardly willing to accept.

Many factors have interfered with developing a mental health care delivery system which uses all of what we know. Any flexible, responsive, and economical health care delivery system must take previous failures into account and must deal with them.

First among the seven factors which have caused failure of health care is the whole issue of social class.[5] Those delivering health care services generally are members of the middle class, holding middle-class values which affect their attitudes towards health, illness and treatment. Even though the middle class is the majority culture in the United States, over 40 percent of the population does not fit into that particular cluster of values. When we add to the differences in social class the differences caused by racial and national cultural differences, then the inappropriateness of many health services becomes clear. Mental health services have been designed by middle-class therapists and planners, using systems which seem particularly appropriate for middle-class patients. These systems include talking therapy, the medical model, appointments and the expectation that patients take increasing responsibility for the conduct of their lives. Treatment services are based on a whole set of assumptions towards therapy, health and illness which are all tied to middle-class values. When the recipients of the care do not share the middle-class values, including attitudes towards time, responsibility, independence, authority, role, illness and health, family, sexuality, upward striving and accumulation of wealth, then programs of intervention based on these values tend to fail. Patients often do not keep clinic appointments, they do not feel they are being helped by someone listening to them. They are frequently not at all interested in taking responsibility for themselves. They do not feel that talking therapy is of any value; they do not see authoritative intervention as benevolent. They tend to see therapists, the hospital, the clinic as establishment interference in their personal lives. They tend not to value intervention as helpful, nor do they necessarily see lack of motivation as sickness. As the result of such class differences between those receiving treatment and those providing it, carefully planned programs fail. Appointments are not kept,[6] patients "do not follow through" or they are "resistant" to treatment interventions and to the gaining of insight.

A second problem is caused by the medical model. We have already alluded to the fact that bedding patients down in a hospital setting because they behave in a way which is unacceptable, or because they think and feel things which are uncomfortable, makes no logical sense.[7] To the extent that we are tied to the medical model by tradition, by professional territoriality and by reinbursement and funding procedures, we are also tied to useless expenditures and rigidities of approach. That is not to say that the medical model of intervention is not a useful one. It has served us well, in part. The medical model should not be abandoned. However, when the medical model becomes a strait jacket as it has with us in psychiatry, then it is time to consider alternative approaches. The continued use of hospitalization for the treatment of psychiatric illness is one good example of this. It is true that many useful and helpful things have been done in hospitals for psychiatric casualties. It is also true that each of the useful and helpful functions that have been carried out in psychiatric hospitals are better and less expensively carried out in other settings. Yet we continue to hospitalize psychiatric patients because of tradition, because of the availability of hospitals, because of medical reimbursement and funding, and because of lack of alternatives to hospitalization in most of the country. The medical model holds us to the hospital as the place of treatment. It also holds us to "treatment" as the basis of intervention and it defines those who should do the intervening.

A third factor which seriously interferes with the development of cost-effective and outcome-effective treatment programs is the multitude of divergent and nontreatment-related professional agendas. Quite understandably each profession, be it nursing, social work, clinical psychology or psychiatry, is interested in preserving its territory and its financial status. Most professions are interested in raising their educational requirements resulting in increased financial rewards to graduates, and finally increasing the size of the territory which "belongs" to them. We have developed a partial answer to some of the cost-effectiveness problems created by this professionalism by employing the well-trained, well-supervised paraprofessional. But new issues have arisen. The paraprofessionals have organized unions which have the same ambitions as the professional groups. They point out that many people performing the same services get paid very differently for these services depending on what professional group they belong to or what training they have had, regardless of whether this training is applicable or not to what they do. They point quite correctly to the economic fact of our free enterprise system that a tradesman or craftsman gets paid the same whether he has graduated from high school, or from college, or has a Ph.D. in English. In short, he gets paid for his work and the scale of pay is commensurate with his expertise. In mental health care, the degree determines the salary for the services rendered. Thus the problems of professional and paraprofessional agendas are complex. Unless they are distinguished from treatment issues and are solved, these problems will continue to interfere with the development of a health care delivery system which is cost-effective and outcome-effective.

A fourth problem area is the whole issue of reimbursement.[8] Private insurance and government funding are based on procedures, practices and attitudes at the level of the common denominator. This ensures that most funding and reimbursement are geared to the practices of twenty and thirty years ago. Attempts at innovation in health care delivery tend to be thwarted by the slowness to change large bureaucratic institutions such as government agencies and insurance companies. Since the mental health field, more than any other field of medicine, is dependent on third-party payment, this factor has significantly slowed the development of health care delivery systems. Even with the backing of federal health planning, changes in funding mechanisms are slow. Whatever else one may say about the planned neglect and the lack of funding for mental health by the current federal administration, the administration did a major service by producing a White Paper entitled "Towards a Comprehensive Health Policy for the 1970's."[9] In that paper it is written:

> . . . In every study of facilities, one finds varying percentages of patients who should be using more appropriate facilities. Patients who could be treated in the offices of physicians or could receive x-rays and other laboratory services from ambulatory care facilities are found, instead, occupying hospital beds. Other patients in hospital beds could be equally well cared for in extended care facilities or nursing homes. And there are patients in nursing homes who should be in residential facilities or boarding homes, or who would benefit from services delivered to them in their homes. Moreover, there are patients in hospitals and other facilities who stay longer than they need to for proper care. Finally, too many hospitals maintain expensive facilities that are rarely used. In 1967, 31 percent of the hospitals that had open-heart surgery facilities had not used them for a year. In addition to the cost of maintaining such facilities, they also pose a risk to the patient—the capability, when used, is likely to have deteriorated in quality.
>
> The extent to which health care resources are poorly utilized throughout the Nation has not been measured nor have the costs of mismanagement been calculated. Just a 10 percent improvement in efficiency would yield a saving of more than $5 billion."

In order to deal with some of the problems we have outlined here, the government proposes the creation of the health maintenance organization (HMO). They state,

> . . . HMOs simultaneously attack many of the problems comprising the health

care crises. They emphasize prevention and early care; they provide incentives for holding down costs and for increasing the productivity of the resources; they offer opportunities for improving the quality of care; they provide a means for improving the geographic distribution of care; and, by mobilizing private capital and managerial talent, they reduce the need for federal funds and direct controls.

Yet, even this paper, which has the authority and the weight of the federal government behind it, has had relatively little impact on health care delivery systems in the United States over the past five years. It has had little impact because it did not change reimbursement procedures or funding mechanisms. Thus hospitals continue to be overused, expensive professionals tend to be working where they are not needed, and standards of care for reimbursement and certification are set up on the basis of procedures and techniques fifty years out-of-date.

A fifth factor interfering with the development of a delivery system as good as we can make it is the resistance of the public. We have not adequately educated the public. Such education is necessary to change laws, to change public and patient and family expectancies, and to bring pressure on reimbursment and funding agencies. Forcing new approaches to the treatment of mental illness on a public which is not adequately prepared, ensures the failure of these approaches.[10] Not only do our patients and their families need to be educated to a changing expectancy, but also the community at large must be greatly involved if we are to change attitudes which allow us to treat patients in nontraditional ways. For us to know that there are better ways of helping mentally ill individuals than hospitalizing them in asylums or state hospitals is not enough. We must let the public know; we must convince them and show them how and why the mentally ill are better cared for in alternatives to hospitalization. The need to educate the public is a particular problem to psychiatry, but it is also shared with the rest of medicine. Medicine has never really faced the fact or the impact of the knowledge that approximately 40 percent of prescriptions which are issued by physicians are never filled or never taken by the patients. Yet the physician and the patient act and evaluate the outcome as though it were the result of the pharmacological intervention which the physician had intended. The medical transaction has been so thoroughly embedded in the authoritarian system that the publication of studies which demonstrate the low correlation between prescription writing and medicine taking has had little impact. Physicians continue to act just as though prescribing medication is synonymous with the patient taking it. Thus, part of the public education must also be for physicians. They must become increasingly aware of the reality of their patients' lives and of the reality of the impact they have on those lives. Physicians tend both to underestimate and overestimate their impact on patients.

A sixth factor which has interfered with the development of an effective health care delivery system in the field of mental illness is our failure to develop adequate techniques for outcome studies and adequate techniques for cost analysis. In part, this failure can be attributed to the long prejudice of medicine against apparent concern with money. In part, it is because the liberal humanistic traditions of psychiatry have taken the stance that ''more is better,'' whether it be the training of personnel, the spending of money or the delivery of services. Those of us who have questioned this approach have quickly been branded as conservatives and reactionaries. Interest in exposing the useless expense and the waste of the health care dollar caused by an archaic bureaucracy, an inflexible professionalism and an unbelievably ineffective cost control has been viewed by many colleagues as a hostile attack on our noble intent and God-given status of omniscience and omnipotence. We are beginning to have tools which allow us to look at outcome and which permit us to do useful cost analysis. We must use these new tools to develop treatment programs which are outcome-oriented and cost-effective.[11]

A seventh factor in the development of a system of health care delivery must take into account the issue of prevention.[12] It is in this area that we have the least knowledge and the fewest techniques. The cause of mental illness remains unknown. All factors of human life ranging from genetics to biochemistry, from diet to child-rearing practices, from social conditions to pressures of civilization, from educational methods to religious affiliation, have been indicted as causative factors. We do know some facts about secondary and tertiary prevention; that is, preventing the complications of treatment and preventing the complications of prolonged illness. We know nothing about preventing illness. Unfortunately, members of our profession have been seduced into taking giant leaps of faith into the area of primary prevention and thus advising on politics, economics, child rearing, diets and genetics.[13] Some advice may have been useful. Much of it was nonsense. All of it is unknown in terms of cause and effect. Our efforts in health program planning should be restricted to the areas which are known to us. We should prevent harm from treatments which are known to be harmful, such as prolonged hospitalization, psychosurgery or the use of certain drugs. We can aid in possible primary prevention by making available our data for retrospective reconstruction in the lives of psychiatric casualties. These data are now available to experts in education, sociology, child rearing, public administration and politics. When we ourselves as physicians venture forth into these fields, we tend to forget that we are dilettantes and that our contribution at best is that of the intelligent layman.

DETAILS OF THE PATIENT CARE PROGRAM

Responsiveness to the patient population is the most important aspect of any treatment program. Not only is this clinically necessary for a minimum of therapeutic effort to do a maximum of good, it also becomes the basis of cooperation between the population served and the servants. Goodwill is established when the clients feel that the program is responsive to their needs rather than bound to bureaucratic procedures. If the clients feel well taken care of, they will come for treatment early and they will respond to their own positive expectancies. For example, with a working-class population it is nonsense to have outpatient appointments available only during the usual clinic hours. With a working-class population it is essential that the bulk of routine clinic appointments should be offered during evening hours and on weekends. This is inconvenient for staff but an absolutely necessary response for the working population. Furthermore, for many client populations the whole concept of appointments is not meaningful. It is necessary to work out procedures so that a patient can be seen by his own therapist when he drops in too late, too early, or even without an appointment. One way this scheduling can be accomplished is to give therapists three apointments back-to-back, then have one appointment free. This free time can be used for drop-ins, emergencies, phone calls, dictating, etc. This type of scheduling can allow for the system to be responsive. Although it makes sense to the middle-class therapist to say to his patient who is too late for his appointment that he must wait until next week, this makes little sense to a non-middle-class patient who does not value time or appointments in the same way. After all, the patient has come for help with his problems in living, not to be trained into the middle-class value system of the therapist. In many public institutions it is precisely this which is the greatest error. Not only do we demand of a poor, socially disenfranchised and schizophrenic patient that he give up his schizophrening, but we also demand that he become like us, a middle-class citizen with middle-class values.

The employment of well-selected, carefully trained and meticulously supervised paraprofessionals can become the backbone of a treatment program. For some patient populations it is necessary first to deal with their expectancy of seeing a doctor. But after this has been worked through, all populations seem to be willing to see a paraprofessional, if this is appropriate. For some lower-class populations it is helpful to use a non-middle-class paraprofessional as the representative of the helping situation. He is more like the patient and can interpret the patient to the system and the system to the patient in an effective way. Frequently, his rapport with patients is much better than that of the professional therapist.

Willingness to intervene in any way necessary without being bound by the usual rules of psychotherapeutic interaction is essential in providing a responsive system. This must include emergency home visits, planned therapeutic home visits, or intervention in the patient's real life—his job, welfare problems, family problems[14] or psychiatric medical problems.[15] It is important that the therapist be well enough trained so that he is always flexible in his type of intervention while at the same time always aware of the possible counter-transference interference when the ritualistic safeguards of the consulting-room psychotherapy model are given up. All therapeutic interventions are acceptable as long as they are put through the filter which asks, "Is this for the patient?" "Is this therapeutically indicated at this time with this patient?" "What are the possible anti-therapeutic effects of this intervention on this patient and does the possible gain outweigh the possible anti-therapeutic factors?"

The medical model has served us well as a platform for intervention in mental illness. However, slavishly adhered to, it interferes with providing necessary services. Within the medical model there is room for both continuing care as well as episodic care. It is essential to recognize that there is a need for both of these approaches. The chronic patient, such as the chronic schizophrenic, needs continuing care. Some of that supportive care can be provided within the medical model, some of it must be provided in the educational model. The purpose of such care within the medical model is the prevention of complications and the maximizing of function. This is similar to care provided to a diabetic or cardiac patient. The purpose of continuing care must also include retraining of environmental manipulation.

Episodic care as in crisis intervention fits many psychiatric disorders. It is important, however, that diagnoses and treatment plans be carefully made so that the treatment fits the need. For example, when there is argument about treatment of schizophrenia, part of the difficulty of looking at outcome is that the natural history of the illness is not taken into account.[16] We have known for at least a century that of a hundred acute schizophrenic episodes about twenty-five will get well regardless of what is done, that twenty-five will not improve much no matter what is done, and that fifty will improve depending on the treatment. Careful diagnosis and evaluation will lead to applying episodic care to the correct 25 percent, supportive chronic care to the correct 50 percent, and palliative care to the remaining 25 percent. Such understanding of the natural history of disease will help us to mobilize our research effort in a useful direction.[17] Episodic care can take a variety of forms, including the psychiatric emergency team, family crisis treatment, overnight shelter in crash pads, motels, medical and nonmedical detoxification units or partial hospitalization such as day treatment or evening treatment. All of these must be a part of a versatile and responsive treatment program. Absence of any one of these aspects of treatment will overtax the rest of the program and will cause inappropriate use and therefore expensive and ineffective use of other treatment modalities.

An effective and economically appropriate treatment program must clearly differentiate a variety of professional agendas. Health education is separate from health restoration and health maintenance. Research is separate from health-maintenance and health-restoration services. This does not imply that these two functions are not vital for a total health system. It is only that they must be recognized as separate and separately funded and planned for. Those of us who have worked in the public sector have learned to be dishonest: bootlegging training and research functions while using treatment service dollars. We justify all this because research and education are important and worthwhile activities. Yet these mixed agendas have led to bad treatment for patients and exorbitant expense and confusion as to outcome. For example, it makes sense to collect a group of schizophrenic patients in one place such as an asylum for a prolonged time in order to study them or in order to allow them to be studied by trainees. This does not make prolonged hospitalization a treatment. If we differentiated the agendas clearly, we would not hospitalize schizophrenic patients for treatment, but we might set up schizophrenia colonies for research and training where schizophrenic participants understand the agenda and get paid for participating in these activities.

One of the most difficult aspects of any program development, particularly when the program is innovative and attempts to be responsive, is the issue of reimbursement and funding. As mentioned previously, mechanisms for funding and rules for reimbursement tend to lag several decades behind practice. If programs are to survive they must find money, and if they need to find money they tend to tailor their program to where the money is. Thus new approaches and new ideas are not easily begun. Only a continued effort in educating the public, the legislature, the profession and the third-party payers, showing each of these groups how new approaches are beneficial to them specifically, will result in changes of reimbursement and funding mechanisms.[18] This will be a long, difficult and often discouraging task. A new approach to funding like prepaid care has much to offer. Successful experiments with prepaid psychiatry have been carried out by Philip Wagner of the Kaiser Health Plan of Southern California,[19] the Group Health Cooperative of Puget Sound, the United Auto Workers of Detroit, as well as the Health Insurance Plan of greater New York. Recently major experiments in prepaid psychiatric care have been carried out by the Western Institutes of Human Resources in Phoenix, Long Beach and San Francisco.[20] Prepaid psychiatry has important consequences in the delivery of services. Health care is available for a regular monthly fee whether the services are used or not. There are no additional charges when services are delivered. An advantage of this system is that both the patient and the provider of the mental health care have the same goal of keeping the patient well. There is no financial reward for ineffective prolonged treatment, and there is considerable motivation for prevention, whenever this is possible. This system also allows for nontraditional approaches and avoids the difficulty of reimbursement of third-party payers. The advantages of prepaid psychiatry are many. The cost is spread to the total population. Both the program and the population have expenses which can be anticipated for the length of the prepaid contract. An emphasis on prevention is possible, and a substantial portion of the money collected for a population might be used for such services. Flexibility of services is feasible. The utilization of expensive and frequently useless services can be prevented. Reward for overtreatment is not built into the system. Costs can be kept down by encouraging the use of the more effective and less expensive techniques and more appropriate personnel. Both the program and the patient population are rewarded for not using expensive treatment.

The issue of public education is an important one in beginning an innovative treatment program. By definition, individuals who are signified as mentally ill have decreased adaptive capacities. They, their families and the community are stressed by the illness. Their ability to assimilate new approaches is more severely limited than that of a general and healthy population. Great effort must be taken in explaining all services and approaches so that everyone understands why and what is going to be done. There is considerable need for regular newsletters, lectures, written handouts and educational programs, so that the cooperation of the population to be served is enhanced. In health educational programs, it must be remembered that there are large populations who distrust all professionals, all agencies and all facilities. We cannot make the naïve assumption that those people whom we are trying to help are going to love us because we are good guys or because we mean well. This is another area in which social-class difference is an important factor and must be taken into account.

In evaluationg a flexible and responsive non-hospital patient treatment program, it is essential that from the beginning the goals of each treatment transaction with each patient are specifically defined so that evaluation is possible. In the last few years a host of new techniques have been developed which are particularly suitable for this purpose. A combination of the problem-oriented record[21] and the technique of goal-attainment scaling provides us with the necessary format in which to evaluate outcome of treatment.[11] It is necessary that the evaluation, problem-listing and goal-setting clinicians be separate from the treatment clinicians. The way this works is that the patient can be seen in intake evaluation for a thorough workup. A feasible goal is then agreed to by the evaluation team and the patient. The patient is then transferred to a treatment program which is appropriate for that goal and the clinicians agree to the goals set and the time specified. It is then possible, by using Kiresuk's techniques, to follow up the progress of treatment towards attaining the goal and to translate the progress into numerical scores which can become the basis of an effective evaluation process. When this is tied to critical incident costing,[4] the actual cost for obtaining a specific treatment goal, we have all the tools we need to study outcome as well as to compare various treatment modalities.

In the area of prevention we have the most to learn and know the least. We have some knowledge in secondary and tertiary prevention. Yet it is the area of primary prevention which requires much research, and it is possible to begin some of that research when we deal with the continuous care of a fairly large population which receives all of its medical and psychiatric interventions from the same organization. For example, just as the intake physical and laboratory screening examination is routine in some health plans when a member joins, a psychosocial survey of each member family is possible to provide basic data before any need for help has been voiced or any diagnostic label has been attached. The health maintenance organization is particularly useful for the study of primary prevention because it can serve as a population laboratory for the study of techniques and knowledge of prophylaxis.

SUMMARY

A patient care program can be effective and economical if it maintains the basic principles of flexibility and responsiveness. It must perform the task of intervening helpfully while at the same time assessing the outcome of the intervention.

Treatment must be cost-conscious. This is good economics as well as good medicine. The least amount of treatment which does the best job is the best treatment. Effective and economic use of resources saves funds and personnel for more treatment. Rituals and repetition compulsions which are a part of the history of psychiatry must be avoided. For any treatment program to survive, reimbursement problems and funding mechanisms must be solved. The most effective vehicle which allows the greatest latitude and the best opportunities for innovation and experimentation is the funding mechanism known as prepaid psychiatry, which is tied to the concept of the health maintenance organization. Psychiatric health maintenance has now been proven to be effective and economical for a variety of populations. The treatment program must be sophisticated in its knowledge and its response to social class disference and cultural differences of populations. It must provide a range of services from chronic to episodic interventions.

REFERENCES

1. Cameron, D. E. Psychiatry and citizenship. APA Presidential Address, *American Journal of Psychiatry*, 1:1-9, 1953.
2. Wolf, S., and Wolff, H. Evidence of genesis of peptic ulcer in man. *JAMA* 120:670-675, 1942.
3. Malan, D. The outcome problem in psychotherapy research, *Archives of General Psychiatry*, 29:719-729, 1973.
4. Mendel, W. Prepaid psychiatry. In Jules Masserman (ed.), *Current Psychiatric Therapies*, Volume XIV, May 1974. New York: Grune & Stratton, Inc.
5. Hollingshead, A. D., and Redlich, F. *Social Class and Mental Illness*, New York: John Wiley & Sons, 1958.
6. Adler, L.; Goin, M.; and Yamamoto, J. Failed psychiatric clinic appointments. *California Medicine*, 99:338-392, 1963.
7. Mendel. W. On the abolition of the psychiatric hospital. In Leigh Roberts, et al. (eds.) *Comprehensive Mental Health*, Madison: The University of Wisconsin Press, 1968, pp. 237-247.
8. Taylor, R., and Torrey, E. Mental health coverage under a national health insurance plan. *Unpublished paper* presented at the American Psychiatric Association annual meeting, May 1973.
9. *U. S. Department of Health, Education and Welfare*. A white paper: towards a comprehensive health policy for the 1970s.
10. Mendel, W. Lepers, madmen, who's next? *Schizophrenia Bulletin*, NIMH, Washington, D.C., 11:5-8, 1974.
11. Kiresuk, T., and Sherman, R. Goal attainment scaling: a general method of evaluating comprehensive community mental health programs. *Community Mental Health Journal*, 4:6:443-453, 1968.
12. Caplan, G. *Principles of Preventive Psychiatry*. New York: Basic Books, Inc., 1964.
13. Mendel, W. The seduction of the therapist. Editorial in *Existential Psychiatry*, 7:28:3-4, 1970.
14. Langsley, D.; Machotka, P.; and Flomenhaft, K. Avoiding mental hospital admission: a follow-up study. *American Journal of Psychiatry*, 127:10:1391-1394, 1971.
15. Goldbert, I.; Krantz, G.; and Locke, B. Effect of a short-term outpatient psychiatric therapy benefit on the utilization of medical services in a prepaid group practice medical program. *Medical Care*, V8:5:419-428, 1970.

16. Parfitt, D. N. The neurology of schizophrenia. *Journal of Mental Science,* 102:429: 671-718, 1956.

17. Bellack, L. (ed.) *Schizophrenia: A Review of the Syndrome.* New York: Logos Press, 1968.

18. Greenblatt, M. Historical forces affecting the closing of mental hospitals. In *Proceedings of a Conference on the Closing of State Mental Hospitals,* Encino: Plog Research, Inc. and Stanford Research Institute, April 1974. NIMH Grant No. 5 ROI MH 19222-02. Pages 3-17.

19. Wagner, P. S. Psychiatry for everyman. *Psychiatry,* V30:1:79-90, 1967.

20. Mendel, W.; Rapport, S.; Glasser, J. The psychiatric health maintenance organization. *World Journal of Psychosynethesis.* 6:10:24-30, 1974.

21. Grant, R. L., and Maletzky, B. M. Application of the Weed system to psychiatric records. *Psychiatry in Medicine,* 3:119-129, 1972.

4

The Right to Patienthood

V. M. RAKOFF

Michel Foucault coined the phrase "the grand incarceration" to describe that period in the late sixteenth and seventeenth centuries when social deviants of all kinds were placed in institutions. Since World War II an opposite process, a grand excarceration, has been under way. The custodial mental hospital has been discredited in its tranditional form. Where it still survives it is thought to be only because of administrative lethargy or obscurantism. Indeed, in their book *Institutionalism and Schizophrenia*,* J. K. Wing and G. W. Brown, in considering the future of the mental hospital, wrote: "To some psychiatrists this book must seem an anachronism reviving echoes of forgotten problems. To them the long-stay question is solved. Once the present, steadily decreasing number of long-stay patients has finally disappeared the new accumulation will be negligible. Chronic schizophrenia can be prevented by drugs or by family therapy, or by a combination of various community treatments and the long-stay patient will be relegated to psychiatric history."

But by now we have available many empirical situations in which the best hopes and the theoretical positions underlying the excarceration may be examined. There are by now many patients outside the institutions, who are living in foster homes, or with their families, working or not working, in contact with institutions, or as free agents. Their situation can be examined from the point of view of the major critical positions which so effectively undermined the mental hospital: the criticism of the institution qua institution and the philosophical questioning of the process whereby patients were labeled mentally ill. The question that must be answered by the new programs is simply stated. Are patients who have previously been hospitalized or who might have been hospitalized a few years ago leading more human, happier, productive lives under the new therapeutic regimes?

At this point it should be made clear that the intention of this paper is not to plead even in the most minor way for a return to the discredited mental hospital, the huge "total institution," but to examine some aspects of, what has by now become in some sectors, a polemical orthodoxy.

---

*Institutionalism and Schizophrenia. A Comparative Study of Three Mental Hospitals. J. K. Wing and G. W. Brown. Cambridge University Press. 1970.

Among the more poignant studies of the way in which patients really lived away from the institution is that conducted by Murphy, Pennee and Luchins,* who examined the conditions of ex-hospital patients in foster homes in Canada. The study was carried out against the background of events outlined above, particularly the proliferation of foster homes for mental patients. Murphy and his co-workers, Pennee and Luchins, studied the "measurable changes in patients' mental and social functioning from the time they left the mental hospital for such a home until eighteen months later when it was presumed that a tendency to improvement or deterioration would have shown itself." The team specifically avoided homes with geriatric or deficient patients; the most common diagnosis for those patients seen was schizophrenia. Pennee and Luchins each visited different groups of foster homes. Pennee visited twenty-nine foster homes and directed his attention principally at the efficacy of the homes in providing a family setting for the residents, while Luchins was primarily concerned with the lives the patients led.

Pennee spent a complete day in most of the homes he visited and occasionally stayed overnight. The homes varied in size, having from two to twenty-two boarders. In almost three-quarters of the homes he visited he found that the promise of a family setting was not fulfilled in the most simple aspects of the home's organization. In most of the homes he visited, the psychiatric boarders had their meals separately from the proprietor's family. They ate rapidly and quietly "showing almost no interaction during meals either with the foster mother or with each other." He remarked that it was only in the smallest homes that the family and the boarders really ate together and "passed food to each other as in a normal family." Pennee seems to have been profoundly impressed by the mealtime silence and the pre-serving of portions. He notes that the boarders were not distressed by the silence and that they were as well fed as the proprietor's family.

In eleven of the twenty-nine homes the sitting room was shared with the family, but in the other eighteen homes a separate sitting room was set aside for the boarders "and there the foster mother or staff rarely came." There was always a television set, and almost none of the boarders was seen to read. They passed their days passively, limiting their social interaction to the passing and lighting of cigarettes. Only a quarter got involved in household activities to the extent of taking their plates into the kitchen. Even though the male proprietors of the homes were busy men with outside jobs, none of the residents was involved in the most ordinary forms of household maintenance.

With very few exceptions, the living conditions of the boarders as shown in their bedrooms were regimented and uniform (in the original text of the paper, Pennee underlines the words "regimented and uniform"), and in many instances the daily activity such as bath times and smoking times was subject to strict regulation.

The lack of activity and spontaneity in the home was only in a few cases

---

*Murphy H. B. M., Pennee B., Luchins D.: Foster homes—the new back wards? Canada's Mental Health 20: Suppl. 71, 1972.

compensated for by activity outside the home, and this was only an extension of his observation that "only a minority of proprietors and foster mothers saw it as their function to develop a more social type of household."

In only six homes did any of the boarders have outside work, and non-work-related outside activity was almost as scarce. Pennee comments, "I had the impression that some of the boarders had more liberty to do things in the hospital than they had now." Geographical isolation of many of the homes and the residents' lack of money contributed to this state of affairs, and there was little or no reaching out to patients by others in the community.

Although all the homes visited were affiliated to hospitals which retained "considerable power over the boarders," much of the hospital supervisor's time during visits to the foster home was spent with the foster mother rather than with the patients. In only two of the settings did community volunteers bring patients from several homes together for "entertainment and refreshments." The hospitals were clearly not neglectful and admitted to using their available staff as best they could. There were occasional visits by occupational therapists, and in one location women boarders were given the chance to visit the hospital hairdresser. However, the occupational therapy programs in general "lacked vitality, and although about half the boarders worked with the occupational therapist when she came and although material might be left with them, their activity ceased when she left."

In the simple matter of dental care for chronic patients there was very little care given.

Luchins made similar observations in the homes that he visited. He too was struck by the poor social relationships between patients and found a lack of relationship between the patients and the foster parents and between the patients themselves. Although Pennee and his group had observed that in homes that had fewer than six boarders there tended to be more interaction between proprietors and boarders than where the homes were larger, this was balanced by his observation that there tended to be "more rivalry or hostility within the boarder group in the smaller homes." And Luchins noted that when patients asserted that they had friends in the patient group he could find no support in most cases. Only twice did he find anything resembling normal friendship, and in both these cases the friendship was between two women who shared bedrooms in an otherwise all-male group. There seemed to be a deliberate attempt to avoid small groups. When patients were sitting in the living room, they addressed people sitting far away from them rather than people sitting close to them. In two of the homes Luchins visited, the patients did not know each other's names "and in no home did I ever find a group playing cards or other indoor games, though such games may be lying there for use." Only once did he hear a discussion on any topic at all. His definition of discussion is modest: "more than three consecutive remarks on the same subject."

The general impression he gained of these homes was an avoidance of intimacy.

Indeed animosity was almost but not quite as absent as friendship. He never once saw a patient confront another patient about difficult behavior: . . . "they structured situations so that there was a minimum of contact and confrontation. People knew which chairs 'belonged' to whom, and they would wordlessly leave them unoccupied pending their 'owners' reappearance." The ubiquitous television set was used as a device to prevent intimacy rather than as a principal source of entertainment. The patients left it tuned to the same station for hours at a time, and in one remarkable instance the patients left an alternate television set tuned to a French program which they did not understand simply because there was a French-speaking helper who came in three times a week and sometimes liked to look at that program. In general, the environment was changed rather than the patients' behavior. He cites the one example in which a French-speaking patient who was judged too garrulous was simply transferred to an English-speaking home where he found no listeners. In general, the routine of the homes was structured and predictable, and the patients went to sleep early, echoing the hospital routine, and there was very little contact between the patients and the world outside the foster home.

Luchins had the impression that the homes with the poorest interaction did not necessarily have patients who were intrinsically more hopeless than the average. The commonest reaction of the foster parents was to regard the patients as incompetent children who were messy or irresponsible and who needed everything done for them. An extreme example of this was in one home where all the patients wore floor-length bibs at the table. Of course, other homes did allow more freedom, and as Luchins says, "the average foster parent seemed to show much goodwill towards the patients, but ended up by running the patients' lives for them in order that matters might be properly under control." Festivals such as Easter and Christmas produced little spontaneity in the patients' behavior. "I sometimes heard talk of the patients' 'own garden' but it was the foster parent who seemed to decide what would be grown there and what fertilizer would be used." Keeping control of the patients seemed to be a prime goal of the foster parents. One foster parent told Mr. Luchins that she was afraid to address the patients with the same informality as they addressed her lest she should lost their respect.

The conclusions Luchins drew from his observations were that the patients who had been discharged from the hospital were not ready to take advantage of more normal roles without assistance. They were not given the encouragement, nor were they given the opportunity, to make mistakes and to try again. They were denied that alternative of reward and punishment that constitutes the normal socialization process.

Luchins summarizes his impressions: "It was my opinion that those who think foster home placement enables a patient to escape the disadvantages of an institutional life are mistaken. Foster homes can be as institutionalized as hospitals are while lacking the compensatory advantages that some hospitals may possess."

His opinion is echoed by Murphy in his discussion: "It is still true that foster homes provide better living conditions than the old back wards. However, it is quite doubtful whether they provide a better means of stimulating the patients' residual capacities than the longer stay ward of the hospital with the various re-involvement programs which many of the latter now attempt.'' Murphy emphasizes that foster parents require professional back-up, and that the urban settings are likely to be more conducive to a more active life than the rural life where the patients will be relatively more conspicious. He adds one hopeful note: he feels that with more responsible professional effort the patients' lives in the foster homes need not be as bleak as they appear to be in this study.

I have presented a lengthy summary of the above paper because it is one of the few published investigations that have attempted to report on the realities of the patient experience in the foster home. It is free of polemic and a valuable addition to the numerous reports from British psychiatrists—particularly Grad and Sainsbury, and Brown and Wing—who have attempted objectively to examine the effects of different models of treatment on families with a psychotic member, on the community and on the patients themselves.

In their 1968 paper in the British Journal of Psychiatry,* Grad and Sainsbury studied the degree to which schizophrenic patients were a burden on their families. They compared the different management systems of the Chichester Community Case Service, in which attempts were made to treat patients outside the institution, and Salisbury, where admission to hospital was more commonly practised. ''The comparison was made in terms of the relief that was afforded to the two groups of families over a period of two years.''

In Chichester a 48 percent reduction in hospital admissions was noted in the years following the establishment of community services. And it was notable that only 14 percent of patients were admitted to Chichester, whereas 52 percent of patients were admitted to Salisbury. After two years, 52 percent of the Chichester patients, as compared with 28 percent of Salisbury patients, were rated as ''a problem to look after'' at some time during the preceding two years. Even after two years at least twenty percent of the families were still affected. They concluded the social cost of psychiatric care was still higher in the community-care service than in the hospital-based one. It was higher principally because of the greater family burden caused by a group of patients who are not commonly retained in hospital even in a non-community service. They make a plea similar to that made by Murphy some years later: ''Our findings therefore emphasize the importance of supplementing the clinical care of the patient treated outside the hospital with adequate social support from his family.'' All the measures used showed that the community service which favored extramural care left the patients' families more heavily burdened. An interesting feature of this study is

---

*The Effects that Patients have on their Families in a Community Care and a control Psychiatric Service—A Two Year Follow-up. Jacqueline Grad and Peter Sainsbury. Brit. J. Psychiat. (1968) 114, 265-278.

that it was not the psychotic patients who caused the most trouble to their families, but the younger neurotic patients who caused the most burden and who may not in most instances be hospitalized.

In a recent report* Creer and Wing summarize their considerable experience with schizophrenic patients in the home setting. Their group consisted of 50 middle-class patients and 30 working-class patients.

The picture they presented was not very different from that reported by Murphy et al. Seventy-four percent of the relatives were troubled that the patients were withdrawn from social contacts. Some did not go out, or by their behavior they prevented the families from having friends in. Many patients spent hours every day doing nothing or sleeping inordinately. Most families reported that they could not get patients to take up a hobby.

Sixty-six percent of the patients behaved embarrassingly in some ways, and nearly three quarters had great difficulty in mixing outside the home. Forty-eight percent of the relatives felt the effect on their own well-being of living with the patient had been severe or very severe, and they all reported that the most severe strain was the unpredictability of the patient. Some family members achieved a sad resignation summarized in the statement, "Once you realize he will never be cured you start to relax."

These studies do not suggest that there should be a return to the large mental hospital. The findings of Goffman are probably still valid and will be an inevitable concomitant of any institution that grows beyond an optimal size for humane interaction. But they do criticize a current orthodoxy which holds that deinstitutionalization inevitably leads to better lives for those whom we previously called chronic psychotics. They emphasize that being in the community is not in itself a sufficient end if it is not accompanied by an energetic, constantly monitored service to the patient and those who provide a setting for the patient, whether it be in the family or in a foster home. Furthermore they emphasize that there is a continuing strain on the community and the family, a strain that is both economic and psychological. Community care, properly conducted, is clearly more expensive than centralized institutionalization.

In our proper respect for civil liberties, many people who require care may drift outside the social network of caring institutions, not because of active personal choice and existential freedom, but as a result of passivity, lack of social skills and poor capacity to handle the complex mechanics required to move in the world that are the behavioral manifestations of their illness in many schizophrenic patients. The fate of many of these de-institutionalized patients is described in a by now famous letter in the *New York Times* of December 9, 1973: "In hotels and rooming houses once built for the well-to-do who came to spend their vacations along the sea, hundreds of former mental patients now sit, heads sunk into their

---

*Schizophrenia at Home. Clare Creer and John Wing. Supplement to the British Journal of Psychiatry. Vol. 125. December 1974.

hands, oblivious to grim, often filthy surroundings. It is estimated that there are 300 to 800 former mental patients in Long Beach, which has a population of 34,000. And many residents worry about the growing numbers . . . The impact of taking a block of people like this from an institution and throwing them in a facility where there is no counterbalancing force of hospital personnel builds up a kind of pathological milieu. They also tend to put people who are under stress, like our elderly and those never made for the world, under more stress, so that we've seen people—little old ladies who were formerly managing with their ongoing associations—ending up in our mental-health clinic . . . The community's hostility added to the former patients' feelings of isolation, but the community had the right to determine its own make-up. Long Beach had 2,500 of the 3,500 licensed beds in Nassau County approved by the New York State Department of Social Services for all types of adult care. In addition, Long Beach has 500 unlicensed beds in hotels and boarding houses, where some of the worst conditions prevail.'' Clearly, these patients have in important ways been abandoned and the community feels threatened. The community has not been prepared to receive the ex-inmates of the hospitals.

And from Britain an even more distressing example of what may happen to patients who drop out of the care-giving network is described by Tidmarsh in the *British Journal of Psychiatry* of April 1973. He reports that 1,225 men and 190 women were sleeping out in London, the highest figure since 1907. Taking into account factors such as the reduction of lodging house accommodation and increase in the number of the unemployed in Britian, surveys showed that at least a quarter of this population is mentally ill, the majority being schizophrenic. He suggests that many of these patients would formerly have been treated in mental hospitals. Furthermore, the common lodging houses (cheap doss-houses run by municipalities) are de facto after-care hostels, accommodating more patients than the officially designated after-care hostels. In view of this, Tidmarsh warns psychiatrists that they should think twice before depriving their patients of the asylum of their hospitals.

Up to now we have dealt with patients who are still caught up in a traditional care-giving system. Although the forms of care giving are changed and questioned, there is fundamental social acceptance of the roles of patients and care givers. But there has been a sophisticated and powerfully expressed current of criticism questioning the very labeling of the psychiatrically disturbed person as "sick" or a "patient." Concomitant with this criticism is its logical consequence: a criticism of the physician's role as labeler, diagnostician, an agent (in this formulation) of a form of societal psychic violence. Laing and his associates, Cooper and Esterson, have given particular psychiatric examples and formulations of the historico-sociological criticisms of Foucault. They have dissented from the commonly held view that aberrance falling into patterns conventionally diagnosed as madness is at best distressing and, at worst, a danger to the sufferer or the people about him.

Laing's earlier work was concerned with schizophrenic patients in traditional mental hospitals. In his writing he deepened the description of Barton's carefully described "institutional neurosis," and made more explicit pleas for humane, individually attentive therapy. He is a skilled and passionate writer whose style of exposition is often close to the polemical. The total institution and assumptions of traditional psychiatry were subjected to scornful reanalysis; as in his well known reexamination of Kraepelin's interview of a schizophrenic patient. Laing explicitly condemns Kraepelin and subsequent psychiatrists following his mode of practice for their clinical obtuseness and lack· of moral imagination. He demonstrates an attempt to understand rather than to label the patient. In the process of understanding the patient, the aberrant behavior is no longer perceived as arbitrary, fragmented—and by implication—beyond humanity.

The understanding of this private and different perception of the world follows from a major source of the Laingian position derived from existential philosophy. By accepting the uniqueness of personal experience and the inevitable distortion of others' experience, he arrives at a Sartrean conception of "the other" (the other who is always in some way alien to one's own existential experience.) "Hell," Sartre wrote in his play *No Exit*, "is other people," a view that he elaborated into a delineation of the group as being a collection of mutually limiting and tyrannical individuals. It emphasizes the loneliness and uniqueness of every individual's "being in the world" and the tyranny of others who attempt to impose their world view on any aberrant individual.

In its extreme version, this point of view implies that all members of a group are potentially tyrannical towards all other members of the group.

The family became for Laing the epitome of the tyrannical group. In his case histories of individual families, he writes with a novelist's eye for personal interaction and the nuances of language. The histories are more vivid than most psychiatric writing, and they give flesh and blood to the theoretical concepts of Bateson and Jackson. They outline the process by which Laing believes families mystify their vulnerable members into behavior which will be described as sick. And in David Cooper's *The Death of the Family* the view of the family in the capitalist world is pushed to its radical limit. Cooper describes the family as a microcosm of the authoritarian society; like the society, it is a system of hierarchical nay-saying authority. Even when the family acts as benevolently as it can—within the limits of its structure—it serves, in Cooper's terms, only to deprive the inidividual by protecting him from the experience of his ultimate loneliness and private terrors. Without this terror he believes there is no true attainment of individual liberty or a full awareness of the self.

One can see how such existential concepts support a conviction that all modes of individual experience are equally valuable. As a consequence, no single person,

---

*Institutional Neurosis (2nd edition). Russell Barton. John Wright and Sons Ltd., 1966. pp. 68.

however he is socially defined, has a right to invalidate any other individual's experience. And all individual experience represents an attempt to come to terms with a particular life situation into which the individual has been thrown. Neither the parents nor (more crucially for this paper) the physician may question or deny the validity of a particular mode of experience.

Once such a position is accepted, the description of unusual or idiosyncratic behavior as psychotic or sick is inaccurate and invalid and the nonsymmetrical relationship between physician and patient is untenable. The best a physician helper can do is to serve as a compassionate companion in the particular experiential journey of the troubled person. This journey is seen as an attempt to adapt to a dictated environment. Laing and Cooper have at various times stated that the "psychotic" experience may be profound and valuable, and as a mode of being may be superior to the flat self—denying experience of those whom society accepts as adjusted and sane.

By being undefined as patient and redefined as spiritual voyager, the psychotic patient is removed from the medical model or structure. It would be inappropriate to use a hospital for an existential option, or indeed to treat a spiritual exercise with medication. There are probably some people who have made a Laingian existential use of a psychotic experience, but one remembers Tidmarsh's vagrants and the people sitting on the seaside benches, and the patients in Wing and Brown's studies who remain alienated from the world under even the best circumstances. The problem remains that there is a residual core of patients who remain, by all but the most extreme existentialist definitions, "sick people." From clearly organic cause or for reasons of gross psychological or cognitive disability they are unable to care for themselves in the day-to-day world, and are manifestly not engaged in a psychic voyage of discovery of the kind imagined by Laing. And they still seem to require the benign license attached to the sick role as defined by Talcott Parsons: they need to be exempted from some or all of their normal social responsibilities; it has to be accepted by society that their illness is involuntary and that their cure is not dependent upon an act of will; they suffer in their sickness. It is true that some of the Parsonian components may be lacking in the chronically ill, but this does not invalidate their position. They may not be fully aware of their condition, and in some rare instances they do not appear to suffer because of their disability and they do not always voluntarily seek help.

It is this last group of patients which most clearly requires precisely that traditional form of physicianship, which has been caricatured and dismissed by Laing.

In addition to Laing's idiosyncratic caricature of the psychiatrist, there has been a narrow definition of the medical model which has held sway in recent times: the physician in this model is seen to be the agent of rational therapy, who attempts cure by medically treating disease with a readily identifiable somatic cause. But the role of physician antedates the scientific discoveries of the eighteenth and nineteenth century. It is independent of such basic sciences as physiology, pharmacology or pathology. The authority of the physician (and the psychiatrist is a physician) which Patterson has labeled Aesculapian authority resides in a socially ascribed and accepted response to suffering. Unlike the priest, whose function has often paralleled that of the physician, he applies (in the ideal), without moral judgement, the total available technology of a given period to the alleviation of suffering, whatever its cause.

If a category of human suffering has been placed within the moral rather than the illness category of experience, then it is not amenable or available to the medical armamentarium as I have just attempted to define it. The radical assumption that madness may be a form of virtue renders the response to it aesthetic or moral. The problem of the aesthetic response is that it is characterized by much ''feeling with'' but no action. (We weep when the heroine dies in the movies, but we do not try to save her.) This is the exact opposite of the physician's response. He must cultivate—again in the ideal—a decent neutrality so that his action is directed towards helping his patient, rather than being an expression of, or an alleviation of, his own emotional state.

At its worse, this form of medical authority may appear to be, or may actually be, a disguise for heartlessness, but more frequently it provides a psychological framework within which the healer may aid anyone, whether he likes him or dislikes him, whether he is personable or ugly or whether he is defined as friend or enemy—and from the point of view of this paper—whether he behaves acceptably or in a way that would be disgusting to uninvolved people.

Whichever model is used, our technology—whether it be psychological or somatic—is not yet adequate to the problem of the chronic psychosis. One can understand the affront chronic patients represent to the ''omnipotence'' of the healer. While it may not be intended, redefining these patients as spiritual voyagers removes them from the arena of physicianly responsibility and they are made to disappear by a rhetorical psychological trick. Those who claim to have the most benign interests of the ''mad'' at heart may have deprived them of the imperfect, partial technology of healing which is available. This is in contrast to the modest pragmatic approach of those who accept the limits on expectation so often necessary with the chronic psychotic. Without this pragmatism they are denied, in the most perennial sense of the word, asylum. And in conclusion, all I am attempting to say in this chapter is: we will continue to require sanctuaries to provide shelter and treatment. In these new versions of the colony or asylum, both the physical and social concerns of the fragile and helplessly aberrant will be appropriately met. And we require careful and continuing back-up support when they are in the world of the ''community.'' We must not bluff ourselves by our statistics to satisfy a dominant rhetoric or government granting agency that we have performed a social miracle and there are no more mad men in the world.

5

A Day-Night
Psychiatric Unit
In A Rural General Hospital

RONALD C. YOUNG, BOB WILLIAMS AND NORMAN P. PETERSON

BACKGROUND

Mental health services prior to 1958 in northwestern Minnesota were virtually nonexistent. A state hospital and limited private practice in psychiatry were the identified treatment services for 94,000 people in an agricultural setting of small towns in eight counties covering 12,000 square miles.

In 1956, Minnesota passed pioneering mental health legislation that made possible 50 percent grant-in-aid funding for community mental health services. This financial assistance prompted the commissioners of the eight northwestern counties to listen to a proposal for locally operated mental health services. A community-based program emerged in 1958 with a staff of five people located at Crookston, Minnesota. This county coalition, operating through an area board, had the agony and the satisfaction of molding their very own program. They tried it all—one central clinic, several clinics, circuit riders, and consultation by the few mental health professionals. Some of the efforts had measurable impact, but usually they fell short of meeting the needs of the people. Funds were not sufficient to carry out extensive programs, so emphasis was finally placed on the consultation model.

By late 1966, a fairly solid base had emerged of consultation services and backup for the ever-present first line of care givers, including clergy, physicians, welfare, public health and legal agents. The small mental health center staff usually acted as therapists only when others in the unorganized cadre of care givers were unable or unwilling to establish a client relationship. The area board and staff were able to include prevention within their program plan. They also realized that another continued need was for a middle range of local care. Something was needed beyond the growing skills of local care takers for problems so severe or complex that people had to be sent to specialized treatment centers miles away. The questions about providing middle range treatment and adjustment included the design of the care pattern, how the program could be financed, whether one location would suffice or there should be an attempt to provide treatment at several locations in the large geographic and sparsely populated area.

Middle-range treatment efforts could not be boldly begun because there was too little information or program experience available close at hand and too many unanswered questions. Trips were made through Kansas, Massachusetts, Colorado, California and Canada by staff and board representatives in an attempt to learn from others who had developed middle-range treatment programs and tried to integrate a patchwork of human services into a network. Questions centered on locating and integrating new social services into a community and possibly into an existing hospital.

After resifting local needs, sorting the innovative experiences of other people, and considering the possible creation of an expensive legacy, it was decided to apply for federal funds to provide a small, flexible multiple-purpose treatment unit with the capability of hospitalization. This matrix was the womb into which federal seed money might be planted. (As in most scenes of conception there was excitement, murmured promises, hints of fear that those promises might be for the moment and that there was no certainty in the expectations for the future.) In the background was the sober fact that someone was going to have to be responsible to nurture, guide and support any viable offspring from that union.

The decision about location for this new service was not without complications, resentment and high-pitched competition between two communities of similar size but located forty-five miles apart. Agreement was finally reached on sanctioning an addition to Northwestern Hospital Services, a community nonprofit general hospital of 150 beds located at Thief River Falls, Minnesota. The hospital had already had experience with several areas of specialty care, and exhibited interest in the new community mental health supplement to the original consultation services.

The resources that were present in the area on which the new proposed comprehensive services were built included the following:

1. The Northwestern Mental Health Center at Crookston, which provided and emphasized consultation, education and coordination of services.

2. Traditional care givers in every community, such as physicians, school personnel, welfare workers, clergy and law enforcement groups, who assumed primary responsibility for point of entry treatment, referring only those cases which they could not manage without consultative. help.

3. A state mental health hospital at Fergus Falls, Minnesota, willing to tailor its programs to augment local psychiatric services and emphasize treatment rather than custody.

With these resources identified, the plan for additional service was gradually formed. The area mental health system at that point was visualized as a three-tiered pyramid whose base represented the first-line community care givers; a second level consisting of specialized psychiatric services at the Thief River Falls hospital; and a third tier devoted to the small percentage of people who would require specialized longer-term, intensive care in a state hospital. The point of entry for most of the consumers was the first level, since the majority of problems were adequately handled through the usual community channels. People requiring more intensive and time-consuming treatment were referred to another tier for evaluation or treatment and then were returned to broader levels for follow-up services.

Several operational principles were set forth to fit the foregoing realities:

1. There was need for a system which emphasized communication rather than limiting decision making. Meaningful interactions and decisions occurred at all times throughout the system, with or without "official" sanction. There were too few professionals to "bless," let alone, "direct," all therapeutic relationships. Consequently, all participants, including patients, and non professionals, were encouraged to take responsible action, providing they were able to communicate the content of the transactions to other significant participants. It was felt that in this way the system could be monitored for potentially harmful events and the skills of all participants would be upgraded. It was also felt that this was a natural addition to the consultation model already well established.

2. The flattened treatment hierarchy encouraged open communications and was effective.

3. The "trapeze transfer" concept of continuity enhanced patient care. The shifting of treatment or follow-up from one care-giver to another contained overlap, so the referring persons did not detach themselves from the case before the accepting worker had a firm grip on the situation. This principle of temporary redundancy prevented losing the patients "between the cracks."

4. Just as the decision making in care and treatment was kept close to the patient, the patient was kept close to his environment of reference for maximally effective intervention efforts.

Following the decision on the program concept and the physical location of facilities, this new addition to the area mental health services was identified as the Day-Night Unit of Northwestern Hospital Services. Questions remained by the hundreds. What kind of architecture? What kind of bedrooms? How many? What kinds of activity rooms? Should there be conventional offices for staff? What kinds of staffing patterns would fit our needs the best? What would be the effectiveness of staff members who would be in the classifications other than the historic social scientists? What contractual agreements are needed? How would services be paid for?

Following closely behind the myriad questions was a full parade of consultants. Many were helpful, others seemed to be transmitting their private ideas into the ionosphere, and some were a part of the conditions in the acceptance of the funds for construction and staffing. After much time spent with federal grantors and state agency representatives, the facility and program plan, like an embryo, slowly began to assume some shape. With additional architectural and mental health consultation, parameters were formed against which to gauge necessary decisions and ultimately use as benchmarks to measure achievement. Some of these 1967 rough parameters are listed, and for continuity, we are providing our 1974 assessments of them.

Parameter No. 1:
We do not know what will be needed in ten years for either facilities or program.
Assessment:
There were no totally acceptable models or plans for physical facilities available to us when the design discussions started with the architect. There were to be approximately 11,000 square feet added to a general acute hospital.

A program in Yorkton, Saskatchewan, was visited, as it was a recent facility attached to a similar-size general hospital. The Denver area facilities were of a historic type found in general hospitals or non-hospital attached programs. Kansas City had a model that used a physical corridor connection to a general hospital linking a day hospital program to the general hospital facility. It was apparent to us that one factor was evident in the majority of the facilities we viewed and researched. The psychiatric programs did include various aspects such as day or night services, partial hospitalization and outpatient services, but the physical facilities for the services were separate and distinct parts of a building and were identified as such. There was not a feeling or indication that the psychiatric service was really integrated into the entire hospital or health services facility. Many fine features and aspects of design and good planning were evident in these facilities, but this separateness did exist and was a feature we did not want.

We were able to add the floor addition so that one main corridor of the unit connected and flowed into a nineteen-bed medical unit that became the inpatient services for psychiatry. By this means, there was an immediate integration of what was a historic and classical hospital service with the new psychiatric service. A roof deck on the new addition was provided for group recreational programs. This was another interdigitating device, as this area was to be used by all patients for diversional therapy and by staff for lunch and coffee breaks. We felt that we had a good start on integrating this new service into the total physical fabric of the general hospital.

The interior design and space allocations of the unit were carefully planned to provide flexibility and lend support to the adopted philosophy and concept that we didn't know exactly what would evolve as an effective program and treatment, and *there would be changes.* The physical facility would have to accommodate change, and the designers were able to accomplish this without the installation of movable walls.

The initial staff was recruited quite rapidly and again we maintained a pivitol stance so we could change direction or emphasis as program developed. This was accomplished in part by plan and in part out of necessity. With a part-time psychiatrist living three hundred miles away and flying in each week for two or three days as medical director, one MSW social worker and one BS social worker, one master's degree psychologist and a master's degree recreational therapist, we filled in the balance of fourteen staff members at the hospital unit with technicians, diploma RN's, LPN's and nurses' aides. This minority of higher-trained staff precluded too many program contributions based on entrenched, rigid concepts. Flexibility and a climate for new ideas were present and enhanced the philosophy of reasonable experimentation.

Specific personnel shortages influenced and shaped some aspects of program planning. By necessity, more responsiblity for case management, counseling, evaluation, crisis intervention and community liaison was shifted onto paraprofessionals, who subsequently performed with maturity and intuitive skill.

An arrangement where each direct care staff member served as coordinator for a case load assigned by the team proved to be an effective way to ensure individual administrative supervision for each patient. These staff people also functioned as therapists and group leaders in various aspects of the program.

The special skills of psychiatric social workers, recreational therapists, psychologists, occupational therapists and nurses were exploited in organizing and supervising segments of the program appropriate to their areas of expertise, and they were also expected to assist their colleagues to become proficient therapists in these areas.

There were numerous advantages and some disadvantages to this kind of staffing pattern. The assignment of explicit responsibility for case management to paraprofessionals, as well as professionals, stimulated their vocational growth and engendered a deep sense of pride and involvement in the program. These staff members conscientiously looked after the details of therapy and manifested themselves in strong patient advocacy. Placing both the responsibility and authority for treatment decisions in the hands of all staff members is an inherent challenge to perform at a high level.

The most obvious shortcoming to this staff configuration is that there is sometimes no adequate substitute for professional expertise. In-service sessions, consultations, personal devotion and years of experience cannot always take the place of an extensive formal education. Concern, personal involvement and intuitive insight are not always sufficient to solve human problems.

Community acceptance was another important consideration. In a rural "fish bowl" setting, the mental health unit and staff were highly visible, and became the subject of interest scrutiny and discussion. The community, and particularly its leaders and professionals, quickly assessed the strengths and weaknesses of the Day-Night staff and took this into consideration when considering a referral. The communication network in a rural area makes it relatively easy to determine whether or not patients are being helped by the program. Also, rightly or wrongly, the community, and especially referring physicians, placed a high value on professional training, and in the absence of other criteria, tended to equate it with competence. Most of the staff eventually enjoyed a high degree of professional acceptance, but it was a measured process of proving ability.

In retrospect, it would have been easier and perhaps more effective to have had a somewhat larger percentage of staff with advanced training to make diagnostic decisions and structure therapy. The basic organizational format and staffing plan were sound; the mix of professionals and paraprofessionals could have been somewhat different.

Parameter No. 2:
We want to avoid the traditional hospital or insitutional atmosphere and tone.
Assessment:
We accomplished the departure from the usual austere, bleak and institutional setting for our treatment unit by telling the designers and architects that this facility was going to be different in both program and surroundings. The focus was going to be on the patient and those close to him. The architectural firm had knowledgeable people who could listen well. They had another advantage in that they had not been involved in the planning of a psychiatric unit in a hospital setting before.

The excellent results were: the use of bright colors, a combination of textured finishes, stone, heavy dimension wood, openness, glass for see-through visibility, and barbecue units in the snack bar, back to back with an efficient kitchen facility. Folding sound-retardant dividers in place of some walls provided the room-size flexibility. Patient rooms took the appearance of motel or studio rooms and provided multiple use in a limited number. Offices were provided in limited number and averaged less than one per three staff members and were used for consultation, reading, dictating and treatment activities. This promoted co-mingling of staff with patients to a greater extent and in addition to scheduled treatment and group activities on the unit. These very attractive facilities in close touch with the patient contributed to effective treatment. National recognition has been given to the total normative effect of this facility design and furnishings.

Parameter No. 3:
We must guard against the trap of limiting treatment options for patients exclusively to the practices of general hospital settings.
Assessment:
The inpatient services that are an integral element of the treatment scheme and are located within the area of a former nineteen-bed medical service and provide the only resemblance to the classical general psychiatric service in a hospital. The usual semiprivate rooms equipped with hospital furniture along with three security or "safe" single rooms are supplemented by utility rooms, a diet kitchen, medication unit, storage and nurses station. The staff, their training, dress and functions fit in with the day hospital closely and the inpatient rooms are the dormitory or bedroom areas. The patients in this service are totally involved in the day-hospital or partial-hospitalization programs.

All physicians having privileges on the hospital staff can admit their patients to the psychiatric inpatient service, and they continue alongside the staff of the Day-Night Unit. The patient, his attending physician and the Day-Night Unit staff combine desires, expertise and recommendations so that a treatment plan takes shape. Admissions to the inpatient services are deemphasized and used only for the following reasons:

1. Severe personality disorganization, psychosis or potentially dangerous behavior that would not be adequately or safely treated in the patient's own environment.
2. Administration of special somatic or milieu therapies.
3. Diagnostic questions that could not be explored outside a hospital.
4. The need for concomitant medical and psychiatric care.
5. Social and domiciliary crises requiring temporary refuge.
6. Court commitment for psychiatric treatment or temporary hold orders.

Short-term inpatient stays are demonstrated by an average length of stay of less than twelve days. The combined staff efforts carry out rapid psychodynamic and medical evaluations while arranging appropriate dispositions with transfer to day hospital or outpatient services being used most frequently. The atmosphere of the inpatient services is kept open and community-oriented with daily influx into the day-hospital and partial-hospitalization programs.

Parameter No. 4:
We would have to develop acceptance and understanding of this program which would be new, slowly evolving, and a vast departure from the usual services found in a rural community and a comparatively small general hospital setting.
Assessment:
The first organized programs in mental health started in the Crookston location touched lightly on direct services and treatment and placed emphasis on consultation and education. This concept did not cause any great concern, and there was little interest or attention exhibited in the general area population, as the mental-illness scene to most people was miles away behind the walls of the state hospital.

Now that direct services, including the overnight housing of people for psychiatric treatment in one of the quiet rural communities had come into being, there were mixed feelings about providing services of a type that would bring in and attract to one center those persons whose behavior was questionable and who might even act dangerously.

Every subdivision within a hospital—surgery, intensive care, central supply, X-ray—has a unique architectural environment and a specialized staff to carry out a particular mission. This deliberate uniqueness, while promoting efficiency, also establishes territories that discourage the free flow of outsiders across its borders. This is often more noticeable and intimidating with psychiatric units than other hospital elements whose daily tasks share a common ''medical'' aura.

Too much separateness and distinctiveness were considered undesirable by the unit executive staff and hospital administration, and a great deal of time and effort was spent integrating it into the general hospital family. These efforts were not totally successful, but after three years the Day-Night Unit rested comfortably in the hospital matrix.

An early mistake was made in discouraging, rather than encouraging, inspection visits by hospital staff during the construction phase. This policy, although practical at the time, accentuated the separateness and prevented other employees from feeling that the unit belonged to the rest of the hospital. Many inservice sessions and informal interactions were necessary to overcome this original deficit in rapport.

Most employees were acutely aware of the unit, but had little to do with it. Although no attitudinal studies were done, their avoidance seemed to stem from active discomfort with psychiatric illness rather than passive disinterest. A few openly admitted fears about going ''up there'' or ''third floor,'' and for many months there was intense curiosity and nervous joking about the unit and the staff.

This phenomenon is also seen in urban hospital psychiatric units, but usually to a lesser degree because of the city's general climate of anonymity and privacy.

The director of nursing was an important force in promoting integration of the Day-Night Unit into the hospital. Her supervisory responsibilities cut across most departments and she used this leverage to encourage participation in in-serivce programs and to improve daily communication.

The Day-Night staff's outreach program floundered initially because they came across to other employees as consultants and experts rather than as fellow employees engaged in a mutual task. Once this subtle kind of putdown was recognized and dealt with, the consultation program became more effective.

The nurse in charge of the inpatient service also played an important role in interpreting the unit to the rest of the hospital and vice versa. Her successful prior experience as a medical nurse and her current position as a mental health professional enabled her to understand both perspectives and encourage rapprochement.

The physicians on the staff were quick to welcome the promise of treatment facilities and psychiatric services that would fill a vast void between ''doing nothing'' and commitment to the state hospital program. Full and general acceptance of the program services is not yet evident. This assessment is based on the reactions of the doctors to the absence of a full-time psychiatrist and the predominance during the first four years of the program of nonpsychiatric trained staff. With the shift in the past year to greater depth of trained professionals, this attitude of the medical staff is changing. Referrals from doctors outside of the community are not as prevalent during the absence of a psychiatrist. A full-time psychiatrist on the unit staff is necessary and is being recruited.

Acceptance of this service as a part of the general health facilities for the area had to be gained from social workers in the county welfare offices, clergy and the state hospital serving this region. Persons in those categories had been the official front-line care givers in the mental health problem areas for several years and were now being exposed to a newly organized program effort that would take over in some cases. The clergy have responded positively and participated in joint efforts including individual case consultation and treatment and educational programs. The county social workers have been willing to share their cases and to trade paperwork. There is an ongoing search for role definition and program responsibility that has not been resolved between the state hospital system and any of the community mental health programs. The relationships are cordial and discussions are frequent, but the final decisions as to role will probably not be settled until a legislative edict is issued in the near future.

Parameter No. 5:
We would have to be attentive to various payment mechanisms and sources of sponsorship for patients in all programs, but especially in the day-hospital, partial-hospitalization and outpatient services.
Assessment:
Our federal staffing grant program was not available when the 50 percent construction grant was awarded. Subsequently, when the staffing grant was applied for on March 10, 1969, the completion of the construction facility was only seven months away. The concept that mental health services were to be considered as public health services lulled some into a false impression that public (state and local) funds through the state community mental health program would provide necessary financing.

The staffing grant narrative did project that approximately 30 percent of the operating budget for the new psychiatric service would be derived from fee for service. The fee schedule recognized the same payment charge system for psychiatric inpatients that was in effect for general medical patients. The day patients or partial-hospitalization patients would be charged $15 for a day program and $6 for an evening program participation. All other non-inpatient psychiatric services would be charged on an hourly basis using the community mental health centers charge schedule of 1 percent of the federal income tax liability for the patient or family head per hour, with a minimum of 50¢ per hour. Fees for these charges were estimated to produce no more than a maximum of 50 percent of the income budget requirements.

Specific mention was made that third-party coverage would be a potential source of payment for services provided to non-inpatients. These sources included commercial insurance, welfare, Medicare and vocational rehabilitation purchased services. Other payments would be from private funds and resources. A reasonable volume of free services was anticipated to be provided as required under the various grant awards and the federal tax-exempt status of the non-profit hospital association sponsoring these services. A further potential source of financial support that was to be developed included special foundation grants for development and operational funds.

The commercial health insurance policies and the Blue Cross nonprofit plans have not, as of 1974, been very helpful or willing to write in their contracts coverage for psychiatric services other than inpatient service.

There is a sprinkling of private insurance firms that offer limited outpatient psychiatric coverage or have a substantial deductible requirement. The Minnesota Blue Cross plan does provide a plan of first dollar coverage for outpatient psychiatric services and specifically recognizes day- and night-hospital programs and the services provided by mental health professionals other than psychiatrists. This plan is also carried in federal employees' contracts written through national Blue Cross plans.

The welfare system in the state, on a county administration basis, provides that welfare recipients who require psychiatric treatment can be admitted to state hospitals, either voluntarily or by court commitment. In these cases the county welfare office responsible for the patient is charged only $10 per month for each patient to cover total inpatient services. This system and the ridiculously low service charge present a problem. Some welfare office directors attempt to resist the utilization of local community services where charges are considerably higher than the state hospital fee system.

The low incidence of health insurance plans that cover non-inpatient psychiatric services, and the present state welfare system covering near free services at state hospitals, have made it very difficult to secure payments for non-inpatient services. The day-hospital and partial-hospitalization programs have sustained losses each year since the program opened in 1969.

A possible solution for adequate financing for community psychiatric services based in a general hospital appeared in Minnesota as of 1972. A token allowance was made from state funds in the grant-in-aid program for community mental health centers. This same source (made possible through contracting with the Northwestern Mental Health Center in this area program) will provide another small grant for two years coinciding with the biennium budget. Looking forward to the time when the federal staffing grant is scheduled to run out, the inclusion of this hospital-based portion into the state community mental health funding appears to be the most logical answer to financial survival.

PROGRESS AND PLANS FOR THE FUTURE

With the addition of the Day-Night Unit, there was a sizable increase in direct services. For a time after the Day-Night Unit opened, there was a disproportionate number of difficult cases referred for treatment. These were clients who had been seen without success by a variety of agencies and professionals. Referral to the Day-Night Unit program was another attempt to solve their chronic and complicated problems. After this group was processed through the Day-Night Unit, there was a decline in the percentage of multiproblem chronic cases and an increase in those with acute and recent symptomatology.

Also, in the early days of the Day-Night Unit there was a higher percentage of welfare cases. This might be explained on the basis of a "wait and see" attitude taken by middle- and upper-class families who wanted to evaluate the competence of the Day-Night program before they sought help for themselves. In the meantime, they used other direct services in cities such as Minneapolis, Fargo or Duluth.

The poor, the rurally isolated, Indians, and the aged make relatively little use of direct services. This level of utilization does not correspond to the incidence of mental disorders in these groups. In the case of those over sixty-five, utilization does not correspond to the large number of aged in this catchment area. To compensate for this underutilization of direct services, the Center staff spends vast amounts of time in the field consulting with nursing homes, hospitals, welfare departments, ministers, physicians and other agencies who have daily contact with these groups. In this way, mental health expertise can be brought to bear on relevant social and psychiatric problems. There are relatively few Indians in the region, and their use of both direct and indirect services is low.

Geographical distance from direct treatment facilities at Thief River Falls and Crookston determines, to some extent, patterns of usage. Those living closest are most likely to avail themselves of direct services.

EMERGENCY SERVICE

Emergency services are related to other Center services. The primary goal of the crisis service is to provide readily accessible face-to-face and telephone service to any person in our catchment area. The focus is to provide intervention at the point of crisis to an individual and/or his social system at a time when they are in need of and receptive to intervention that will restore the situational homeostasis.

The staff providing the service also provides the consultative and clinical aspects of the program. The advantage here is that if further services are needed, the patient or consultee can easily flow through the program without being "lost" or dropped from treatment or consultation because of gaps in those services.

Staff members receive approximately three to four crisis calls per week. In addition, approximately three people per week avail themselves of the 24-hour service by coming to us during day and night time hours, to discuss their situation face to face. The nursing staff of the inpatient service responds to calls and visits during evening, weekend and night hours. If it is felt that further evaluation and/or treatment is necessary, the day staffs of the inpatient, outpatient and partial-hospitalization programs are on call to speak with the patient on the telephone or come to the hospital for a face-to-face conference. During the day hours, the primary resource is a full-time MSW who can respond to these emergencies with back-up if he be unavailable.

The Glenmore Foundation Treatment Center provides three- to five-day evaluation service for alcoholic and drug patients. The entire staff is on 24-hour call. Emergencies are seen at the hospitals, agencies, police departments, in the home, and only seventeen were seen at the Center and labeled as emergencies. Frankly, many emergencies are not labeled as such. At the present time, the Center has no data collection system or retrieval method to collect specific information on the crisis intervention system. Contacts are noted in team notes where a chart exists, or are recorded and kept in a file folder for persons having no prior contact with the Center.

Referrals for emergencies come from lawyers, MD's, ministers, friends, school social workers, law enforcement, welfare, self. There is no adequate data retrieval system other than time sheets. Most emergencies are seen by primary care givers who may refer or request consultation. The emergency services include diagnosis, treatment, and hospitalization.

The forty-nine member staff consists of counseling aides, addiction coordinators, nurses, mental health educators, prevention coordinators, psychiatric social workers, psychologists and psychiatrists.

The full staff is available twenty-four hours a day, seven days per week, with assigned staff on call. Staff handles emergencies weekdays and the inpatient psychiatric service also assumes responsibility evenings and weekends with a back-up call schedule.

The most frequent psychiatric crisis symptom is depression; the most frequent problem is acute family crisis.

The strongest feature of the emergency service is the responsiveness of the Center staff. The weakest features are incomplete organization, coordination and publicity.

In summary, there are several crisis intervention services: the Northwestern Mental Health Center, including the Day-Night Unit; Glenmore Foundation (alcohol and Drug problems); Emergency Home Services (a multi-agency project). The Northwest Directory is a listing of emergency telephone numbers for the entire catchment area and provides numbers that can be called on a 24-hour basis. A well-established emergency resource system, backed up by Center staff consists of our community hospitals, peace officers, family physicians and clergy.

OUTPATIENT SERVICES

Treatment alternatives for children, adolescents and adults include individual, group, family and couples therapy, psychodrama, OT, RT, medications, videotape techniques, emergency services, collaborative therapy, bibliotherapy and community meetings.

The staffing pattern includes those in the field being on call. Coordination with every outpatient service—individual and group consultation, education and program development—is seen by the staff as a prevention opportunity to be exploited. An example is the High Risk Clinic. We took the forms from the School Diagnostic Clinic, counted the children and read the charts to find out how many were high risk babies. After the statistical survey, we went into a rural

area and did a pilot project and then proceeded to apply for federal funds to get this program off the ground. This is our pattern for prevention programs.
We receive referrals from:

Self, family, clergy or friend 157
Physician 172
Court 16
School 22
Welfare 61
Other 62

Others that comprise the total are employers, police, probation officers, Veterans Administration, Catholic Social Services, Manpower Services and Crippled Children. We do not have a waiting list.

Others that comprise the total are employers, police, probation officers, Veterans Administration, Catholic Social Services, Manpower Services and Crippled Children. We do not have a waiting list.
For reasons that are yet to be clarified, there were relatively few referrals from area ministers. Workshops, seminars, personal contacts and other outreach efforts were enthusiastically received by this group, but did not stimulate any significant volume of referrals. It may be that the Mental Health Center's previous consultation and education program for ministers helped them maintain most of their disturbed parishioners in counseling relationships, while referring only the most difficult and refractory cases to family physicians or other facilities who then might call upon the services of the Day-Night Unit.
A much discussed question during the planning stages was whether physicians, who traditionally refer problem cases to specialists, would send patients to the Day-Night Unit, where psychiatric treatment was under the medical supervision of family physicians and where a specialist was available only two days a week. More specifically, would physicians in the region refer patients to a generalist working in a specialty unit? The response was varied. Some were apparently not concerned with this issue, focusing instead on the advantages of having a nearby mental health resource for their patients and accepting rather uncritically the professional credentials and aura of the unit. Old inter-city rivalries were probably convert factors that influenced referrals. Old animosities, jealousies and competitive feelings between Thief River Falls and surrounding towns at times tipped the scales away from referral. Any doubts, including those about staff qualifications, might then justify referring a patient to another center. A significant number of physicians continued to send their patients to the psychiatrists they had used before the Day-Night Unit opened. Geographic proximity was not always a compelling reason for either the patient or his physician to break off established ties with medical specialists in distant cities.

PARTIAL HOSPITALIZATION

A full range of partial-hospitalization alternatives is available, including half-day, evening and weekend programs and night hospital. Any combination of these possibilities is available for the staff's prescription, and "trapeze transfer" from one category to another is easily accomplished.

The length of partial hospitalization is individualized according to the patient's needs, always with the realization that iatrogenic morbidity can occur with overutilization of psychiatric services. The major diagnostic category served by the partial-hospitalization program has been neurotic depression. Night hospitalization is seldom used because it has been found that patients able to function effectively during the day rarely need overnight hospitalization.

It is a well-known fact that partial-hospitalization programs often fail because of transportation difficulties. This is particularly true in a region that is sparsely populated and has no comprehensive transportation system. Whereas occasional outpatient appointments or the visits associated with 24-hour hospitalization usually present no insurmountable travel problems, the daily trips or special lodging arrangements usually required for partial hospitalization are much more of an obstacle to continuing treatment. Granted, a number of very ill patients have shown remarkable ingenuity in getting back and forth to day hospitals, but this tends to be the exception rather than the rule. Usually the family or another interested party must assume some responsibility for assisting a disorganized, withdrawn or poorly motivated patient with daily travel or lodging plans.

These problems were apparent during the planning phase of the Day-Night Unit, but for a time it appeared that a serendipitous situation would essentially solve the transportation problem. Unfortunately, the scheme failed for unexpected reasons.

One of the nation's largest snowmobile manufacturers headquarters is in Thief River Falls and draws a work force from a radius of fifty to seventy-five miles. With employees converging from all parts of the area each day, it held promise of being an ideal travel network for partial-hospitalization patients. The company's personnel department was very cooperative and agreed to put their employees in touch with Day-Night patients needing rides.

In a number of cases this matching plan worked beautifully, but utilization was limited for two main reasons: 1) incongruity of hours, and 2) failure to match geographic locations.

With respect to the first reason, the morning shift at the snowmobile plant began at 7:00 A.M.; the formal program at the Day-Night Unit opened at 9:00 A.M. Many patients were unwilling to arise that early, travel to Thief River Falls before 7:00 A.M. and then wait two hours at the hospital for the first therapy session.

The second problem was even less predictable. Despite the large number of employees who lived in the region, it was often difficult to find one who traveled close enough to a patient's residence to obviate the need for some kind of intermediate transportaiton. The system, though somewhat flexible, was not personalized and exact enough to be acceptable to many patients.

Consequently, a significant percentage of nonresident partial-hospitalization patients either supplied their own transportation or were quartered in local hotels and rooming houses.

INPATIENT SERVICE

The inpatient service is an integral part of the total program and inpatients participate in activities with other categories of patients as prescribed by the treatment team.

There is a core staff consisting of nursing personnel and psychiatric aides assigned primarily to the inpatient service. It is their responsibility to provide coverage for those patients unable to leave the inpatient area to participate in other activities and to staff the evening, night and weekend shifts. Much of their time is spent in informal interactions with patients, one-to-one conferences, recreational activities and some community meetings.

Referrals to the inpatient program come from:

Family	55.1%
Self	14.6%
Physicians	12.1%
Police Officers	12.1%
Mental Health Center Staff	2.7%
All other areas (court, clergy, schools and welfare) were approximately	1% each

Neurotic depression	29.5%
Anxiety neurosis	13.5%
Alcoholism - chronic	8.7%
Schizophrenia, paranoid type	6.9%
Schizoid personality	4.6%
Alcoholism - acute	4.6%

It is the practice not to exclude any citizens of our area from service for any reason. The diagnostic groups showing the lowest incidences are hysterical neurosis, adjustment reaction to adult life, acute schizophrenia, nonpsychotic acute brain syndrome with epilepsy, drug addiction, adolescent situational reaction, cerebral atrophy and mental retardation. There is a problem in serving the aged because of their inability to come to the Center, the distance being considerable in this rural area.

The major resources used for patients discharged from the inpatient service were our outpatient and partial-hospitalization facility, 118 or 43.1 percent. 102 or 37.2 percent were discharged home without need of an agency follow-up plan. The next group were people sent to long-term care facilities, such as nursing homes or convalescent nursing care of the VA hospitals. There were 18 in this group comprising 6.4 percent. Seven patients were committed to Fergus Falls State Hospital (2.6 percent).

The nearest non-center psychiatric service has been the Fergus Falls State Hospital. We are fortunate that our relationship with them is good, and they strongly support community-based psychiatric services.

Referral and continuity of care have been matters of high concern for both facilities, and as a result there has been no loss of care due to inadequate relationships.

ADDITIONAL DIRECT SERVICES

Diagnostic Services: The School Diagnostic Clinic is designed to meet the primary and secondary prevention needs of our schools in providing comprehensive diagnosis, treatment and planning for children. The purpose of the clinics is to provide medical, psychological and educational consultation to school personnel on children with learning, reading, emotional, social or physical problems. Children are referred to the clinic by doctors, school social workers, teachers and parents.

Conventional psychological and psychiatric diagnostic services are available through the Center staff to the entire area, including its school psychologist and school social workers.

Rehabilitation Services: There are two sheltered workshops in the area providing rehabilitative services to the handicapped. The Center staff provides consultation to this program and the alcohol and drug program at Glenmore.

Pre-Care—After-Care: Both direct and consultation services are offered for pre-care and after-care problems. Contacts are maintained with a number of other agencies, including the state hospital, welfare departments, county nursing service, peace officers, Division of Vocational Rehabilitation, etc.

INDIRECT SERVICES

Staff members act as encouragers, educators, direct caretakers, enablers, stimulators and consultants on program and curriculum changes. The staff is the mediator between individuals, families and agencies in the community. This philosophy allows everyone to get into the mental health picture and urges community citizens to be concerned with their neighbors. Our philosophy emphasizes the social model and de-emphasizes the disease model.

The Center developed local resources in the community to carry out mental health functions because of their nearness to the situation and more ready availability. The board and staff decentralized services to increase availability.

Our federal funds are decreasing. Our hope, as this decrease occurs, is that there will be a corresponding increase in the state and local communities' gradual assumption of program responsibility. This applies to hospitals, nursing homes, welfare officers, ministers, law enforcement, Day Activity Centers, etc., as these agencies are dealing directly with emotional and social problems.

We continue to assist programs and people in prevention, diagnosis and treatment of mental illness, retardation and addiction, through education, consultation, assistance in program building, joint funding and to provide direct services when others say they cannot or will not become involved.

The extent of our commitment to indirect services is reflected in the following table:

	Mental Health	Mental Retardation	Alcohol & Drugs	Total
Consultation	5,758.25	1,904.75	2,907.50	10,570.50 hours
Direct Services	9,761.50	168.75	534.25	10,464.50 hours

FUTURE PROGRAM PLANS

Though the basic philosophy of our program has not altered since the start, there have been many administrative and program changes incorporated into future program plans.

1. Considerably more staff time is now being spent on comprehensive planning and coordination of relevant programs in this catchment area.

2. There has been improvement in business administration practices and in coordination of services.

3. Planning and implementing programs for developmental disabilities and alcohol and drug programs has been greatly increased.

4. More emphasis is being placed on programs devoted to children.

5. Some funded staff positions which were unfilled are now filled.

6. The present board is reevaluating the administrative structure to facilitate planning, coordination and implementation of services.

7. A joint data collection system with Fergus Falls State Hospital is currently under way and will provide a much clearer picture of patient flow patterns throughout the regional mental health system. This will provide a basis for future comprehensive planning and rational utilization of existing facilities.

8. There are advisory committees for coordination. Both the Comprehensive Mental Health Center and State Hospital programs are represented on five area-wide advisory committees. Coordination of two programs and discussions about joint patients are done in meetings and through telephone consultations.

9. Statistics show that consultation and education services are used in proportion to population percentages in each county. Minority groups use services slightly above their percentage of the population, but their need is more than other groups'. The rate of service to alcoholics is accelerating, but is inadequate for their needs. More service is being provided to the aged than previously, but it is still not proportionate to the relatively high percentage of the aged living in this region.

10. From the standpoint of disability groups, more staff time is spent with young people, those with chemical dependency problems, the retarded and persons with developmental disabilities. Both direct service and consultation time are involved in this effort. Much of this changing emphasis can be attributed to federal and state program initiatives. With a larger staff, the Center is able to be open evenings and serve working people who cannot come during the day. Many of the staff are younger and more responsive to teenagers and their problems. Many special programs have been created for younger age groups.

11. Planning for inservice training is an ongoing process limited only by availability of staff. Existing inservice is provided to community agencies (nursing homes, peace officers, day-care center staff, ministers, hospitals, welfare offices, schools students, teachers, PTA's, school social workers), and some are designed for the community at large. We are consistently being asked for more inservice training by these agencies. This service competes with the constant demand for direct service and crisis intervention programs.

12. The system used in maintaining patients' records is a simplified filing system. Since early 1974 we have been doing inservice with other agencies to do the Lawrence-Weed Problem Oriented charting. We have comprehensive data on charts, and we exchange data with other agencies. We are in the process of exploring methods for more ready retrieval of statistical and other data.

The Day-Night Unit chart is an integrated, continuous record of contacts with the patient during outpatient and partial-hospitalization treatment. Also included are summaries and excerpts from his inpatient record. All testing, correspondence, initial evaluation, telephone contacts, medications and team notes are included in the patient's chart.

The chart is automatically available to all Center staff, and there is frequent communication between the two offices as to new referrals into the system.

Appropriate exchange of records with other agencies is considered to be part of good patient care, providing the patient authorizes this communication.

13. Consumer participation in planning and services of the Center is very important to us. We have consumers on our Youth Councils throughout the area. We have many consumers on our Area Board and Advisory Boards: the

Mental Health Board, the Mental Health Committee, the Developmental Disabilities Committee and the Northwest Council on Alcohol and Drug Problems, Inc. We have several consumers on the Group Home Board and the Sheltered Workshop Boards which function in the area. The Board for Special Education also has consumers, along with the superintendents. We receive feedback from consumers on the Day Activity Center's Board, and daily feedback from primary care offices. Our board members, who live in the area and our county commissioners hear daily feedback from their constituents and report back to us.

Our primary consultation and education goal is to reduce the incidence of mental illness, addiction and retardation (developmental disabilities) through education (prevention) and early intervention. An emphasis of our consultation and education is to achieve necessary updating or expansion of existing programs and implementation of new programs.

We utilize individual case consultation to support caretakers' ability and confidence in providing services. Concurrently, we are alert for information and motivation for necessary new programs or expansion of existing programs, as well as opportunities to improve the coordination of area services available for mental health, retardation and addiction.

A current prime priority goal of consultation and education, accelerated by state and federal interest, is to achieve sanction and coordination of all agencies within our region for comprehensive planning and implementation of our service delivery system and budgets.

14. Parent study groups: Eight parent study groups which include three ten-week sessions with four to five sets of parents and three three-week sessions with larger groups.

15. Public education: Projects for public education include Child-Rearing Principles for PTA's, Family Disorganization for Rotary Club, Child-Rearing Principles for Northland Community College, Legal Drug Abuse for women's clubs, women's seminars for the Red River Valley Winter Shows on Parent and Teen Communication and Personal Enrichment. Attendance at these functions ranges from twenty to eight individuals. Requests for such seminars and programs are increasing at a rapid pace.

16. Sheltered Workshop: The developmental disabilities specialist consults with the workshop in providing inservice and coordination. The board has seventeen members serving as the governing body. The workshop was implemented by the Division of Vocational Rehabilitation, Red River Valley Medical Society and the Mental Health Center. Two facilities, one in Thief River Falls and one in Crookston, operate to serve a total of 44 clients.

17. Day Activity Workshops: Workshops and inservice training are given by the staff psychologists and the developmental disabilities specialist. Testing procedures are explained in workshops, and individual staffs call for consultation on their individual problems.

18. Home Extension Programs: The Home Extension Services in our area co-sponsor many programs; examples—Parent-Teen Communication, Active Listening, and Mental Health Information are covered for radio and television audiences in the area. Weekly sessions are held in coordination with community resources. The community responds with telephone calls to the station to be answered on the air. A Women's Worry Clinic was conducted in an all-day session with thirty-five women coming from all walks of life and ranging in age from the twenties to eighty-six. This project was well received and will be continued with community resources.

19. Inservice in the Welfare offices: This monthly program is being conducted in the Pennington County Welfare Department in Thief River Falls by the staff social workers. Other welfare offices prefer inservice on a regular one-to-one basis.

20. Inservice in the Public Health nursing services, nursing homes and hospital staffs: Inservice training is provided on a regular monthly basis with the Polk County Nursing Service in Crookston. The nursing homes and hospitals in our area request inservice training regularly. Subjects range from depression, suicide and grief to techniques of active listening.

21. AA groups: Addiction coordinators provide consultation and coordinate the AA groups in the area.

22. Advisory committees: The Developmental Disabilities Advisory Board and the Northwest Council on Alcohol and Drugs have been in existence for many years. The Mental Health Committee was revived last year and held four meetings.

23. Monthly consultations: Consultations each month are held with schools, law enforcement, nursing homes, hospitals, physicians, welfare departments, parents, private agencies, ministers and other primary caretakers.

24. Alcohol and drug consultation: Alcohol and drug counselors are working in the area. The Center staff provides consultation and coordination in this program and assists in recruitment. The comprehensive community approach to the alcohol and drug program has been substantially implemented with at least one reception center in operation.

One of the major functions of the advisory committees is evaluation. The Comprehensive Mental Health Center Board also serves in this capacity.

The program evaluation project staff from Minneapolis has discussed the application of their techniques to this program. Using staff time studies we found that field staffing patterns would have to be changed because some areas were getting less service than they needed. This was changed. A Group Home Committee was formed after a survey was done, and it was found there was a need for group homes in each county in our area.

As a result of a questionnaire about the need for more direct services, the school psychologist and school social worker programs were initiated and the volume of direct services available through the Center Staff was increased.

Based on a survey, individualized statistical reports are sent to each county listing the types and numbers of services given to their residents. The least effective service is the High Risk Newborn Clinic because of insufficient funds to provide staff. The most effective is the Community Consultation Program.

CONCLUSION

At this point in the program's development it is clear that there is a need for clarification of administrative relationships and coordination of program planning.

In historical perspective, a great deal has been accomplished since the program first began. There are many more professionals and services available to the area and these elements are working together quite harmoniously. The Center has been successful in helping to establish a number of community programs that subsequently hired professionals who now live in various localities throughout the region.

Perhaps the most outstanding achievement of this program is its success in carrying out a mission defined in the original staffing grant and in maintaining harmonious relationships within the program and with other community agencies. It is also perhaps somewhat unusual to have a program of this size successfully carry out missions in both direct service and consultation. Also of note is a viable partial-hospitalization program operating in a predominantly rural region.

It is apparent to us that the early premise that was probably the unstated rationale for the federal staffing grant program—i.e., that there were no singular models or approaches to community-based mental health services that could be identified for nation-wide application and pattern recognition—was real and very true. The federal and state funding programs have been the "help from home" that was essential to make possible the seek, search, experiment and educate activities by the many agencies that have participated in or been in touch with this program. Through these continuing and sincere contributions to put effective program pieces together while maintaining the focus on the people with problems, we are developing quality human service programs.

In summary, our open-ended "see-if-it-works" pattern is repeated over and over again in the mental health service systems of northwestern Minnesota. This has led to refinement of many kinds of service delivery with a minimum of exclusion, and a maximum of inclusion of as many people as possible in the planning, delivery and revision of mental health systems.

A rural mental health program must be designed for responsive change. In concept and structure it must be in constant touch with the population it is designed to serve and be able to respond to changed need as it occurs. Without continued external monitoring, there is a relentless drift toward meeting the needs of staff rather than of patients. The original plan was to freeze nothing into permanency, to make no part sacred, and to build machinery for easy revision of the network. Scrutiny sharpens as subsidy money shrinks.

As can be seen in the preceding material there are many parts to the care system, and the trick is to keep them articulated yet be able to dismember those which may be redundant or unnecessary. The projected phasing out of federal subsidy funds, and the concomitant pressure to close state hospitals, place facilities such as the Day-Night Unit in a crunch of increased demand for services coupled with decreased funding. A readiness for adaptive realignment is therefore built in.

Despite minor boundary skirmishes, temporary "pet" projects, and the specter of amputation of unnecessary services, the people seem to have faith that their interests in building positive mental health are well served.

Part III

The Changing
Mental Health Scene:
The Edge of the Art

In Part I we used a low-power lens to bring population-oriented program issues into focus. In this section we focus with a higher-power lens upon the individual and his social network in search of innovative approaches that can strengthen the armamentarium of the mental health worker serving individuals and families "in the field."

A major problem in the diagnostic assessment of patients' needs and resources is the definition of the "perimeter of concern." To what extent—and under what circumstances—should appraisal and treatment encompass the social life space of troubled persons?

Recent advances in patient management stress factors that conduce to "health" as well as "illness," strengths as well as weaknesses. There has been a concomitant emphasis upon adaptation-promoting resources. Such resources have traditionally been sought as "ego strengths" *within* the individual; there has been relative neglect of resources available from attachment figures. In noting the redemptive power of human attachments, renewed appreciation has grown for the remedial qualities of human connectedness. This appreciation is reflected in the recent dramatic realization of professionals of the therapeutic and preventive potential of mutual help groups and community support systems. The perspectives so induced and their application to service delivery—are discussed in this section.

Therapeutic intervention is being further refined by strategies that capitalize on the leverage provided by the "openness" of a living system as it strives to adapt to demands for change. *Hansell* describes this as the "adaptive interval." In a series of publications, he has developed a unique application of systems and adaptation theory to mental health services. In his chapter, he describes the assessment of a patient's "predicament" by evaluating the state of his "seven essential attachments."

Hansell envisions service as an "encounter" arranged to yield "expansion of an individual's adaptational capacity." Service resources are organized to capitalize upon the "adaptive interval" so that the individual is helped to master the situation precipitating his distress. Hansell has refined the techniques for such intervention as "decision counseling." The helper supports a troubled person, whose vision of reality has become temporarily obscured, so that he mobilizes innate ego capacities for appraising his situation and acting upon it. The temporary relationship provided to a troubled person is used to speed him through a process in which the sources of his adaptive difficulties are defined; a strategy for action is elaborated and implemented and any strategic errors are subsequently monitored and corrected for.

Rakoff and Lefebvre review the state of the family therapy arts. They describe the evolution of family therapy, comparing the accents and emphases of existing schools. They suggest that the distinction between so-called "conductor" and "reactive" therapists is probably more artificial than real, implying that effective family therapists display similar skills; differences appear to reflect personality styles rather than ideologies. (There is suggestive confirmation of this hypothesis from research on individual and group psychotherapy. Differences in personality rather than ideology appear to distinguish the effective therapist from one who is ineffective or does harm.) They note that existing parameters for the definition of indications, contraindications or prognosis in family therapy are inadequate, and call for precise research to refine these issues.

They approach the family field with tempered objectivity and do not fall prey to the impassioned zealotry of some of the family therapists they discuss. In spite of the limited ability of family therapists to predict likely outcomes, they stress that family therapy is by now a tried-and-true technique; our relative ignorance of how and why it works should not obscure the fact that it does. Their discussion therefore concludes that "family therapy is a pragmatically useful technique." They warn that family therapy not be regarded as "a quasi-religious system or universal panacea."

Pattison presents us with a comprehensive description of the evolution, present state and applications of psychosocial systems theory. He describes the gradual extension of the mental health professional's perimeter of therapeutic vision which now transcends the boundaries of the psychobiological system to encompass the psychosocial field. He indicates how family therapy, group therapy, Lewinian field theory and ecological systems approaches have contributed to this extended vision. As he lays the multidisciplinary cornerstones upon which his models are constructed, he guides us to an understanding of the potential of social systems intervention in modifying the alternatives, responsibilities, role demands and tasks available in a multiperson field of forces.

Pattison's position is buttressed with case examples. His researcher's analytic orientation leads him to suggest that person-oriented and social-system-oriented models of intervention be seen as complementary. His comparison of these two models has rich heuristic potential.

Lieberman, in a chapter on the use of groups, addresses one of the most crucial issues in human services delivery: quality assurance. From his study of groups, he provides data about some ostensibly therapeutic group endeavors. We learn that some groups—or therapists—*can do harm*. The "encounter group" study of which he was co-investigator noted that certain professional styles produced "casualties," while others did not. For example, a tape-led group did no harm and, parenthetically, produced more effective outcomes than did 50 percent of the human leaders.

Lieberman answers other important questions. Who participates in encounterlike groups? What are they seeking? He finds that these people are little different from those who seek conventional psychotherapy. Many encounter group members are, or have been, in psychotherapy. For others, the encounter group experience functions as a sensitizing "dry run" for subsequent psychotherapy.

He also discusses some of the emerging "alternatives" to institutionalized services, and speculates about their significance.

Reflecting Lieberman's interest in the growth of alternative group service vehicles, *Hirschowitz* describes specialized groups tailored to the needs of people in states of transition. His approach involves definition of the *tasks*, general and specific, appropriate to particular role transitions. Since these tasks tax the *coping* resources of people, the coping process is described, defined and analyzed. He then describes how his concepts are actualized in group vehicles to "help people cope with the tasks of transition." Illustrative groups are discussed, and helping ingredients identified. In his discussion, he emphasizes that some of these ingredients can be made available only in groups—their availability is limited in traditionally conceived dyadic service structures.

On the basis of his analysis, he suggests that groups to ease people through the tasks of transition be presented as educational rather than "service" or "therapy" vehicles. Such definition is based upon feedback from consumers who identify two principal elements in help received: the sharing of relevant information and mutual support. The unique demands upon such an educational structure and its leader are discussed. The helping vehicle is viewed as a purposively constructed temporary support system for the promotion of cognitive mastery and its translation into adaptive action.

Maley and Hunt review the development and present position of the behavior modification "movement." They believe the movement has suffered from the evangelical excesses and occasional "abrasiveness" of its true believers who have promoted "behavior mod" as too all-embracing a panacea for human ills. They remind us that the only orthodoxy is heterodoxy, and call for a pluralistic, pragmatic approach to service delivery. They are critical of the practice of defining patients and their problems by "force fit," the Procrustean process by which problems are defined to meet the needs of a therapeutic provider with an impassioned investment in his own technique. Solutions, they suggest, should fit problems—not the other way around.

Maley and Hunt's chapter holds promise for the more effective integration of behavior modification into the broader streams of human service delivery. They also emphasize the need for conceptual bridges between behavior modification and general systems theory.

With *Ahr*'s chapter on "Community Television and Community Mental Health," our "multifocal lens" rotates once more to bring the community macrocosm into focus. Ahr's approach reflects the community mental health orientation; with this orientation, a population's needs and potential resources are explored so that creative linkage can be forged. The orientation encourages the mobilization of latent resources. In seeking imaginative collaboration with existing community resources, Ahr highlights our underutilization of the mass media in general and of community television in particular. He underscores the media's vast potential for the promotion of mental health and impact upon primary and secondary prevention programs. He describes an approach to fruitful collaboration with community television and offers a logical model for systematic, collaborative planning.

Finally, a chapter by *Rasmussen* gives encouraging information about nationwide program activity in primary prevention. She evaluates primary prevention programs, illuminates what is being done, notes what is not being done and suggests what might be done. She also offers specific strategies to improve the contributions of mental health agencies to prevention. She asserts that the defensive response of many mental health professionals to pleas for the evaluation of preventive programs is groundless, and offers criteria for such evaluation. In common with other contributors, Rasmussen emphasizes the need for clearly stated assumptions and goals in the design and delivery of programs. Without these, neither objective evaluation nor corrective learning can occur. She makes her assumptions clear, indicating that prevention goals are feasible, legitimate and sanctionable.

She emphasizes that goal setting and program evaluation are not excrescences upon the body politic of mental health but organic to its survival, growth and perpetuation.

She reminds us to enlist the support of publics and legislatures, suggesting that this is best realized by clear communication in a comprehensible public language. Prevention goals are achieved *indirectly*, with contributions from social institutions and agencies that may have little or no formal connection with mental health. In working with them—and for them—sanctions, Rasmussen stresses, should be carefully established and maintained.

Enhancing Adaptational Work During Service

NORRIS HANSELL

ADAPTATION AS A THERAPEUTIC CONCEPT

The Random House Dictionary defines adaptation as ''an alteration in the structure or function of an organism by which it becomes better fitted to survive within its environment.'' For the word ''adapt,'' it lists additional meanings, such as ''to conform,'' ''to adjust,'' ''to modify so as to respond to altered conditions.'' The concept of adaptation is a central one in modern biology. It is a beginning point, for example, in the study of the differentiation of life forms into species. In physiology, the notions of homeostasis, feedback and regulation are arranged around the concept of adaptation. The study, for therapeutic purposes, of an individual's growth and development in a particular cultural and familial context is quite practically rooted in consideration of the detailed mechanics of adaptation. Several notions of the origin of symptomatic behavior are grounded in concepts of accommodation to prior circumstance. Some earlier life adjustments are visualized to carry forward and yield in new circumstances a disability. Adaptation concepts also show themselves in several notions of treatment. Therapists often attempt to discover the key elements of a challenging situation so as to allow the patient to more precisely focus his efforts. Or, therapists work to identify what is the no longer present prior problem to which the current behavior may be a lingering response. For example, fixed suspicion, fixed anger or fixed sadness are in some situations understood as a presently nonadaptive pattern reactively established in the context of a prior challenge.

Although concepts of adaptation are not newcomers to clinical work, sometimes they have been fragmented in their application by not being recognized as centering in the physiology of adaptation. For example, such notions as ''neurotic anxiety'' and ''chronic institutional dependence'' clearly arise from adaptational concepts. But the grounding in adaptational mechanics is less clearly expressed in the usual strategies for managing these problems.

Several examples of the application of adaptational concepts to treatment strategies may suggest the nature of the practical line of discovery which is under way. Many of these applications emerge quite easily once the adaptational focus of a service design is recognized. Therefore, let us start with a definition. *A service is an encounter, purposefully arranged, occupying a short interval of life, and yielding an expansion of an individual's adaptational capacity, one which persists after the termination of the encounter.* Such a definition of service emphasizes the fact that the presentation for service arises when prior behaviors, including the adaptational residues of previous challenges, are no longer satisfactory in managing the current circumstance. The goals of treatment include the establishment of such new patterns of behavior as will yield a reduction in distress combined with the continued survival and flourishing of the organism in the new or altered circumstance. The most effective methods for the reduction of distress flow from new behavior which "faces" the challenging situation and manages it. Let us take a look at some consequences of placing adaptational concepts at the center of our clinical designs.

SEVEN ESSENTIAL ATTACHMENTS

As therapists explore the consequences of rooting their service activities in efforts to enhance adaptational work, they find themselves seeking a greater clarification of the normal operations of adaptational behavior. For example, it is often helpful to have available a method for assessing an individual's life-supporting transactions with his environment. It is helpful if the method for assessing these transactions directs the observer's attention broadly across an individual's life pattern, but at the same time, is simple enough to be useful within the ordinary pace of clinical work.

For the purposes of clinical work, we arrange the assessment of transactions with the environment into "seven essential attachments." It would be possible to organize such an inquiry into five, or eight, or ten attachments. More critical than the exact number is the notion that the survey be sufficiently broad to provide perspective, yet show a parsimony which would allow action within the space of an evolving situation.

The seven categories of necessary transaction with the environment are deeply interrelated: as a set, they describe a life support system. On the other hand, they are "cantilevered": the interruption of any attachment for more than a brief interval yields a damage which spreads beyond this attachment to gradually involve all the attachments. For example, if the organism loses its "attachment," or exchange, with oxygen for more than a few seconds, it dies. This consequence follows even if the other attachments, as to food and water, remain intact.

Here, then, are the seven essential attachments (1-16):

1. *To food, oxygen and information of requisite variety:* biochemical and informational supplies;
2. *To a clear concept of a self-identity,* held with conviction;
3. *To persons,* at least one, in persisting interdependent contact, occasionally approximating intimacy;
4. *To groups,* at least one, comprised of individuals who regard this person as a member;

5. *To roles,* at least one, which offer a context for achieving dignity and self-esteem through performance;

6. *To money or purchasing power* so as to participate in an exchange of goods and services in a society specialized for such exchanges;

7. *To a comprehensive system of meaning,* a satisfying set of notions which clarify experience and define ambiguous events.

1. *The attachment to food, oxygen and information.* This primordial attachment includes material exchanges which provide the supplies for the construction of the body and the inputs of sensation which comprise the building blocks of personality and cognitive life. The pace of the damage consequent to loss of this attachment is variable, but the outcome, without repair, is invariable. If the supplies of oxygen are interrupted, death or damage follows quickly. When supplies of sensation and information are interrupted, the disorganization of the personality begins almost as promptly and spreads progressively. Such situations are demonstrated, for example, in the chemical interruptions to sensation which occur during general anesthesia, or with the anatomical interruptions which occur in spinal injuries, or with the situational interruptions which accompany confinement to bed, imprisonment or hospitalization. A flow of information appears necessary to the organism, not only to yield the raw sensation of experience, but to provide a portion of the organizational integrity of personality itself. Although all individuals regulate the flow of information to themselves through using, for instance, a pattern of diurnal rest and activity, or as in arrangements for privacy or vacations, any substantial, sustained interruptions of the flow of information lead to a consequent disorganization of personality and performance.

In clinical settings, an individual's attachment to supplies of information is monitored through observations of the presence of the affect of *curiosity.* Curiosity appears to accompany the physiological activities involved in the registry of sensory experience. It provides a specific signal to an individual, and to his social surround, that he is in active contact with a sensory flow. When such a flow is interrupted, he automatically signals his social surround, for instance, with the affects of boredom and apathy. Such displays signal that he is at risk of having separated from his sensory flow. The searching, scanning qualities of the transaction with sensation illustrate the "two-way" nature of the flow which is characteristic of all the attachments. The organism is active in maintaining the attachment and, as well, signals the condition of the attachment at any time. Major clinical utility is appearing in new efforts to monitor the status of the attachments via observing such signaling.

2. *The attachment to a clear notion of identity, a picture of the self.* Human beings organize the flow of ongoing perceptions and actions around a more enduring picture or map of the self and its possibilities. A stable notion of the self, one which shows clear outlines, seems to comprise an essential feature of the machinery which defines ongoing experience. The self-identity is constantly being

constructed and repaired. Some components of identity are observations an individual makes about himself. Some are abservations others have offered to him. Some are decisions he has made which fix critical features and define "the essential self." Some are beliefs an individual may hold about his probable future behavior in various conceivable circumstances. Such beliefs constitute a type of planning.

An individual needs to know what kind of a person he is and needs to know it with conviction. To the extent that he loses a clear notion of who he is, or loses a sense of conviction about any such notion, he becomes immobilized from decision. He may be said to be "disassociated." Individuals in distress frequently demonstrate a loss of clarity to their experience of self. They do not seem to know who they are, nor where they are going. Older individuals can lose a sense of identity when life events remove them from a social field of people who know them or from a flow of experiences of a type they are competent to master.

We assess the presence of a sense of personal identity by noting the *degree of clarity or certitude* accompanying its operations. With such practices, we are monitoring the effectiveness of the self-view as a gyroscope within the flux of experience. Does the individual appear to know what kind of an individual he is? Can he consider certain possibilities for action which are forbidden, or others which are required by the circumstances? Does he say about some possibilities, "That's not me," or, "Yes, that is a situation in which I can see myself"?

3. *The attachment to persons.* An individual requires a persisting attachment to at least one other person. A personal attachment is recognizable when the individual and another person react in a manner dependent upon their recollections of past and future behaviors of each other. Does the individual regularly make arrangements to be in the presence of a particular other person? Does the other person make *arrangements to be near,* or to exchange language, or to feel contact or sensation with this person? When an individual can report no repeating meetings, or "presences," with another person, we can assume there is no person-attachment. Ordinarily, an individual cannot with dignity report the absence of friendships. Most often, he signals such a fact within clinical contacts by offering descriptions of his solitary status which are buried in the recollected events he offers. The report of even a small number of events of private, unique communication set in close space can inform us of the intact nature of the basal attachment-to-persons.

4. *The attachment to groups.* An individual needs an attachment to at least one group fully as much as the attachments to oxygen or to persons. The presence of an attachment to a group is revealed by any repeating activity with a cluster of persons who regard the individual as a member. Usually, the individual also regards himself as a member. The attachment to groups can include, for example, enmeshment in work groups, religious groups, social groups or political groups. The dominant grouping for many persons is one based on the family or upon kinship. All individuals require at least one group attachment which can assist them with the tasks of provision of food, shelter and recreation, and which can

assist them in the regulation of their adaptational work during intervals of challenge. A central feature of all such primary groups is a capacity to generate the affect of *solidarity*. Solidarity-linked conduct is a signaling system. It has the effect of informing the members of a regularly clustering set of persons concerning the availability of the group-oriented attachment interest of each of the others in the set. It is a multilateral marker of readiness for continuing attachment. The existence of this group-directed signaling activity provides to the clinician a handy marker that an individual has available to him a group attachment. If he can report regular activity, in specific settings, with clusters of persons, accompanied by sentiments of solidarity, the group-attachment is intact.

5. *The attachment to social roles.* Each person needs to have available some opportunities to perform at least one persisting social role in congruence with the requirements of that role. The role which constitutes an attachment seems to need to be one for which publicly accessible standards of conduct are established. Whether milkman, teacher, mother, child, steel worker or friend, each person needs to have available skills and opportunities to show that he "can do." An individual needs to show that he can accomplish tasks, attract people and generate interest among others in helping him perform such tasks. He needs to demonstrate that he can serve a purpose useful to others. From such experiences and observations as are gained in the performance of such roles, he comes to regard himself with esteem. Others come to confer value and dignity onto his public presence. *Self-esteem and dignity* are acquired, at least in the early portions of the life cycle, within contexts of role performance. Later in life, they may become more free-floating as an individual acquires some "credit" or repute. The personal experience of self-esteem has the effect of creating a signaling field which can draw others "in close." It seems to attract them into enlarged contacts with a person. Dignity originates in the social surround, but, thereafter, alters the individual's out-going signaling. Among other effects, it seems to elicit a kind of promissory note of assistance, or of dutiful conduct by members of the field, should the need arise.

Linkage to a persisting social role, with the personal availability of skills and opportunities for its performance, are so basic to survival that clinical work regularly requires the assessment of this attachment. The presence of any situation which confines an individual to an institution or which drastically constricts his physical excursion will sever the role attachments. Any situation which holds little opportunity for ordinary role conduct, or which limits a person to the role of patient or of casualty, will sever the attachment to roles. Migration, social upheaval and personal injury also can break vital role linkages.

6. *The attachment to the cash economy.* Most human beings are resident in areas of the earth's surface which are organized into one or another national system of trade and economic exchange. Such exchange greatly increases the material standards of food, shelter, clothing, goods and services for those participating. It expands their options and security much over what could be created by their solitary labor. But the amplification of human energies made possible by such

exchange is available only to persons who are actually linked, through cash or purchasing power, to the economic engine. The situation of an individual who is without such purchasing power is similar to that of a primitive hunter and gatherer, though often one without the skills for such gathering.

The fact of non-attachment to the economy results in a disturbance which is profound and progressive. This situation is background to the disappointing results of mental health services to persons who are socially isolated, migrant, aged, or resident in households without a breadwinner. Whatever specific help a narrow, sectoral service might offer, if it does not repair the linkage to the economy, its benefit may fade before larger forces.

Assessing the integrity of the economic linkage can usually be accomplished by considering a person's *clothing or shelter*. Or it can be discovered by examining an individual's weekly activities and daily schedule. Employment, purchasing power or membership in a family which is linked to the economy reveal themselves easily in such an examination. If the status of the linkage is still in doubt, the observer can ask himself *whether he would lend* this person a thousand dollars. If he would worry about the individual's capacity to repay, he has likely answered his question.

7. *The attachment to a personally experienced, comprehensive system of meaning.* All persons carry a residue of notions, some in words, some in images, which guide their decisions in the ongoing conduct of affairs. They carry a "general purpose map" for movement through life. The work to maintain such a map is a continuing activity of cognitive life. "Guide-post observations," when put into words, are discussed under terminologies variously called "religious," "ethical," "life-style" or "common sense." The observer knows of this guidance system primarily through affects associated with its operations. Experiences of sentiments of "offense" or "properness" or "meaningfulness" are examples. Any individual in a state of attachment to his comprehensive system of meaning has a regular flow of such experiences. These affects signal to him what is important, proper or conventional, or what is wrong or outside his concept of properness.

In assessing whether an individual is in contact with his comprehensive system of meaning, the observer looks for *options within the current predicament which the individual regards as either forbidden or required.* The observer may also look for reports of activities which are associated with a deep sense of self-expression or of gratifying importance. Also helpful in assessing this attachment is the presence of ritual activity, or of celebrations, or of reaffirmations of valued beliefs. Human beings appear to spend a significant fraction of their time keeping a core value-system alive so that it may be "ready" to them when called into decision-making activity during episodes of challenge. The presence of ritual and festive activity often provides a handy marker for detecting the integrity of the attachment to a personal system of meaning.

The clinical concept of the survey of essential attachments is one based upon the consequences of such attachments for survival and for the performance of adaptational work. The clinical utility of an assessment method which allows the rapid detection of severances in these attachments resides in the governance it may give to clinical efforts. Methods are evolving to assist distressed persons repair such attachments so as to be able to proceed with their adaptational activity. The concept of "seven essential attachments" is further designed to direct the attention of helpers into a broad scan of an individual's current situation. It makes less likely a premature focus on the distressing "plumage" regularly attending anyone passing through the adaptational episode.

BEHAVIOR DURING THE ADAPTATIONAL INTERVAL

A handy picture of the usual physiology and behavior during the adaptational interval is helpful to clinicians who are working to assist in the conduct of problem-solving work. In recent years an increasing number of clinicians have been using the observation of several regularities during the adaptational interval to alert them to the presence of crisis behavior in the situation and to assess the effectiveness of an individual's responses. Individuals faced with episodes of substantial adaptive challenge show a set of behaviors which, taken together, comprise a major dynamic governing what others can do that will work. In particular, the crisis picture includes a characteristic pattern of attention, identity, affectional attachments, memory, role performance, decision making and distress signaling.

Much of the behavior expressed during a profound crisis interval is common to all persons experiencing such an interval and for whatever reason. We use the term "crisis" to identify any rapid change or any encounter which provides an individual with a "no-exit challenge" to alter his conduct in some manner. A situation is problematic to an adaptational degree for an individual when it does not stimulate him to directively react to it with any response he has available. It does not call forth a ready response.

Consider the range of challenges which can stress an individual. The loss of a beloved person, or situation, or movement in geographic space can provide such a challenge. Losses in health, or limb, or life ideal can provide such a challenge. Catastrophies of flood and weather, as well as social catastrophies of unemployment, war and pestilence, can present such a no-exit situation. All these situations call for personally novel, rapid change.

For these several reasons, it may be useful clinically to become familiar with the regularities in crisis behavior, particularly in regard to services based around the provision of assistance with adaptational work. We can use such regularities to detect that an individual is in an adaptational interval (17-28). We use the term "crisis plumage" to include all varieties of this behavior. We use the detection of such behavior to signal ourselves that we are dealing with a person who is wrestling with a radical adaptational challenge.

1. *The individaul shows a narrowed, fixed span of attention.* He is not scanning his whole environment but is focused on a few items. He may be ruminating about a few details of a complex predicament. His attention is fixed or frozen for intervals of minutes and is constrained from its usual flow through an organized sequence of thought. It jumps around without any strategy of scanning. The narrowed, constricted pattern of attention during distress is a liability because it displaces the more ordinary and vital pattern in which an individual sticks with a new fact and works on it. Whereas an individual ordinarily arranges his thoughts until he develops an action which will work, during a crisis he can sometimes "get stuck" or "cycle" in thought. Some such cycling notions would include: "I am helpless." "I am incompetent." "People are after me." "My life is no good." "I'm a victim of particular circumstances." As we observe such an individual, he seems to be preoccupied. He presses upon the listener a "topic of choice." Topic-of-choice and fixity-of-attention are two aspects of the same process. Such findings indicate that an individual is in the early phases of an adaptational sequence.

2. *The individual shows loosening and widening of his affectional attachments.* His social connections and stable patterns of activity toward persons, groups, families and projects show a characteristic decay in precision and a loss of their usual pattern. Whereas ordinarily there is a regularity to the distribution of an individual's sentiments and interests, in crisis such attachments become weak or intermittent. As an individual's pattern of socially directed activity breaks down, individuals report feeling separated, distant or "unhooked" from the primary figures in their lives.

Of equal importance during crisis is the extraordinary activation seen in behaviors of the type which initiate new attachments. Prominent among such behaviors are activities like moving up close, seeking eye and skin contact, and offering unguarded, intimate language. Each of these behaviors is part of sequences of conduct which reach out for new attachments. Coincident with the decline in order, stable attachments, the individual appears to develop a random, migratory, search-and-attach pattern. The individual feels, and signals, as if in readiness to "latch on and hold."

People working in clinical settings of a type which receive many individuals in distress experience a large measure of this urgent signaling for attachment. Clinicians active in reception work often report a clingy, clutchy, demanding component to the behavior of individuals presenting in profound panic. Such individuals give the appearance of wanting to attach to anyone who is immediately present or to anyone willing to respond. Such attachments are less an organized choice than an automatic mooring in panic. From a more general, biological viewpoint, the picture of the attachments during the adaptational interval is one of an altered distribution. The individual is loosening or "randomizing" his previous attachment behavior and "opening" himself in readiness for new attachments.

The heightened attachment activity at crisis has profound consequences for individuals who are social isolates. Individuals without a family or friends, and beset with a crisis, are often caught in a context which is accidental or impersonal. Sometimes they are located in a surround peopled mainly by treatment or agency staff. Such treatment staff, whatever skills they may have, often lack direct knowledge of an individual's prior personality or performance. The individual is then in the risky position of passing through an adaptational crisis while set in a context of persons who do not know his regular appearance. The persons of such a context can only perceive the current, atypical, often unattractive appearance. Consequently, isolated people are often in the situation of having to direct their attachment energies exclusively toward people who are either temporary or strangers, toward persons whose view of them is confined to the atypical behavior of the crisis interval. One consequence of this narrow view is an unwarranted clinical pessimism. Another is that many persons who make contact with treatment systems during crises "latch on" and permanently attach to the particular people and settings traversed during such crises. In such a set of practices, the service activities often recruit troubled people quite securely into continuing linkages with social networks comprised of treatment staff who might better have done their work and bade farewell.

The degree of hazard that this transfer of attachments may occur during service can be raised or lowered by several design features of the service provided. Particularly hazardous are ideologies which encourage professional helpers to send signals inviting their clients into shelter or asylum. Of similar hazard are practices of such type as emanate from notions describing bad families, schizophrenogenic mothers or toxic environments. Professional beckonings about bad environments have the effect of offering shelter. Signals offering shelter are every bit as interesting to persons in distress as are mirages to weary desert travelers. Fortunately, the loosened and randomized attachment activity at crisis can just as well be used to lead to improved friendships as to approach asylum.

3. *The individual in distress experiences a profound loss of moorings to a vision of his identity.* During the period of crisis, the personal experience of identity becomes diffused and volatile. The individual appears unaware of his notions of who he is. He shows difficulty in reporting his usual experiences and satisfactions. Most people can experience, when they so desire, a clear notion of an identity, one held with conviction. Most of the time, people can summon a defining set of impressions of who they are and what capacities they demonstrate. But during crisis, individuals appear to lose these clear orienting notions. They appear stranded and without a map of the possibilities.

The loss of the experience of identity manifests itself particularly in indecisiveness. Individuals cannot decide whether to do this or do that. They cannot reckon whether this or that is going on. In addition, individuals in crisis seem exquisitely tuned in to picking up signals from their surrounding social field, especially signals about who they are and what is happening. If an individual does not know who he is, and if people around him appear to know who he is, such people acquire a special importance to him via their effects on defining his future. During the crisis interval, an individual's identity lies substantially in the social surround. An individual is vulnerable in crisis not just to what may happen to him but to the longer-term impact of what he may decide is true about himself.

Ordinarily, an individual's persisting social network takes action to remind him during a crisis of who he is and who he has been. As a consequence of recollecting what kind of person he has been, the ordinary social network tends to restore the individual during the flexibility of crisis to a kind of individual very much like the one he has been. This "stabilizing reconversion" is one of the main helping activities conducted by friends during the interval of crisis. This stabilizing effect by persisting social networks, within the otherwise chaotic events of crisis, constitutes one of the dominant dynamics governing the adaptational interval. This effect is one of the origins of the vitality of friendships and of the drama of conversion experiences. Networks familiar with the usual behavior of an individual regularly place a moratorium on offering judgments based upon an individual's atypical and currently unattractive performance. They will say, "George is not having a good day." The existence of such a moratorium has the consequence of placing an envelope around crisis behavior. But for an individual who is isolated, or migrant, or brought in by the police, there is no such persisting social surround. There is no network available to recollect such a cherishable past. It is from such a dynamic that "accidental networks," ones having only "the now" for reference, wreak such personal havoc without any malicious intent. Networks not possessing any past they might recollect in behalf of an individual can offer only a mirroring of the decayed behavior of the present. They can only visualize a future looking much like the present. This sequence of events has extraordinary importance in human affairs. It is a situation which regularly has the consequence of converting the transitory behavior of a crisis into a persisting identity and into a stable career. What is seen within an event acquires a governance function in creating a pattern.

As professionals become cognizant of the durable sequelae of this problem, they are exercising much more vigilance to detect the signals of the prior and ordinary identity through the noise and plumage of the current distress. This effort is known as "the signal-on-noise problem."

4. *The individual in distress quite regularly offers a socially unsatisfactory performance of his usual roles.* The repeating activities which individuals offer as milkmen, breadmen, mothers, students, etc., contain intricately patterned behavior. An individual knows well what he is supposed to do each day, as do those around him. A significant fraction of those behaviors which repeat daily is in service to a persisting cluster of roles. This set of roles defines many of an individual's primary social connections and comprises a portion of his identity. But during the adaptational interval, role behavior and much of other behavior becomes randomized. Patterned role-states decay toward unpatterned, less

differentiated pieces of behavior. Things an individual might ordinarily do, he doesn't do. Things he would seldom do are more likely to appear. Unlearned, built-in patterns, like fear-display, approach-display, or combat behaviors, become more prominent.

From the standpoint of members of an individual's regular social network, the presentation of decayed role-behavior sometimes acquires a threatening, hostile or deteriorative meaning. The biologic value of such de-differentiated behavior, value as a step toward change or redefinition, is seldom visible to the surrounding network. Typically, the social surround reads decayed role-behavior as a herald of general and perhaps permanent loss of competence. The longer such a decayed state lasts, the more pieces of behavior are involved, and the less is known of an individual's past, the more the surrounding network reads deterioration. But professionals who are charged with altering the course of events can most easily do so if they regard an episode of decayed role behavior as an opportunity for making choices. The future situation could involve new role acquisition, old role reac-quistition, or prolongation of this currently decayed state.

5. *The individual in distress experiences an altered state of consciousness which often includes a random-access memory.* Normally, there are filters on memory which affect the recall of stored memories to consciousness. Certain areas of the registry of prior experience are, at any time, prevented from recall. At the same time, other aspects of previous experience are made to vigorously press upon attention. They come into consciousness accompanied by affects of certitude and conviction. During the adaptational interval, the controls on recall, of both the filtering-in and filtering-out types, are reduced. Resultingly, the flow of memory seems random and chaotic, an experience William James called "the whir and blur." This randomizing mode of the controls to memory is similar to the migratory quality of the flow of attention during crisis, to the decayed nature of role-behavior, and to the acquisitive quality of affectional attachments during the interval.

Observers can become aware of the presence of the random-access mode of memory when an individual reports his experience flow with an accompanying affect of perplexity or with a marked lack of certitude. Individuals in the im-mediate context of the person in distress usually find such a state of mind at once interesting and worrisome. Some members of the network will regard this altered state of consciousness primarily as bizarre or as frightening. Professional helpers who have become accustomed to its outlines, or who use it as an instrument of therapy, find it somewhat less worrisome.

The biologic value to survival of occasional episodes of random-access memory is most evident when such an individual is interactive with the orderly thoughts of another person, one not in crisis. Under such a circumstance, the readiness for change can be used. Perhaps the basal requirement for the constructive use of crisis, for helping, is a situation allowing the interaction of a person in crisis with a person not in crisis. The productivity of many activities called "helping" is rooted in such an interaction. This is so because the malleability of the random-access memory only becomes an asset when combined with the task-drive and regulatory actions of a person not floating in the same state, one who can push it toward problem-solping. The fact that the random-access memory, with its disorganizing whir and blur, is a hazard for the isolated person arises from its lack of social regulation. Isolated persons conduct a distinctly inferior quality of adaptational work growing from their lack of a regulatory context during the interval of the work. On the other hand, individuals possessing a regulative social context use the random access memory as a part of the substrate for change. Treatment activities and psychiatric services almost universally employ designs to arrange for the presence of a social context which has the effect of regulating adaptational work.

6. *The individual in distress experiences a drastically reduced ability to make decisions.* Decision making involves the steps of inventory, appraisal, decision, action and review. Although it ordinarily proceeds inexorably—like respiration— in profound crisis, and especially for persons who are isolated during crisis, it meanders falteringly. The readiness in crisis to consider many notions, including ones previously thought absurb or unthinkable, is only a useful component of adaptation if it can be combined with an ability to select and to act. The act of deciding entails selecting from among competing mental notions via the use of some criteria. The halting, meandering character of decision work, particularly as shown by the *solitary* person in crisis, is a benchmark of the crisis-in-transit state. The striking increase in the ability to decide and to act when an interacting second person puts the special crisis consciousness to work is equally a benchmark. The necessity for input by the social surround in order to release the productivity of crisis is the radical center of designs for service, professional and folk. People in crisis bring a readiness for change which does not galvanize into decision and action without input from persons around them who are themselves not in crisis.

7. *Individuals in distress send signals of distress.* All the primates and many colonial species send characteristic signals of distress at the discovery of situtations of threat to their survival. This signaling seems to have the effects of alerting the group to such hazard and also of mobilizing activity in behalf of the sender of the signals. Such signals often stimulate clustering assemblies around the troubled signaler and sometimes stimulate cooperative activity. Such activity is most often an attempt to fix, remove or flee the situation.

Distress signaling is transmitted by several channels—posture, smell and sound. Humans also employ role and language behavior for such signaling. Members of the same species apparently can quickly recognize each other's distress signals. Humans appear to have in almost continuous readiness certain learned, as well as unlearned, crisis attitudes. These regulative activities come out of semiautomatically in the context of such signaling. The general activities called forth by such signaling are clustering, assessing, embracing, helping, if possible, or extrusion of the signaler, or flight if no satisfactory response can be developed. Much of our work as professional helpers is related to attempts to modify and orchestrate the built-in responses of humans to distress signaling.

A handy awareness of the above regularities in the behavior of individuals in distress can assist professionals in recognizing the adaptational interval when it is present and in using it for the growth of their patients. Clinicians are increasingly vigilant to detect these characteristic alterations of attention, identity, affectional attachments, memory, role definition, decision making and distress signaling. More and more precise application is being made to such classical clinical objectives as enhancing adaptational capacity. In particular, the biologic flexibility of the adaptational state is increasingly recognized as a hazard for the individual who is isolated, or socially unregulated, and as an asset when brought into contextually regulated use as the substrate for problem-solving behavior.

Several regularities within problem-solving work during the adaptational interval affect any efforts to influence such work. The above-mentioned properties of attention, affectional attachments, decision making and memory are background for a sequence of activities sometimes termed "problem solving." Many observers have concluded that the major body of such activity is transcultural and common to all mankind. Many aspects appear to arise in an unlearned fashion, although there may be some refinements by the workings of personal development and cultural structuring. Consider such activities as contacting the castastrophe, figuring out what is happening, considering the possibilities for action, deciding from among those possibilities, taking action, assessing effects. Every challenge involves the same steps and the same ordering of steps. Whether the type of challenge is large or small, whether presenting slow or fast, whether met easily or calling for major innovation, a similar set of adaptational mechanics can be observed (29-43):

1. *The discovery of the presence of a challenge event:* the discover of a no-exit challenge; the dazed search for bearings; the anguished call of distress; the discomfort of the discovery of the fact of a catastrophe.

2. *Recognizing the nature of the challenge event:* the experience of perplexity, of search; the movement to define what is going on; the identification of what is lost, hurting or different; the quandary; the sadness and reminiscence while surveying what is no longer present.

3. *Constructing and considering several possibilities for action:* The experiences of suspicion and vigilance while one figures the consequences of each path; reckoning what of the past is most valued, and most deserving to be carried ahead so as to arrange a future worth living.

4. *Deciding: selecting from among possibilities that which is best for action:* the complaining arising because no action possibility seems perfect; the comparison and cross-testing with others to recognize which option shows the most promise and feasibility.

5. *Taking action according to selected plan:* doing; the holding of hope, faith and resolve while seeing it through; enduring, struggling and "hanging in."

6. *The evaluation of the results of action:* Is it okay? Is it not okay? Outcome

monitoring, waiting, checking, testing; recycling the problem-solving process because it hasn't worked.

7. *Returning to the ordinary state*: celebrating, relaxing, taking pride; moving back to the ordinary patterns of life.

Each step is carried on in the context of specific affect states which appear to biologically facilitate the activities of that step. Each of the affect states also appears to signal the social surround of the nature and pace of the adaptational work in process. Let us examine the same seven steps again.

Step 1. The discovery of the presence of a challenging event. Problem-solving work does not commence unless the individual decides he has perceived a clear and undeniable hazard or loss. The affect signals of anxiety, panic, terror, dread, daze, the call of distress, the shock of impact, the cry of pain, all seem to signal to an individual that he is moving into a special state. They all as well signal the surround that an individual is moving into the adaptational sequence. The organism does not move into the adaptational sequence for trivial reason. The interval calls for abrupt changes in behavior and for heavy expenditures of energy. There are risks of death and injury. There are risks of extrusion from the social setting during the disorganized middle phases of the sequence. Individuals long remember the pain and terror of the sequence and express little appetite to enter it unless absolutely necessary. Individuals who are regulated by a social surround "gate" the onset. The signaling of an individual moving into the interval slowly used to be called "denial." The persons in the surround will push or "pace" him. If an individual appears not to be "facing his difficulty," he will be prodded to commence. If an individual is moving toward action too quickly, the surround will attempt to slow him down so he does not "run off half-cocked." The regulatory function of the social surround which begins in Step 1 proceeds in a similar manner through all of the steps.

Step 2. Recognizing the nature of the challenging event. No person can relinquish what he cannot identify. No person can arrange to deal with what he cannot detect. The signals of sadness, perplexity, reminiscence, protest, anger, wonder, supplication and yearning appear to assist an individual to enter this phase. The same signals call the social surround to regulate the phase. During Step 2, an individual is figuring out the nature of the problem and recruiting assistance in dealing with the situation. The modes of perception and cognition which are characteristic during the adaptational interval, that is, the random-access memory, the "scanning" activity of attention, appear uniquely suited to defining the outline of what is novel in the challenge. Role behavior is opening to the possibility of major changes in pattern. Affectional attachments to persons and to groups are loosening to be ready for realignments. Of striking significance is the observation that the special behavioral sequence (search, appriasal, decision, action, and review—the problem-solving sequence) appears to start automatically whenever the usual calculus of reckoning is disturbed. But it does not start unless the usual calculus of reckoning is unable to remain undisturbed. It does not start unless the person is unable to explain what is happening.

During the phase of defining the predicament, an individual tries to discover figure and ground. He is engaged in the formation of new concepts. He is trying to figure an edge, then a shape, then a problem. People in the surround seem to recognize the fact that such figuring, or such reminiscence, is an aspect of defining what must be mastered, or relinquished. The social surround takes action to "push" the individual to work on problems, to "get on with life" or to "count your blessings." The social surround also appears to assist the individual in gating the flow of the activity. If it comes along too slowly, takes too long, or proceeds too repetitiously, friends will push it, saying, "The good old days are over."

Step 3. Constructing and considering several possibilities for action. Group connectedness and the experiences of dignity and self-esteem appear intrinsic to the process of opening up the possibilities for major change. The affect signals of suspicion, perplexity, doubt, complaining, anomie, helplessness and supplicance appear to stimulate an individual to construct visions of actions and consequent futures. The same affects stimulate his surround to assist and regulate such envisioning. No person can organize to carry through a response he cannot envision. The adaptational work of figuring out what to do carries that experience of uncertainty which is intrinsic to any examining of the unknown. It is a situation which requires an individual to hold in mind several ideas, or several portions of what may be done. This task is connected with the inherently destabilizing experience of tentativity. Individuals seldom enjoy the concentrated effort which is part of envisioning and probing unfamiliar possibilities. The social surround appears to make a covenant with the individual. It appears to react to the possibilities he raises. It appears automatically stimulated to let him know if he gets too far "off base" from their perceptions.

The affect signals of the adaptational phase when options are being considered include the provocative displays of persons "figuring out something." They display suspicion because they are vigilant to detect cues which would clarify possibilities. They display perplexity because they are suspending premature decision about the best course to take. They display doubt because insufficient sorting has occurred to warrant certitude. They offer complaints because none of the options meets all criteria of attractiveness. They show anomie because they are "in between" the old ways and yet-to-be-decided new ways. They display a category of signaling sometimes called "helplessness" because such signals draw the social surround into performing its intrinsic regulatory activities during the unstable, middle phase. They are supplicant because the supplicant display orients the social field, when drawn in, toward the special activities of helping. The supplicant display increases, in the social field, the dominance of regulatory activity over other, competing activities such as eating, sleeping and resting.

Professional activities to enhance the adaptational work of individuals in distress make necessary use of such affect displays to detect the phasing of the work in process. It is important, therefore, that such displays not be medicated or otherwise ablated. Otherwise the professional helpers, as well as the social surround, lose their requisite signaling frame.

Step 4: Deciding: selecting the best possibility for action. No possibility is worthy of action which is not envisionable as an attractive future. The affect signals of conviction, certitude, discovery-aha and "girding" appear to regulate this phase of problem-solving work. The activities which comprise the task of deciding are those of picturing and comparing for value the futures consequent to particular current actions. Individuals appear to picture what features would be embodied in a satisfactory solution and try to recognize that option which best displays such features. As individuals are moving to make such a decision, they appear to summon their orienting life values: Who am I? Who do I want to become? What is important? The surrounding social field acts to remind an individual of what goals he has pursued in the past. Individuals in the field present recollections of what he has done which might apply to the task of recognizing the best future. When an individual appears stuck on comparing a large number of possibilities, often with sounds of complaining, the surrounding social field will push him with: "Why don't you decide how things should be?" Whereas the isolated individual in a cycling series with complaining seldom appears to move toward decision, a person doing the same cycling within a regulative social context will be pushed by the field to press for the one best decision.

The interplay between a person in distress and his surrounding social field seems to be regulated by the signaling exchange among them. In order for this exchange to take place, it seems necessary that the individual and a surrounding field be in occasional close "face-to-face " contact. The very fact of such contact seems to stimulate behavior which appears as the product of a temporary task-group. The exchanges and responses show all the earmarks of being "automatic," unlearned, and built into the species. The signaling code which assembles and regulates this cluster apparently constitutes one of the heritable faculties of the species.

Step 5: Taking action according to the selected plan. The pattern of persevering in a selected course of action is maintained in the face of uncertainty as to whether it will work by the use of an abiding convenant organized via exchanges of the affect of hope. The affect signals of hope, faith, resolve, enduring, abiding, struggling and hanging-in appear to hold an individual "on course." Equally, they hold a group into sustained support of the efforts of the same individual. The result of the undertaken line of action often cannot be securely anticipated through the main period of the required effort. The signaling affects of hope, faith and resolve, seem to have the consequence of maintaining a pattern of behavior through an interval when its effect cannot yet be known. No outcome feedback is possible during the very interval when the new behavior is acquiring its survival value. In this particular situation, faith and resolve may comprise of variety of "temporary feedback" which may maintain the plan and its labors to the point when its results become visible. Loss of hope is one of the central features of the clinical pattern of depression. Depressed persons express a major abortion in the mechanics of their problem-solving work. This abortion pertains even though their faculties appear otherwise preserved, though sometimes slowed. It is easy to understand why the terms for the affects hope, faith, and resolve are so prevalent in the folk lexicon of coping.

Step 6: Evaluation of results. Efforts to persevere continue until exhaustion sets in or until a marker of success is experienced. The "success marker," because it elicits the stopping process, has a need to be as convincingly secure a signal as was the original experience of threat which started the sequence. The affect signals of waiting, watching, caution, testing, checking, sounding and patience appear to have the effect of "homing" the adaptive work. They regulate its final movement toward its objective. There is a watchfulness for the effects of actions undertaken. There is a testing of observations against intended outcome. Individuals moving through this phase characteristically are active in cross-checking their observations with others. "How does it look?" "Are we okay?" "You're not out of the woods yet." The efforts to start coping are so painful and the efforts to maintain it so arduous that the signal to relinquish the effort must be convincing. The regulatory action at this time appears to hold the behavior on course until the satisfactory resolution unfolds.

Step 7: Return to ordinary state. The costly energies and resources recruited into the adaptational sequence must be relinquished and returned to their more usual patterns as soon as possible. The affect signals of celebration, taking pride, relaxation and taking stock act to regulate the closing of the adaptational sequence. It is necessary to hold the adaptational work in process "long enough" but not one moment longer. Just as a special pattern of thought and behavior becomes established once a challenge has been detected, it is necessary to suspend this pattern when the situation is managed. The daily rhythms of life must resume. Whatever moratorium and special expectancies had been in effect are promptly suspended as ordinary affairs resume. Much of the behavior and biology underlying the switch-overs at entry and exit of the adaptational state remain to be described. What is known suggests that the adaptational state contains substantial hazards if prolonged. For example, bereavement can become prolonged into a state of constricted exhaustion. The "wind-down" and return to more ordinary lines of activity is as necessary at the end of adaptational work as was the "start-up" at the presentation of the challenge.

The work of meeting the challenge with an existing pattern of living follows a sequence made *necessary* by the logic of switching, made *possible* by the physiology of the crisis state, and *regulated* by the social surround. Several dominant activities of professionals are rooted in the requirement that individuals have available to them a regulative social surround so that they might conduct effective problem-solving work.

PROFESSIONAL ACTIVITIES AND ADAPTATIONAL WORK

Activities which attempt to control symptoms primarily through enhancing adaptational capacity comprise an increasing fraction of service designs. Professional activities which increase the likelihood of adaptational success are desirable because they approach the objective of reducing the need for extended intervals of treatment. But it is precisely in the area of practices directed toward enhancing adaptational work that many professionals feel least prepared by virtue of training. Lacking such skills, they may sometimes fall back on the overuse of shelter and asylum or on the conveyance of distressed persons into constraining roles.

Consider several pertinent clinical skills:

1. *Activating the "scanning" property of attention.* Many clinical activities have as their effect diverting an individual's attention toward problem identification, survey of facts, and discovery of more interesting lines of inquiry. An individual often enters service preoccupied with a narrow range of thoughts which recur in a repetitive pattern. This repetition aborts adaptational work. Clinicians regularly work to divert this pattern and restart the scanning activities of attention. Often such a diversion from the topic-of-choice occurs because the interest of the clinicians is somewhat different from the interest of the patient. These interest differences have the effect of diverting the patient from his prior fixity of thought. It may be that budging him from such fixity gains its value from starting his problem-solving work.

2. *Convening fragmenting networks.* Much of clinical work has to do with drawing together families, friends, work associates and other ad hoc groupings. When such groupings include the patient, they can provide the immediate social attachments and context which regulate adaptational work. Sometimes such groupings are comprised of families which previously were fragmenting. At other times, it is more useful to draw together groups of patients or groups of staff-and-patients in order to create this regulative context. The active ingredient in such groupings resides in the essential function of a regulative context in enhancing the performance of adaptational work.

3. *Providing task definitions.* Many clinical activities have the effect of introducing a structure of timing, setting, sequencing and task objectives for an individual whose current experience is chaotic. Also, many ordinary clinical activities have the effect of providing convenient markers of headway and accomplishment. Such activities act to pace individuals who are mainly experiencing the whir and blur of panic.

4. *Assisting socially isolated persons to form new social affiliations.* Because of the extraordinary differences between the adaptational work of isolated persons and persons in a social context, clinical activities which can envelop a social isolate within an even temporary task group can yield life-saving increases in the effectiveness of the problem-solving work he conducts.

5. *Detecting personality.* Professional activities which detect personality and

attractiveness in an individual, amidst the static of symptoms and distress behavior, provide an input which ordinarily would be offered by a stable social network. An individual may be showing abundantly the plumage of the adaptational interval. Often, he cannot detect his own identity nor his comprehensive system of meaning within all this distraction. Clinical activities which detect and mark competent performance have the effect of increasing such performance. Also, actions which detect his identity in the context of the plumage of the interval assist an individual himself to recollect such an identity.

6. *Facilitating decision and action by regulating the onset, pace and focus of adaptational work.* Clinical activities which assist an individual to reconstruct a clear notion of his self-identity, or which draw comparisons of various options against a description of the self, advance the pace of adaptational work when it is slowed or cycling.

7. *Converting several kinds of aborted behavior into useful problem-solving work.* For example, activities which ask an individual to convert long lists of complaints into descriptions of which should really be seem greatly to energize his decision and action. Lines of endeavor which convert vague or multi-valent appraisals of the situation into the single, best, current assessment of what is going on have the effect of accelerating the making of decisions. Actions which convert general, vague objectives into a series of visible steps also accelerate the pace of making decisions.

8. *Rapidly converting requests for shelter and presentations of signals of distress into therapeutic plans.* Professional activities which hear signals of distress and immediately seek,to commence problem-solving work make the best use of the brief interval. Requests for shelter and signals of distress seem to have as their purpose the gaining of entry into a regulative context. The regulative context acts most effectively when it focuses on adaptational work rather than on ex changes around entry, the provision of shelter, or the chemical relief of distress.

9. *De-recruiting individuals from the sick role who have adopted it for imprecise objectives or extended intervals of time.* It seems that some kinds of professional service can have the effect of recruiting individuals out of their ordinary network and into restrictive social roles. A subsequent adaptational interval may offer the possibility for de-recruiting the individual from that role and constricted setting and allowing him to reenter more ordinary, more interesting circumstances. The activities which seem most associated with this objective are ones which present conventional, social expectations rather than ones based on the continuance of the constricted roles.

10. *Managing episodes of decayed performance.* Clinicians are often in the situation of having to preserve life and encourage social order in the context of behavior which is threatening life or the public order. Mental health services which preserve or repair the effects of such self-destructive behavior and, at the same time, keep the focus on a prompt return to adaptational work, offer the most promise for converting the plumage of distress into the occasion of growth.

SUMMARY

Important headway has been made in the identification of requisites for competent adaptational conduct. One requisite appears to be the intermittent presence of a social surround allowed to perform a set of semiautomatic actions. These actions appear to regulate the starting, stopping, pacing and precision of the adaptational work of the challenged individual. Although this system is ordinarily not fragile, several aspects of professional practice may enhance or eclipse its regulatory functions. Clinicians are just beginning to discover what some of these practices and services might be.

In the nineteenth century, the socially regulative context, the connections between services and the enduring affiliations for individuals with disturbances of performance were typically provided within asylum. In the twentieth century, practitioners are working to invent analogous arrangements without resort to asylum. How the system eventually will look is less clear than what it will have to do. It will need to enhance the adaptational work of individuals passing through life challenges. It will also strive to reinforce, rather than eclipse, the regulative fabric of ordinary human society. Doubtless, as the sciences of human biology and behavior advance, the technical activity of professionals will acquire more precision. Modern service practices are allowing many clinicians to rediscover the ancient observation that the satisfactions of adaptational accomplishment may outlast the relief offered by sanctuary.

REFERENCES

1. National Center for Health Statistics. *Medical Care, Health Status, and Family Income*, Series 10, Number 9. Washington, DC: US Dept HEW, 1964.
2. National Center for Health Statistics. Socioeconomic characteristics of diseases persons, US, 1962-63 Deaths, Serial 22, Number 9. Washington, DC: US Dept HEW, 1969.
3. MacMahon, B.; Johnson, S.; and Pugh, T. F. Relation of sucide rates to social conditions: Evidence from US Vital Statistics. *Publ Health Rep 78*:285-293 (April) 1963.
4. ———, and Pugh, T.F. Suicide in the Widowed. *Amer J Epidemiol* 81:23-31, 1965.
5. Malzberg, B. Mental disease among the native and foreign-born white populations of New York State, 1939-1941. *Ment Hyg 39*:545-599, 1955.
6. ———. Rates of mental disease among certain categories of population groups in New York State. *J Amer Stat Assoc 31*:545-548, 1936.
7. Brenner, M. H. *Mental Illness and the Economy*. Cambridge, Mass: Harvard U Press, 1973.
8. Kramer, M. Epidemiology, biostatistics, and mental health planning. In R. R. Monroe et al. (eds.) *Psychiatric Epidemiology and Mental Health Planning*, Psychiatric Research Report Number 22. Washington, DC: American Psychiatric Association, 1967, pp 1-63.
9. ———. *Some Implications of Trends in the Usage of Psychiatric Facilities for Community Mental Health Programs and Related Research*, PHS Publication Number 1434. Washington DC:US Dept HEW, 1967.
10. ——— et al. Patterns of use of psychiatric facilities by the aged: Current Status, Trends, and Implications. In A. Simon and L. J. Epstein, eds. *Aging in Modern Society*, Psychiatric

Research Report Number 23. Washington, DC: American Psychiatric Association, 1968, pp 89-150.

11. Rubin, R., and Eisen, S. B. The old timers' club. *Arch Neurol & Psychiat 79*: 113-121 (Jan) 1958.

12. Gruenberg, E. M. The social breakdown syndrome—some origins. *Amer J Psychiat 123*:1481-1489 (June) 1967.

13. Harlow, H. F., Primary affectional patterns in primates. *Amer J Orthophychiat 30*: 676-684, 1960.

14. ———, and Harlow, M. F. Social deprivation in monkeys. *Sci Amer.* (Nov) 1962.

15. ———. The effect of rearing conditions on behavior. *Internat J Psychiat 1*:43-51, 1964.

16. Wallace, A.F.C. Mazeway disintegration: the individual's perception of socio-cultural disorganization. *Hum Org 16*:23-27 (Summer) 1957.

17. Hinkle, L.E.. and Wolff, H.G., et al. Studies in human ecology. *Amer J Psychiat 114*:212-220 (Sept) 1957.

18. Hinkle, L.E., and Wolff, H. G. Ecologic investigations of the relationship between illness, life experiences and the social environment. *Ann Int Med 49*:1373-1388 (Dec) 1958.

19. Lindemann, E. Symptomatology and management of acute grief. *Amer J Psychiat 101*:141-148 (Sept) 1944.

20. Adler, H.M., and Hammett, V. B. O. Crisis, conversion and cult formation. *Amer J Psychiat 130*:861-864 (Aug) 1973.

21. Darwin, C. *The Expression of the Emotions in Man and Animals.* Chicago: Univ. Chicago Press, 1965 (original edition 1872).

22. Wallace, A. F. C. Stress and rapid personality changes. *Internat Rec Med Gen Pract Clin 169*:761-774 (Dec) 1956.

23. ———. Cultural determinants of response to hallucinatory experience. *Arch Gen Psychiat 1*: 58-69 (July) 1959.

24. Bowlby, J. Separation anxiety. *Internat J Psycho-Anal 41*:1-25, (Parts 1 and 2) 1960.

25. Tyhurst, J. S. The role of transition states—including disasters—in mental illness. *Symposium on Social and Preventive Psychiatry.* Washington, DC: Walter Reed Army Institute, 1957, pp 149-172.

26. Schildkraut, J. J. and Kety, S. Biogenic amines and emotion. A.M. Freedman and H. I. Kaplan (eds.) *Human Behavior.* NY: Atheneum, 1972, pp 90-112.

27. Rahe, R.H., et al. A longitudinal study of life-change and illness patterns. *J Psychosom Res 10*:355-366, 1967.

28. Hirschowitz, R.G., Crisis theory. *Psychiat Ann 3*:36-47 (Dec) 1973.

29. Visotsky, H.M., et al. Coping behavior under extreme stress. *Arch Gen Psychiat 5*:423-448 (Nov) 1961.

30. Bruner, J. S. et al. *A Study of Thinking.* NY: Wiley, 1956.

31. Miller, G. A. The magic number seven plus or minus two: some limits on our capacity for processing information. *Psychol Rev 63*: 81-97, 1956.

32. Coelho, G.V., et al. Coping strategies in a new learning environment. *Arch Gen Psychiat 9*:433-443, 1963.

33. Silber,E.,et al. Adaptive behavior in competent adolescents. *Arch Gen Psychiat 5*:354-365 (Oct) 1961.

34. ———. Competent adolescents coping with college decisions. *Arch Gen Psychiat 5*:517-527 (Dec) 1961.

35. Richter, C. P. The behavioral regulation of homeostasis. *Symposium on Stress.* Washington, DC: Walter Reed Army Medical Center, 1953, pp 78-88.

36. Pribam, K. H. Feelings as monitors. In M. B. Arnold, ed., *Feelings and Emotions.* NY: Academic Press, 1970, pp 41-53.

37. ———. *Languages of the Brain*. Englewood Cliffs, NJ: Prentice-Hall, 1971, especially 99-115, 167-214, and 252-270.
38. Wallace, A. F. C. Mazeway resynthesis: a biocultural theory of religious inspiration. *Trans NY Acad Sci Ser 2: Vol 18: No 7*:626-638 (May) 1956.
39. Caplan, G., Mason, A., and Kaplan, D. M. Four studies of crisis in parents of prematures. *Commun Ment Health J 1*:149-161 (Summer) 1965.
40. Fitzgerald, R. S.Reactions to blindness. *Arch Gen Psychiat 22*:370-379, (April) 1970.
41. Melges, F. T., and Bowby, J. Types of hopelessness in psychopathologic process. *Arch Gen Psychiat 20*:690-699 (June) 1969.
42. Hansell, N.; Wodarczyk, M.; and Handlon-Lathrop, B. Decision counseling method: expanding coping at crisis-in-transit. *Arch Gen Psychiat 22*:462-467 (May) 1970.
43. Selye, H. The general adaptation syndrome and diseases of adaptation. *J Clin Endocrinol 6*:217-230 (Feb) 1946.

7

Conjoint Family Therapy

V.M. RAKOFF and A. LEFEBVRE

Although psychotherapy of the family as a whole is essentially a post-World War II phenomenon, by now there are a number of relatively unquestioned axioms, assumptions and doctrinal quarrels associated with the field. Unfortunately, while there is some empirical research, there is certainly not enough of it to substantiate either the clinical analyses frequently advanced after initial screening interviews, nor to support the various rationales which putatively shape the details of practical technique. This is to imply not that there has been no research at all but that many assertions related to expectation, outcome, suitability for therapy, therapist behavior and manipulation of the family are often stated with a degree of certainty beyond the experimentally validated data. However, in spite of the blend of occasionally grandiose theory and the bewildering variety of approaches within a comparatively new field, conjoint therapy *is* pragmatically useful, and like many therapeutic approaches it is used without a sufficient theoretical base to explain its usefulness. (It may be of some comfort to remember that aspirin, a drug of protean usefulness, has been used in medicine since the late nineteenth century, but that an understanding of its action had to wait until two or three years ago.)

It is surprising that treatment of the family unit in the presence of the therapist had to wait fifty years or so after the initiation of psychoanalysis, since the human household has from its beginnings provided the fundamental dramatis personae of psychoanalysis: father, mother, siblings—and less crucially, nursemaids and so on—are the essential figures in all case histories. Yet the assumption that it was only the fantasied representation of these figures, rather than their "real" presence which was important in the therapeutic relationship, appears to have determined the explicit exclusion of others, however important, from the treatment setting. This applied not only in the analysis of adults, but perhaps more curiously, of children as well.

Common sense and the considerable accumulation of clinical observation have validated the importance of the family in the growth of the individual, and support for these observations does not depend on psychoanalytic theory alone. In this area at least, there is a coming together of a number of contemporary theoretical structures, each of which has contributed important insights into our understanding of human development and the acquisition of behavior.

It is not, for example, a caricature of the clinical phenomenology, nor of the underlying theory to assert that the most simple assumptions of learning theories explain many aspects of the ways in which the family as a whole acts as a conditioning laboratory: by a subtle complex of rewards, punishments, and models, the shaping of behavior occurs with a consistency and power which no artificial situation can match.

More recently ethology has reinforced concepts of a naturally expected environment, and it has given heuristic weight to the commonly made statements that the family is a unity and that family interaction, particularly in the earlier years, will determine both behavior which can readily be related to immediate time and place, and more crucially to patterns of interpersonal response in the comparatively distant future. In this way the more time-bound and mechanical concepts of learning theory are related to insights of dynamic psychiatry. In the light of ethological concepts, interpersonal relationships within the family are not only important as they are verbally reported by a single patient in a dyadic relationship, but are valid and important clinical material as they are displayed in their reality during family therapeutic interviews. Furthermore, the essential findings of ethology that members of developed species require a normative expected environment for optimum development must alter the view that the therapist has of the individual patient. He cannot be understood as independent and self-defining, but should be perceived as part of a necessary system. The interactions observed by the therapist during therapy are therefore the operational expressions of connectedness. The family, in short, is not a unit arbitrarily selected by a clinician in response to a particular fashionable polemic, but can be seen to be a natural and necessary focus of therapeutic attention.

In their historical overview of family therapy, Zuk and Rubinstein characterized the strict therapeutic isolation of the analysand from his family as stage one in the development of the field. And while they describe the concern for the family shown in child guidance clinics as stage two, it is our opinion that they failed to emphasize the continuing concern for family influence and involvement implicit in psychoanalytic thinking from its beginnings. It is true that Adelaide Johnson in 1949 gave a dramatic description of the link between gaps in the parental super-ego and symptom formation in the child; but the earlier experience of Adolf Eichorn is closer to the spirit and technique of conjoint family therapy as it is practiced (albeit in a variety of forms) at present. Eichorn, who was not a simple pragmatist, but was closely associated with the psychoanalytic movement in Vienna, worked with the juvenile court. He frequently visited families and described ways in which parental dynamics contributed to the delinquency of their children.

But delineating an historical process may not be an entirely chronological exercise. The antecedents of a mode of therapy (or indeed of many theories and actions) are frequently latent in preceding practice, and require only a change of emphasis to become manifest. For example, in Zuk and Rubinstein's stage three of family therapy, there was a coalescence of a number of theories and experimental therapies specifically concerned with the individual in relation to others, the "others" being members of any group important to the patient. Sullivan, Horney, Fromm and Erikson, in an historical succession (which would not necessarily be accepted by everyone), emphasized the importance of the interpersonal, the social and historical influences in the formation of personality and behavior, although each of them gave different weight to particular aspects of the huge complexity of the "sociocultural" forces acting on the individual. And at the empirical level many workers attempted a definition of crucial pathogenic relationships.

Perceiving that the individual had characteristic ways of behaving in groups, Slavson, Foulkes, Anthony, Ezriel, Bion and others used the artificially constituted therapeutic group as a treatment modality. Their theoretical positions are again in many ways divergent, but for the purposes of our present concern it may be said that they share the belief that behavior in the group represents a characteristic sample of interpersonal behavior and is material for psychotherapy which can be usefully interpreted. They believe (in common with other psychotherapists) that interpretations couched in the language of their particular convictions will hopefully lead to changes in interpersonal behavior.

Traditional psychoanalysts had, and frequently still have, a concern that a principal focus of individual psychotherapy, the transference—an essentially dyadic phenomenon is violated in the group therapeutic process. But the dynamically oriented group therapists and family therapists believe that the transference is not only, or necessarily, confined to the analytic situation. It is also manifested in the consistent behavior shown to other group members, and within that context, is an interpretable event. In short, the internalized pathology of group members may be modified by understanding and treating the group process.

It is an easy step to move from the artifically constituted therapeutic group to the natural group of the family. If conjoint family therapy has a founding father, it must be Nathan Ackerman who specifically defined family therapy. Parallel with Ackerman's developing theory of roles and their importance in family interaction, there was a efflorescence of concern with the family. For many groups of workers, the main work was with families with a schizophrenic member. Attempts to sort out specific modes of interaction within these families became their predominant activity. Each group, on the basis of clinical investigation, advanced formulations which were attempts to describe interactions they believed to be characteristic; and it was proposed explicitly or implicitly that such interactions constituted sufficient cause for the development of schizophrenia.

Frieda Fromm-Reichman (1948) was probably the first worker to explicitly label the figure who was to become one of the dominant personae in family therapy—the "schizoprenogenic mother." She was described as aggressive, domineering, insecure and rejecting; the father by contrast was described as inadequate, passive and rather indifferent. (Both these descriptions were to become clinical clichés, not by any means confined to families with a schizophrenic member.) Tietze (1949) confirmed Fromm-Reichmann's description in his study of twenty-five mothers of schizophrenic patients. He found them uniformly rigid and rejecting. A year later Reichard and Tillman (1950) subdivided schizophrenogenic parents into three groups: schizophrenogenic mother—overtly rejecting; schizophrenogenic mother—covertly rejecting; schizophrenogenic father—domineering and sadistic. The family as a whole was implicated by Lidz in his study of fifty hospitalized schizophrenics, only five of whom he considered to have an adequate home life. More specific factors were identified by Elleison and Hamilton who found that thirty of their sample of one hundred hospitalized schizophrenics had experienced the loss of a sibling.

In 1959, Haley summarized this phase: "A transition would seem to have taken place in the study of schizophrenia; from the early idea that the difficulty in these families was *caused* by the schizophrenic member, to the idea that they contained a "pathogenic" mother, to the discovery that the father was "inadequate" to the current emphasis upon all three family members involved in a pathological system of interaction."

The Jackson and Satir group espoused the view of the family as a system—which, like all systems, operated by developing a "homeostasis" without which it could not operate—a hypothetical condition in which any change in one family member effects changes in others in the family. Family therapy was claimed to be an opportunity to break up the schizophrenic's communication code. An important theoretical assumption was thus given a central place—namely, that there is a characteristic and definable mode of communication in the "schizophrenic" family.

Haley in his close association with the Jackson-Satir group adumbrated a more specific description of the communication disorder. He concluded that in these families there is an incongruence between what is said and what is intended. Statements are made, then qualified and contradicted (1959). Furthermore, he postulated a disorder of the family system: "a perverse triangle" of intergenerational coalition, in which the separation between the generations is bridged. Two generations of the family combine to victimize a member of the third generation who becomes the identified patient, and this maneuver (as with almost all interactions described as characteristic of the schizophrenic family) is denied by the family members.

It was Gregory Bateson(1956) who formulated what was to become perhaps the most famous of the hypothesized schizophrenic modes of communication—the "double bind": a vulnerable mother copes with the anxiety and hostility aroused by the threat of too much closeness with her child by assuming an attitude that is excessively loving. Her attitude is expressed in characteristically ambivalent messages, in which the overt message is contradicted by a covert message, in a situation from which the recipient cannot escape, and in which recognition of the contradiction is prohibited.

Ronald Laing and his associates incorporated the "double bind" hypothesis into their formulation of "mystification," a process by which the recipient is driven into a position which is labeled crazy, but which is in fact an understandable adaptation to the demands of a distorted environment. Laing developed the core concept of distorted communication to support the philosophical position that the labeling of the patient reflects not only familial but also societal denial of the aberrant individual's right to a self-validated existence. At its most extreme, his position becomes paradoxical, and he asserts that the label of psychosis is really a definition of the societal and familial madness.

In the absence of well-defined language for describing family and group interaction not only as the accumulated actions of isolated individuals but as a truly functioning gestalt, other groups developed schemata which emphasize structural interactional models as compared with the analyses of communication and systems disorders of the Haley, Jackson-Satir group. An important representative of this approach is the Lidz, Cornelison, Fleck and Terry group who studied fourteen families with a schizophrenic member for over two years. As a result, they emphasized the father's pathogenic influence. They described five types of father.

1. The father who undercuts his wife's authority and molds his daughter to fit his needs. He is often sexually seductive with his daughter.
2. The father who is hostile towards his children and belittles his sons.
3. The father with an exalted self-concept.
4. The father who is a failure in life.
5. The passive, inadequate father.

Recently Lidz and Fleck have critically reviewed their work. They have switched from focusing on the father to an emphasis on the failure of schizophrenic families as a whole to differentiate clearly between the two generations most directly involved in nuclear family relationships. They coined the terms "marital schism" and "marital skew" to characterize the disturbed relationships between parents. In both these processes, there is a mutual failure of the marital partners to meet each other's deep dynamic needs. In the first case (schism) the family stays together despite overt scrapping. In the second case (skew), overt harmony masks covert disagreement. Marital schisms and skews pave the way for a seduction of children by one parent or the other into a pathologic alliance.

"Schism" and "skew" are attempts at a language describing a pattern of organization. Unfortunately, they are only two metaphors (given, to be sure, some operational description), but there are many unique, perhaps pathology-inducing, organizational patterns which would each require a metaphor to summarize the characteristic interactions. Particular groups have generated their own distinctive metaphors which have become part of the accumulated but random and disparate vocabulary of family therapy. Another, by now almost classical, metaphor is Lyman Wynne's (1958) "pseudo-mutuality" derived from his work with the families of hospitalized schizophrenics. It summarizes a form of relationship *he* believed to be particularly pathogenic: the family members are preoccupied with fitting together at the expense of individual identity, divergence is forbidden and family members strive to maintain an outward appearance of mutuality. Wynne suggested that the typical organization of a family with a schizophrenic member is one in which there are a limited number of roles, for which the members compete. Subsquently he added the terms "alignment" and "split." "Alignment" is akin to an alliance between two family members who have a positive feeling for each other. "Split" describes an experience of opposition between family members with a resulting negative emotional equilibrium of the family.

Meissner criticized the limitations of these interactional models: interactional theory does not provide explanations of sufficient cause for psychotic breaks and does not explain the differences between psychotic and nonpsychotic communication. Role theory does not explain why one child in a family "inherits" the psychotic role while another does not. The theories, in general, press towards excessive explanation of partially understood clinical phenomena; the described interactions all share the implicit or explicit belief that the psychosis of the identified patient is both a product of distorted interaction and a necessity for the maintenance of a fragile family unity.

THERAPEUTIC GOALS AND TECHNIQUES

In spite of the theoretical welter, there is some agreement among practitioners on the direction and goals of family therapy, probably most succinctly outlined by Nathan Ackerman. He defined family therapy as "the therapeutic interview with a living unit, the functional family group comprising all those who live together as a family under a single roof, and any additional relatives who fulfill a significant family role, even if they reside in a separate place."

In this context, the *unit of illness and health,* the unit of treatment influence, is the family group, rather than the single patient in isolation. In family therapy, one views the psychic functioning of one person in the wider context of reciprocal family role adaptations, and the psychosocial organiation of the family as a whole, both in the here and now, and across the generations.

In the psychotherapy of the family group, Ackerman outlined several main principles:

1. The breakdown of one member of the family (identified patient). The nature of his disablement and the associated symptoms may be viewed as a reflection of the emotional warp of the entire family (i.e., the *unit of pathology* is no single family member, but the family as a unit). One can often delineate a specific correlation between the emotional pathology of the family group and the breakdown of a particular, symptom-bearing member. Often a

core of pathogenic conflict and associated defense patterns is contagiously passed down from one generation to the next. (One must therefore be alert to the movement of a pathogenic disorder across three generations.)

2. In disturbed families as a rule, there are *multiple instances of psychiatric disorder*. It is rarely the case that only one member of the family is emotionally disabled. This places an emphasis on the vicissitudes of interaction in the family as a whole, as well as their effect on the more vulnerable individuals.

3. It is also clear that as one intervenes in the family, here and now, the *focus* of the most intense conflict and disturbance *may shift* from one part of the family to another.

These principles are generally accepted among family therapists. But in themselves they are obviously not specific guides to the process of treatment. In 1970, a committee of G.A.P. proposed some useful distinctions between immediate, short-term goals and overall, long-term goals for family therapy.

Immediate goals include discovering if and how the presenting problem is linked to a definable system of family relationship, and in what way the family members are emotionally and behaviorally involved with one another. Ideally, a central part of each family member's life should be absorbed in wrestling with, fending off or coping with the shared problem. The reason for this is that exploratory family therapy appears to be most effective for the treatment of relationship problems in which all of the participant family members have a vital and continuing stake, on either a conscious or an unconscious level.

A second immediate goal is to assess precisely who will be the participants in family therapy. As with other modalities of treatment, the method of doing this varies from therapist to therapist. Satir, for example, makes each family member voice a specific goal at the beginning of the first interview. She believes that in this way all family members commit themselves to coming to treatment sessions, not only in the interest of the patient but for themselves as well. Other family therapists spend a great deal of the first interview assessing the patterns of interdependence within the family. When these can be demonstrated to the family, the therapist has a rational response to the perennial question of the family involved in treatment: ''Why should all of us come when it is Charlie who is sick?'' The therapist is thus able to involve the family members without having to assert that ''the whole family is sick.'' This assertion may in fact alienate family members from therapy if its sole basis is a theoretical a priori approach independent of the clinical realities.

Long-term goals may emerge during the process of therapy, or in certain cases where there is specific psychopathology, the long term goal may be defined from the very outset. But common long-term goals in almost all family therapy involve the improvement of communication and an increase in flexibility in family roles. Hopefully these changes will allow individual members more autonomy, empathy with other family members and a reduction of conflict.

THERAPEUTIC APPROACHES

Bels and Ferber attempted to classify the wide variety of therapeutic styles and techniques, and produced a rough distinction between the conductors and the reactors: the conductors are generally vigorous, somewhat theatrical personalities who lead the group at all times. They act as theatrical "agents provocateurs." The reactors, on the other hand, are quieter and tailor their approach to the group dynamics of the family.

The reactors were in turn divided into two groups: the analysts, who use the language of psychoanalysis and focus on the internal process of the individuals; and the system purists, who tend to seek out the characteristics of the family network as a system. They couch their interpretations in the language of systems analysis. In spite of their categorization, Bels and Ferber maintained—and we agree with them—that there is not much difference in the technique of the reactors and the conductors. The differences seem to derive more from the personality of the individual therapists than from their various theories. Having said this, one can discern certain differences in the therapeutic approaches of well-known family therapists, and it may be useful briefly to touch on these. Ackerman, as demonstrated by his clinical demonstrations and his legacy of video tapes and films, mobilized family interaction using a blend of confrontation and personal charm. He said that he "tickled" the defenses against what he called "punitive relations" cutting through denial, hypocrisy and projection. He believed that he would achieve his therapeutic goal by forcing the family members to be more open with him than they were with each other.

Virginia Satir, on the other hand, presents herself as a teacher and an expert on communications. Essentially she hopes to teach the family "a new language" which will help them resolve their communication problem.

Bowen and Minuchin have a "stage direction" approach to the therapist-family interaction which, they believe, enforces differentiation of individuals from what Bowen has called the "undifferentiated family ego mass." Minuchin, working with poor, relatively nonverbal families, concentrates upon the demonstration of alternative modes of interaction rather than verbal interpretation. He enacts alternate modes of behavior, and he and his associates have developed techniques using (what may be loosely called) traditional family therapy together with behavior-shaping strategies derived from behavior therapy. They claim notable therapeutic success for this approach in the treatment of psychosomatic disorders in the identified patient. They have reported on their successful treatment of brittle diabetics and anorexia nervosa.

Roland Tharp and the multiple-impact group concentrate on conventional family roles in the areas of solidarity, sexuality, external relations and internal instrumentality. An attempt is made to teach the family new techniques of negotiating on concrete issues from which they can generalize.

Norman Paul's goal is to exorcise "the ghost," a figure from the past who is usually one of the grandparents. This pathological ghost dominates the family life and is responsible for much of its psychopathology.

Among the reactor analysts are Carl Whitaker, Lyman Wynne and James Framo. They believe that the individual carries within him a nonrational and unconscious truth which when exposed in family therapy will help to set him free. They use co-therapists for the working through of parental transference.

The reactors-system purists —Zuk, Haley and Don Jackson—are much less explicit in their definition of the role of the therapist. The therapist is supposed to emerge as the covert leader of the group by a series of implicit rather then explicit therapeutic ploys. It is as though the family is seduced into accepting the therapist's leadership without being aware of the process as it is happening.

In a sense all family therapists adhere to a communications theory of intervention. Bateson has probably elaborated this approach most fully. But in the end he is forced into considerable theoretical conjecture as he attempts to make sense of the "black box" by which the input into the system is transformed into a not always obviously related output.

There are some special approaches to family therapy that deserve to be mentioned. The behavior-therapy approach advocated by Lieberman tends to ignore pathological interaction as the family members learn to give each other recognition and approval for desired behavior. It should be noted that in the pragmatics of the therapeutic situation, this requires considerable skill, since the therapist's cultivation of deliberate deafness to the most common complaining verbalizations, in an attempt to extinguish the complaints by lack of attention, produces an almost comic effect.

Network therapy is a somewhat heroic approach: six four-hour evening sessions are conducted in the home of the "schizophrenic family." Friends, family, neighbors and representatives of concerned agencies are invited to these meetings. The evening is divided into three phases—a pre-session gossip, a main session focused on two concentric groups (the "inner group or family" and the outer group of the others) and a post-session coffee and rehash. The logistics of this approach are obviously very complicated and imply considerable willingness on the part of relative strangers to be involved in a therapeutic process which may not always appear to be relevant to their concerns.

INDICATIONS AND CONTRAINDICATIONS FOR FAMILY THERAPY

There are few objective contraindications or indeed indications for family therapy. It is perhaps unfortunate that much of the early work in conjoint family therapy was conducted with families with a schizophrenic member. In spite of anecdotal case reports of dramatic improvement, the validation of this therapeutic approach has not been sufficiently stringent. Murray Bowen has stated that he doubts if he has ever changed the dynamics of a schizophrenic, whereas multiple-impact therapists claim that all schizophrenics have been improved. Bearing in mind the looseness of the criteria, Wynne states that in general terms exploratory family therapy should be considered for the treatment of relationship problems in which all of the participant members have a vital and continuing stake—e.g., adolescent separation problems manifesting as identity crisis; rebellious deliquent behavior or a failure to emerge from the symbiotic dependency relationship; the trading of disassociations, a complex of intrafamilial problems in which each person sees himself as having a specific limited difficulty which he feels derives from another family member; a collective cognitive chaos and erratic distancing, as in families which exhibit a transactional thought disorder.

There are some therapeutic systems in which the family approach is used as a blanket approach to all new psychiatric cases. Implicit in this approach is the concept of generalized systems theory. It is thought no matter what the presenting symptomatology, the patient is essentially part of an interlocking network of concerned individuals and agenices that are involved, to a greater or lesser extent, either in the pathogenesis or the rehabilitation of the family. It serves the purpose of affirming that no matter how the individual patient is handled, following the initial diagnostic exploration, he is a member of a family and community.

CONTRAINDICATIONS TO FAMILY THERAPY

According to the 1970 G.A.P. Report, these are: the presence of a malignant, irreversible trend towards the breakup of the family; the dominance within the group of a concentrated focus of a malignant destructiveness; one parent who is affected by an organized paranoid condition; incorrigible psychopathological destructiveness or a confirmed criminal or pervert; either one or both parents who are unable to be honest with a therapist or each other; the existence of a valid family secret; cultural, religious or economic prejudice against this form of intervention; rigid defenses which if broken may induce a psychosis, a psychosomatic crisis or a physical assault; the presence of progressive organic disease.

While these contraindications appear to be valid on the basis of clinical experience and common sense, they are not supported or negated by studies. In a series of twenty cases treated in a study by Epstein, Rakoff and Sigal, attempts to predict harm to the family, and success or failure of treatment, were notably unsuccessful. A number of families which appear to be extremely pathological were in fact helped by conjoint therapy. Many anticipated difficulties failed to materialize in the course of therapy. More objectively, a recent paper by Guttman describes a specific contraindication for family therapy: the fragile adolescent with marginal functioning may be precipitated into a psychotic break by conjoint family therapy.

OUTCOME OF FAMILY THERAPY

Bowen feels that he can change the dynamics of most families in four years, although he has the reservations about schizophrenics referred to above. Langsley, in Colorado, has written that he has circumvented hospitalization in 90 percent of acute cases originally thought to require hospitalization. The McMaster University Department of Psychiatry in Canada has similarly had considerable success in maintaining disturbed patients out of the hospital by the use of a family and systems approach. In the study of twenty families referred to above, fourteen of the twenty cases showed considerable improvement after approximately a year of conjoint family therapy.

In the welter of therapeutic approaches, it is difficult to evaluate specific theoretical and therapeutic approaches, but it is clear that an intelligent, empathic therapist working with the family as a whole may achieve therapeutic results beyond his or our capacity satisfactorily to explain the process by which this is achieved. All forms of therapy have in common the clarification of interaction and the exposure of family members to one another in the presence of a figure who, by his authority, may prevent harm being done.

The literature does not contain many objective descriptions of the process of family therapy. However, in the study of twenty families by Epstein, Rakoff and Sigal referred to above, a normative pattern of therapeutic engagement emerges. Most families will accept conjoint family therapy when it is offered, and even families who may initially not be considered suitable for treatment will frequently enter into and participate in treatment. Most family members furthermore will not initiate a move to drop out of therapy, and it is difficult to predict in advance which families will be easy and which difficult to treat, and which resistances will be used during treatment. The frequently expressed fear regarding the application of family therapy to families with fragile defenses does not appear to be valid. Little harm if any appears to be caused by encounter within the family.

In short, family therapy is a pragmatically useful technique, and should not be regarded as a quasi-religious system or universal panacea. It is now a well-accepted technique of the therapeutic armamentarium. But if it is to move beyond the merely pragmatic, it will require careful research projects constructed to examine outcome, indications and contraindications, and therapeutic process. In addition, its applicability to particular syndromes will require exhaustive investigations.

BIBLIOGRAPHY

1. Ackerman, Nathan W. Treating the Troubled Family, New York. Basic Books Inc., 1967.
2. Beels, C. Christian, and Ferber, Andrew. Family therapy: a view. *Family Process*, Vol. 8, No. 2, September 1969, 280-319.
3. Boszormenyi-Nagy, Ivan, and Framo, James L., eds. *Intensive Family Therapy: Theoretical and Practical Aspects.* New York: Harper & Row, 1965.
4. Epstein, N. B. Family therapy today: an observation. *Laval Medical*, Vol. 41, No. 6, 835 (1970).
5. Epstein, Nathan B., and Bishop, D. S. Family therapy: state of the art. *Canadian Psych. Assoc. Journal*, Vol. 18, No. 3, p. 175-183, June 1973.
6. G.A.P. Report No. 78. The Field of Family Therapy. Formulated by the committee on the family, Vol. VII, No. 78, March 1970.
7. Haley, Jay. *A Review of the Family Therapy Field in Changing Families: A Family Therapy Reader.* New York and London: Greene & Stratton (eds.)
8. Haley, Jay. Approaches to family therapy. *Int. I. of Psychiatry*, Vol. 9, 233-242, 1970.
9. Langsley, D. G., and Kaplan, David N. The Treatment of Families in Crisis. New York: Greene & Stratton (1968).
10. Liberman, Robert. Behavioral approaches to family and couple therapy. *Am. Journal of Orthopsychiatry*, Vol. 40, 106-113 (1970).
11. Minuchin, Salvador. The Use of an Ecological Framework in the Treatment of a Child. *The Child and His Family*, E. J. Anthony & C. Kouperhik (eds.), Wiley Interscience (1970).
12. Rakoff, V. M., Sigal, J. J. and Epstein, M. B., Predictions of Therapeutic Process and Progress in Conjoint Family Therapy (to be published in *Archives of General Psychiatry*).
13. Speer, David C., Family systems: morphostasis and morphogenis or is homeostasis enough? *Fahily Process*, Vol. 9, No. 3, 259-377 (1970).
14. Speck, R. V., and Ruveni, V. Network therapy: a developing concept. *Family Process*, Vol. 8, 182-191 (1969).
15. Steinhauer, P. Reflections on criteria for selection and prognosis in family therapy. *Can. Psych. Ass. J.*, Vol. 13, p. 317-321 (1968).

8

Psychosocial System Therapy

E. MANSELL PATTISON

The purpose of this chapter is to describe the clinical and theoretical development of an approach to psychotherapy based on social system theory. (77,78,79) This approach is neither psychological nor sociological. Rather, I view human behavior as the *product* of an interaction between individual psychology and the social field. Hence I use the term *psychosocial* to label the *system of behavior*. A system of behavior is a *gestalt* pattern that is more than the sum of its component parts. Each part of the system exists in reciprocal relation to every other part. Thus a change in one part requires a reciprocal change in every other part.

I define *therapy* as a healing intervention in behalf of a *specific individual* who has identifiable dysfunctional behavior. This may be internal behavior (thoughts, feelings) or external behavior (words, actions). There are other healing interventions in the history of medicine that are quite properly conducted in behalf of people in general, such as water fluoridation, vitamin enrichment of bread, public sanitation, etc. Such general system interventions, without a specific individual target might be termed medical care, but not medical therapy.

In terms of mental health I deem it important to distinguish between levels of system intervention, some of which are therapy, others of which are care. Still other levels of systems intervention that utilize mental health skills and knowledge are not properly subsumed under sickness/health paradigm because different social sanctions and norms operate to regulate professional intervention. For example, organizational consultation is often provided by mental health consultants. The social sanction is not based on a ''sick''organization that requires ''healing.'' Rather, the mental health professional offers skills and knowledge from one professional arena that may be useful in another arena but under a nonmedical set of role norms. (40)

There is a clear social sanction to define certain individual behavior as ''sick'' in terms of mental health parameters. There is also social sanction to ''treat'' the sick individual. Now in the development of mental health concepts we have moved toward a more social view of human behavior. In so doing we seek social sanction to define and treat a social unit comprised of more than one person.

We have gained social sanction to define and treat ''sick'' families as a social unit. At this point there is much conceptual confusion. On the one hand, critics maintain that only an individual can appropriately be defined as sick, and that a social unit cannot be labeled as sick. On the other hand, some family therapists assert that there are no sick individuals, only sick families; the individual psychopathology is defined as a reflection of the family. Thus if the family were well, the individual would be well.

For my part, I take neither position. The social purpose of defining a person or social unit as sick is integral to the social sanction to treat that person or social unit. Thus we may label any social unit, family, neighborhood, community, organization, city or government as sick. But we do not have the social sanction to do so. Nor do we have the social sanction for treatment intervention. We gain social sanction to define and treat to the extent that we can demonstrate appropriate skills and knowledge that justify a social mandate to treat.

The professional mandate for treatment is rooted in the individual. The farther we depart from the individual, the weaker the social mandate to define and intervene. Family therapy did not develop because of the discovery of sick families but, rather, from the demonstration that the family was inextricably linked with the defined sick individual. We have demonstrated that intervention with the family produces healing of the individual. Thus we have gained sanction to define the family social system as sick and engage in family treatment *as a system*.

Therefore, we can define an individual as sick, and we can define a family as sick. But we do not have a mandate to treat a sick family that has no identifiable sick individual. But let us go a step further. The *degree* of intimate relationship between the individual and a social unit is critical to the extension of a treatment mandate. For example, grandparents and cousins of a sick individual may be closely linked and properly involved in treatment. But if grandparents and cousins are not involved in the family life of the individual, they may properly disclaim involvement. The extreme end of this process is the sick worker on an office staff. Here it would be usually difficult to link the social unit of office staff behavior to the genesis and maintenance of individual sick behavior. Likewise the office staff would probably disclaim involvement in the treatment of the individual. And surely we would have an impossible task to gain social sanction to define the office staff as sick and "treat" the office staff.

In this chapter I am concerned with the extension of the social mandate to define and treat *social system units*. However, I wish to carefully differentiate the professional mandate for treatment intervention.

I shall focus primarily on the *intimate and immediate psychosocial system* of an individual characterized by three major factors: 1) a high level of face-to-face personal interaction, 2) a high degree of emotional involvement, and 3) and high degree of instrumental responsibility between members. This psychosocial system is the fundamental matrix within which an individual exists and acts. I propose that we define this system for professional intervention *on behalf of the identified patient*. We may, where appropriate, negotiate a sanction to *treat that psychoso-*

cial system as a system. In other instances we may not seek to treat that system, but collaborate with that system.

To complete this survey, I shall briefly review other social system units that may be appropriately involved in mental health care. In these latter instances I shall not refer to psychosocial system therapy but, rather, to psychosocial system care.

I. CLINICAL DEVELOPMENT

To begin, I shall trace the development of personal psychotherapy from its inception as a two-person social dyad through a series of steps to the *multiple-person, multiple-relation* psychosocial system.

Psychotherapy has its most obvious derivation from Freud. Grounded in the medical milieu at the turn of the twentieth century, it is not surprising that psychotherapy was built upon the medical doctor-patient model. Inherent in that model was the nineteenth-century concept of disease—an affliction of an individual, an affliction that required treatment of that individual. Disease was an individual affair, and so became psychotherapy. (12)

The first step away from the explicit one-to-one model appeared some twenty years after the birth of psychotherapy. Around 1920 the child guidance movement began to develop with the inclusion of the parents of the "sick" child in the therapeutic enterprise. The parents, however, were not conceptualized as "patients," nor were the parents involved in "treatment." Rather, the parents were taken into the psychotherapeutic enterprise under the rubrics of "guidance," "education," casework," "social work," or "ancillary" therapy. This was not incongruous in terms of the existent model of psychotherapy, which was *by definition* a one-to-one relationship.

The second step in the revision of the original model of psychotherapy was the development of group psychotherapy in the 1930's. The early pioneers in group psychotherapy had acquired their clinical experience in the child guidance movement and had already observed the importance of interpersonal relationships in the behavior of the "sick" child. The early experiments in group psychotherapy were modeled on the one-to-one relationship. Hence group therapy was actually treatment of *a* person *in* a group. It was several decades before a thoroughgoing conceptual shift was made to the concept of treatment of *all* persons simultaneously *by* the group. The introduction of treatment in a multiple-person setting and, even more so, the introduction of the concept of treatment *by* the participants, occasioned volatile and bitter arguments, for the proponents of the one-to-one model of psychotherapy argued that this form of psychotherapy did not meet the theoretical requirements for the conduct of psychotherapy. Indeed, group therapy did not meet the required definitions of psychotherapy, based on the premises of one-to-one relationships. (73, 74)

The third step came with the introduction of family therapy, begun gingerly in the 1940's and reaching real visibility in the late 1950's. (69) The introduction of family therapy grew out of the same intellectual and clinical experiences that had spawned group therapy. However, family therapy took longer to develop. One significant reason may be that in group therapy the participants were unrelated to each other, and each group member was identified as "sick." Thus the one-to-one model of psychotherapy was strained but not broken. However, family therapy introduced major problems. It was no longer clear who was sick and who was well in the therapeutic setting, nor who indeed was the patient. Further, the participants were intimately related to each other. This latter factor proved a challenge to traditional ideas of the one-to-one model, such as the development of transference, regression, lack of destructive feedback, etc. It was recognized that family therapy was not just group therapy with a family group, but perhaps the introduction of a therapeutic technique *sui generis*. (41,43)

The fourth step was the introduction in the early 1960's of a further seeming confusion. Clinicians began to organize multiple families into one group for therapeutic purposes, perhaps four to six families meeting together, comprising some sixteen to twenty-five people, both related and unrelated to each other. (9,14,23,55,) A similar mix was produced in the development of married couples group psychotherapy in which four to six married couples met together as a group. (38) As before, the therapeutic situation involved persons who were related in real life, but in addition it included persons who were totally unrelated to each other. At this point it seemed very difficult indeed to conceptualize this mode of psychotherapy under the traditional theories of psychotherapy developed from the one-to-one situation.

The fifth step occurred less explicitly than the rest. It began in the 1950's with the development of home visitation treatment programs, where the mental health professional went into the home of the "sick" person to treat him, and perforce to work with the family of the patient. (72) This was close to the one-to-one model, but even the shift in setting raised conceptual issues. (83) Shortly however, the home visit was rapidly expanded in scope. MacGregor et al (62) introduced the concept of "multiple impact" family therapy where a team of professionals worked with different segments of the family together. A variation, but a significant one, was the conduct of an entire course of family psychotherapy in the families' homes. (93) Interestingly, these therapists reported that friends, relatives and neighbors would occasionally be included in the family sessions because of happenstance, invitation by the family, or even by specific invitation by the therapist because the "extra-familial" person was noted to play an important role in the dynamics of the family. Similarly, other therapists have reported on experiences in living in the homes of families in treatment, or making extensive visits to the homes of families where they participated in various family functions that included friends, relatives, visitors, etc. (43,54,59)

The sixth and final step has been to formalize contacts and relationships between family members and non— family members—to include in the psychotherapeutic situation any number of persons who are related by either kinship, friendship or functional relationship (employer, etc.) or community residence (4,7,8,34,35, 44,46,68,69,88,93,94,95,107). This social network of relationships then has been made the focus of psychotherapy. In all these instances, the focus of therapeutic work has shifted to the social system of the individual patient, and the therapy of the patient is achieved via change in the psychosocial system of the patient.

It is apparent that psychosocial system therapy stands a far distance from psychotherapy as defined from the one-to-one situation. To attempt to "fit" these latter psychotherapeutic techniques into the conceptual schemata derived from the one-to-one model of psychotherapy seems not only herculean, but perhaps more important, merely inappropriate. Rather, I suggest that these psychotherapy innovations call for the development of a new model of psychotherapy that is appropriate to these techniques. This model, which I call the "systems" model would not replace the "personal" model, but would complement it.

II. THEORETICAL DEVELOPMENT OF SOCIAL FIELD THEORY

Gardner Murphy has observed that, from the time of Aristotle until late in the nineteenth century, psychology was the study of individual minds. Group interaction and interpersonal relations were problems for the historian, the moralist, the jurist, the political economist. Psychotherapy was born in an intellectual era in which perhaps only a one-to-one model of psychotherapy could have been built.

However, a social psychology of human relationships built on the work of William McDougall, Cooley, Durkheim, Giddings, Ross, Tonnies and, especially, George Herbert Mead began to stir an intellectual ferment that was to shake psychological thinking loose from its individualistic moorings. (64)

In the 1920's, social scientists began to study "natural groups" in society in the conviction that the solution to "social problems" could be facilitated by the study of social interaction and normal social groupings. (33,47,84,96,110) This empirical research approach was translated into social work practice with groups. But interestingly, the "social group work" method has remained defined as *not* psychotherapy. The empirical study of natural groups in the community also gave rise to social welfare and social action programs. Yet here also, such intervention was not defined as psychotherapeutic. In both instances, because specific people were not identified as "sick," these types of intervention were not seen as having personal therapeutic potential. More recent evaluations to be cited suggest that therapeutic potential was present, but not exploited.

Finally, in the 1930's, Kurt Lewin formulated his now famous "field theory." In brief, field theory posits that each individual exists in an interpersonal field of relationships. Each person exerts an influence on every other person in that field. But in addition, each person exists at a particular place in that field, with a cumulative effect on him from the juxtaposition of all around him. Lewin uses the term "valence" to symbolize the positive and negative tugs and pulls that impinge like magnetic forces upon the individual.

Lewin proposed that the behavior of the individual is the product of two forces. One is the internal psychological structure of the person. The other is field characteristics.

One can change behavior in two ways. First, we can intervene in the internal psychological structure of the individual. This is the traditional model of "personal" psychotherapy. The second method consists of intervention with the social field, such that the individual exists in a different field. This is the model of "systems" therapy.

The early development of multi-person therapeutic situations may be seen as an application of general principles of Lewinian field theory. Other extensions of field theory are exemplified in small-group sociology, social psychology, and role theory. Persons operate in a social field which to a significant extent determines behavior. Thus one can create a social field which can be of therapeutic benefit to the emotionally disturbed person. Cody March, pioneer in group therapy methods, coined a succinct motto of this theory: "By the crowd they have been broken; by the crowd they shall be healed."

However, this concept of social field is an impersonal concept. The destructive or beneficent effects of the social field are not dependent on the particular personalities or relationships of the individual persons that comprise the field— rather, it is the sociological structure of the field that determines its impact. Thus Cody March was quite correct when he used the word "crowd" in his aphorism.

When, however, the focus of clinical concern shifted to families and persons linked together by their instrumental and affective relationships to each other, we observe a more complex and different sociodynamic. For here we have not only the effects of impersonal sociological group function, but also the effects of instrumental and affective linkages that exist between members.

Edward Jay (49), an anthropologist, in his paper "The Concepts of Field and Network in Anthropological Research" attempts to differentiate between the impersonal social field and the personal psychosocial network. He suggests that social field be used to refer to an egocentric system: "There is no hierarchy, no nucleated denser focus of relationship or center. The only center would be the unit from which we are looking outward in a given arbitrary distance. Every unit is in this sense a center. We might say that such a system is always egocentric . . . the units of the field may be individuals, families, communities, or other social aggregates, but the field as such does not constitute a 'group' with corporate qualities and cohesiveness." In contrast, Jay defines a network as the totality of all the units *connected by a certain type of relationship.* A network has definite boundaries and is not egocentric, and a major focus of study of such a psychosocial network, then, is on the nature and quality of these specific connecting relationships that set the particular pattern of the network. For example, a family is a social network that is characterized primarily by specific affective connections, whereas a factory work team is a social network characterized primarily by specific instrumental connections.

What we have observed over the past thirty years is a step wise recognition of the psychosocial network in which the patient is embedded; moving from parents and child to nuclear family, to extended family, to finally a complex social network that may include nuclear family, various kin, friends who have "affective" links, and persons like ministers and bosses who have "instrumental" links. (16,17, 22, 30, 48, 56)

The major conceptual shift, so far as therapy is concerned, revolves around the focus of therapeutic intervention. In the one-to-one "personal" model the assumption is made that psychotherapy will effect change in the individual that will enable him to behave differently in his social fields and social networks. But, in the multiple-person "systems" model we assume that by tightening or loosening the affective and instrumental linkages that exist in the network, different options for behavior will be presented to the "patient" and consequently the patient will behave differently. Thus the focus of psychotherapy in the "systems" model is to change the interactional characteristics of the psychosocial network. This model explicitly assumes that human behavior is significantly determined by the characteristics of the social field or social network; hence the therapeutic emphasis lies here, rather than on changing the individual per se.

There are at least two major corollaries to this thesis. First, in the one-to-one "personal" model the definition of normality is essentially an *idealistic* one, i.e., the mature genital character, whereas in the "systems" model the definition of normality is an *adaptive* one, i.e., capacity to operate effectively in the person's social field and network. Second, the "personal" model focuses on characterological change, whereas the "systems" model focuses on behavioral change.

III. EMPIRICAL DEVELOPMENT OF PSYCHOSOCIAL SYSTEM DEFINITIONS

The rationale for a focus on social networks also arises from a series of empirical studies. Anthropological studies of kinship systems had demonstrated that the kin social network in primitive societies was a major determinant of affective and instrumental relationships. The same was shown to hold for the agrarian small-town enclaves that characterized the living patterns of Western societies until the late nineteenth century. However, with industrialization and the dramatic shift of the population balance to large-city living patterns, it was observed that traditional kinship relationships were severed both by geography and rapid shifts in social and economic status between members of the kinship system. By the 1940's sociologists such as Talcott Parsons concluded that the former affective and instrumental functions of the kinship system had vanished and been replaced by social organizations (29) It was concluded that the extended kinship system typically had been replaced by the so-called nuclear family, i.e., mother father, and pre-adult children. It was concluded that the nuclear family could not provide all of the necessary affective and instrumental needs necessary for effective family function, and fears were expressed for the demise of the nuclear family, as it was an unstable social structure.

However, the pessimism of the 1940's did not bear fruit as even more industrialization and urbanization occurred in the subsequent decades. In turn, a number of more refined studies of urban kinship systems demonstrated that the earlier sociological view of the nuclear family required revision. (98) It was shown that in working-class and even in lower-class families in urban areas a kinship system was present and powerful. Further, it was shown that kinship systems existed in urban middle-class and upper-class families. (2,3,11,20,22,25,30, 36,37,42,53,60,61,70,87,97,99,100,101,102,108,109)

Thus at the present time we have extant at least four variants of kinship systems:

1. The traditional extended family structure that is an interdependent social and economic unit, each nuclear subfamily living in geographic proximity and depending on the extended kin for major services in life.

2. The dissolving or weak family in which most kin functions have been taken over by large-scale formal organizations, leaving the family with little to do—all that is left is a very tenuous husband-and-wife relationship.

3. The isolated nuclear family, composed of husband, wife and small child. Fewer but essential function are concentrated in the nuclear family, sufficiently powerful to provide stability.

4. The modified extended family structure consisting of coalitions of nuclear families in a state of partial dependence.

In most of the sociological literature the study of kinship systems has been confined to the study of blood-related kin. Yet studies from a sociopsychological perspective have demonstrated that in urban settings, and especially among middle-class families, the kinship system, usually of a modified extended type, consists not of blood kin but of *affective kin*. That is, friends, neighbors and associates in informal social groups assume the functions of bloodkin in an affective and instrumental network of relationships. In summary, then, in urbanized living patterns *the blood-kin system has been replaced by a friend, neighbor, associate, kin system.* (30,56,89)

These kinship considerations assume clinical importance both in terms of the social network conditions that may produce symptomatic behavior and as a social system to which therapeutic efforts may be addressed.

The importance of family relations in the genesis of disturbed behavior in one member of the family has been extensively discussed in the family therapy literature. The family dynamics involved, however, may not just be the dynamics of the nuclear family. For example, Mendell et al (65,66,67) have reported several studies on the communication of maladaptive behavior over multi-generations—in one instance, over five generations. They conclude from their studies that the focus of therapeutic intervention must aim at this ongoing social system: "When the individual comes to a therapist for help, we assume that he is admitting the failure of his group as an effective milieu in which to find the solution he seeks [to his problems]. Our data suggest that the individual seeking help frequently approaches the therapist to protest against the ineffectiveness of the group to which he belongs."

The importance of kinship systems as a framework for psychotherapy is emphasized in the clinical treatment of families with schizophrenic members, where it has been noted that affective kin relations often play a determinative role in the behavior of nuclear family members. In some instances, the schizophrenic family is unable to utilize the affective and instrumental resources of a kinship system, whereas in other instances the kinship system serves to perpetuate and reinforce psychopathological family dynamics. (58)

The lack of an effective kinship system or malfunction in the kinship system has been suggested as an etiological factor in nuclear family dysfunction.

A study by Kammeyer and Bolton (50) compared a group of normal families and a group of families applying for treatment at several family service agencies. They found that the client families, by comparison, had fewer memberships in voluntary associations, fewer friendships with relatives, and fewer relations living in the same community.

In another, more extensive study, Leichter and Mitchell (57) focus on the necessity for a diagnostic focus that extends beyond the nuclear family: "We have argued that family diagnosis must not end with the nuclear family, because the family is no more a closed equilibrium system than is the individual . . . Knowledge of the relationships between the family and its external environment are vital . . . this knowledge applies to kin, to occupational associates, to friends, and other non-familial relationships. Leichter and Mitchell then turn to discuss treatment intervention. They suggest that the kinship network might be the appropriate unit of treatment, yet, interestingly, though writing in 1967, they were apparently not aware that clinicians were actually embarking on a treatment course they could only suggest: "Perhaps a group of kin could even be an effective unit of group treatment. This unit would differ radically in some of the characteristics of externally impersonal relationships that pertain in group therapy . . . A group of kin might be an effective unit of treatment precisely because they are in-terrelated, and changes in one would have actual relevance for changes in the others . . . the possibility that this unit might be effective in some instances is no more far-fetched than the notion that the family rather than the individual is sometimes the appropriate unit of treatment . . . The notion that under some conditions it might be beneficial to treat more extended segments of the kin network sounds removed from present thinking, but is a possibility that should not be arbitrarily excluded."

It is of historical interest, however, that N.W. Bell (10) had suggested the kin social network as a focus of psychotherapy as far back as 1962. He observed that "well" families had achieved resolution of the usual problems of ties to extended kin, and therefore had the resources of the kin available, whereas "disturbed" families had been unable to resolve conflicts with the extended kin outside the nuclear family. Bell observed that the pathological families used the extended families 1) to shore up group defenses, 2) provide stimuli for conflict, 3) as a screen for the projection of nuclear family conflict and 4) as competing objects of support.

Meanwhile, a number of family sociologists had been pointing to the existence of the modified extended family system as a potential mental health resource. Eugene Litwak (31,60,61) suggests that mental health professionals avail themselves of the kin network instead of trying to provide solely professional treatment resources. Speaking of *family* in the modified extended kinship sense, he summarizes: "there are several classes of situations where the trained expert is of little use: in situations which are not uniform where the minimal standards set by society are not involved. By contrast, the formal organization might be more effective in uniform situations where high social values are involved. The question arises as to whether the family as a primary group might not be superior to the formal organization in these areas . . . the family structure is able to deal more easily with the idiosyncratic event because the family has more continuous contact over many different areas of life than the professional organizations . . . the family has speedier channels for transmitting messages that had no prior definition of legitimacy . . . it is less likely to have explicit rules on what is and what is not legitimate, it is more likely to consider events which have had no definition . . . In most instances the bureaucratic agency in the extreme case is prevented from considering events without a prior definition of legitimacy by law. In most instances the bureaucratic agency is specifically prevented from acting, by explicit rules which define the area of legitimacy ahead of time . . . The family can define much more uniquely what is to be valued. The number of people who must cooperate are much fewer, and because they are involved in affectional relations, they are most inclined to accept each other's personal definition values."

Translated into clinical idiom, Litwak's observations suggest that the modified extended family network may provide a more potent therapeutic organization in some instances than the placement of a nuclear family in a bureaucratic mental health treatment system.

The application of therapeutic intervention, however, will depend on the clinician's assessment of the type of kinship system which exists for a given family, and furthermore, the clinician must apply therapeutic intervention techniques applicable to that type of kinship network.

The most obvious example of the problem is to survey most of the clinical literature on family therapy. Almost all such literature only describes the psychotherapy of a nuclear family. Yet the typical family of the slum ghetto is probably of the dissolving-weak type. The use of nuclear family psychotherapy techniques became inappropriate and useless when applied to dissolving-weak family and kin systems. The best illustration of this is given in the work by Minuchin et al (68,69) with slum families in New York and Philadelphia. They found that there were a variety of subtypes of dissolving-weak family and kin systems, none of which were like the typical nuclear family so familiar to most upper-middle-class American psychotherapists and clinics. Minuchin and his group found that they had to devise strikingly different methods of therapeutic intervention with these dissolving-weak family and kin systems.

Another clear example of the difference which kin social network makes in planning therapeutic intervention is provided by the work of Elizabeth Bott from England.(15,16) Basing her study on observations of family life and the social network of families, she outlines several different types of nuclear families, each of which has a different functional relationship to its social kin network. For our purposes we shall consider only two polar extremes: the close-knit family network and the loose-knit family network.

The characteristics of those two polar types will be categorically compared.

1. The close family lives in geographic proximity to area of rearing and blood kin. The loose family lives geographically distant from area of rearing and blood kin.

2. The close family is linked along gender lines with preceding and succeeding generations. There is little socioeconomic change from one generation to the next, and social values are expected to continue from one generation to the next. The loose family is not linked along gender lines, with primary loyalty being established between marital partners. The nuclear couple typically have changed socioeconomic status from parents and kin. Children are related mutually to the marital couple. Values are not transmitted from one generation to the next, and children are expected to separate from the marital pair when adulthood is reached.

3. The close family has a high rate of intergenerational visitation and primary relationships are along kin lines rather than between husband and wife. The loose family has a low rate of intergenerational visitation and primary relationships are between husband and wife. Visitation here is with other nuclear marital pairs.

4. In the close family, husband and wife have clearly defined instrumental tasks based on gender. Satisfactory sexual relations are not requisite for marital stability. Child rearing is defined by the kin system on each side, not by the marital pair. In the loose family, husband and wife have more diffuse instrumental tasks, the bond is primarily affective and satisfactory sexual relations are a major component of the bond. Child rearing is usually disparate from kin tradition, and is defined mutually by the pair.

5. In the close family, the primary unit is the kin system of which the

nuclear family is a subsystem. Family values and interaction are determined by the kin system. In the loose family, the primary unit is the nuclear family. Family values and interaction are determined by the nuclear family, usually disparate from the blood kin system. However, the *affective* kin system of neighbors and friends, also loose-knit nuclear types, may be important parts of a social system that defines values and· behavior.

This brief review of family sociology does not do justice to the rich literature that has been recently generated. I wish to stress, however, a major shift in focus on the *definition of family*. Until quite recently the sociology of the family was primarily focused on different types of nuclear families. In turn, family therapy has developed with a primary focus on the treatment of different types of nuclear families.

The *new* family sociology has rediscovered the fact that there is a rich and complex kinship system even in contemporary America. There is provocative empirical data to demonstrate that this *extended system of social relations* plays a critical role in individual function. Thus the psychosocial field of the individual is not just the nuclear family, but is a larger more complex field of personal relationships.

For the traditional extended kinship family, which is characteristic of minority communities, rural communities and much of working-class communities, the psychosocial system comprises not only the nuclear family but other blood kin, grandparents, in-laws, cousins, aunts, uncles and, to a certain extent, close friends and neighbors.

In contrast, the modern urban nuclear family also has an extended kinship. This is less formal and less visibly structured, but it is real nonetheless. In this case the kinship system consists of neighbors, friends and work associates, who form the *functional* kin. We have not yet socially recognized this psychosocial network for what it is. Yet its function is just as potent, influential and critical as that of the traditional kin system based on blood and marriage definitions.

Psychosocial system therapy, then, goes a step beyond the definition of the nuclear family. Here we seek to define the psychosocial extended system of intimate personal relations that comprise the larger system matrix of the individual. Therapy is addressed to this defined psychosocial system in the same way as is addressed to the nuclear family.

How does the clinician define the psychosocial system? To date, this has been a matter of clinical judgment, based on information provided through contact with the nuclear family. However, my colleagues and I are working on a clinical method to provide a reliable definition of the psychosocial system.

Although I cannot provide technical details here, I will summarize our preliminary work on an instrument, the Pattison Psychosocial Kinship Inventory. The inventory is based on the empirical social psychology of interpersonal relations. (1) Stable interpersonal relations are based on the following. First, there is a relatively high degree of *interaction,* whether face to face, by telephone, or by letter. In other words, a person invests himself in those with whom he has contact. Second, the relationship has a strong *emotional intensity.* The degree of investment is reflected in intensity of feeling toward the other. Third, the emotion is generally *positive.* Negative relationships are maintained only when other variables force the maintenance of relationships, such as a boss or spouse. Fourth, the relationship has an *instrumental base.* In other words, the two persons can potentially call upon the other for concrete assistance. Fifth, the relationship is *symmetrically reciprocal.* That is, the other person reciprocates strong positive feeling, and reciprocates in instrumental availability.

The healthy person will have high ratings on each of these dimensions for each person in his psychosocial network. With a greater degree of emotional dysfunction, there will be less evidence of each dimension in the psychosocial system.

Preliminary data, drawn from urban populations, allow us to propose some further aspects of the psychosocial system. The healthy person has twenty to thirty persons in his psychosocial network, in which there are predominantly high dimension ratings. His network has a high degree of interaction. The neurotic has usually about ten persons in his psychosocial network, including negative and absent members. His network has a low degree of interaction as a system. The psychotic has only five members in his psychosocial system. The dimensions are ambivalent and nonreciprocal. The system is totally interactive, excluding all others.

Thus far, on a clinical basis, we have been able to complete this inventory with the identified patient with a high degree of reliability. The next task is to then assemble the persons in the psychosocial system in relation to the patient. Finally, the therapist commences to negotiate a treatment contract, either to work directly with that system or to collaborate with that system.

IV. EXAMPLES OF OTHER THERAPEUTIC SYSTEMS ANALOGOUS TO THE PSYCHOSOCIAL SYSTEM

To look back briefly on the progression outlined, the concept of psychotherapy has moved from a concept of psychotherapy as an intervention with one person to change his character structure, to a concept of psychotherapy as an intervention with a social system that in turn changes the options, roles and functions of one person as part of a multi-person field of behavior. The same progression has occurred in three other systems of intervention. These four systems reflect a more general pattern. Hence each will be sketched out to illustrate the general principle.

If the individual psychotherapy system is the first, then we may call the mental hospital system the second. In the second system the intensive therapeutic approach to the patient began with one-to-one intensive psychotherapy of a patient who lived on a hospital ward. (An example might be Frieda Fromm-Reichman's intensive psychotherapy of schizophrenic patients at Chestnut Lodge.) Then attention began to focus on the quality of the ward living experience. Attempts were made to humanize ward living experiences with open-door policies, social activities, etc. This might be termed the creation of therapeutic milieu. Conceptually the next step was the introduction of group discussion among patients, and patient self-government programs. Following this came the concept of *milieu therapy*, that is, the deliberate management of the entire social system of the hospital in which the psychotherapist does not treat a specific patient, but focuses on directing the social system so that it will operate in a therapeutic fashion. This shift has been so pronounced that some would not describe milieu therapy as psychotherapy, but rather as *sociotherapy*. This labeling maneuver may be seen as one attempt to deal with the failure of the one-to-one personal model of psychotherapy to provide an adequate conceptual base for this broadening of the intent of psychotherapy. (6,26,27,28,)

The third system may be called the community mental health system. Early attempts at intervention in the community to improve the mental health of community members was based on the identification of individual persons in distress. Perhaps classic individual case work in community welfare agencies may be seen as a prototype. Here attempts were made to help persons with their rent, child care, clothing, food, etc. The second step was taken with the development of local community groups to deal with common problems, and to assist natural community groups to function more effectively. This may be seen as the classical group-work approach. And the final step has been to use community mental health programs to launch broadscale social-action programs aimed at changing basic social programs, social policies and social organizations of an entire community. The critics of such community mental health endeavors rightly state that social action does not seem to fit the paradigm of traditional mental health concerns. However, from a social systems viewpoint, such social action foci would be a logical part of the model of intervention. (52,75,76,80,81,82)

The fourth system might be called the educational-organizational system of intervention. I have here in mind the development of the programs of the National Training Laboratories. The NTL began as an attempt to provide group sensitivity experiences that would change the personality function of educators and work supervisors. It was soon observed that the benefit of this experience focused on change of the individual was quickly vitiated by the social system requirements to which the individual returned. The next step at NTL was to bring members of the same educational or work group together for group experiences. This proved more effective, but still it was observed that a small work group also returned to a larger organizational structure. Thus the final step taken by NTL has been to develop programs of social system intervention that aim at producing changes in the structure of the entire organization. Thus the movement here has also been a shift from intervention with the individual to intervention with the social system. (5,19,39,105)

In summary, I have attempted to develop a rationale for a social system focus of psychotherapy. This focus is in concert with a more general frame of reference, including examples from three other systems of intervention. As suggested at the outset, this progression may be seen as the clinical reflection of a larger scientific movement, namely, a general human psychology which in 1900 framed human psychology as an individual matter, and has since moved toward a human psychology which is a social psychology. As a corollary then, we have moved from a model of psychotherapy as an individual enterprise to a model of psychotherapy as a multi-person enterprise.

V. THE SYSTEM MODEL OF PSYCHOTHERAPY
AND THE PERSONAL MODEL OF PSYCHOTHERAPY

In this section I shall briefly outline some distinct differences between a "personal" and "system" model of psychotherapy. My aim is to illustrate that the two models do not compete, but rather are complementary models, for each is addressed to different psychotherapeutic goals.

The "system" model of psychotherapy is actually the older. It is the model of the shaman, the primitive healer, the folk healer. In his studies on primitive healing procedures, Ari Kiev (51) has suggested that psychotherapy is a public affair.

In the primitive society, if a member became "sick" this was matter for public concern, for a necessary worker was lost to the small society. Hence it was in the interest of everyone to see to it that the sick person was restored to function. There was little margin for functionless members of the community; everyone was needed to keep the small society functional. When a person became emotionally "ill," there was a generally accepted societal explanation for the cause of the illness. Further, everyone in the small society knew what healing procedures needed to be carried out. And everyone knew what the shaman would do in his healing rituals. Kiev and others have provided examples of the shaman-society healing rituals.

The goal of the healing was to restore the ill person to his usual mode of operation and function in the social system. There was no questioning of the values or patterns of function of the social system. In other words, there was a value consensus between healer-patient-society. And there was a healing consensus between healer-patient-society. And the healing procedures were a multi-person enterprise that involved healer-patient-society. (12,13)

In contrast, the "personal" model of psychotherapy developed with quite a different rationale. The goal was not to help the patient return to function in his social system in the same old way. Rather, it was to help the patient to examine his social system, examine his pattern of function in his social system, and perhaps function in a different social system altogether.

Now, the "personal" model could only come into existence in the face of several other social considerations. First, the person was not immediately required for the society to function; he could remain dysfunctional for extended periods of time. Second, the person had available to him a variety of value systems from which he could choose, i.e., he did not live in a one-value society. And third, the person had available alternative social systems into which he could move.

In the "system" model, privacy is anti-therapeutic, for it is the public pressure, public response and public support that enable the person to move rapidly back into

TABLE I

Two Complementary Models of Psychotherapy

	Personal Model	*System Model*
GOAL	To change personality structure	To reinforce adaptive personality structure
PATIENT RELATIONSHIP TO SOCIAL SYSTEM	May choose to change social systems	Seeks to return to social system
THERAPIST RELATIONSHIP TO SOCIAL SYSTEM	Is given social sanction to stand apart and question	Is given social sanction to help social system function better
PSYCHOTHERAPY VIS-A-VIS THE SOCIAL SYSTEM	Occurs at a distance	Occurs in ongoing system
PRIVACY OF PSYCHOTHERAPY	Of paramount importance	Anti-therapeutic
MEMBERS OF PSYCHOTHERAPY	Therapist and patient	Therapist and social system
FOCUS OF PSYCHOTHERAPY	Individual patient (Patient directly)	Total social system (Patient indirectly)
ROLE OF PSYCHOTHERAPIST	To catalyze capacity of patient to develop self direction	To catalyze capacity of social system to function more effectively
DEFINITION OF PATIENT	A person only is defined as dysfunctional.	A person and his system are both defined as dysfunctional.
DEFINITION OF THERAPIST	A professional in a treatment role is the therapeutic agent.	A professional and the system share in creation of a system as therapeutic agent.

his accustomed social function. In the "personal" model, privacy is paramount, for it is the privacy which enables the person to achieve distance and perspective on his behavior in his social system. It is the privacy of the "personal" model that allows the patient to explore alternatives without public pressure.

Thus we can see that if our psychotherapeutic goal is rapid return of a "sick" person to accustomed social function, then we may choose the "system" model to capitalize on the "public" that comprise the patient's social system. This is psychosocial system therapy. It is a public therapy. The difference between the primitive shaman and the psychosocial system model therapist is that the therapist may aim at changing some characteristics of the social system and not merely use the social system as does the primitive shaman.

If our psychotherapeutic goal is change of personality with the concomitant development of capacity to choose among alternative social systems, then the "personal" model of psychotherapy in the traditional psychoanalytic sense becomes the model of choice.

The advantage of having two models of psychotherapy is that the psychotherapist may be freed from the attempt to make very different types of therapeutic interventions fit into a model that is inappropriate, and hence experience conflict over a variety of technical, social and ethical issues. Further, the psychotherapist can clearly take advantage of the strengths of either model as indicated instead of comprising one model to achieve the goals of the other model.

The differences between the two models are charted in Figure 1 for comparative purposes.

VI. PSYCHOSOCIAL TREATMENT SYSTEMS AND PSYCHOSOCIAL CARE SYSTEMS

As clinicians in mental health experiment more with the extension of treatment programs into a variety of social systems, many innovations have appeared. Therefore, it may be appropriate to provide a preliminary framework within which to cast a variety of social system interventions. The following is based in hierarchical order on the basis of *psychosocial connectedness.* In other words, the most intimate psychosocial system is characterized by a high degree of psychosocial interpersonal relatedness—the five dimensions of interaction, intensity, positiveness, instrumentality and symmetrical reciprocity.

The Intimate Psychosocial System

This social system comprises the nuclear family, but is not limited to the nuclear family. This is the system of the most important people in a person's life. This is the system to which psychosocial system therapy is addressed.

A sub-set of this system is extended blood and marriage kinship system. Treatment of this system has been subsumed under family therapy, but is really an extension of nuclear family therapy. The recent work by Minuchin, et al (68,69) and Bozormenyi-Nagy (18) on extended families is directed to this sub-system.

Another sub-set is the functional kin of neighbors, friends and associates that comprise the psychosocial kin of the urban nuclear family. The network therapy of Speck (93,94,95), Attneave (7), and the Psychosocial Systems Therapy a la Pattison herein, are directed to this sub-system. (76,77,78,79)

The Temporary Psychosocial System

This social system comprises therapeutic social systems such as hospital units, day-care centers, resocialization programs. Here the patient is provided temporary membership in a psychosocial matrix that provides a combination of both affective and instrumental relations based to some degree on ongoing face-to-face interaction. (106) The concept of the "therapeutic community" sums up the nature of this social system. The therapist does not "treat" this system, but directs this system to have therapeutic impact on the patient in this system. (6) Multiple family therapy is another example. (55).

The Ecological System

This social system is not a discrete unit, but consists of patient linkages to a variety of organizations, persons and other social units. Representative therapists in this category would be Auerswald (8), Polak (85), and Hansell. (44) Their treatment program involves helping the patient to make use of various persons and agencies in order to function effectively in their community. Each sub-unit has its own ecological niche, to which the patient is brought and taught how to utilize. (63,90,91) Volunteers and paraprofessionals may serve an ombudsman role in assisting the patient to adapt to his ecological terrain. (21,24,103,104)

The Kin Replacement System

In this instance we look at social systems in which the patient has partial participation. Here the patient is lacking certain critical members to provide affective or instrumental care. Hence part-time replacements are provided.

Self-help groups are a sub-type of a kin replacement system. The self-help group does not become involved with the totality of the person's life, but does offer help, in regard to specific sectors of life behavior, on an *on-going basis.*

Substitution systems are another sub-type. I have in mind Big Brothers, Big Sisters, widow-to-widow programs, etc. Here a more specific personal relationship is offered on a *time-limited basis.* Crisis intervention groups are another example.

The Associational System

These social systems offer both instrumental and affective resources to the individual on the basis of voluntary association in relation to activities and interests. Examples would include the tavern group, the street-corner gang, church groups, Great Books clubs, social clubs and recreational associations. Although such social systems have other social aims and functions, they also provide a social matrix within which less intimate but nonetheless important human relationships are established and maintained. (86)

To summarize: each of these five levels of social systems provides a matrix for the individual. As we move from the most intimate system to the least intimate system, the embeddedness and connectedness of the individual in that system decreases. The mental health professional likewise has the strongest mandate for intervention with the most intimate system, and his mandate decreases and changes on down the line. Each type of system may be important, though, in patient care. The role of the professional changes from one of treatment agent, to treatment director, to system coordinator, then system collaborator and, finally, system cooperater. I should not like to see us define each of these systems as "treatment" systems. Nor should I like to see each system as the object of treatment. Rather, I hope to illustrate how the mental health professional may play a variety of roles, vis-à-vis the patient, in making appropriate utilization of each type of social system.

VII. CASE EXAMPLES

Case #1. Treatment of a psychosocial system

On December 17, the University Hospital psychiatric consultation service received a consultation request from the orthopedic ward regarding an eighteen-year-old single white girl who was being treated for multiple injuries sustained in a motorcycle accident. The previous evening the patient was found to be overly drowsy, slow to respond to conversation, with slurred speech. She had taken an overdose of sleeping medications, which she had been accumulating surreptitiously. When questioned, she said, "It didn't matter, I don't want to live. Don't bother me. I want to join my boy friend, my husband to-be."

In the past several years the patient had been attracted to the hippie movement and had adopted a "drop-out" attitude toward life and her family. She had been dating a boy twenty years old who had similar interests. The girl's parents did not approve of the relationship and openly expressed their dislike of the boy friend. The couple took off for Wyoming against the wishes of both sets of parents. On October 7, while riding a motorcycle together, they were involved in a head-on collision. The boy friend was killed instantly, while the patient sustained serious injuries. A large body-encasing cast was placed on her for orthopedic injuries.

At the University Hospital she was polite but distant to her parents, as well as to the nursing staff. The one relationship that seemed meaningful to her was that with the orthopedic resident in charge of her care. On the evening of December 16 this resident had made arrangements to change the traction on her leg. She stayed away from a ward Christmas party to await him. However, on the way to the hospital the doctor himself had an accident. The patient was informed of this accident in somewhat ambiguous terms, since the extent of his injuries was not known. The patient showed no demonstrable reaction to this event. But one hour later she was found in the depressed suicidal state described. (In retrospect the accident of the physician reactivated the same reaction as the death of her boy friend, the physician having been ascribed a transference-determined role, that is, she and he had a relationship that existed in opposition to the rest of the world.)

The ward staff found the girl increasingly uncooperative the next morning, and during the day the medical staff and nursing staff became increasingly angry with each other for failing to establish rapport with the girl. A psychiatric consult was requested. The psychiatric resident interviewed the girl, but she refused to talk to him and told him to leave her alone. He wrote a dejected consultation note and told the orthopedic staff that he could be of little use to them because the patient would not talk to a psychiatrist. The girl became more lethargic. The staff thought she was surreptitiously taking more pills, which they assumed were being brought in by her hippie friends. She was placed in an isolation room and forbidden visitors. Her mental condition seemed to deteriorate.

I interviewed the girl late on the second day after her suicide attempt. She was resolutely negativistic toward anyone she perceived as part of the establishment or who represented any type of authority. I was able to find out that she did like to talk to the Presbyterian minister from her family's church, and that she was angry at not being able to visit with her hippie friends, several of whom also had a social relationship with the same Presbyterian church.

At this point I elected to explore the characteristics of the social network of this girl both within the hospital and outside it. A plan was worked out with the psychiatric resident to systematically interview all the persons we could determine had some current relationship with the girl.

First, we found that the medical staff and nursing staff had given up on any attempt to establish a working relationship with the girl. Each staff blamed the girl for creating a problem with the other staff. Thus we found the girl was being made the scapegoat for interstaff conflict.

Second, we found that her parents and the dead boy friend's parents were both trying to visit her, but were avoiding each other in the hospital. Each set of parents blamed the other parents for the fate of their child. However, each set of parents also blamed the girl for her current behavior, which they asserted made it impossible to talk to the other set of parents. Thus the girl was the scapegoat for the interfamily conflict.

Third, we found that the Presbyterian minister was interested in talking with the girl, as were her hippie friends whom he knew. However, in view of the suicidal attempt, neither the minister nor the hippies felt that they should interfere with staff or parents. Further, they were fearful that if they visited with the girl, they might somehow precipitate further depression and another suicidal attempt.

Fourth, we found that the medical staff and nursing staff had no communication with either set of parents, the minister or the hippies. Both the hospital staff and the kin and friends were reluctant to approach each other. The staff viewed the family and friends with suspicion, as possibly contributing to the girl's depression, while the family and friends were suspicious of the hospital staff as being hostile to them and not caring about the welfare of the girl.

With the information at hand regarding the scapegoating and blockades in the social network, we decided to inform the girl that we would not conduct any psychiatric treatment with her, but that the psychiatric resident would be visiting with her family, friends and staff to work out a hospital program for her. Thus the social network of the patient, which consisted of multiple blockades in a dysfunctional network, was defined as the focus of therapeutic intervention.

First, a meeting was arranged with the minister at his church that included all of the hippie friends that had visited the girl. The girl's problem was thoroughly discussed with this group, and they agreed to a program of daily visitation with the girl. Second, several meetings were arranged with the medical staff and nursing staff, together and separately, to outline the problems in her social system which had been uncovered. The issues of interstaff conflict were aired and discussed. Concrete plans for specific nursing care were devised and reviewed daily with both the medical and nursing staff. Further, meetings were held between the two sets of parents and the medical and nursing staff to discuss and determine the management of the patient. Specific roles for the behavior of the parents were established. Subsequent meetings between the parents and hospital staff were held to maintain the agreed-upon role contracts. The hospital staff also met with the minister and the hippie friends, and their roles were defined and agreed upon by both groups. Third, meetings were held with each set of parents and with both sets of parents together. Their mutual hostilities and projections were explored and resolved in several joint sessions. Their mutual roles in visiting with the girl were outlined and agreed upon. Subsequent meetings were held with the parents to reaffirm and sustain their roles with each other and with the girl.

All these network contacts were made within several days. Within the first week the girl became brighter, more communicative, less depressed. She became demanding and engaged in very active, albeit hostile, interactions with many people. Her clinical depression rapidly cleared, and she was able to go home on a weekend pass—the weekend was uneventful. A subsequent surgery and hospital stay in February was also uneventful, and the patient was considered by the hospital staff to be a ''good'' patient during her second hospitalization. Subsequent follow-up revealed a satisfactory convalescence and no recurrence of her clinical depression.

Case #2. Treatment via construction of a temporary psychosocial system

A fifty-year-old woman called the alcoholism clinic asking for help. She stated that she was so intoxicated from a drinking binge that she could not take care of herself and that she was suicidal. Two clinic staff persons drove out to the woman's house, which was located twenty miles away in an isolated canyon. The woman was found to be living alone. She was both isolated and lonely. Her recurrent depressive moods led to alcoholic binges, which in turn reinforced her guilt and depression. She had no friends or relatives. She was not currently working. There were four neighboring homes; however, the woman stated that although she knew the neighbors casually, she had never wished to impose on them. She felt both guilty about and ashamed of her condition and tried to hide from her neighbors.

After this situation was discussed, and permission was granted by the woman, the two staff members went to call on the four different neighbors. In this particular circumstance the women all knew each other and had casual friendly relations. They all expressed concern for the alcoholic woman who was their new neighbor. However, they had not wished to impose themselves because of her apparent desire for isolation and lack of interest in making friends with the neighbors.

The four neighbor women were invited to the home of the alcoholic woman, and a group discussion was held for the rest of the afternoon. The neighbor women were eager to volunteer their help. They each volunteered to provide for cooking and home care until the alcoholic woman was able to care for herself. They arranged a schedule of daily visits in rotation.

The clinic staff returned every week to meet with the entire group, while also maintaining daily telephone contact with both the alcoholic woman and the four neighbors. After several weeks of intimate involvement, the woman was able to resume the management of her own home. She entered therapy in the alcoholism clinic and obtained a job. She has continued to maintain a close relationship with the group of four neighbor women who assisted her through her crisis.

Case #3. Coordination of an ecological system

A forty-year-old mother called the outpatient clinic seeking help in regard to her seven-year-old son who refused to go to school. A staff member made a home visit. The clinical history provided a clear diagnosis of school phobia. The situation was discussed with the mother, who then expressed her incapability to deal with the situation. There was no father in the home. There were two younger children, aged three and one, who consumed much of her time and attention.

The staff member received permission from the mother to engage the help of her neighbors and to assist in negotiations with the school. One neighbor next door readily agreed to take care of the two younger children while the mother would accompany the son to school. Another neighbor agreed to care for the children while the mother did her necessary shopping. Still another made arrangements to provide activities for the son with her own children several days of the week in order to engage him in socialization close to his home, yet near the home base. The staff worker accompanied the mother to school to discuss the situation with the principal and teacher, so that a coordinated plan for management of the phobia could be implemented. The staff worker then accompanied the mother and son on the first day of return to school, and monitored the separation of the son from mother at school so that the situation was handled in an emotionally appropriate manner. At first, daily contact was maintained with the mother and the neighbors, and then weekly contact, until the school phobia was successfully resolved over the next month.

VIII. SUMMARY

This chapter has described the clinical theoretical development of an approach to treatment based on social systems theory. A systems model of therapy is described for multiple-person, multi-relational social systems which are the target of therapeutic intervention. It is pointed out that the psychosocial system that is the fundamental matrix of life is more extensive and complex than just the nuclear family. A method for defining the members of the psychosocial matrix system is described along with preliminary findings on the relation between the psychosocial system and levels of emotional dysfunction. A preliminary classification of different types of psychosocial systems is presented, along with indications of the role the professional may play in each type of social system for appropriate patient care.

REFERENCES

1. Adams, B. N. Interaction theory and the social network, *Sociometry* 30: 64-78, 1967.
2. Adams, B. N. *Kinship in an Urban Setting.* Chicago: Markham, 1968.
3. Aldous, J. Intergenerational visiting patterns: variations in boundary maintenance as an explanation. *Family Process* 6: 235-251, 1967.
4. Alissi, A. S. Social work with families in group-service agencies: an overview. Family Coordinator 18: 391-401, 1969.
5. Argyris, C. On the future of laboratory education. *J. Appl. Behav. Sci. 3*: 153-182, 1967.
6. Astrachan, B. M.; Flynn, H. R.; Geller, J.D.; and Harvey, H. D. Systems approach to day hospitalization. *Arch. Gen. Psychiat. 22*: 550-559, 1970.
7. Attneave, C.L. Therapy in tribal settings and urban network intervention. *Family Process 8*: 192-210, 1969.
8. Auerswald, E. H. Interdisciplinary versus ecological approach. *Family Process 7*: 202-215, 1968.
9. Barcai, A. An adventure in multiple family therapy. *Family Process 6*: 185-192, 1967.
10. Bell, N. W. Extended family relations of disturbed and well families. *Family Process 1*: 175-193, 1962.
11. Bell, W., and Boat, M. D. Urban neighborhoods and informal social relations. *Amer. J. Sociol. 62*: 391-398, 1957.
12. Bernstein, L., and Burris, B. C. (eds.). *The Contribution of the Social Sciences to Psychotherapy.* Springfield, Ill.: C.C. Thomas, 1967.
13. Blackman, S., and Goldstein, K. M. Some aspects of a theory of community mental health. *Comm. Ment. Hlth. J. 4*: 85-90, 1968.
14. Blinder, M. G.; Colman, A. D.; Curry, A. E.; and Kessler, D. R. MCFT: Simultaneous treatment of several families. *Amer. J. Psychother. 19*: 559-569, 1965.
15. Bott, E. Urban families: conjugal roles and social network. *Hum. Relat. 8*: 345-384, 1955.
16. Bott, E. *Family and Social Network.* London: Tavistock Publ., 1957.
17. Boszormenyi-Nagy, I., and Framo, J.L. (eds.). A theory of relationships: experiences and transactions. Chap. 2. in *Intensive Family Therapy.* New York: Hoeber, 1965.
18. Boszormenyi-Nagy, I., and Spark, G. M. *Invisible Loyalties.* New York: Harper & Row, 1973.

19. Bradford, L. P. Biography of an institution. *J. Appl. Behav. Sci. 3*: 127-143, 1967.
20. Cohen, A. K., and Hodges, H. M., Jr. Characteristics of the lower-blue-collar class. *Social Problems 10*: 303-334, 1963.
21. Collins, A. H. Natural delivery systems: accessible sources of power for mental health. *Amer. J. Orthopsychiat. 43*: 46-52, 1973.
22. Croog, S. H.; Lipson, A.; and Levine, S. Help patterns in severe illness: the roles of kin network, non-family resources, and institutions. *J. Marr. Fam. 34*: 32-41, 1972.
23. Curry, A. E. Therapeutic management of multiple family groups. *Inter. J. Grp. Psychother. 15*: 90-96, 1965.
24. Curtis, W. R. Community human service networks. *Psychiat. Annals 3*: 23-40, 1973.
25. Dotson, F. Patterns of voluntary associations among urban working-class families. *Amer. Sociol. Rev. 16*: 687-693, 1951.
26. Fairweather, G. W. (ed.). *Social Psychology in Treating Mental Illness: An Experimental Approach.* New York: J. Wiley, 1964.
27. Fairweather, G. W. *Methods for Experimental Social Innovation.* New York: J. Wiley, 1967.
28. Fairweather, G. W.; Sanders, D. H.; Cressler, D. L.; and Maynard, H. *Community Life for the Mentally Ill.* Chicago: Aldine, 1969.
29. Farber, B. *Family: Organization and Interaction.* San Francisco: Chandler, 1964.
30. Farber, B. *Kinship and Family Organization.* New York: J. Wiley, 1966.
31. Faris, R. Interaction of generations and family stability. *Amer. Sociological Review. 12*: 159-164, 1947.
32. Feldman, F., and Scherz, F. *Family Social Welfare*, New York: Atherton, 1967.
33. Festinger, L.; Schachter, S.; and Back, K. W. *Social Pressures in Informal Groups*. New York: Harper, 1950.
34. Finlay, D. G. Effect of role network pressures on an alcoholics approach to treatment. *Social Work 11*:71-77, 1966.
35. Friedman, P. H. Family system and ecological approach to youthful drug abuse. *Family Therapy 1*: 63-78, 1974.
36. Gans, H. J. *The Urban Villagers*. New York: Free Press, 1962.
37. Gans, H. J. *The Levittowners*. New York: Pantheon, 1967.
38. Gottlieb, A., and Pattison, E. M. Married couples group psychotherapy. *Arch. Gen. Psychiat. 14*: 143-152, 1966.
39. Gottschalk, L. A., and Pattison, E. M. Psychiatric perspectives on T-groups and the laboratory movement: an overview. *Amer. J. Psychiat. 126*: 823-839, 1969.
40. Griffith, C., and Libo, L. *Mental Health Consultants: Agents of Community Change.* San Francisco: Jossey-Bass, 1968.
41. Grosser, G. S., and Paul, N. L. Ethical issues in family group therapy. *Amer. J. Orthopsychiat. 34*: 875-884, 1964.
42. Hader, M. The importance of grandparents in family life. *Family Process 4*: 228-240, 1965.
43. Handlon, J. H., and Parloff, M. B. The treatment of patient and family as a group : is it group psychotherapy. *Inter. J. Grp. Psychother. 12*: 132-141, 1962.
44. Hansell, N. Patient predicament and clinical service: a system. *Arch. Gen. Psychiat. 14*: 204-210, 1967.
45. Hansen, C.C. An extended home visit with conjoint family therapy. *Family Process 7*: 67-87, 1968.
46. Hoffman, L., and Long, L. A systems dilemma. *Family Process 8*: 211-234, 1969.
47. Homan, G. C. *The Human Group.* New York: Harcourt, Brace, & World, 1950.
48. Jackson, D. D. The individual and the larger contexts. *Family Process 6*: 139-147, 1967.
49. Jay, E. J. The concepts of 'field' and 'network' in anthropological research. *Man. 64:* 137-139, 1964.
50. Kammeyer, K. C. W., and Bolton, C. D. Community and family factors related to the use of a family service agency. *J. Marr & Family 30:* 488-498, 1968.

51. Kiev, A. *Curanderismo: Mexican-American Folk Psychiatry.* New York: Free Press, 1968.
52. Klein, D.F. *Group Dynamics and Community Mental Health.* New York: J. Wiley, 1968.
53. Komarovsky, M. The voluntary associations of urban dwellers. *Amer. Social Rev. 11*: 686-698, 1946.
54. Landes, J., and Winter, W. A new strategy for treating disintegrating families. *Family Process 5*: 1-20, 1966.
55. Laquer, H.P. General systems theory and multiple family therapy. In J.H. Masserman (ed.), *Current Psychiatric Therapies*, Vol. 8. New York: Grune & Stratton, 1968.
56. Lebowitz, B.D.; Fried, J.; and Madaris, C. Sources of assistance in an urban ethnic community. *Human Org. 32.* 267-271, 1973.
57. Leichter, H.J., and Mitchell, W.E. *Kinship and Casework.* New York: Russell Sage Fdn., 1967.
58. Lidz, T.; Fleck, S.; and Cornelison, A.R. The limitations of extrafamilial socialization. Chapter 18 in *Schizophrenia and the Family.* New York: International Universities Press, 1965.
59. Laskin, E. Breaking down the walls. *Family Process 7*: 118-125, 1968.
60. Litwak, E. The use of extended family groups in the achievement of social goals: some policy implications. *Social Problems 7*: 177-187, 1959-60.
61. Litwak, E. Extended kin relations in an industrial democratic society. Chapter 13 in Shanas, E., & Streib, G.F. (eds.), *Social Structure and the Family: Generational Relations.* Englewood Cliffs, N.J.: Prentice— Hall, 1965.
62. MacGregor, R.; Ritchie, A.M.; Serrano, A.C.; and Schuster, F. P. *Multiple Impact Therapy with Families.* New York: McGraw-Hill, 1964.
63. Mannino, F.V., and Shore, M.F. Ecologically oriented family interaction. *Fam. Process 11*: 499-505, 1972.
64. Mead, G.H. *Mind, Self, and Society.* Chicago: Univ. Chicago Press, 1934.
65. Mendell, D.; Cleveland, S.E.; and Fisher, S. A five-generation family theme. *Family Process 7*: 126-132, 1968.
66. Mendell, D., and Fisher, S. An approach to neurotic behavior in terms of a three generation family model. *J. Nerv. Ment. Dis. 123*: 171-180, 1956.
67. Mendell, D., and Fisher, S. A multi-generational approach to treatment of psychopathology. *J. Nerv. Ment. Dis. 126*: 523-529, 1958.
68. Minuchin, S. The use of an ecological framework with treatment of the child. In E. Anthony & C. Koupernik (eds.), *The Child in the Family.* New York: Wiley-Interscience, 1970.
69. Morrissey, J.R. *The Case for Family Care of the Mentally Ill.* Comm. Ment. Hlth. J. Monograph No. 2, 1967.
70. Muir, D.E., and Weinstein, E.A. The social debt: An investigation of lower-class and middle-class norms of social obligation. *Amer. Sociol. Rev. 27*: 532-539, 1962.
71. Nadler, E.B. Social therapy of a civil rights organization. *J. Appl. Behav. Sci. 4*: 281-298, 1968.
72. Pattison, E.M. Treatment of alcoholic families with nurse home visits. *Family Process 4*: 75-94, 1965.
73. Pattison, E.M. Evaluation studies of group psychotherapy. *Inter. J. Grp. Psychotherapy 15*: 382-397, 1965.
74. Pattison. E.M. *A Brief History of the American Group Psychotherapy Association.* New York: Amer. Grp. Psychother. Assn., 1969.
75. Pattison, E.M. The role of adjunctive therapies in community mental health center programs. *Therap. Rec. J. 3*: 16-25, 1969.
76. Pattison, E.M. Group psychotherapy and group methods in community mental health. *Inter. J. Grp. Psychother. 21*: 214-225, 1971.
77. Pattison, E.M. Systems pastoral care. *J. Past. Care 26*: 2-14, 1972.
78. Pattison, E.M. Social system psychotherapy. *Amer. J. Psychother. 17*: 396-409, 1973.

79. Pattison, E.M. Group treatment methods suitable for family practice. *Inter. Publ. Hlth. Rev. 2*: 247-265, 1973.
80. Peck, H.B. The small group: core of the community mental health center. *Comm. Ment. Hlth. J. 4*: 191-200, 1968.
81. Peck, H.B., and Kaplan, S. Crisis theory and therapeutic change in small groups: some implications for community mental health programs. *Inter. J. Grp. Psychother. 16*: 135-149, 1966.
82. Peck, H.B.; Kaplan, S.; and Roman, M. Prevention, treatment, and social action: a strategy of intervention in a disadvantaged urban area. *Amer. J. Orthopsychiat. 36*: 57-69, 1966.
83. Perry, S.E. Home treatment and the social system of psychiatry. *Psychiatry 26*: 54-64, 1963.
84. Phillips, M. *Small Social Groups in England*. London: Methuen, 1965.
85. Polak, P. Social systems intervention. *Arch. Gen. Psychiat. 25*: 110-117, 1971.
86. Pringle, B.M. Family clusters as a means of reducing isolation among urbanites. *Family Coordinator 23*: 175-180, 1974.
87. Reiss, P.J. The extended family system: correlates of and attitudes on frequency of interaction. *Marr. & Fam. Living 24*: 333-339, 1962.
88. Rueveni, U., and Speck, R.V. Using encounter group techniques in the treatment of the social network of the schizophrenic. *Inter. J. Grp. Psychother. 19*: 495-500, 1969.
89. Salloway, J.C. and Dillon, P.B. A comparison of family network and friend network in health care utilization. *J. Comp. Fam. Stud. 4*: 131-142, 1973.
90. Siporin, M. Social treatment: A new-old helping method. *Social Work: 15*: 13-25, 1970.
91. Siporin, M. Situation assessment and intervention. *Social Casework: 6*: 91-109, 1972.
92. Shanas, E., and Streib, G.F. (eds.). *Social Structure and the Family: Generational Relations*. Englewood Cliffs, N.J.: Prentice-Hall, 1965.
93. Speck, R.V. Family therapy in the home. *J. Marr. & Fam. Living 26*: 72-76, 1964.
94. Speck, R.V. Psychotherapy of the social network of a schizophrenic family. *Family Process 6*: 208-214, 1967.
95. Speck, R.V., and Rueveni, U. Network therapy—a developing concept. *Family Process 8*: 182-191, 1969.
96. Sprott, W.J.H. *Human Groups*. Baltimore: Penguin, 1958.
97. Sussman, M.B. The help pattern in the middle-class family. *Amer. Sociol. Rev. 18*: 22-28, 1953.
98. Sussman, M.B. The isolated nuclear family: fact or fiction. *Social Problems 6*: 333-340, 1959.
99. Sussman, M.B., and Burchinal, L.G. Kinship Family network: unheralded structure in current conceptualization of family functioning. *J. Marr. & Fam. Living 24*: 231-240, 1962.
100. Sussman, M.B., and Burchinal, L. Parental aid to married children: implications for family functioning. *J. Mar. Fam. 24*: 320-332, 1962.
101. Sweetser, D. Asymmetry in intergenerational family relationships. *Social Forces 4*: 346-352, 1963.
102. Sweetser, D. Mother-daughter ties between generations in industrial societies. *Family Process 3*: 332-343, 1964.
103. Torrey, E.F. The case for the indigenous therapist. *Arch. Gen. Psychiat. 20*: 365-373, 1969.
104. Umbarger, C. The paraprofessional and family therapy. *Fam. Process 11*: 147-162, 1972.
105. Winn, A. The use of group processes in organization development. *J. Grp. Psa. & Process 2*: 5-19, 1969.
106. Woodbury, M.A. *The Healing Team and Schizophrenia: From the Psychiatric Hospital to Community Centered Intervention*. Springfield, Ill.: C.C. Thomas, 1969.
107. Woodbury, M.A., and Woodbury, M.M. Community-centered psychiatric intervention: a pilot project in the 13th arrondissement, Paris. *Amer. J. Psychiat. 126*: 619-625, 1969.
108. Young, M. The role of the extended family in disaster. *Hum. Relat. 7*: 383-391, 1954.
109. Young, M. The extended family welfare association. *Social Work 13*: 145-150, 1956.
110. Young, M., and Willmott, P. *Family and Kinship in East London*. London: Routledge & Kegan, Paul, 1957.

9

The Use of Groups
in the Changing
Mental Health Scene

MORTON A. LIEBERMAN

In today's urban (and even not so urban) America, almost any bulletin board contains testimony that groups are "in" as a medium of choice for changing people. It has been estimated that upward of five million Americans have at one time or another participated in some type of group activity aimed at personal growth or change in encounter groups. A few million others are members of self-help groups; tens of thousands have been patients in some form of group psychotherapy. What sorts of groups, what sorts of members, what sorts of problems and what sorts of people assume the function of helping others to change? These four questions require somewhat lengthy answers to convey some sense of the current scene, because the range of applications, methods, participants, and agents of change has increased geometrically over the last two decades.

Who comes to groups and why do they come? The most reasonable answer is: nearly every kind of person, with almost every conceivable psychological or social complaint. The goals of group clients vary all the way from reducing juvenile delinquency in others to reducing weight in themselves. Some among the clientele of current-day healing groups bring problems once taken almost exclusively to mental health professionals—severe personal or interpersonal concerns; others face no immediate serious stress, but seek the group in the hope that it will provide them with clues to personal enrichment—that participation in a shared effort at growth will help them actualize unused but available personal potential. Another sizable group of the clientele are those who see themselves as limited not by general aspects of their own personalities or personal situations, but by specific problems that impinge on them because of their relationship to a social order which they feel suppresses them because of sex, sexual mores, race, age and so on. Finally, groups can be found which contain members who claim no motive for belonging other than to widen their experience, to share, to enjoy or to learn to enjoy communion with others.

When one turns to the question of *what sorts of groups* make up the current scene, the divergence seen is equal to that of the types of clients and their goals. The litany of labels—Gestalt, Transactional Analysis, Confrontation Therapy, Marathon, Encounter, Sensory Awareness, T-Groups, self-help groups, consciousness-raising groups, all in addition to the more traditional forms of group psychotherapy—does not aid in clarifying what sorts of things are thought by each school to be the essential elements of change or cure. Some group leaders on the current scene believe passionately in the healing qualities of group-generated love; others believe just as passionately in the curative powers of hate, seeing the basic stuff of change as stemming from the experience of primary rage. Some depend solely on talk therapy; others use music, lights and the clench of human bodies. And many groups have no formal or appointed leaders.

Can the current use of groups be described by who it is who leads them? Can the sense of confusion be reduced by organizing the array of forms and techniques according to the background, education or professional discipline of those who purvey group people-changing services? No, for those who have made themselves available to lead such groups may have been prepared by long years of training in prestigious professional institutions, by participation in two-week institutes, or purely by personal commitment. Nor would a sense of order stem from examining the location of such activities. Many personal change-oriented groups are to be found in traditional help-giving institutions, such as mental hospitals, schools or social agencies; some take place in the offices of mental health practitioners in private practice. Many are found in growth centers, a new institution specifically formed for conducting such groups. Church basements, dormitories and living rooms have also become the scene of people-changing groups.

The diversity of goals, clientele, form of activity, leadership and setting of people-changing activities in groups may suggest why attempts to evaluate the consequences or effects of all these activities have yielded equal diversity—from ably documented findings suggesting major behavioral, attitudinal and personality changes (the reconstruction of individuals) to equally well-documented examples of the severe debilitation of individuals growing out of their participation in change-oriented groups.

This chapter aims to apprise the reader, both descriptively and analytically, of the current use of groups in all their diversity, and to establish some reasonable signposts which may help to organize the vast array of activities now characteristic of healing groups. What are the historical as well as current forces that have shaped the group practices so abundant in our society? Why do therapists, leaders or organizations place people in groups for healing purposes? What is seen as the role or task of the leader or therapist?

Why use groups? The use of groups for systematically helping individuals in distress is of relatively recent origin in modern mental health practice. It is perhaps helpful to recall, however, that small groups have always served as important healing agents; from the beginning of recorded history, group forces have been used to inspire hope, increase morale, offer strong emotional support, induce serenity and confidence, or counteract many psychic and bodily ills. Religious healers have always relied heavily on group forces, but when healing passed from the priestly to the medical profession, the deliberate use of group forces fell into a decline concomitant with the increasing sanctity of the doctor-patient relationship.

The strangeness experienced by many seekers of psychiatric help, when confronted with the help-giving conditions of groups, is the result of a complex process affecting both those who seek the help as well as those who give it. The development of psychiatry as an entrenched part of modern medicine was in part predicated on the idea that "scientific medicine" must at all costs distinguish itself from healing which stemmed from nonscientific traditions. Modern Western psychiatry was even more plagued than other branches of medicine with the need to become "scientific." In its beginnings the medical treatment of psychological problems required, for its legitimization as a branch of medical science, a clear differentiation between its methods and those that preceded it in folk societies, where highly developed group-based techniques were used for curing psychological illness within the framework of the family, the group of similar sufferers, the village or the religious community. This association of "prescientific" therapies with group forms perhaps influenced psychiatry away from utilization of group techniques.

Until the recent advent of the new group therapi. s, it has been expected in Western culture that personal help be given by *one* person—it may be the corner bartender, a personal friend or a professional such as a lawyer, doctor or clergyman, but what is important is that it is expected that the context in which it is rendered will be private, intimate and exclusive. Even in such congregate bodies as the family or the church, it is generally assumed that personal help will be offered and received in a private, two-person relationship, not through the congregate as a whole. The genesis of modern psychiatry within the general Western cultural context in the first half of the twentieth century did not, in other words, contain conditions suitable for the flourishing growth of group-based healing technologies.

In the early 1900's, Joseph Pratt, a Boston internist, organized classes for tubercular patients: "The class meeting is a pleasant social hour for members . . . made up as a membership of widely different races and different sexes, they have a common bond in a common disease. A fine spirit of camaraderie has developed. They never discuss their symptoms and are almost invariably in good spirits . . ." (1907). Pratt's therapy had many similarities to current-day inspirational group psychotherapy; he hoped to overcome the pessimism of the patients, to discourage neurotic secondary gains from illness, and to encourage self-confidence.

Isolated individuals in the early 1900's reported sets of experiences similar to those of Pratt. In Europe, for example, Alfred Adler established guidance centers that used group concepts in treating working-class patients. An early and important influence in the development of group psychotherapy was the use of the healing group by Jacob L. Moreno, who is best known for his development of psychodrama (1953). The analogies between Moreno's approach to the healing groups and those described in anthropological literature are impressive. The patient is provided with the opportunity to express himself freely through drama, trying the role of himself or others he feels significantly related to his present problems. The patient often enacts scenes from his past, while other persons (whom Moreno called alter egos) articulate feelings, moods, responses and so on which may not be evident to the patient himself (a kind of Greek chorus orchestrated by the therapist). The work of Trigant L. Burrow was an important, but unfortunately unrecognized, influence in the area of the use of groups. Burrows, a psychoanalyst, became dissatisfied with the emphasis psychoanalysis placed on the individual, an emphasis that he felt excluded examination of social forces. In the early twenties, Burrow initiated the use of the group context for the analysis of behavioral disorders in relationship to social forces and coined the term "group analysis" to describe the treatment setting (1927).

Thus, the techniques characteristic of current group treatment practices were clearly evident in the first quarter of the century. The inspirational character of Pratt's groups has many modern counterparts in the self-help movement, such as Alcoholics, Anonymous; Recovery, Incorporated; and Weight Watchers. The employment of the expressive part of the person through dramatization as part of the curative process forms a major component of many current group methodologies. Finally, the use of the group social context for psychoanalytically oriented analysis is still very visible as a major direction in current practice. By and large, however, the efforts of the early proponents of group methods were isolated; their predominantly pragmatic concerns did not lead them or others to explore the conceptual grounds underlying the use of groups for therapeutic benefit.

Thus, it would seem reasonable to raise the question, Why place patients in groups? It should perhaps be noted that at different times and in different cultures the forces might be just the opposite, and it would seem "abnormal" or unusual to have one healer and one patient. The examples of healing cults in folk societies amply express that in many societies the ordinary or the usual way of healing may be within a social or multiperson context. It does seem sensible to ask, nevertheless, how it is that patients began to be placed in groups for treatment in this culture. Although there is no single answer to this question, there are several important factors that have helped to accelerate the use of groups for healing purposes.

The current use of group psychotherapy did not develop in full force until the 1940's. Although, as the history of the forces impinging upon group therapy indicates, there were clear-cut signs of a movement to the use of groups for healing functions prior to that time, these were small and isolated attempts without much reverberation within psychiatric circles. Foremost on the list of reasons are the simple pragmatics or economics of the situation. In times of short supply, such as that created by World War II, of psychiatric personnel, and increased need for service, the "reasonableness" of treating patients in groups came to the fore. This "discovery" has been made over and over again in various segments of the healing professions; the spread of group forms was much influenced by the social pragmatics of picking professionals to treat larger numbers of people and, to some extent, shaped by the economics of fee structures—forces that cannot be ignored in explaining the development and spread of groups for healing functions.

A second major impact directing the professional to the use of groups developed out of the changing nature of theory with regard to both the nature of man and the genesis of his psychological ills. An increasing emphasis on an interpersonal view of man and the suggestion that psychological disturbance might be intrinsically related to problems of relationships among people—a social rather than intrapsychic phenomenon—made the jump from a dyad to multi-person treatment situations an easy one.

The practice of the healing professions is littered in its history with examples of serendipity—the chance discovery that groups seem to be potent constructive forces in the healing of psychological illness. This is a theme that cannot be omitted when examining the question of why therapists do place patients in groups. Psychotherapists are a restless lot, and the practice of healing is never stabilized. Inner doubt, feelings of failure, discouragement and frank therapeutic despair are the common lot of the mental health professional. The search after new techniques, modalities or procedures is unending, a theme that may explain in part the current popularity of group practice.

Finally, the personal needs and gratification of the healer—a topic fraught with apprehension, concern and frequent avoidance—also is present as one of the factors that move therapists to place patients in groups rather than dyads. The excitement, stimulation and the need for novelty are a few of the "reasons" that have directed therapists toward the use of groups. For many practitioners the sanctity and the privacy and the ability to concentrate totally on one other human being, and the opportunity that such an intimate relationship offers for exchange, are a prime attraction of the individual psychotherapeutic relationship. There are others, however, who need different arenas, and for whom an audience, a chance to observe rather than to hear about behavior and an opportunity to wield a different form of influence are more attractive.

AN ILLUSTRATION OF THE NEW AND NOT SO NEW

Before proceeding to examine the various systems of people-changing that occur in groups, it may be useful to have some image of group psychotherapy both as it has commonly been practiced within traditional mental health settings and as it operates in some of the "newer therapies." The initial session of a traditional therapy group, for example, would be something like this:

About nine people file into a room slowly, tentatively. Each has seen only one other person in the room: the therapist—a week earlier in a diagnostic interview. Some appear reluctant, some enthusiastic, but all have come to this first meeting with at least the willingness to go along with the therapist's belief that the group could be useful to them. They sit in a circle, quiet and expectant. Their posture seems anxious. What will go on here? What can go on here? What will the therapist do? Several in the group have had previous psychotherapy. One woman begins the interaction by describing the disappointments she has experienced in previous treatments. A note of desperation and near panic is discernible in the responses of others to her wail of self-negation and helplessness. Sympathetic offerings of similar tales of woe are heard from various people in the room. From time to time the therapist comments, pointing out the fearful expectations of the various group members.

Underneath the "stories" and histories offered by various members, the therapist "hears" the patients asking each other a set of questions only hinted at in what they are saying. And underneath the questions about others in the room lie still another set all having to do with the person himself. Why did you come? What are your hopes? What forms does your 'sickness' take? Do you feel that this may do me any good at all? Are you as sick as I? Am I as sick as you? How strange, perhaps even insane, is the arrangement whereby I come to a group of neurotics to get better. Above all, what is the "doctor" over there planning to do for me? I don't like people—why must I be here? Who are these others and what have I to do with them?

Thus, group therapy beings. The patients begin an experience in treatment which they may understandably feel violates expectations they bring from their experience in other doctor-patient relationships. Often group therapy patients cannot see what good it will do an unhappy neurotic person to share his "problems"with other neurotic sufferers. Is it enough to reassure him, as some therapists indeed believe, that "a problem shared is a problem helped" or to provide a context founded on the assumption that misery not only loves but is relieved by company? What of the therapist? Will he, by virtue of some rare professional training and intuitive attributes, be able to understand, diagnose and change the troublesome personality problems of a lifetime? And, at that, of a roomful of people simultaneously? He (the therapist) obviously expects something useful to come from the interactions of these people, but how does he see the members being of use to each other when he remains silent and passive so long? What does he expect will happen?

At the other end of the group treatment continuum we can imagine another group of people temporarily migrating to a growth center. Their arrival is noisier, more buoyant, more playful; they are in vacation garb, their talk is more free and more reminiscent of the first evening of summer camp than the still, anxious scene of the group therapy session. They are likely to have speaking knowledge of Maslow, Rogers, Berne and Perls, and of the latest people-changing procedures. They express their desire for change freely and seem eager to get to know one another. They seem hardly able to await the morning's beginning; if some appear a bit anxious, others are enthusiastic about the drama that will unfold. All know in general what they can expect to happen but seem restless to generate the specific emotions and events which will form the content of their shared experience.

What will the leader, whom they have never met, be like? What will he do or expect of them? In the back of their minds is the accumulation of images based on what they have heard from friends and from the popular press—images which are mixed with desires to become changed people. Will it work for me? What about the others? Will they really get to know me? Can I trust them? Will they help me?

They do not have long to wait: the leader begins with an explosion of his inner feelings. He may be sleepy this morning, he may not have wanted to come. He may look around the group and find it full of "unattractive" people and "tell it like it is" without pausing. On the other hand, he may express his total positive regard for all and quickly exhibit a readiness to accept any behavior expressed. He may then launch into a set of instructions, perhaps suggesting, "All of you look so 'up tight' that we ought to loosen up and begin by playing a childhood game".

The images evoked by these two settings are intended to suggest that the group-based people-changing business in our society today has diverse assumptions, allegiances and expectations, to an extent that it might appear sheer folly to consider them under the same rubric.

COMPARISONS AMONG CURRENT-DAY HEALING GROUPS

A scanning of the field of group-based activities whose central task is the psychological and behavioral alteration of individuals and the relief of human misery would suggest that the range of such activities might be grouped under four major types which are distinguished from one another mainly by whom they see as appropriate clientele and what they regard as the major function(s) of the group. At one end of the continuum would be those activities that formally fall within the purview of societally sanctioned, professionally led groups— *group psychotherapy*. Group therapy explicitly employs a *medical* model. Its avowed public goal is "cure," or the production of mental health, and it seen as its relevant population those who define themselves as seeking release from psychological misery. The group members are generally called "patients," who are thought by the therapist (and probably themselves) to be psychologically "ill" and to exhibit "sick" behavior. An important implication of this emphasis is that some individuals would be considered as appropriate candidates for the method and others (the "psychologically healthy") and would not.

At the opposite end of the professional continuum is a variety of *self help movements*: Alcoholics, Anonymous; Synanon; Recovery, Incorporated; and so forth—up to perhaps as many as 216 separate organizations. By intention, these groups are not professionally led. As lay movements, however, they share with group psychotherapy some restrictive notions of appropriate clientele. The definition of appropriate clientele is usually much narrower than in group psychotherapy, but there are clear-cut inclusion/exclusion principles. One must be an alcoholic, an abuser of drugs, a child abuser, a parent of a child who has a particular disease, and so forth. The range for any particular self-help movement's attention is limited to individuals who have a common symptom, problem or life predicament.

A third set of healing groups occurs under the rubric of the *human potential movement*, including such variously labeled activities as sensitivity training, encounter groups, and so on. Although there are many instances where such groups are led by nonprofessionals, they usually do involve professionals, whether legitimized by traditional psychological and psychiatric training or by newer short-term training institutions. A major distinction between the previously mentioned activities and encounter or growth groups is that the latter view themselves as having universal applicability. Unlike group therapy—which implies psychological illness and patient status—or self-help programs—which are directed at a common problem of members—the encounter movement considers its activities relevant to all who want to grow, change and develop.

Finally, we come to *consciousness-raising groups*, which share with the self-help groups the insistence on nonprofessional orientation and peer control but, unlike the self-help groups, have broad criteria for inclusion. Although they do not take in everyone, as does the human potential movement, consciousness-raising groups are formed on the basis of certain *general* demographic similarities—sex, race, ethnicity, age or sexual behavior. The tie that binds is not a common psychological syndrome but the general social characteristics of a large subgroup of people; the membership criteria, in other words, permit wide latitude regarding personal particularities.

STRUCTURAL AND TECHNICAL DIFFERENCES AMONG GROUPS

Perhaps the most important technological change reflected in the newer forms of healing groups as compared to more traditional psychotherapeutic groups is reflected in techniques for *lessening the psychological distance between the leader and the participants*. A variety of modes serve this function: the transparency of the therapist (he reveals his own personality), the use of informal setting, the trend of leaders to assume the stance of participant, the diminution of the importance of the leader, his presentation of self more nearly as a peer and, finally, the use of physical contact—touching—are all innovations which seem calculated to reduce the psychological distance between the changer and the changing.

Few guides exist to assess the importance of such a change from the traditional patient-therapist relationship. Perhaps all that can be said for sure is that such changes reflect current changes in social mores, which have increasingly moved away from emphasis on the priestly status of healing professionals and other experts. The new forms, having developed more recently, could be said to be more sensitive than the old to current cultural expectations.

A second major distinction between therapy and encounter groups, on the one hand, and most self-help and consciousness-raising groups, on the other, relates to their conception of the function of the group as a mechanism for personal change.

Both psychotherapy and encounter groups of almost all theoretical persuasions share, as a fundamental assumption, a view of the group as a *social microcosm*. It is this aspect of the group—that is, its reflection of the interpersonal issues that confront individuals in the larger society—that is the most highly prized as the group property which induces individual change. Varying types of encounter and psychotherapeutic schools of thought differ, of course, over which transactions are most important—those between patient and therapist or those *among* patients. They also differ regarding which emotional states are most conducive to positive change. But underneath all the activities that fall into these two types lies the assumption that cure or change is based on the exploration and reworking of relationships in groups.

Self-help groups and consciousness-raising groups develop a rather different stance toward the issue of the group as a social microcosm. The interaction among members as a vehicle for change appears to be somewhat de-emphasized. The group provides a supportive environment for developing new behavior not primarily within the group, but outside. The group becomes a vehicle for cognitive restructuring, but analysis of the transactions among members is not the basic tool of change.

Another characteristic that contrasts these four systems is the degree to which they stress *differentiation* versus nondifferentiation among their members. "Being neurotic," having psychological difficulty or being a patient are vague and relatively unbounded identifications compared to being a member of a racial minority group or a woman in a consciousness-raising group. Being interested in growth and development is obviously a more vague, indistinct basis for forming an identity with a communal effort than being an alcoholic or a child abuser. It is easier for consciousness-raising groups and self-help groups to stress identity with a common core problem than it is for psychotherapy and other groups. Although it is typical for psychotherapeutic group to go through a period of time in which similarities are stressed, this is usually an early developmental phase and represents an attempt of the group to achieve some form of cohesiveness. It is not the *raison d'être* of the group, as it may be for a consciousness-raising group or self-help group. In fact, there is some evidence that encounter group participants who remain committed to a sense of similarity are less likely to experience positive change (Lieberman et al., 1973). The potency of both self-help groups and consciousness-raising groups, on the other hand, appears to stem from their continued insistence on the possession of a common problem; their members believe themselves to derive support from their identification with a common core issue.

An obvious distinction among the various systems of group-based healing rests in their *attribution system*—the interpretive theories explicitly and implicitly communicated regarding the source of human misery and how one resolves it—for example, the degree to which the systems emphasize internal versus external sources of the problem. Psychoanalytically oriented psychotherapeutic groups attribute the source of psychological difficulty to the personal past. Women's consciousness-raising groups emphasize an external locus of the problem: an impersonal, sexist society. In our attempt to understand what processes may be psychotherapeutic, I believe we have paid too little attention to the effect of varying attribution systems on change. In comparing several theories of personal change employed in encounter groups (Gestalt, Transactional Analysis, Rogerian and so forth) it was found (Lieberman et al., 1973) that it made little difference which theory was "taught," as long as *some* cognitive structure was taken away from the group to explain one's problems and how to resolve them. Whether this observation would fit the larger differences in attribution systems one can assume between, for example, psychotherapeutic groups and women's consciousness-raising groups, is a major unknown.

Of course, one may reasonably ask, although all of these activities are taking place in groups, is it reasonable to assume that they are serving similar functions as alternatives to traditional mental health systems? Are such groups the relevant concern of psychiatry? The question can be answered in several ways. The issue of just what is a relevant concern of psychiatry is heavily value-laden. There are many who believe that the only legitimate concerns of psychiatry are the mental illnesses. I feel neither competent to deal with, nor believe it is appropriate, to join this issue here, but rather would sidestep it by noting that much of what is the current practice of mental health does concern itself with a broad range of troubled individuals who come to us occasionally with classical neurotic problems, perhaps more and more frequently with problems that we label "existential concerns," and certainly with concerns about various unhappinesses or disturbances in their interpersonal world. If we look at such people, I can offer you some evidence that at least one such institution-using group-based change system outside of traditional psychotherapy attracts people who are in many ways similar to patients who enter formal or traditional mental health systems.

A STUDY OF GROWTH CENTER PARTICIPANTS

During the past decade, a new form of institution, the growth center, has spread across the United States, as well as other Western countries. A major theme of this new institution has been to move away from defining people who need psychological help as "patients." Yet, some recently developed information suggests that perhaps the newer forms which emphasize growth and the development of human potential may not be attracting a different population from that engaged in psychotherapy. This study provides survey information on the users of these new activities: Why do they come? What do they expect? How, if at all, do they differ from the users of traditional psychotherapy? Specifically, do the goals and the expectations of patients entering traditional mental health institutions differ from the goals and expectations of participants who enter activities in the Human Potential Movement?

Self-administered questionnaires were sent out to 656 prospective participants at five growth centers. A contrast sample was generated from similar questionnaires given to 150 applicants to five private psychiatric clinics. The questionnaires for both samples were completed prior to participation in activities at the growth centers or clinics. Return rates of 65 percent for the growth centers and 59 percent for the clinics brought the final sample size to 426 growth center participants and 89 psychotherapy patients.

A broad range of questions about motivations, perceptions and attitudes were asked. Two measures of psychological disturbance were included which, in previous studies, differentiated psychiatric patients: Life Stress and (self-reported) Psychiatric Symptoms. Assessments were also made in the following areas: motivation, such as help-seeking, educational, social, recreational; attitudes toward, and perceptions of, growth center leaders (or therapists) in terms of authority, egalitarianism and expertise; time orientations; amount of expected change; and images of growth centers and psychotherapy in terms of their participants, process and outcome.

The growth center population was examined for its help-seeking characteristics. A national probability sample provided normative data on stress and symptoms for contrasts with the clinic and growth center samples.

Growth center participants had significantly higher stress (p < .001) and symptoms scores (p < .0001) than did the normative population. Social class and age were statistically controled. Help-seeking was widely endorsed as a motive for attending such centers, and 81 percent of the prospective participants had either been or were currently in psychotherapy. Thus, the "patientlike" characteristics of those attending growth centers emerged strongly on all the variables examined, and the phrase "therapy for normals" would not characterize most of the sample. They resemble a clinic population much more than they do a normal population. Nor do the data support a hypothesis that growth centers are an alternative pathway for getting help. Most applicants are currently experiencing distress in their lives and have sought outside help with it, both in psychotherapy and from growth center groups. They seem not so much to have chosen one over the other as to have chosen both.

The myth that the Human Potential Movement appeals to hedonistic, playful seekers after joy is not borne out by the data. Rather, their goals are instrumental and focus primarily around issues of obtaining help with personal problems. Participants' stated reasons for attending for one-half to three-quarters of the sample include bringing about change in themselves, dealing with current life problems, improving their relationshaps with people, solving long-term personal hang-ups, becoming a new person, seeking increased meaning in life, expanding their consciousness and increasing their self-awareness and body awareness. Only a handful come for a vacation, to get away, to turn on, to have intense emotional experiences or to seek new sexual experiences. Nor do they seek primarily to cope with alienation. Few come to meet people, find community or relieve feelings of loneliness.

The appeal of the growth center's egalitarian qualities—the diminished status and power differentials between client and leader in contrast to the supposedly more authoritarian relationship which exists between patient and therapist—has frequently been cited as a reason for the rising popularity of the centers. Our data do not support such a distinction, however. There are no differences between the samples in their perceptions of leaders' (or therapists') special power or expertise. Furthermore, those who enter growth centers with the avowed purpose of relieving their distress do, more than all other groups including therapy patients, seek expert help when faced with interpersonal problems. There is little evidence, then, to suggest that growth center goers represent a unique population of egalitarian-oriented individuals who have rejected the traditional structures of society for getting help. Despite the existential rhetoric of the human potential movement, those who seek out these activities are instrumentally rather than existentially oriented. They believe that technologies for solving all human problems exist.

Participants in growth center activities, compared to therapy patients, place more emphasis on the present than the future and on immediate rather than delayed gratification. They feel that present joys are more important than a distant good and are not willing to endorse the position that present sacrifices lead to future rewards. When one looks at their actual expectations for change over time, however, they are not wildly optimistic. Their time span is somewhat shorter, so that by the end of one month, growth center participants expect to make significantly more progress than therapy patients do. However, this difference disappears in ratings of progress by six months, and by one year it is the psychotherapy patients who expect to make more progress toward their goals. Thus the adherence to an existential, "live for today" ethic is more rhetoric than reality, and the myth that growth centers appeal to the miracle seekers is not supported by the findings.

The strongest differences between therapy patients and growth center participants were found in their respective views of the process by which change occurs. Growth center participants expected, much more than did therapy patients, to experience feelings of excitement and joy and to experiment with new forms of behavior by doing and saying things they had not previously done.

The particular form of growth center activity these participants attended seems to have little to do with their motivation for entering—whether their "thing" is a Gestalt encounter, a week of meditation, a course in biofeedback or any of the other widely ranging cafeteria of people-changing activities offered in a typical growth center. In some subsequent work, based on in-depth interviews, two important themes emerged. Those who have selected themselves out to be participants in such settings, as compared with more traditional patients, have an orientation to change which implies the absence of pain in the change process. Those who attend growth centers do form a unique subculture in our society—they are attuned, in almost a life-style way, to reliance on institutional structures for helping them with interpersonal and personal problems. In this sense, they are much more dependent upon institutional structures for resolving their psychological misery than are the general population and even those who enter traditional mental health systems. Typically, they have spent long years moving from one form of institutional change or therapy to another. It is a repetitive pattern, towards which life is focused almost as if they have little belief that they will find solace solace, but are committed to the process of looking.

THERAPISTS' CONTRIBUTIONS TO THERAPEUTICS

Theories of personal change in groups usually give great emphasis to concepts addressed to the relationship of the leader to the patients. Similar to theories of individual therapy, they emphasize the central importance of the therapist. It is through his actions or abstinence from action that change processes are initiated, are set in the right (or wrong) direction. Theories are maximally distinguishable by the particular dimensions of the leader/client relationship they emphasize. For some, the core concepts relate to the interpersonal conditions the leader creates between himself and each participant—positive regard, genuineness and so forth. Others stress the leader's symbolic properties, such as the specific transference relationship between each individual patient and the leader, while others stress the symbolic relationship of the leader to *the group as a whole.* Still others, although also stressing the unique relationship of each patient to the leader, emphasize negative rather than positive interaction between and through such devices as the "hot seat," in which the group acts as Greek chrous or background to this primary relationship. Despite such fundamentally different conclusions about what the crucial leader "inputs" are, however, all these theories agree on the centrality of the leader to the change process: it is he who sets up the learning experience, who makes the interpretations or analysis resistance, who sets up the norms, who is the "model" and so forth. The specific content of the leader's actions and responsibilities may differ, but the underlying assumption is that the central factor in what changes people is what the leader does or how he expresses himself.

It is possible, however, that the behavior, personality and skill level of the leader has taken on mythic proportions as a basic causal force explaining successful/unsuccessful personal change in groups. Some obvious factors in the history and development in the use of groups for people-changing may have contributed to this view. Theories of group change of individuals naturally have given great prominence to the role of the leader—after all, most of these theories have arisen from leaders who have often also been highly charismatic individuals. It is understandable that the clinicians who have developed what little theory there is on changing people through groups might be somewhat myopic and could easily be pardoned if they have overestimated the contribution of the leader (i.e., themselves) to the curative process. No theories of group personal change are broadly accepted that have developed out of the thinking of the patients or out of experimental psychology—perhaps with the exception of some applications of behavioral modification theory that are used in group contexts. Thus the assumption of leader centrality found in most theories of group personal change may represent an understandable overestimation on the part of the theorists, based on their unique perspective on the process about which they attempt to theorize.

But what about transference? Could anyone who has ever worked with a people-changing group realistically ignore the magical expectations, distortions, overestimations that are directed toward the person of the leader? No matter what one labels the feelings and thoughts of members toward their leader, it is hard to ignore transference as a central phenomenon common to all people-changing groups. I see no reason to question that the complex, convoluted, super-charged feelings that focus on the person of the therapist do not exist. Many would agree that the leader need not do anything more than be there to become enhanced with the aura of professionality—a person capable of giving help, of performing a priestly function. Whether or not transference is a universal product of psychotherapeutic contact, however, the fact of transference reactions where indeed they do occur does not, in an of itself, *demonstrate* that the leader is central to the curative process. That supercharged feelings toward the leader are usually generated in a group context does not permit one to jump to the conclusion that transference is intrinsically a curative factor in the group context. In other words, no unquestionable cause-effect relationship relative to outcome is demonstrated merely by the evidence that leaders usually become objects of transference.

In addition to the observation that most theories of group personal change have grown out of the experience of leaders or therapists themselves, and that the virtual omnipresence of transference has been taken as proof that the leader is central, several other conditions may be observed which may ''account for'' the strong belief that the leader is central. Professionalization, the length of time invested in training, the sharp boundaries surrounding the help-giving professions, the distinctive languages, the fee structures and so forth, are all conditions that would imply the ''helpfulness'' of considering the leader to be central, prominent, critical in the curative process. It seems reasonable to think that to the degree that an activity in our society becomes professionalized, so will the role of the professional who conducts the activity become enhanced in the minds of both the professional and the layman. Consider for a moment the full implications of discovering that most of what helps patients in groups stems from the relationships members have to one another and to processes that are only tangentially related to the behavior and person of the leader. Such a view would in all certainty present difficulties for continued dismissal of questions regarding whether profession-alization is necessary—or how much.

It is natural that theories of group personal change, as a latter-day development, should have been influenced by images of the obvious influence and control leaders exercise in dyadic therapy. This historical fact probably accounts, to some extent, for the prevalent assumption that the person and behavior of the leader are critical in group personal change.

Thus many forces exist for creating mythology surrounding the person of the leader. Journals and professional meetings endlessly encourage debates which support the "prominence" of the therapist or leader through disucssions of such issues—what he does, how he does it, when he does it, how he feels, what are his hang-ups, how aware he is, what is his theory, whether he works alone or with a co-therapist; whether "he" is he or she, black or white, kindly or hostile and so forth.

What data, then, can the field bring to bear on this issue—not whether groups help people, but whether what the therapist or leader does is central in that help-giving process and, if not, what precisely can be specified as essential leader inputs?

The empirical findings available in the literature offer only a few crumbs, and cannot provide evidence for a reasoned position on the question of how much the therapist or leader contributes to the outcome of patients. Some perspective on the question is offered via the analogy from individual psychotherapy relative to the nonspecific treatment of placebo effects. For the groups, the analogue to placebo effects are certain events that frequently occur in small face-to-face intensive groups that can provide experiences which *in themselves* are curative. Because these events occur in concurrence with the presence of a leader—and, at that, one often perceived as in possession of magical qualities—their curative power is attributed to the leader.

The data available only serve to legitimize raising this question; they are insufficient to answer it. Studies reporting no differences in the effectiveness of naive therapists compared to experienced professionals could be interpreted to mean that the group situation within rather broad limits is useful regardless of the specific behavior of the therapist. Studies in which large outcome differences were found among experienced therapists might, on the other hand, suggest an alternative conclusion—that the behaviors of the therapist are critical. If we look closely at these studies, however, an alternate explanation could be offered. Suppose for a moment we make the assumption that the major impact of therapists or leaders is to make people worse. Let us also play with the assumption that there are only two major factors operating in therapeutic groups—the intrinsic beneficial effects of the group itself, and the inputs of the leader, most of which are nonbeneficial. The notion behind these assumptions is to establish as the appropriate zero point for assessing the leader contribution not a nontreatment control situation, but rather a treatment situation minus the leader.

In the encounter group study, sixteen leaders who had ten or more years of experience in conducting groups were compared to groups which had no leader other than Berzon's peer tape program. Of the sixteen leaders only four exceeded the mean score of the two tape groups; the other twelve leaders did less well than the tape groups, some considerably less well. While the tape groups, of course, were not leaderless groups in the strictest sense, only a minimal structure is offered to the participants in the tape situation. Thus, it seems reasonable to assume that the tape group creates conditions reflecting the curative power of the group under minimal leader "input," and therefore has implications regarding the constructive potential of a group without the intervention of a professional leader. Data such as these could, of course, be interpreted—similer to the data in which naïve therapists are compared to expert practitioners—as suggesting that most therapists are relatively incompetent. This has in fact been the usual approach to such "disturbing" findings when they appear in the literature. The background and professional esteem of the sixteen therapists compared to the tape groups make it hard to argue for such an interpretation. These men were clearly competent in executing practices appropriate to their theories of change, but perhaps they were not competent in using maximally the inherent curative powers in a group for benefiting patients. Indeed, it is possible that they may have intervened in such ways as to obstruct these naturally beneficial attributes within the group. Findings such as these raise a more important issue: I believe there are processes within a group that in and of themselves are help-producing, so that to demonstrate that people can get better in groups does not answer the question of just what are the contributions of the group leader to the therapeutic process.

Evidence for the positive effects of intensive small group experiences external to the behavior of the leader comes from an examination of specific "curative mechanisms" and particular psychosocial conditions which often lie outside the direct influence of the leader. Normative characteristics of the group—the informal, often inarticulate and undiscerned social agreements which regulate the behavior of members— were demonstrated in the encounter study to be strong and perhaps more important influences on overall outcome scores than leader behavior. The findings further suggested that leaders contributed a smaller share to establishing the normative structure than what would be expected. Therapeutic mechanisms, such as similarity and "spectator therapy"—the ability of a person to identify with the experiences of another without directly participating in them, or experiences of finding similarity between oneself and another human being—were demonstrated powerful mechanisms for change, mechanisms which arise more from the intrinsic characteristics of intensive peer group experience than from the behavior of the leader. The role and status of the individual in a group—for example, whether he was a deviant in the group or a central person—were also demonstrated to account for successful outcome more than almost any other elements of the change process.

Findings such as these point to the importance of opening debate on the question of the importance of the leader to the group, an assumption that may have thus far served more to confuse than to elucidate.

Such findings also re-raise the classic question that has plagued psychotherapy for many decades—can expertise be operationally defined? One of the major impediments to quality studies of skill in people-changing groups has been the inability of the field to define the meaning of expertise. Many are satisfied with the definition of an expert as one who applies the right intervention at the right time to the right person. Changing people involves a complex sequence of events, and what evidence is available suggests very clearly that no particular experience will be uniformly profitable to all people. The appropriateness of a particular experience to a particular person is highly dependent on the state of the person at that point and on the context (the characteristics of the social system) in which the person finds himself. Such a view of skill implies that the leader be able to gauge more accurately the states of both person and social system, have within his grasp a wide variety of intervention strategies, and be able to diagnose both the individual and the group so that what he does can be useful to both. The social microcosm that is the group is a complex, dynamic, changing entity. It can be, even to the highly experienced leader, an often bewildering set of contradictions and frank mysteries of what is going on. Cognitive maps are difficult to find in groups, and the leader must work hard in order to make sense of the myriad of behaviors, thoughts and feelings that are rapidly generated in any group aimed at personal change. Groups offer a great opportunity for projective error—the ascription by the leader of his own thoughts or feelings to the amorphous, complex, supercharged collectivity that is the group. More often than not, leaders will ascribe their own inner state, their boredom, their anger, their warm feelings to the group.

Groups have considerable persuasive force, and it is not uncommon for the leader to find himself carried along by particular group emotions.

Groups generate primitive fears in their members and can do so in leaders as well. A common error made by many who conduct groups is to join the members when they focus in on a particular member—in scapegoat fashion; this is an easy error to make in change groups because the goals are to try to get the person to change, to reveal himself and so forth. Examples like this could be multiplied tenfold, but the essential issue is that the supercharged collective feelings that so often characterize people-changing groups cannot help but impact on the leader. Crucial, therefore, is the ability of the leader to disentangle his own feelings and thoughts from those that dominate the group at a particular time so that he can maintain enough distance to observe what is happening and be useful to the participants. Such skills are not automatic for most people; education and training and the development of a perspective on one's role and position are critical to their development.

Skill or expertise also implies the ability to develop adequate sources of feedback. One cannot be useful to the group or to the individuals in it without having some means of knowing how his interventions have affected the group. The leader must develop some way of assessing the impact of his interventions. Again, this is a most important skill that requires training and expertise.

Perhaps the most useful way of illustrating some of the problems of circumventing expertise would be to review briefly some of the newer assumptions of the "new group therapies." In a very real sense, the human potential movement has attempted to shortcut training issues by developing strategies for conducting groups that minimize training requirements. The human potential movement assumes that everyone who comes to encounter or sensory-awareness groups has the same underlying needs because all the moderns are alienated, isolated and cut off from their feelings. Groups can provide a sense of communion and relatedness to others without the aid of highly trained leaders. The generalized view that all people need the same thing serves to diminish the attention to the complexity of the change process, for it obviates the problem of determining particular needs of a particular person. Change then becomes a simple matter of providing a context through the group for expressing those feelings assumed to be blocked; leadership becomes simply a matter of providing experiences for psychological and physical closeness to allow participants to sense that they are not alone. Such a monothematic approach to people and their needs and how they can be changed flies in the face of considerable evidence to the contrary.

A second solution has been to develop a highly specific set of techniques (usually termed *structured exercises*), which are primarily sets of prescriptive behaviors by which the leader creates particular feeling states and experiences in the members. Numerous books presenting such techniques have appeared in the last five years. They also serve to simplify the task for the leader, for he now has a set of highly specific activities which he can offer the group in order to be facilitative. When such leader interventions were studied (Lieberman, Yalom, and Miles, 1973), it was found that they were not highly successful, and served more to increase the group's esteem for the leader than to change the individuals in the group. Leaders who used such devices were both liked and perceived by the participants as competent, but they were not particularly successful in changing people.

Probably the most serious error of the newer therapies is the assumption what group members like is what is useful and productive. The new therapies generally generate *enthusiasm* in their members—it is common for those who have engaged in encounter and other growth-oriented groups to proselytize—to tell their friends they should join a group led by their leader. Thus leaders are caught in a closed cycle in which they increase their behavior to produce enthusiastic responses from members. By and large, they are successful in such interventions and do create enthusiastic groups. Unfortunately, the evidence at hand is that level of enthusiasm is not equivalent to productive learning and change. In fact, they are orthogonal; some of the most enthusiastic participants are among the least changed. *Change* and enthusiasm are not the same thing; when they are confused, the leaders endanger their chances to provide a setting where people can learn and grow.

Thus, despite the absence of direct evidence that expertise is a crucial element in facilitating change in groups, some of the solutions which have been designed to bypass the issue of expertise have not proven to be useful. The question is still open and demands sophisticated research on the elements of expertise, and on how much expertise in the person of the leader contributes to developing the social microcosm in which the change process is to take place.

10 Groups to Help People Cope with the Tasks of Transition

RALPH G. HIRSCHOWITZ

INTRODUCTION

This chapter discusses groups for people in states of transition. In developing these groups, we pursued multiple interests. These included innovative *services, training* opportunities for community mental health professionals and *research.* Research had a dual focus: we hoped to learn about some states of transition from our "subjects," the consumers of services, and to discover the optimum mix of content, structure and processes for particular groups.

In pursuit of these interests, we devised pilot groups for diverse populations. Of these, groups for recently separated spouses, school newcomers, first-year medical students and married couples in mid-life are discussed here.

Before discussing groups to help people cope, we pause to clarify our choice and usage of the concept "transition." We deliberately avoided the more familiar professional concept of "crisis" because of its annexation by the clinical community. Clinicians have, in attitude and behavior, *often subverted the content and intent of seminal crisis theorists like Tyhurst, Erikson, Lindemann and Caplan. Techniques of "crisis intervention," usually practiced after entry into a service-treatment agency, have too often connoted passage through a sickness-wellness transition for the client. We have also noted, with some dismay, the tendency of clinical professionals to "treat" clients in crisis states with "techniques" such as "brief therapy" or "supportive medication." This often fails to meet legitimate needs for specific coping guidance while giving the person in transition a false——and ultimately, self-defeating—definition of his experience.

A further disadvantage of "crisis intervention" in the context of clinical care-giving stems from the heavy reliance of clinicians upon one-to-one service with its built-in danger of dependency or transference problems for the client. This danger often occurs outside the awareness of the servicing professional, and can occur even when he attempts consciously to prevent it. While the clinician may assume that he is not perceived in the clinician role, the setting, his own unconscious elitist habits and the *social* definition of the event usually carry the role-defining day. (For this reason, among others, we attempted to decontaminate our own structure

---

*A study by Bloom (1963) demonstrates that there is little coherence or consistency about the concept or its translation as "intervention" within clinical ranks.

by the participation of nonclinicians.)

When service is conceived and delivered on a "treatment" model, it contains within it the occupational hazard of defining the psychological concomitants of transition states as pathological. Our approach defines the "symptoms" of transitional stress as expectable, and conceives of service on an adaptation-promoting and educational guidance model. Because of the absence of the sickness-treatment undertow of "crisis," we prefer the more neutral concept of *transition* state.

TRANSITION

Transition derives from the Latin *trans* and *ire*, to go across. This connotes a state of movement and implies a point of departure and a destination. Transition is thus a *temporary* state bridging *from* a former state *toward* a future state. This in-between bridging state permits us to conceive of movement from a stable role and identity to one which is new, changed or extended. The *tasks* of transition can then be construed as detachment from a former role and the structuring of roles appropriate to a new situation. A state of transition, in our definition, places a significant *adaptive* demand upon someone to surrender, modify and/or extend aspects of his habitual identity, image and roles. Adaptive demands are generated by conditions involving significant newness, strangeness, unfamiliarity and inescapability. The transition from home to school *for the first time* thus qualifies as a role transition demanding an adaptive response; as it becomes practiced and familiar, it loses its response-demand quality. We are concerned with those states of transition that involve such high levels of uncertainty and ambiguity that the person cannot draw upon previous knowledge or experience for an immediate coping response.

The Transititon State: Description

The state of transition "goes across" from a situational context in which life has been patterned and balanced to a context so unfamiliar that appropriate person-environment niches have yet to be fashioned. In the state of transition, the lack of habitual ease and balance is manifest by *pattern* disruption in all systems, physiological, psychological and interpersonal. Habitual ease becomes un-ease and can easily become dis-ease. During transition, habitual patterns of organization, control, equilibrium-maintenance and integration become labored and difficult. As the person struggles for adaptive mastery, he experiences fragmentation of his sense of self and identity, and will have this uncertainty mirrored in the reflected appraisals of those who know him.

His interactions with people will have a groping, awkward quality as he attempts to respond to the dictates of a life script, the role instructions for which are only dimly perceived. In his movement from a familiar but obsolete role to a new but unfamiliar one, the individual is literally betwixt and between. His behavior will oscillate between the role behavior characteristic of his past situation and tentative attempts to enact the required new role. The greater his uncertainty, the more likely it is that "role clinging" will occur. In the new, untried situation, the person unwittingly shows the role behavior characteristic of his previous position. In situations involving major loss, there may be oneiric lapses in which the person finds himself sleepwalking "as if" the world is no longer changed and the previous stable world (with his valued attachments) is restored to him.

Identity

As the person struggles to master new role demands, anticipating and rehearsing where he can, security and self-esteem are threatened. As he attempts to stake a claim to his future identity, cards of past and aspirant identity may whir through his mind in adolescent-like disorder. Like the adolescent, endeavoring to relinquish an existing identity while unable to claim a new one, his behavior is punctuated by fluctuations of mood and self-image. "Identity diffusion" is therefore by no means confined to adolescence or its re-evocation in "middlescence." It occurs to some degree in all significant role change.

As in adolescence, the search for identity anchors is accompanied by marked introspection and egocentric absorption. An internal dialogue is generated around such questions as "Who am I? Where am I going? Why do I suffer so? What am I to make of my life now?" Introspection wanders kaleidoscopically through Time Past, Present and Future with questions like "Where have I been? How did I reach this point? How can I ever feel worthwhile again?" When such egocentric preoccupation becomes overcast with the gloom of despair, severe withdrawal may occur. At this point, cognitive operations may become paralyzed and "hopelessness, helplessness and giving up" impairs adaptation. Thinking becomes concrete, unrealistic and ruminative. Limited segments of the total space-time landscape are brought into view so that the "total picture" cannot be seen. Typically, intrusive, repetitive rumination then substitutes for scanning and planning. The struggle to establish a new, more congruent self-image and identity while achieving the necessary reorganization of space and relationships is reflected in these observations of Weiss on the recently separated.

> In these ways and in still other ways, separation forces a redefinition of fundamental assumptions in the relationships individuals maintain with others and their understandings of themselves. It is a time of transition from one organization of life to a quite different organization. During the transition the individual is like someone visiting a foreign country, constantly encountering new customs and new practises, constantly off balance as he searches for cues that will tell him what is happening around him. But the individual in separation is even more adrift than this, because there are no signs to tell him that his world has changed. People who once were friends behave differently now, but continue to define themselves as friends; his children are still his children, although the relationship is different; the language; the places; the people, all are the same, and yet they all are different. (1974)

THE TASKS OF TRANSITION

We suggest that there are two major tasks in transition: demolishing the old (patterns, role, identity . . .) and building the new. While engaged in these adaptive tasks, there are intermediate psychological "maintenance" tasks en route to the new situation. Of these, the maintenance of emotional equilibrium, self-esteem and automony loom largest. The dimensions of the tasks of transition vary with the habitual competencies, roles and relationships that have to be relinquished and, commensurately, the new knowledge, patterns, roles and skills that have to be acquired.

The Old and the New

Old structures are demolished as new structures are built. The psychological task of demolition is accompanied by processes Janis (1958) has described as the "work of grieving"; reconstruction involves his "work of worrying." The demands of the immediate situation usually dictate the sequence in which these psychological tasks will be confronted. The needs of immediate, emergency survival may obscure, or postpone, grief tasks.

Some of the confusion of the person in transition stems from the bewildering oscillation between past and future, grief and worry, that he experiences. The "work" often proceeds discontinuously subject to the presence or absence of disorienting, triggering cues in the person's immediate environment. In a situation where he can "bury himself" in accustomed activity, the person may compartmentalize himself, experiencing little affective or role disruption, only to be overwhelmed by grief and worry in a context where the reality of his changed situation engulfs him. For example, the recently separated spouse may function effectively in his familiar work environment only to experience emotional devastation when he returns to what is now a new, unfamiliar "home"—or returns to his old home in the new role of "ex" or visitor. In transition, the person is unsure of himself. He and/or others, will report that he is "not himself." As he emits fewer cues of disorganization and begins to surmount his adaptive tasks he will be seen as "his old self again."

Any situation of change involves losing ("missing") familiar components of a past habitual universe. The amputation of habitual aspects of the self is akin to the dismemberment of an amputee. Like the amputee, the person in change struggles to comprehend changes in self-image which are not immediately assimilable. The person may be protectively numbed by "phantom limb" experiences which dim his appreciation of the loss or its significance. As appreciation of the loss intensifies, the emergency emotions that accompany grief are experienced. These include rage and resentment, fear and apprehension, guilt and depression. These are repetitively reexperienced in the process of "remembering" as the person looks back and "remembers when . . ." He sustains a continuing, sometimes unconscious, dialogue with his phantoms as he reviews the life he has led with these objects that are now lost to him. By such remembrance he dismembers; he buries what has been and lays the past "to rest." He must repetitively leaf through the book of his once stable life, recalling, reevoking, reenacting and remembering as he does so. This review of past associations metabolizes the emotions of grief so that, with every effort of reminiscence, some energy is withdrawn from past investment; this energy can then be invested in the construction of a changed self and web of relationships.

Anticipatory Grief Work

Grief can be experienced in advance of an anticipated change-loss event. When the "work of grieving" is done prior to the actual separation from valued associations and roles, more energy is available for immediate and prospective tasks. (In a study by Hamburg and others of parents of leukemic children, healthy adaptation involved the experience of anticipatory grief and suffering, protected by partial denial; as acceptance grew, suffering became muted. Preparatory detachment from the leukemic child thus eased the eventual mourning tasks.)

The process of grief work is perforce slow. The more devastating the anticipated loss, the greater is the likelihood of overwhelming rage, guilt and depression. To maintain some equilibirum, reduction of emotional intensity is achieved by partial denial. The facts of dismal reality are assimilated slowly, and all its implications are equally slowly appreciated. The reality of loss is thus alternately confronted and avoided; Weissman (1972) describes this alternation between denial and acceptance as analogous to sand trickling back and forth in an hourglass. Some denial appears to be adaptive in the early weeks of assimilating "bad news" so that a measure of hope is maintained while exploratory reconnaissance and reorganization proceeds. Some early denial thus serves adaptive ends. However, when denial continues for many months, it no longer serves these ends; if significant reality is not confronted, no "prophylactic," anticipatory grief work is done.

The Work of Worrying

In our conceptual approach to the strategies appropriate to "worry work" we are indebted to White (1974) for his formulation of defense, mastery and coping. *Defense* pursues immediate survival: safety and protection. Defensive maneuvers occur in situations which arouse high anxiety; the anxiety is triggered by threat cues in an environment suddenly suffused with much uncertainty and ambiguity. Since these cues signal danger and the task terrain is poorly defined, tactics of psychological defense are more likely to serve the end of immediate self-protection than reckless, impulsive engagement. Defense, adaptively, can "buy time" in the interest of future mastery. However, when defense is the only tactic available, exclusive reliance upon defensive tactics may prove maladaptive; the person attempts to preserve a steady "as is" status in the hope that the threat will "blow over." The adaptive repertoire becomes gravely limited to one of habitual withdrawal-avoidance. *Mastery*, on the other hand, involves tactics of approach and attack, the determined exercise of aggressive initiative. Mastery proceeds through sequential phases involving reconnaissance of a potentially hazardous situation followed by planned attack. Mastery vanquishes threat while defense shields against it.

The concept of *coping* includes, but transcends, mastery. Studies of coping behavior have focused upon such radical role transitions as college entry, menopause, retirement, marriage and death. Behavior prior to, and/or following disaster states, surgery and disfigurement has also been extensively studied. Coping patterns have been explored with changes in the family structure, such as accession or dismemberment. White says, "It is clear that we tend to speak of coping when we have in mind a fairly drastic change or problem that defies familiar ways of behaving, requires the production of new behavior, and very likely gives rise to uncomfortable affects like anxiety, fear, guilt, shame or grief, the relief of which forms part of adaptation. Coping refers to adaptation under relatively difficult conditions." (1974)

Coping in response to perceived danger demands the immediate mobilization of ego resources to ensure survival (defense) while engaging the autonomous ego in the "intelligence" functions of perception and reception, information gathering and processing, scanning, planning and rehearsal for action. As action ensues, reflective processes continue to correct for error. Adaptive coping thus requires adequate mechanisms of defense *and* mastery. Some of these are generic, applying to all situations of adaptive challenge, some are more situation-specific.

In adaptation, the organism must simultaneously orient itself to its environment; maintain the necessary conditions to move in pursuit of perceived interests (by ensuring some autonomy and freedom of movement) and regulate potentially disruptive emergency emotions so that psychological balance is preserved and enough energy marshaled for the ego to seek, receive and process information. The "work of worrying" is influenced by multiple factors including the reality of change demands, their subjective appraisal, and the level of fear and anxiety generated. Effective coping is most likely to occur under conditions where the level of anxiety experienced is neither too high or too low. Also, information-seeking and processing does not proceed randomly. Everyone has an optimum rate of information input that is conducive to unconfused, straightforward action. Both higher and lower rates will tend, for different reasons, to make action difficult. Every person therefore seeks to regulate information input so that it can be processed without overload. When the mental apparatus is flooded with anxiety, the ego's cognitive operations become paralyzed. On the other hand, a state of low, or no, anxiety can only occur when the *realistic* dangers in a situation are denied, misperceived or inadequately appraised. A *working* level of emotional arousal accompanies realistic coping.

The Management of Dependence

In transition, the loss or threat of loss of familiar attachments arouses heightened needs for dependency and closeness. The person needs actual or symbolic others for sustenance and reassurance. While he needs to preserve autonomy and some capacity for independent initiative, his survival often depends upon access to adaptive resources other than his own. He needs to know his limits, where external help is, and how to avail himself of it.

The person's characteristic dependency stance is therefore a crucial determinant of his coping behavior. In the management of dependency, people are either appropriately *dependent, overdependent* (when behavior is characterized by a search for blanket reassurance, for someone to "take over") or *counterdependent* (exaggeratedly overindependent). This latter posture, while perilous for adaptation, is culturally expected of most males and exacts the sacrifice of legitimate dependency needs. The counterdependent personality is compelled to obey internalized demands to "stand on his own feet." These demands carry with them taboos against the experience of "unmanly" emotions such as pain, hurt and grief. When this occurs, emergency affect is repressed and overcontrolled: as Hansell (1975) emphasizes, the advantages that accrue from signaling via the "cry for help" are then lost to the organism. Signal affects become mangled and their help-evoking adaptive potential may be unrealized.

It is necessary for effective adaptation that the person maintain psychological equilibrium while responding to the multiple needs converging upon the organism in a time of transition. Balances must be struck by the ego in the emotional, cognitive and executive spheres between defensive stability-maintenance operations and active, exploratory efforts at mastery. In adaptation to change, energy-expending "worry work" is punctuated by episodes of "turning off," recuperation and re-creation. Some stability must necessarily, be maintained while anticipating, planning and implementing change. Psychological security operations must be adequate enough to maintain self-esteem, meet needs for dependency, maintain autonomy and channel aggressive energy toward mastery. In the absence of such operations, the syndrome of "helplessness, hopelessness and giving up" is likely to occur. We emphasize the oscillating quality, therefore, of psychological reorganization in coping with the tasks of transition. The person searches for acceptable compromises between mastery and defense, advance and retreat. Few critical role transitions are absolute emergency situations requiring that immediate battle be joined. Coping with transition usually alternates between approach and avoidance, attention and inattention, impulse gratification and stern impulse control, overdependent searches for reassurance and overindependent denial of dependency. This pattern occurs in anticipation, as well as during a transition state.

In summary, effective "worry work" requires a mental apparatus with adequate capacity for perception, cognition, volition, planning and action under the emergency psychological conditions of transition. In addition, emotions must be regulated so that energies are available for constructive problem-solving. Impulsiveness must be curbed, self-esteem maintained and autonomy, with freedom of movement, preserved.

An important component of "worry work" is the anticipatory rehearsal of behavior that will be required in the new situation. White says, "The use of strategies of adaptation in advance, in anticipation of problems that still lie ahead, would appear to be a peculiarly human attribute." The advantages that can accrue from these strategies are demonstrated by the work of Egbert with pre-surgery patients (Egbert et al, 1964) and the NIMH group that studied the coping strategies of pre-college students (1961). Pre-rehearsed patients recovered quicker from surgery; effective student coping was characterized by adequate prior information seeking, projection of the self into the anticipated image and role, and rehearsal of the behavior perceived as appropriate to the aspirant college status.

HELP: OUR PHILOSOPHIC UNDERPINNINGS

As Darwin (1872) cogently argued one hundred years ago, the expression of emotion by man and animals (through highly elaborated expressive systems in primates) serves many purposes, including signaling the need for help. The "cry for help" is a programmed survival-serving communication of the need for support and assistance. The aggression released in situations of disequilibrium is similarly adaptive in energizing the locomotor behavior of attack, withdrawal or retreat. The affects of fear and apprehension establish a state of vigilant ego alertness that triggers exploration of the environment. This exploration hunts for areas of danger and safety. The heightened vigilance is accompanied by increased needs for reassurance. The resultant *search behavior*, the goal of which is the pursuit of sources of authoritative support and reassurance, has its origins in the infant's search for parental protection when threatened.

The contributions of significant other people in the environment are, therefore, crucial to effective adaptation. They meet needs for authoritative guidance, support self-esteem and maintain self-confidence. Other people provide opportunities to test and appraise the reality of a changed situation and its demands. They offer consensual validation, encourage anticipatory rehearsal and neutralize emotionally distorted introspection. Heightened needs for support and dependence, particularly when the individual has lost his attachments or has limited access to them, signal the need for alternative transitional supports. Our helping vehicles have been constructed to meet these heightened needs for temporary support while coping with the tasks of transition. Our approach has been based on the assumption that adequate knowledge of transitional tasks and the mobilization of generic problem-solving skills are basic to effective adaptation. In addition, persons in transition require access to people who can offer support and provide authoritative guidance across transitional bridges. Their availability reduces the stress and discomfort of the transition state and significantly attenuates the magnitude of the adaptive task.

A person coping with critical role-transition tasks cannot expect—or be expected—to cope unless his basic 'biophysiological equipment is intact and energy reserves are adequate. If not, he functions in a state of psychological malnutrition. He needs energy or the capacity to mobilize it; if he is physiologically depleted or ill, his energy reserves are eroded. He also needs an intact mental apparatus and a fund of learned "programs"—generic coping strategies—to draw upon as he negotiates the new, strange or unfamiliar. When he has little or no experience with strangeness, his needs for proximity and contact comfort are higher than that of the average individual.

Help Through the Seminar Process: The Achievement of
Coping by Learning, Rehearsal and Action

Our helping groups have recognized the power of group solidarity in enhancing the ego's coping equipment of "common sense, realism, inventiveness and courage" (White, 1974). The groups' goals have been to stretch ego by mobilizing and practicing coping skills. While recognizing the likelihood of variation in the ego strengths of a group of people in transition, we assumed that, given the opportunity, existing strengths could be refined and new strengths acquired in an appropriate vehicle. We assumed that coping skills could be acquired and reinforced by *learning*. We designed our learning-teaching strategy on White's ego-oriented proposition: "When we speak of strategies of adaptation, however, we are referring more particularly to the realm of behavior, the realm that is directly controlled by the nervous system and that is in various degrees open to learning through experience." (1974)

Studies of behavior in such life-cycle transitions as adolescence, menopause and retirement have guided our "seminar" approach to *helping* people acquire the knowledge and skill to cope with the tasks of any specific transition—and simultaneously enhance generic coping ability. Our conceptual foundations guided our construction of a helping structure in which relevant information would be processed, plans elaborated and action rehearsal occur. We recognized also that the helping vehicle would have to support the maintenance of internal equilibrium, keeping physiological and emotional distress within bounds so that the mental apparatus could have energy available for its worry work. We also appreciated the need for people in transition to be *actively* involved in the architecture of their adaptive strategies so that personal autonomy could be sustained. We wanted to encourage personal initiative and provide sufficient psychological space and freedom of movement so that people could approach or withdraw as they needed to. We needed a structure which would combat, not promote, feelings of helplessness. Our ideal structure had to promote the scanning, information processing, planning and action components of effective coping; simultaneously, it required a secure, safe emotional matrix. Since the task was to promote, learn and teach coping, we decided that our structure—and "service contract"—should be unequivocally defined as educational, usually in the form of a "seminar."

GROUPS TO HELP

As we clarified our conceptual approach to transition, coping, coping tasks, strategies and helping, we were challenged to develop *group* vehicles which would speed and support people through the tasks of transition. How could we devise effective group structures that did not require prohibitively high resource investments? This question had to be addressed in the context of our search for particular populations in transition with significant coping tasks, whose numbers were multiplying and whose needs did not appear to be adequately met in the society. What group structures could be devised to serve some of these populations? The structures, we reminded ourselves, should meet multiple needs. In our judgment, these included:

—access to relevant information and guide maps about the transitional terrain through which people were passing.

—opportunities to process the information at an individualized pace, avoiding overload or underload, so that it could become personally relevant.

—the maintenance of internal balance while struggling with the tasks of transition.

—meeting needs for legitimate support, reassurance and contact comfort.

—the maintenance of internal psychological security operations, self-esteem and core identities.

—the provision of feedback.

—opportunities to test out and validate perceived expectations from strangers in new environments.

—opportunities to plan and rehearse role-appropriate action in response to the demands of new or changing environments.

The Seminar Model

Our seminar vehicle was devised to meet the needs we have listed. In our approach, we shared White's conviction that "fairly simple and direct methods of influencing behavior can produce a good deal better result then we have been taught to suppose." (1974)

We decided to build a learning-teaching vehicle in which people would learn about their coping options. We decided that such a vehicle would be effective if enough support was available to allay overwhelming anxiety or depression, and if the structure provided opportunities for anticipatory rehearsal and subsequent playback of action based upon such rehearsal. Our structure would have to build in enough cohesiveness and strength to ensure that persons did not habitually avoid or retreat from the tasks of transition. While providing for reality confrontation, it would need sufficient "holding power" to insure against "dropping out" so that the person in transition did not flee from painful feelings released as he attempted to master his situation. The structure should "lend ego." With a formal focus upon cognitive mastery, it needed to build in enough emotional support for participants to be able to confront the emotional experience of their shared condition. Leadership would therefore have to ensure substantive inputs of relevant information and opportunities to digest these, while maintaining sufficient psychological safety, support and security to permit the sharing of personal pain. We were after a model for adult learning and education under conditions of such uniqueness that no existing model of "androgogy" was likely to be entirely relevant. As we first translated our ideas into action we were uncertain about the duration for which such a temporary system should be erected and what provision, if any, would have to be made for formal continuity. With increasing experience, we have answers to some of these questions. A description of a typical group seminar now follows with a discussion of the lessons we have distilled. Our paradigm is "Seminars for the Separated" where experience has been extensive and intensive. We also mention similar group structures that were designed to serve other populations.

Seminar Groups for the Recently Separated: A Paradigm

These seminars were conducted under the auspices of a university psychiatry department and the prevention office of a state mental health department. Consumers were recruited by advertisements in local newspapers inviting recently separated spouses to participate in a knowledge-sharing discussion of separation. Prospective applicants were screened to balance the number of men and women and to ensure that applicants were *recently* separated.

The staff resources included a sociologist with considerable knowledge of disrupted social ties and community health professionals who led small group discussions and conducted research interviews.

For each seminar program, some twenty-five participants were recruited. Eight consecutive weekly meetings began with a 45-minute lecture by the sociologist. The group then divided into three small groups for one and a half hour's discussion. Meetings were preceded, and followed, by informal interaction in a congenial living room atmosphere.

The lectures were designed to provide relevant *information* about the psychological experience of separation, the associated disruption of life patterns and the dislocation of preexistent relationships. Information was given about the varied strategies used by the recently separated in reorganizing their lives. The likely costs and consequences of particular strategies were discussed so that effective coping maneuvers could be compared with those that were less effective and sometimes hazardous. Lectures therefore dealt with such topics as the emotional impact of separation upon the person, his children and members of his family. Changes in the relationship with kin and friends as well as continuing relationships with the spouse were explored. The organization of life in such areas as dating, sex and work was specifically addressed. Participants were given an introduction to what awaited them in "the world of the formerly married" and the accompanying changes in identity and self concept. Assistance agents and agencies available to the formerly married were discussed and evaluated.

The final lectures were used for purposes of review, evaluation, feedback and formal closure.

Each lecture was used to springboard small group discussions by the participants. In constituting the small groups, attempts were made to achieve a heterogeneous balance of age, gender, occupation and personal style in each group. In the groups, participants reviewed the history of their separations, discussed their immediate experiences, processed the lecture material, and rehearsed strategies for coping. The lecture content invariably stimulated relevant "case" material from the participants' recent experience. Group leaders would often be quite directive in stimulating generalizable "real life" discussion. The leader's role was to clarify information, help people review the immediate past and plan ahead; promote peer learning and support; and divert available emotional energy into constructive planning and eventual action. The structure provided by the lecture, with its substantive information about the "natural course" of separation, provided guide maps for the participants so that they could invest their energies in reality-based planning rather than drain off energies into defense against unrealistic fears or the pursuit of overoptimistic fantasies. At the same time, the leaders explicitly avoided gambits to play psychiatrist or group therapist, or respond to parentifying attempts to achieve "Doctor, tell me . . ." dependency gratification. They maintained theme centrality and relevance so that direct or vicarious learning was always occurring. Groups functioned best when they had able, stable, well-informed group discussion leaders who encouraged participation, prevented scapegoating of individual members and curbed monopolistic meandering by dominant or anxious members. Group leaders required substantial knowledge of separation, the management of transition and group processes. They needed skill in group tension management so that groups did not become flooded with contagious emotions of paralyzing or flight-promoting intensity.

In one experimental group, no formal instructional input was provided, and "free floating" discussion was invited. While participants in that group reported the experience to be helpful, the number of drop-outs was unusually high. We therefore recommend the more formal lecture-cum-discussion structure which makes for optimal psychological safety. We believe that the structure speeds group development so that the group can rapidly perform effectively without paying the penalty of the tension associated with excessive process "looseness."

The seminar was evaluated by telephone interviews between meetings and after the seminar's completion. In their responses, participants emphasized the value of the information they received and the reference group support provided by the seminar structure. The principal investigator has recently conducted a long-term follow-up in which many former participants reported that the seminars proved helpful in coping with specific problems subsequently encountered.

Groups for School Newcomers

This project was designed to provide services to school children new to schools on an Air Force base. We designed small group vehicles to greet, orient, support and guide school newcomers through the transition of school entry. We were particularly interested in the low-cost dimension of using volunteer-mothers as small-group discussion leaders; our mental health professionals played complementary roles as teacher-consultants.

Children joined the small groups soon after their entry into the school system. The volunteer group leaders were accepted on the basis of effective mothering experience and evidence of sensibility, sensitivity and empathy without over-involvement. They were trained (and, to some extent, screened out) through lectures, role playing and case discussions. They received anticipatory guidance and on-the-job supervision. The school newcomers and their parents were told that the children would participate in group discussions to help them become familiar with their new situations. Participation was for eight continuous weeks, with children leaving and entering in open-ended fashion. The effects of these discontinuities were neutralized by the advantages of having, at any one time, children experiencing the white heat entry crisis mingling with veteran-peers who were well past this point and could act as models and guides. The children stayed eight weeks, on the assumption that adaptive strategies would be sufficiently learned and practiced in that time. This proved on evaluation to be generally true. The few cases where children appeared to be coping poorly were almost invariably associated with conflicts between malcoping parents whose frustration and depression then descended upon the children. Our student malcopers were usually victims of situations where parents were "not together" about the move—or much else.

The leaders of groups of very young children communicated through such media as puppets, play and stories; with older children, there was focused discussion of "what it had been like" at the previous base. Children talked about the "good old days" and were encouraged to release emotions bound up in lingering attachments to the past. Children talked about topics like best friends and pets. By such reminiscence, they were able to share and work through feelings of grief and loss. Meetings were also devoted to Time Present with discussions of the school, and "what life was like" on their Air Force base in the immediate community.

In our evaluation of the impact of the experience on the children, we relied on the testimony of the children and discussion leaders and on more detailed evaluation by teachers and parents. The consensus was that the experience was helpful and well worth incorporating into the school structure. A serendipitous finding was this program's unique value to the volunteer group leaders. Their supervisory group meetings became support structures in which they shared some of their own problems. Many were in mid-life transition, seeking new avenues for mothering skills which their growing children now underutilized. For some, the experience in the program was followed by formal entry into "new careers" or professional human service programs.

Groups for Married Couples in Mid-Life

Under the auspices of a university adult education division, a course was offered entitled "The Human and Marital Condition in the Temporary Society." Its formal content dealt with the adaptive demands of changes in the family's "life cycle" and such transitional events as geographic relocation or mid-career change. Temporariness, loneliness and uprootedness were specifically explored. The seminar began with formal lecture presentations. As a language for shared discussion emerged, participants contributed "real life" case material about their own struggles.

The "instructors" for the "course" were a husband-wife team who lectured, participated actively in structured exercises (acting both as mentors and role models) and conducted the open discussions that eventually emerged. Two-hour meetings were held weekly for eight weeks. A need was then spontaneously voiced for longer meetings; the seminar concluded with three meetings, each of six hours, held at intervals of three weeks. This group decision permitted more openness and vicarious learning as couples elaborated individualized strategies to cope with the multiple transitional demands that were converging upon them. Seminar participants were struggling with such varied transitions as job changes or career plateauing for the husband; new career decisions for the wife; relocation; and "nest-emptying."

The experience was emotionally intense, demanding sensitivity, skill—and stamina—of the instructors. It rapidly emerged that most couples habitually denied or avoided the pain and grief accompanying change in their life situation. Many were also struggling with their "mid-life" crises, questioning the meaning and purpose of their lives and searching for existential anchors. The seminar experience provided them with models for effective affective communication, helped them to draw boundaries around their adaptive tasks and to share coping alternatives. Over the weeks of the seminar, they moved from habitual patterns of withdrawal-avoidance or restrictive conflict resolution to more direct confrontation of their feelings, values and fundamental concerns. Marital systems thus began to function as mutual support systems. Skills in effective communication, negotiation and conflict-resolution were practiced and learned. Roles were reexamined: in many cases, these were renegotiated. In a supportive seminar context of "mutual help," they worked through conflicts which had been suppressed. As participants struggled to practice more adaptive habits, they received supportive responses from the entire group. The opportunity to "reality test" by consensual validation was a significant learning ingredient.

On evaluation, the participants reported a stressful but rich and compelling learning experience. The instructors continued to hear informally from the couples who continued to make good use of their newly acquired skills and requested continuance in some form of "advanced" seminar. Some couples formed their own "support systems" by continuing to meet together.

Our Seminar Model and Adult Education

This particular seminar model is of general application to groups of families that are experiencing—or anticipating—any significant change in their external or internal environments (such as relocation, job termination or retirement). A constructive aspect of this seminar was that it was offered under the auspices of a university adult education division. This definition of participants as consumers of an educational service has many advantages over a definition of service as "help" or "treatment." If identical services were provided by a care-giving agency, inevitable stereotypes of "client" or "patient" would be evoked in the minds of some consumers, staff, families or friends. A mental health professional's presentation of himself as an educator more accurately communicates his intent and preferred role in this situation.

Based on this experience with groups of married couples, we are presently developing similar programs to support people—and their spouses—through the critical transitions of retirement and job termination. These will be described in later publications.

Groups for Students

We have used our generic "adult education" model in conducting a time-limited group for first-year medical students. Students were recruited soon after their arrival and attended assiduously. The group provided information and support, meeting needs for a transitional "home" and family, including surrogate parents and sibs, until the students had settled into their new roles and were "at home" in their strange environments.

For some years, we have conducted groups for new psychiatry residents and other students "in transit." While ostensibly providing "laboratory learning" about group process, we are satisfied that more significant needs are met as the students give and receive support in navigating the troubled waters of their shifting roles, identities and situations.

DISCUSSION

We have described some groups which illustrate our approach to helping people cope with transitional tasks. Our list is neither inclusive nor exclusive; similar principles inform many "transitional groups" such as Hamburg's group for adolescents. (1972) We have now conducted or supervised groups with a variety of populations not all of which are described here. All groups share in common the basic structure of a learning experience. While leaders are instructors, the role requires exquisite sensitivity to levels of emotional arousal in the group; the leader must steer vigilantly enough to avoid excessive emotional flooding (with likely flight from the group) and situations of under-arousal (which often makes for friendly, popular exchanges—but zero learning). Navigating carefully, group leaders introduce information about the tasks confronting the participants and discuss strategies for coping with them. Recognizing that participants enter a group while in transitional dysequilibrium, the balance between information-based guidance and equilibrium-maintaining support is delicately titrated. A week's interval is usually provided between one meeting and the next to provide time to assimilate information and translate it into personally relevant plans for "installment plan" mastery of the transition state. The small group meetings provide abundant opportunities for informal engagement between participants before, after and between meetings. Three structures for temporary emotional support are thus available: the total seminar structure, the small group structure and the informal structure in which temporary "buddying" often occurs among participants. This temporary bonding varies with the needs of different people. It has, however, been our general experience that small group members who signal extreme distress usually receive concerned, reassuring calls between meetings.

The leader must have knowledge and ability in two primary areas: the tasks of a specific transition and skills as a group conductor. While providing information about transition tasks, he must simultaneously develop and maintain an administrative matrix in which safety, support and security are assured for all participants. When leaders can draw upon personal experience of any particular transition state, they provide authentic evidence of its successful resolution and amplify the credibility of presentations. The personal styles of staff persons should be such that they function as role models for generic problem-solving mastery. In addition, they should be responsive and objective enough to model the process of empathetic concern without overidentification.

While staff are supportive, participants provide and receive strong *peer* support. This mutual interdependence should be actively encouraged by staff leaders, since participants are considerably strengthened by sharing their emotional experiences with others in the same situation. The "veterans" in any group, who are furthest along any transition path, enrich the information made available in a seminar; the fund of shared experience multiplies possibilities for action and charts possible courses—and dangers. When participants cope well from one week to the next, group members provide supportive reinforcement; when they fare less well, the group is an objective, nonjudgmental arena in which to plan for error correction.

Why Groups, Not Dyads?

Discussion of the advantage of group structures over dyads must first address "For what?" We have emphasized the need for a structure which provides *information* and *guidance* for planned action while simultaneously affording opportunities to meet transitional emotional needs so that personal autonomy, self-esteem and equilibrium are maintained. We appreciate that a dyadic structure can address these needs. However, we suspect that dyadic counseling is *less* effective than a group structure *and* has more attendant hazards. We believe that the dyad cannot provide the consensual validation available in a group containing people "in the same boat." The dangers of significant transference—and countertransference—occurring are considerably mitigated in a group. There is a very real dyadic hazard that the counselor or therapist may, insensibly, "take over,'' generate undue dependency and become a substitute for a lost object, such as a separated spouse and/or a nonavailable parent. This hazard is diminished in a group by the *exchange* of guidance and support among co-equal participants; the temporary interdependence that occurs is between peers and is achieved without loss of autonomy. While giving and receiving peer help, the participant can continue to value himself as a source of use to others, which is reflected in the appraisals of other group members.

The "staff" in a group provide structure; they manage and administer; while they provide care and concern, they function primarily as managerial thermostats to regulate an emotionally supportive matrix in which group members give and receive support *from one another*. Personal needs for support, concern and validation of self-worth are substantially met by other members. The group thus provides a unique opportunity for consensual validation. The structure is one of *mutual* support and help for which there is no analogue in dyadic professional help.

Groups also exercise regulatory influence inasmuch as group members who report, display or plan behavior which is potentially self-destructive have their impulsivity curbed, learn from past errors and rehearse future behavior. This increases the likelihood of constructive outcomes. Group members splint one another and provide auxiliary controls when needed.

In the maintenance of emotional equilibrium, the group structure provides multiple opportunities for meeting heightened dependency, affectional and attachment needs without loss of face. The remarkable properties of emotional contagion in groups can generate intense warmth, closeness and tension-reducing solidarity sentiments. (Emotional contagion may also spread anxiety and rage; here, emotional thermostatic regulation by the leader is crucial.)

For people who are in transition and for whom new roles have not yet solidified, the group structure provides a reference group haven in which to divest themselves of previous roles and support one another in the rehearsal of new ones. The group provides an arena for giving and receiving feedback in response to specific questions like "How am I doing?" and "Where ought I to be?" The awareness of a weekly meeting stimulates the maintenance of grooming behavior and provides an opportunity to compare the person's impression of himself with the appraisals of fellow sufferers, who are usually accepted as trustworthy neutrals.

The groups thus
—consensually validate reality.
—provide "group mirrors" in which to correct distortions of the self-image.
—provide a temporary, safe, warm shelter in which to experience inclusion and acceptance.
—sustain equilibrium through the grief and worry of transition.
—link fellow suffers so that they can be "co-counselors" to one another.
The dyad meets very few of these needs.

The group structure we have elaborated differentiates a role for staff persons as "Experts" who provide relevant information in ways that are timely and with content that is relevant and assimilable. The staff also provides small group discussion leadership so that information is clarified, shared and personalized. The leader monitors group process, maintains a level of appropriate working tension and promotes general participation. He ensures that no one is "out of field," maintains thematic flow, models support and ensures that no member is scapegoated. His role is more complex than that of the conventional "chairman" or "instructor"; he builds a supportive matrix, participates actively and is sufficiently informed about the transitional task to answer questions and provide new information. When he has himself successfully navigated a particular transition state, he can offer data from his own experience testifying, as a living model, to the successful mastery of transition.

BIBLIOGRAPHY

Bloom, B. L. Definitional aspects of the crisis consultation, *Journal of Consulting Psychology,* 27: 498-502, 1963.
Chodoff, P.; Friedman, S.; and Hamburg, D. A. Stress, defenses and coping behavior. Observations in parents of children with malignant disease. *American Journal of Psychiatry,* 120: 743-749, 1964.
Egbert, L. D., et al. Reduction of post operative pain by encouragement and instruction of patients. *New England Journal of Medicine,* 270: 825-827, 1964.
Hamburg, B. and Varenhorst, B. Peer counseling in the secondary schools: a community mental health project for youth. *American Journal of Orthopsychiatry,* 42: 566-581, 1972.
Hansell, N. Enhancing adaptational work during service, this volume.
Janis, I. L. *Psychological Stress,* New York: Wiley, 1958.
Weiss, R. S. Mimeo, Laboratory of Community Psychiatry, 1974.
Weissman, A. D. *On Dying and Denying.* New York: Behavioral Publications, 1972.
White, R. W. Strategies of adaptation: an attempt at systematic description, in Coelho, G. V., Hamburg, D. A. and Adams, J. E., eds., *Coping and Adaptation,* New York: Basic Books, 1974.

New Directions and Recent Advances in Behavior Modification

ROGER F. MALEY AND SHARON HUNT

INTRODUCTION

Behavior modification is a generic term used to label the process of changing human behavior by the use of experimentally derived psychological principles. Although there are disagreements concerning the precise definition of behavior modification, most would accept one which includes a strong emphasis on learning theory principles. In contrast to more traditional therapeutic approaches, the behavior modifier explicitly manipulates the client's environment to produce the desired behavior change. Consequently, the grist for the behavior modifier's mill is the relationship between changes in the environment and changes in a client's behavior.

For the purpose of this chapter, the labels "behaviorist," "behavior therapist" and "behavior modifier" will be used interchangably. Although subtle differences between the terms have been proposed (e.g., Kanfer and Phillips, 1970), their similarities far outweigh their differences, and they all stand in at least partial opposition to dynamically oriented, traditional intervention approaches.

Whether the approach being used is patterned after the operant conditioning paradigm, as in token economies, or based on respondent conditioning principles, as in aversion therapy, or combines elements of each, as in interpersonal training, the clinical focus is on behavior which can be observed or measured either by scientific instruments or by the client himself. Ullmann and Krasner (1965, p. 1) state that the behavior therapist basically ask three questions: "(a) what behavior is maladaptive, that is, what behavior should be increased or decreased; (b) what environmental contingencies currently support the behavior (either to maintain undesirable behavior or to reduce the likelihood of a more adaptive response); and (c) what environmental changes, usually reinforcing stimuli, may be manipulated to alter the behavior?"

Despite several recent attempts to generate a comprehensive appraisal of behavior modification and behavior therapy (e.g., Franks, 1969; Karen, 1974; Rimm and Masters, 1974), the field has grown at such a rapid rate that a precise overview is next to impossible. New journals devoted to the application of behavioral principles to solving human problems have sprung up all over the world. In 1972 an international symposium on behavior modification was held with participants from several countries. The influence of behaviorism as a philosophical position has been felt in such diverse areas as systems analysis, program evaluation, educational psychology, management practices and the entire community mental health movement. Even the radical behavioral viewpoint, as exemplified by Skinner, is receiving serious attention in academic as well as nonacademic settings, and is seen by many observers as having profound significance on many aspects of our society.

As a result of this behavioral movement, more and more practicing clinicians are now conceptualizing deviant behavior patterns in objective and quantifiable terms. Such vague criteria as "personal growth," self-actualization," "increased insight," etc., while not necessarily denied all validity, are held in abeyance in favor of more observable and specific descriptions of problematic behavior and treatment outcomes. The "psychological model" of behavior disorders, with its emphasis on learned behavior patterns, has generated a large number of successful treatment strategies and has contributed to the gradual erosion of the "medical model."

Many of the factors that have contributed to the increasing application of behavior modification principles are related to the failures of alternative approaches. Deficiencies in the medical model, poor mental health institutions and the failures of the community mental health movement have created a demand for more accountable, effective procedures. Consequently, behaviorally oriented clinicians have become quite credible and are very much in demand in all types of clinical situations. Concepts such as learning, relearning, discrimination learning, etc., are now applied in practically every clinical setting and indicate the increasing acceptance of behavioral approaches in dealing with problems of deviance.

In this chapter we will point out both the strengths and the weaknesses of behavioral treatment strategies and attempt to indicate what we see as the major new directions in which behaviorists will head. The reader is reminded that the literature and research reviewed in this chapter include many treatment approaches which have gone under a variety of labels in the past. The general field is anything but solidified and constant. While we view this state of affairs as being extremely healthy, it nevertheless leaves the reviewer in an organizational nightmare and makes remote the likelihood that any summary of the field will be seen as totally accurate by all behaviorists.

THE GROWTH OF BEHAVIOR MODIFICATION

Even without a totally appropriate model for the delivery of human psychological services, we do know some of the things that must be done to improve the situation, and most of these are augmented by a behavioral orientation. For example, recent successful treatment packages have been able to clearly specify the goal of intervention, have directly dealt with the presenting problems, instead of conceptualizing them as symptomatic of an underlying disease process, and have built into the treatment strategy ways of evaluating the treatment and the means of maintaining therapeutic gains in the client's natural environment.

The Decline of the Medical Model

At this point in time, it would be a case of overkill to join the long list of professionals (e.g., Szasz, 1961; Ullmann and Krasner, 1965; Wolpe, 1958) who have attacked the "medical model of mental illness." Suffice it to say that the medical viewpoint has been gradually replaced by more accountable orientations and more practical conceptual systems designed to facilitate the rational delivery of mental health services. By necessity these new orientations have focused on: (a) observable outcomes, (b) short-term intervention strategies, (c) the use of non-doctoral-level treatment specialists, and (d) the optimal use of the client's natural environment instead of total reliance on office psychotherapy for one hour a week.

The decline of the "medical model" certainly has been accelerated by the overall poor outcome results obtained from the research studies of psychodynamically-oriented psychotherapy. Even though many practicing clinicians go their merry way without considering the research evidence upon which their endeavors rest, increasing numbers of professionals are looking for more effective and scientifically validated intervention strategies. Problems involving the unreliability of diagnostic efforts (Ward, Beck, Mendelson, Mock and Erbaugh, 1962; Rosenhan, 1973), and the unrelatedness of diagnosis to treatment or treatment outcome (Mischel, 1968), have further weakened the psychodynamic model.

At the same time, many treatment programs based on behavioral principles have shown remarkable success with vastly differing types of clients afflicted by a variety of problems. Procedures such as desensitization, aversion therapy, modeling, token economies, implosive therapy, contingency contracting, negative practice, counter-conditioning, etc., have been experimentally validated in numerous studies. Although there certainly remain clinical and social problems resistant to the skills and knowledge of the behavior modifier, the contribution of learning theory positions and therapy derived from this vantage point is securely established.

Some Illustrious Treatment Failures

For hundreds of years the problem of managing deviants while protecting the public interest has remained largely unsolved. Then, as now, institutions were constructed to house people who had violated the norms of community life. Ineffective treatment methods have been used, at least in part, to create an illusion of treatment. This has been particularly true in the operation of large public mental hospitals. Although more subtle, the same sets of conditions have created problems in private treatment systems and for the entire community mental health movement. Overall, research would suggest that, when mental health clients are treated with these illusory methods, they probably fare no better or no worse than if they were not treated at all. Whatever changes do occur seem to be more a function of the social environment in which the patient lives, rather than being related to the received treatment.

Indeed, some researchers, such as Stuart (1970), believe that the existing research evidence on dynamically oriented psychotherapy shows that some clients are actually harmed by treatment. They are not merely wasting their time and money.

Looking at the research evidence on the effects of psychiatric hospitalization, one can easily conclude that for many patients "treatment" is harmful. The only effect that can be consistently shown in research studies is that of psychological deterioration over time for long-term patients (Mahrer and Mason, 1965; McInnis and Ullmann, 1967). As Perrow (1965, p. 924) has observed, "there is no appropriate treatment technology available for the large public mental hospital." It is obvious that many forces within a psychiatric institution promote deterioration. In fact, there is proof that time-in-hospital is linearly related to the development of the patient's "social breakdown" (Gruenberg, 1967) and increasingly "regressive" behavior. In other words, the longer a person remains in a mental hospital, the poorer are his chances of ever being released. If a patient has been in continuous hospitalization for two or more years, the probability of his being released and never being readmitted is about 6 percent (Honigfeld and Gillis, 1967).

These conditions will not be improved until mental institutions stop seeing their mission as the treatment of "disease" in a hospital setting and begin to conceptualize their activities as educational and see their function as more like that of a school than of a hospital.

In the early 1960's it appeared that the emerging community mental health movement would be a most promising enterprise. However, a decade later, most of our earlier expectations and beliefs have been dashed upon the hard rocks of reality. The community mental health movement never really dealt with the problems of most concern to society. Many of the movement's failures were due to omissions, others to the fact that it promised itself and society far too much. For example, our efforts in the field of delinquency prevention did not reduce crime; the plight of the mentally retarded and the chronic mental patient was not dramatically improved; and the cost to society of the multiple-problem family, which is seemingly impervious to intervention, has not been significantly reduced. The social movement called community mental health and its spiritual sibling, the war on poverty, have not been very effective in achieving their stated goals, and the successes of behavioral treatment strategies seem even more inviting in the light of these failures.

The Etiology of Disorders

Most forms of traditional, psychodynamically-oriented psychotherapy provide only one method of treatment, regardless of the specific nature of the client's problem. The underlying theory of the etiology of the disorder dictates the treatment. For example, in the case of psychoanalysis the theory dictates that the client's present problems probably stem from a lack of insight into critical childhood experiences and, thus, the achievement of insight becomes the paramount therapeutic goal. Similarly for a Rogerian therapist, client problems are seen as reflecting a need for "unconditional positive regard" and, consequently, this technique becomes the principal mode of treatment.

On the other hand, the behavior therapist is willing to assume a quite varied etiology, as long as a learning history is stressed. And, in fact, conducting behavior therapy does not even require that the precise learning conditions giving rise to present difficulties be known. As a result, behaviorists have little difficulty in avoiding what Bandura (1969, p. 89) has called the "all-purpose, single method" type of therapy.

If a therapist views all psychological disorders as emanating from a common internal process that is basically "unconscious," the client's presenting problems will seldom be accepted as the *real* problem. Behavior therapists, however, are quite likely to accept the client's presenting complaints as valid and to see the client as a competent source of pertinent information.

Thus, it can be readily seen—even if it comes as a surprise—that the clinical orientation of a behaviorist leads to more flexibility in terms of treatment approaches and puts the behaviorist ahead of the traditional therapist in terms of dealing with complex clinical problems.

The Use of Nonprofessionals as Change Agents

Perhaps one of the major advantages of the behaviorist's position is the ease with which nonprofessionals can be trained to help in the therapeutic process. It seems quite remarkable that all of the mental health fields have gone as far as they have on the basis of individual treatment models without ever having formulated clear conceptual plans for the integration of nonprofessional change agents. For example, the extremely complicated problem of the generalization of treatment benefits from an office to a client's natural environment will remain essentially a mystery until we can program the natural environment (especially the natural, interpersonal environment of peers, family and friends) to be the primary agent for behavioral change and maintenance (Tharp and Wetzel, 1966). Behavioral approaches are thus valuable because they promote the development of new sources of manpower and lead away from total or even primary reliance on doctoral-level practitioners and one-to-one forms of office psychotherapy.

The Issue of Accountability

Many young practitioners are convinced that the mental health professions are dedicated to a grand societal rip-off. These feelings have arisen at least partially in response to the demonstrable lack of effectiveness in practically every area of professional involvement. Although this is probably a harsher conclusion than the professions deserve, it is not one that is totally irrational. To argue that our mission of changing complex human behavior is just too complicated and too difficult to be effectively evaluated is begging the issue, and amounts to a colossal evasion of our current difficulties.

Our students are aware of the "credibility gap" in mental health endeavors and sense the need for renewed commitments to public stewardship through systems of professional accountability. Because most mental health systems have a captive market with little or no competition to provide treatment alternatives, the systems have not been subjected to independent outside reviews which might have promoted competency and responsiveness. In addition, the leadership in mental health has frequently been exercised by professionals who have refused to accept public criticism and demands for explaining failures. Such a situation cries out for accountability systems which hold professionals responsible for the results of their intervention efforts and reward them according to the outcomes they produce.

The resulting lack of demonstrable effectiveness has made us vulnerable to political maneuverings, both by evil men who want to keep certain types of deviance under tight social control, and by honest men who are genuinely confused as to what mental health services should be. Most politicians are interested in promoting effective systems. Yet, when professionals cannot specify what it is that they are doing and how they will evaluate success, one should not be surprised when these activities slip into the political realm and become highly charged emotional issues.

Like it or not, the future is at hand. To meet it, we are equipped only with what we have and what we know. These inadequacies are modifiable to the extent that we are willing to subject our knowledge of treatment techniques and delivery systems to critical analyses, and based on those analyses, to change our modes of operating.

Our old conceptual systems, based mostly on psychodynamic approaches to problems in living, have not provided effective platforms for intervention. Other models, such as the behavioral model and the public health model, have shown considerable promise of success. It seems reasonable that we now place far greater reliance on these new models and use them as our guiding conceptual lights to see what dark corners they might begin to illuminate.

PROBLEMS IN BEHAVIOR MODIFICATION

In spite of the obvious successes of many behavior modification procedures, the field has been hampered by a number of problems stemming from the characteristics of the practitioners as well as of those of the methodology. With some justification, behavior modifiers are often viewed as "arrogant" and "belligerent" by both other professionals and lay people. Resistance to the approach is often evidenced when attempts are made to implement treatment programs and, upon occasion, we suspect many behavior modifiers have identified themselves to a sensitive audience by some other term. Historically, the belligerence and arrogance of many behaviorally oriented clinicians have stemmed in part from a strongly felt conviction they they possessed the "truth," and efforts to reconcile behavioral principles with those of other schools were considered pointless. This self-imposed exile from the mainstream of academic psychology has produced a rather cultish, inbred group of professionals (Krantz, 1971), with a terminology that is sometimes unintelligible to practitioners of other approaches.

A further contribution to the belligerence of the behaviorist has undoubtedly been his traditional distance from actual clinical practice. Initially, behavior modifiers were dependent on clients in closed institutions, clients who constituted an essentially captive population. Because this population had been virtually abandoned by other mental health professionals, behavior modifiers were allowed to try out their unorthodox treatment strategies. Thus, their early successes with the mentally retarded and the chronic schizophrenic patient bolstered their self-confidence and their conviction that behavioral approaches provided the only viable and efficient treatment approaches. This conviction, backed by their marked successes, has forced the entire spectrum of clinical services to pay attention to behaviorists, however reluctantly.

The rather enviable position of behavior modification today is weakened by several deficiencies in the model. The restrictions imposed by adherence to the laboratory heritage, the failure to deal conceptually with the role of private events in human behavior, the excessive reliance on demonstration projects and the concentration on rather simple clinical problems have become sources of considerable concern to behaviorists. Increasingly, behaviorists are coming under the control of contingencies exercised by society as opposed to those of fellow professionals.

The Laboratory Heritage

Perhaps as a result of their experimental, laboratory heritage, behaviorists have been tied too closely to operant methodology. The strong emphasis on empirical and experimental validation, buttressed by misguided notions of scientific purity, initially led behaviorists to tackle only those problems which lent themselves to this type of analysis. Clearly specified responses, subject to observation and measurement, were considered a prerequisite to intervention. Thus, much of the literature to date documents success in eliminating disruptive behaviors, in training more appropriate interpersonal behaviors, and in increasing the rate and accuracy of academic responses. Until a few years ago, clinical problems that were not *clearly* a function of antecedent and/or consequent conditions were left to nonbehavioral practitioners. Davison (1969) has discussed some of the problems with the narrowness of the operant model of behavior change, and the reader is referred to his excellent article for a more detailed discussion than can be given here. Suffice it to say, that more and more behaviorists with training and experience in applied settings have abandoned the near-total reliance on the operant model and operant methodology, and are now seriously trying to integrate knowledge from other social sciences into their clinical practices.

Another weakness in the early attempts by behavior modifiers to treat deviant behavior has centered around their reliance on individual organism research design to evaluate their treatment effectiveness. Because of the fear that group designs obscured important individual differences (Sidman, 1960) leading to treatment results that had statistical, but not clinical, significance, behaviorists have used reversal and multiple baseline designs almost exclusively. Excessive adherence to this methodological approach had led to the neglect of viable program evaluation studies which focus on the comparative efficiency of different types of treatment programs for different groups of clients. Thus, until recently we could not state with certainity that token economies produce beneficial behavioral changes of a greater magnitude or with greater efficiency than alternative therapeutic procedures (Olson and Greenberg, 1972). With some notable exceptions (e.g., Phillips, Phillips, Fixsen and Wolf, 1973; McMichael and Corey, 1969; Cole, Martin and Vincent, 1973), behaviorists have not attempted large-scale evaluations of innovative educational, rehabilitative or correctional programs, even though they have contributed much of the treatment theory underlying them. New methodologies must be developed in response to increased societal demands for information pertaining to the efficiency and cost of programs which are publicly financed.

Private Events

An additional deficiency in the behavioral model has surfaced as behavior modifiers have begun treating more complex and subtle clinical problems. The emphasis on overt behavior as the focus of treatment, to the exclusion of "inner events," has both limited the types of problems with which many behaviorists have been willing to work and has retarded the development of methodologies appropriate for monitoring and modifying such covert variables.

Dollard and Miller (1950) have presented a convincing case for regarding covert responses as behaviors that follow the same laws as overt muscular responses. Since that time, increasing evidence has strongly indicated that one can be a "behaviorist" without focusing exclusively on overt behavior (e.g., Jacobs and Sachs, 1971). Consequently, we are left with some sort of mediational S-R position (e.g., Davison, 1969; Mowrer, 1960; Osgood, 1953). This means that we can conceptualize behavior on the basis of functional relationships which go beyond the immediate observables. However, as Davison (1969) cautions, one must make certain that the intervening variables are securely tied to behavior on both the antecedent and consequent ends. It is, indeed, possible that some behavior, both covert and overt, is controlled by processes which have little to do with operant conditioning. In other words, the assumption that all deviant behavior is a function of its consequences remains to be proven. At least part of the problem lies in the wholesale application of Skinnerian techniques derived from laboratory work with animals to verbal, symbol-producing humans. Again, there is no doubt that operantly based treatment approaches have produced tremendous clinical benefits. Our concern at this point is with the narrowness of the model. There are many other social learning principles that can be utilized in clinical settings.

The Demonstration Project Syndrome

Since many behavioral programs have been experimental, attempts to im-plement the findings in applied, natural environments often produce disappointing results. Demonstration projects are designed to maximize the probability of success of a given experimental model: the staff-client ratio is high, the equipment budget is lavish, the treatment facility modern and the staff and clients frequently handpicked. These conditions do not typically reflect the resources available to the real world practitioner. One can't blame a classroom teacher with thirty-five students for protesting that she can't implement individualized programs, no matter what the gain to her pupils. Nor can one be unsympathetic to the mental hospital aides, who must supervise sixty to ninety patients, when they object to the time involved in running a behavioral program with a disruptive resident. Professionals who run demonstration projects are spoiled and often do not direct enough of their efforts to adapting their highly successful programs for im-plementation in the typical classroom or the typical hospital ward. Clearly, demonstration projects perform a valuable function in allowing the development and evaluation of new treatment procedures in an atmosphere free of the bother-some interference of unsympathetic administrators, skeptical staff and money shortages. But continued support of such projects should be contingent on the general applicability of the new techniques, as well as on their "social value."

Complex Clinical Problems

In spite of its marked early successes, and perhaps because of those successes, behavior modifiers have only recently begun to undertake more complex prob-lems. Few would argue the effectiveness of behavior modification in reinstating concern for grooming in chronic mental patients, in keeping schoolchildren in their seats and improving their academic performance, and in ridding people of snake phobias. Behaviorists have dealt with these and comparable problems admirably. And as might be predicted from reinforcement theory, success with a given procedure in a given area perpetuates that procedure. Behavior modifiers have focused on classroom and institutional problems because they've been so successful in those areas, but this concentration has led to criticism that behavior modification deals with only relatively simple, monosymptomatic problems such as those referred to above.

Most of the objections concerning the "narrowness" of behavior modification are rapidly becoming dated. Recently, behaviorists have begun dealing with extremely complicated clinical and social problems, such as marriage counseling (Azrin, Naster and Jones, 1973; Stuart, 1969, 1972 [b]), alcoholism (Bigelow, Cohen, Liebson and Faillace, 1972; Cohen, Liebson and Faillace, 1971; Hunt and Azrin, 1973; Nathan, 1971; Schaefer, Sobell and Mills, 1971; Sobell and Sobell, 1973; Sobell, Sobell and Christelman, 1972), drug abuse (Melin and Götestam, 1973; Wolpe, 1965), juvenile delinquency (Phillips, Phillips, Wolf and Fixsen, 1973; Stuart, 1971, 1972 [a]), ecological engineering (Clark, Burgess and

Hendee, 1972; Hayes, Johnson and Cone, 1974; Kohlenberg and Phillips, 1973; Powers, Osborne and Anderson, 1973; Willems, 1974), racial integration (Hauserman, Walen and Behling, 1973) and employment practices (Jones and Azrin, 1973). While the attempts are highly tentative in some of these areas, and while some serious methodological problems have yet to be resolved, the behavior modifier nevertheless is rapidly moving into areas of greater social concern.

NEW DIRECTIONS IN BEHAVIOR MODIFICATION

The New Behavior Modifier

The first generation of behavior modifiers were, for the most part, trained as clinical psychologists. However, their dissatisfaction with traditional clinical practices led them to seek alternative treatment strategies, discarding in a fairly wholesale fashion any concept or technique based upon subjective evaluations of emotional states.

Behavior modifiers have been, until very recently, an inbred group, with students receiving their training either in independent, behaviorally oriented institutes or in university graduate programs with limited representation of other approaches. Thus, most graduates have left school with a well-nurtured disdain for "traditional" clinical psychology and psychiatry, and very little appreciation of their possible contributions. The result has been a certain "naïveté" in terms of understanding the complexity of the assessment of and solutions to many clinical problems.

Armed with the "truth," behavior modifiers have typically kept their distance from practitioners representing other approaches and disciplines. This has obviously made it difficult for the behaviorist to be integrated with other mental health professionals. However, the increasing tendency to deal with more complex clinical problems has made it imperative that the behavior modifier develop more sophisticated evaluative methodologies and treatment techniques. It seems reasonable to re-visit the traditional clinician to attempt an incorporation of his knowledge and skills. To this end, behavior modification is now being relocated in the training of mental health clinicians.

From the beginning, behaviorists have been trying to convince people that the "law of effect" really works. This has resulted in the "demonstration project syndrome," and as discussed earlier, demonstration projects have proved that the proper manipulation of environmental contingencies could change the behavior of clients in settings in which the therapist had a tremendous amount of control. This seemed to be the primary goal of behavior modification for many years, and only recently have behaviorists come to question the overall value of demonstration projects. Increasingly, the questions behaviorists are asking are much more sophisticated, and strongly focus upon the generalizability of treatment results in the client's natural environment, the importance of the selection of the target behaviors, and the cost-effectiveness of behavioral treatment as compared to other types of treatment modalities.

Like all clinicians, behavior modifiers have had serious problems with maintaining treatment effects and have not yet engaged in the type of long-range follow-up research which is absolutely necessary to ultimately decide which treatment approach is best suited to specific problems. The failure of many behavioral approaches to generalize to different settings (Kazdin, 1974) has also highlighted the need to consider other theoretical and methodological approaches.

In addition, the refusal by early behaviorists to acknowledge the role of inner events had led to premature exclusion of many areas of the social sciences. This seems to be slowly being corrected, as evidenced by the work of psychologists such as Homme (1965), who view inner events as "covert operants," which are just as subject to control as "overt operants."

Improved Public Relations

Behavior modifiers have frequently demonstrated an appalling lack of political expertise and sophistication. Survival in an institution often has more to do with a clinician's skills in interpersonal impression management and his dealings with administrators than with the scientific correctness of his treatment program. Failure to recognize this reality has led to the abortion of many treatment projects that were well designed from a technical viewpoint and would have worked had the staff been willing or able to carry out the treatment. Increasingly, the successful behavior modifier is analyzing the behavior of staff and administrators, in the same fashion as he would that of a client or patient, by asking questions about the contingencies operating on the individuals involved.

For example, what controls a mental hospital attendant's behavior? A few years ago the behaviorist would have assumed (mistakenly) that his training methods did, or that improvements in the target population's behavior were all that was necessary to control staff behavior. The problem was analyzed in terms of developing better in-service training programs or therapeutic approaches. Only slowly did the behavior modifier waken to the fact that there are virtually no contingencies operating in the typical institution to support ward staff who actually engage in treatment rather than custodial care.

In addition, behavior modifiers have been very poor public relations managers. Criticism of behavioral techniques, some of it valid, most of it based on mis-understanding and misinformation, appears in the mass media with increasing frequency. Termination of valuable though controversial programs has occurred in several states. While no one would advocate the continuation of compulsory, abusive techniques, there is a clear danger that in the concern for eliminating abuses, many administrators and public officials fail to discriminate between "good" behavior modification and "bad." Court cases, such as *Wyatt vs. Stickney* (the Alabama decision), have challenged, if not threatened, the existence of some widely used behavioral procedures. Many of the back-up reinforcers used with chronic mental patients in token economies, for instance, have been declared by the judiciary to be constitutionally guaranteed, and thus not available for contingency management. Faradic shock and other forms of aversive control have been outlawed in a few states and in many institutions. If the outcome of these challenges is a tightening by behavior modifiers of their evaluation procedures, then the field will have benefited. But behaviorists must take more seriously their responsibility to educate the public and to monitor their colleagues in order to guard against fraudulent practices.

Contributing to the problem of public relations is the tendency of many newspaper and magazine writers to lump a number of vastly different techniques together under the general rubric of "behavior modification." Thus, we read in the newspaper that psychosurgery, chemotherapy and electroconvulsive shock are forms of behavior modification. And in one sense they are, since they decidedly do produce changes in behavior. The relevant question here is whether the term "behavior modification" has, by being linked with so many diverse treatment approaches, lost its capability to communicate information about treatment approaches. Do professionals who belong to the ASSOCIATION FOR ADVANCEMENT OF BEHAVIOR THERAPY, read the JOURNAL OF APPLIED BEHAVIOR ANALYSIS and BEHAVIOR THERAPY and reject psychosurgery and chemotherapy have the right to the exclusive use of the term "behavior modification"? On what grounds can this be claimed? To sidestep the issue, some behaviorists are now suggesting the development of a new term that would clearly distinguish their practices from those of the psychosurgeons. Though no resolution is in sight the problem has been recognized, and increased discussion will ensue.

The naïveté of the behavior modifiers is also demonstrated in their failure to recognize the incongruity between behavioral philosophy and the social ethics of Western culture. In a society where individualism and competition are highly encouraged, where people are raised on concepts such as free will, where the motivation for an individual's behavior is attributed to inner emotional states, it is not surprising that there is difficulty in reconciling the tenets of the more radical behavorist schools, as exemplified by Skinner (1971), with traditional cultural values. Behavior modifiers talk about behavior in ways that confuse and frighten people, expecting the logic of their position to overcome vastly different conditioning histories. Again, behaviorists must begin to analyze and attempt to change the behavior of the public by using the same terms that have proven so successful in dealing with client populations.

Use of New Concepts and Strategies

Another new direction for behavior modification centers around the use of concepts and treatment technologies from other areas of the social sciences. Behaviorists' earlier defensiveness has given way to the realization that other areas just might have something to offer in the design, execution and evaluation of treatment programs.

A primary new direction for behaviorists is the use of group approaches and a much stronger focus on interpersonal behavior. Group methods of treatment and training are one of the fastest growing areas of clinical practice, and behavior modifiers are becoming convinced that individual psychological problems are not really "individual." Instead, people's problems are conceptualized as resulting from faulty or inadequate interpersonal learning. Interpersonal problems and conflicts are now seen as more important than intrapsychic ones, even at the peak of an individual's disorder. Individuals are firmly locked, far more than what we once thought, into a matrix of social habits and cultural institutions which narrowly determine the nature of their lives and the social behaviors available to them.

As adults, we manifest behaviors determined in many ways by our interpersonal learning in past small groups and the role demands of our present small group or institutional situation. Man is, indeed, a social animal whose behavior is in large part determined by group memberships. The effect of group experiences upon an individual's behavior and his attitudes about himself and others appears to be so pervasive that numerous theorists believe an individual becomes what he is because of the roles and behaviors he has assumed in various groups.

Thus, for many behavior modifiers, group treatment approaches are not merely seen as less expensive and more desirable alternatives to individual treatment. These behaviorists believe that the individual is currently having psychological difficulties *because* of inadequate, harmful prior interpersonal learning and, consequently, the most direct form of treatment must revolve around group processes and the learning of new interpersonal behaviors.

The success of the behavior therapies in general, the growing evidence that changes in interpersonal skills (resolving "problems in living") results in intrapersonal changes, rather than the other way around, the lack of evidence to support "symptom substitution," and the growing dissatisfaction with the old "medical model" of treatment have all facilitated the rise of group behavior modification techniques. Groups are now seen as active agents of therapy and not merely the environmental setting where other agents (techniques) are brought into play.

Lack of System Orientation

Behavior modification has also suffered from the lack of a system orientation. At an abstract level, behavior analysis and systems analysis seem to have proceeded along different paths toward common goals. These paths might be described as differing in general approaches to problem-solving which stems from the use of inductive-empirical approaches in behavioral analysis and deductive-conceptual approaches in systems analysis. In the real world, for example, in a particular mental health organization, the two groups' problem-solving behavior probably proceeds in the following manner: the systems analyst is likely to map out a conceptual model of the organization, its internal and external resource exchanges, feedback loops and the social policies establishing the flow of rewards to the organizational environment. He will concern himself with aggregate data on programs and staff/client behavior, and should it be desirable to change the organization, he is likely to choose points of intervention that can be viewed as molar elements of the system—for example, changing policy to retard the acceptance of clients or to accelerate client discharge. The systems analyst is likely to proceed using a reductionistic model, focusing on the behavior of particular individuals after having examined aggregate group or subsystem data.

The behavior analyst, on the other hand, is likely to begin problem-solving on the reverse side of the organizational system. His first focus is likely to be the behavior of individual staff and clients, and he will probably proceed inductively and additively to construct subsystem and, later, large system operations based on the examination of aggregate data. His conceptual model of the organization is built from the bottom up, rather than from the top down. Should he choose to develop organizational change efforts, the behavior analyst is likely to first focus on attempting to alter the contingencies affecting individual staff and/or client behavior. He will proceed upward through the organization to alter group or subgroup contingencies to the extent that it is necessary to bring about the desired behavior change. Given the nature of human service delivery systems, it is highly probable that before reliable individual and subsystem behavior occurs, the behavior analyst will find himself concerned with broad organizational policy as a contingency management problem, and the systems analyst will find himself concerned with individual behavior as a derivative of organizational contingency management or social policy (Harshbarger and Maley, 1974).

The point here is not merely that these two groups of problem-solvers will unavoidably be concerned with similar problems; rather, that from the outset they are dealing with different aspects of the same problems. The sooner this is realized, the greater the likelihood that their efforts will be complementary and mutually supportive. Effective behavior change strategies in organizational sub-systems are doomed without the appropriate changes in social policies. Effective social policy rests upon its resulting in a more adaptive, rewarding, individual behavior.

There is thus a growing awareness by behaviorists that a systems perspective is absolutely necessary for the ultimate solution of treatment programming. This integration of behavior analysis and systems analysis, although in its infancy, is quite exciting, and already promises to be fruitful for both groups. Behavior analysts find their problem-solving strategies enriched and expanded through the integration of the larger, more encompassing conceptual models of systems analysis, and human service delivery systems are improved because of this integration (Maley and Harshbarger, 1974).

SUMMARY

In summary, then, we see that behavior modification is now well established within the discipline of psychology, as well as within the mental health professions as a whole. Distinguished from more traditional clinical approaches by its focus on specifiable behavioral change, by the questions it asks concerning the etiology and treatment of deviant behavior, by its emphasis on data-based treatment decisions and by its use of paraprofessional change agents, behavior modification has responded to the decline of the medical model and to increasing social demands.

The success of behavior modification treatment programs has been hindered by a number of problems which seem to be related both to the characteristics of some behavior modifiers and to their dominant methodology. Behaviorists have rightly expressed pride in their successes; unfortunately, this confidence has often led them to excessively belligerent stances and rather arrogant pronouncements of possessing the "truth." Thus, some of the resistance to behavior modification has been generated by the behavior of behavior modifiers. Too rigid an adherence to laboratory procedures, particularly operant methodology, overreliance on single subject research designs, neglect of program evaluation studies, a failure to explore the role of private events in human behavior, too much effort expended in developing demonstration projects, and a heavy focus on treating relatively simple, monosymptomatic behaviors have all slowed down the assimilation of behavior modification into the mainstream of clinical practice. The good news is that these problems seem to be lessening and that behaviorial treatment strategies can be expected to form an increasingly strong and visible force in tomorrow's mental health programs.

REFERENCES

Azrin, N. H.; Naster, B. J.; and Jones, R. Reciprocity counseling: A rapid learning-based procedure for marital counseling. *Behaviour Research and Therapy,* 1973, *11,* 1-18.

Bandura, A *Principles of behavior modification.* New York. Holt, Rinehart and Winston, 1969.

Bigelow, G.; Cohen, M.; Liebson, I.; and Faillace, L.A. Abstinence or moderation? Choice of alcoholics. *Behaviour Research and Therapy,* 1972, *10,* 209-214.

Cohen, M.; Liebson, I. A.; and Faillace, L. A. The modification of drinking in chronic alcoholics. In N. K. Mello and J. H. Mendelson (eds.), *Recent Advances In Studies of Alcoholism.* Rockville, Md: National Institute of Mental Health, 1971, 745-766.

Cole, C.; Martin, S.; and Vincent, J. A comparison of two teaching formats at the college level. Presented at the First Annual Conference on Behavior Research and Technology in Higher Education, Georgia State University, Altanta, 1973.

Clark, R. N.; Burgess, R. L.; and Hendee, J. C. The development of anti-litter behavior in a forest campground. *Journal of Applied Behavior Analysis,* 1972, *5,* 1-5.

Davison, G. C. Appraisal of behavior modification techniques with adults in institutional settings. In C. Franks (eds.), *Behavior therapy: Appraisal and status.* New York: McGraw-Hill, 1969, 220-278.

Dollard, J., and Miller, N. E. Personality and psychotherapy. New York: McGraw-Hill, 1950.

Franks, C. *Behavior therapy: Appraisal and status.* New York: McGraw-Hill, 1969.

Gruenberg, E. M. The social breakdown syndrome: Some origins. *American Journal of Psychiatry,* 1967, *123,* 12-20.

Harshbarger, D., and Maley, R. F. (eds.). *Behavior analysis and system analysis: an integrative approach to mental health programs.* Kalamazoo, Michigan, 1974.

Hauserman, N.; Walen, S. R.; and Behling, M. Reinforced racial integration in the first grade: A study in generalization. *Jouranl of Applied Behavior Analysis,* 1973, *6,* 193-200.

Hayes, S. C.; Johnson, V. S.; and Cone, J. D. The marked-item technique: A practical procedure for litter control. Presented at the Association for Advancement of Behavior Therapy meeting, Chicago, 1974.

Homme, L. E. Perspectives in psychology - XXIV: Control of coverants, the operants of the mind. *Psychological Record,* 1965, *15,* 501-511.

Honigfeld, G., and Gillis, R. The role of institutionalization in the natural history of schizophrenia. *Diseases of the Nervous System,* 1967, *28,* 660-663.

Hunt, G. M., and Azrin, N. H. A community-reinforcement approach to alcoholism. *Behaviour Research and Therapy,* 1973, *11,* 91-104.

Jacobs, A., and Sachs, L. B. (eds.), *The psychology of private events.* New York: Academic Press, 1971.

Jones, R.J., and Azrin, N.H. An experimental application of a social reinforcement approach to the problem of jobfinding. *Journal of Applied Behavior Analysis,* 1973, *6,* 345-353.

Kanfer, F. H., and Phillips, J. S. *Learning foundations of behavior therapy.* New York: John Wiley, 1970.

Karen, R. L. *An introduction to behavior theory and its applications.* New York: Harper and Row, 1974.

Kazdin, A. E. A review of token economy treatment modalities. In D. Harshbarger and R. F. Maley (eds.), *Behavior analysis and systems analysis: An integrative approach to mental health programs.* Kalamazoo: Behaviordelia, 1974.

Kohlenberg, R., and Phillips. T. Reinforcement and rate of litter depositing. *Journal of Applied Behavior Analysis,* 1973, *6,* 391-396.

Krantx, D. L. The separate worlds of operant and non-operant psychology. *Journal of Applied Behavior Analysis,* 1971, *4,* 61-70.

Krapfl, J. E. Accountability for behavioral engineers. Presented at Drake Conference on Professional Issues in Behavior Analysis, Drake University, Des Moines, 1974.

Mahrer, A. R., and Mason, D. J. Changes in number of self-reported symptoms during psychiatric hospitalization. *Journal of Consulting Psychology,* 1965, *29,* 285.

Maley, R. F., and Harshbarger, D. The integration of behavior analysis and systems analysis: A look at the future? In D. Harshbarger and R. F. Maley (eds.), *Behavior analysis and systems analysis: An integrative approach to mental health programs.* Kalamazoo: Behaviordelia, 1974.

McInnis, T. L., and Ullmann, L. P. Positive and negative reinforcement with short and long term hospitalized schizophrenics in a probability learning situation. *Journal of Abnormal Psychology,* 1967, *72,* 157-162.

McMichael, J.S., and Corey, J.R. Contingency management in an introductory psychology course produces better learning. *Journal of Applied Behavior Analysis,* 1969, *2,* 79-83.

Melin, G. L., and Götestam, K. G. A contingency management program on a drug-free unit for intravenous amphetamine addicts. *Journal of Behavior Therapy and Experimental Psychiatry,* 1973, *4,* 331-337.

Mischel, W. *Personality and assessment.* New York: Wiley, 1968.

Mowrer, O. H. *Learning theory and behavior.* New York: John Wiley and Sons, 1960.

Nathan, P. E. Basic research in behavioral aspects of alcoholism. Presented at the Eighth Annual West Virginia School on Alcohol and Drug Abuse Studies, 1971.

Olson, R. P., and Greenberg, D. J. Effects of contingency contracting and decision making groups with chronic mental patients. *Journal of Consulting and Clinical Psychology,* 1972, *38,* 376-383.

Osgood, C. E. *Method and theory in experimental psychology.* New York: Oxford University Press, 1953.

Perrow, C. Hospitals: Technology, structure and goals. In J. G. March (ed.), *Handbook of organizations.* Chicago: Rand McNally, 1965, 910-971.

Phillips, E. L.; Phillips, E. A.; Fixsen, D. L.; and Wolf, M. M. Behavior shaping for delinquents. *Psychology Today,* 1973, *7,* 74-79.

Phillips, E.L.; Phillips, E. A.; Wolf, M. M.; and Fixsen, D. L. Achievement Place: Development of the elected manager system. *Journal of Applied Behavior Analysis.* 1973, *6,* 541-561.

Powers, R. B.; Osborne, J. G.; and Anderson, E. G. Positive reinforcement of litter removal in the natural environment. *Journal of Applied Behavior Analysis.* 1973, *6,* 579-586.

Rimm, D. C.; and Masters, J. C. *Behavior therapy: Techniques and empirical findings.* New York: Academic Press, 1974.

Rosenhan, D. L. *On being sane in insane places. Science,* 1973, *179,* 250-258.

Schaefer, H. H.; Sobell, M. B.; and Mills, K. C. Baseline drinking behaviors in alcoholics and social drinkers: Kinds of drinks and sip magnitudes. *Behavior Research and Therapy,* 1971, *9,* 23-27.

Sidman, M. *Tactics of scientific research.* New York: Basic Books, 1960.

Skinner, B. F. *Beyond freedom and dignity.* New York: Alfred A. Knopf, 1971.

Sobell, M. B.; Schaefer, H. H.; and Mills, K. C. Differences in drinking behaviors between alcoholics and normal drinkers. *Behaviour Research and Therapy,* 1972, *10,* 257-267.

Sobell, M. B., and Sobell, L. C. Alcoholics treated by individualized behavior therapy: One year treatment outcome. *Behaviour Research and Therapy,* 1973, *11,* 599-618.

Sobell, L. C.; Sobell, M. B.; and Christelman, W. C. The myth of "one drink." *Behaviour Research and Therapy,* 1972, *10,* 119-123.

Stuart, R. B. Operant-interpersonal treatment for marital discord. *Journal of Consulting and Clinical Psychology,* 1969, *33,* 675-682.

————. *Trick or treatment: How and when psychotherapy fails.* Champaign: Research Press, 1970.

————. Behavioral contracting within the families of delinquents. *Journal of Behavior Therapy and Experimental Psychiatry,* 1971, *2,* 1-11.

————. Behavioral contracting with delinquents: A cautionary note. *Journal of Behavior Therapy and Experimental Psychiatry,* 1972 (a), *3,* 161-169.

————. Behavioral remedies for marital ills: A guide to the use of operant interpersonal techniques. Presented at the International Symposium on Behavior Modification, Minneapolis, 1972. (b).

Szasz, T. S. *The myth of mental illness: Foundations of a theory of personal conduct.* New York: Hoeber-Harper, 1961.

Tharp, R. G., and Wetzel, R. J. *Behavior modification in the natural environment.* New York: Academic Press, 1969.

Ullmann, L. P., and Krasner, L. (eds.), *Case studies in behavior modification.* New York: Holt, Rinehart and Winston, 1965.

Ward, C. H.; Beck, A. T.; Mendelson, M.; Mock, N. E.; and Erbaugh, J. K. The psychiatric nomenclature. *Archives of General Psychiatry,* 1962, *7,* 198-205.

Willems, E. P. Behavioral technology and behavioral ecology. *Journal of Applied Behavior Analysis,* 1974, *7,* 151-165.

Wolpe, J. *Psychotherapy by reciprocal inhibitions.* Palo Alto, Calif.: Stanford University Press, 1958.

————. Conditioned inhibition of craving in drug addiction: A pilot experiment. *Behaviour Research and Therapy,* 1965, *2,* 285-288.

12

Community Television
and Community
Mental Health

PAUL R. AHR

Community television* has matured in a quarter-century from a scattering of lone antennas erected in isolated areas to a nation-wide distribution of franchises which serve more than 6 million subscribers in large cities as well as small towns. Initially developed to improve the reception of broadcast or over-the-air commercial television programming, the present community television systems both import existing broadcast channels of regional and national scope and originate many hours weekly of supplemental local programming of community interest and with community input. At the present time the full impact of community television in terms both of the range of market penetration and of the variety of community-oriented programming has hardly begun to be realized.

The Sloan Commission on Cable Communications (1971) reported that in mid-1971 only 6 million of the nearly 60 million households with television sets were subscribers of the approximately 2,750 community television systems in operation. However, the same report predicted that by 1980 penetration will be in the range of 40 percent to 60 percent of TV households, and that in metropolitan areas penetration is likely to be substantially higher.

Increased penetration without the opportunity for community-originated and community-oriented programming serves only to replicate and enhance the current regionally and nationally oriented broadcast television system. As community television has developed, however, there has also been a parallel development in the responsibility of the local community television system to be responsive to its host community. No longer solely an importer and booster of weak broadcast signals, new community television franchises are now required by the Federal Communications Commission to provide channels for public service programming in the following three areas: local and state government, public access and education. In addition, the Sloan Commission has recommended the inclusion of a fourth mandatory channel for health. The availability of these channels in conjunction with the cooperation of interested community television managers provides the mental health professional with an important medium for regular communica-

---

*In this paper the term "community television" replaces but is equivalent to the traditional term "community antenna television," or CATV. With the decreasing emphasis on community antennas, "community television" has become the preferred term.

tion with an increasingly wider range of individuals in their own community. The maturation of this potent resource comes at a time when the trained personnel and available funds necessary for successful mental health programs are both unevenly distributed and in short supply. Proper utilization of community television can provide those professionals who have been mandated to deliver mental health services a unique opportunity to offer a range of indirect services to a wide variety of individuals, especially including those potential clients who are not currently being served as a result either of their distance from or lack of interest in available facilities and services.

The purposes of this chapter are to suggest a series of mental health education and ancillary services which can be effectively provided via community television, to discuss a choice of roles which will be available to the mental health professional in utilizing community television, and to delineate a series of tasks this professional person will encounter in utilizing community television to provide these services. While the present discussion is limited to population-oriented mental health programming via community television, it should be borne in mind that these services and this television modality represent a limited range of mental health and related services which can be delivered through the full range of television systems, which also include two-way interactive television, closed-circuit television, video tape recording, instructional television fixed service and broadcast television.

MENTAL HEALTH SERVICES APPROPRIATE
TO COMMUNITY TELEVISION

Community television, first and foremost, is a medium for the transmission of audio-visual communications to an audience defined geographically by the boundaries of the franchise area and functionally by the willingness of individuals within that area to subscribe to this service. Although two-way interactive community television systems are currently operational on a demonstration basis (Coltman, 1972) and present community television systems can be adapted to direct selected programming to specialized audiences (e.g., physicians, students, prisoners) in special settings (e.g., private offices, hospital rooms, classrooms), the most prevalent use of community television is for the one-way transmission of a variety of programs to a general audience of subscribers, usually in their own homes.

Each of the defining characteristics of community television has an impact on the ways in which it can be used. Viewed from the perspective of the population-oriented mental health professional, one of the most important features of community television is the opportunity this medium provides to present current mental health issues and principles to a wide audience of families in their own homes.

The mental health professional who has wished to educate or mobilize community members to address themselves to mental health and mental illness topics has typically done so either by delivering public speeches, presenting relevant films or distributing pertinent booklets. Each of these methods has placed some of the burden of information acquisition on the individual, who has been required either to request the materials or to leave his home (and frequently other members of his family) to come to a public meeting place.

Community television, on the other hand, requires only that the subscriber tune in to the appropriate channel at the designated time. Because the community television message is available at home, mental health oriented presentations can be made available simultaneously to all family members in their "natural habitat."

Because the community television audience is restricted to those subscribers who live within the geographical limits of the franchise area, the mental health professional knows in advance many of the characteristics of the persons to whom he will be delivering his televised messages. This foreknowledge should facilitate the preparation of program materials which are relevant to the needs and concerns of the local audience.

Constrained only the uni-directionality of transmission, the availability of resources and the limits of creativity and local mores, mental health professionals can prepare several broad categories of programming which present a range of relevant audio-visual messages and materials. Two important categories of programming, the provision of public mental health education and the development of resources which address the mental health needs of community members, are especially pertinent and well suited to the capabilities and limitations of community television.

Public Mental Health Education

The provision of public mental health education services can be considered under three main headings.

Formal Education. Courses like "Sunrise Semester" or "University of the Air" in such topic areas as general psychology, abnormal psychology, child development, sociology, hygiene, etc., provide an opportunity for the presentation of mental health issues to the wide community television audience. However, such formalized courses of instruction, whether for academic credit or not, frequently have as their major objective the discussion of a broad range of concepts in the specified subject area, and the presentation of mental health principles, when included, tends to be a subordinate objective. In addition, the sequential and formal lecture format of many of these televised courses often appeals primarily to the perseverant and verbally proficient members of the audience. Therefore, unless mental health information is directly addressed to those subgroups who would most profit from it—the less well-educated and less successful members of the audience—it will be effectively inaccessible to them.

Presentation of General Mental Health Information. The presentation of important mental health issues and the identification of human service resources in the community in a televised discussion or documentary format can provide a more informal method for changing public attitudes toward these issues and for stimulating appropriate utilization of these resources. The following formats for the presentation of general information can be presented separately or in combination.

(a) *Discussion of Mental Health Issues.* Research on public knowledge about mental health problems has characterized the average citizen as more uninformed than misinformed about such problems. Despite being surrounded by mental-health and mental-illness phenomena the typical community television viewer is unlikely to recognize or to characterize them as such. But despite his lack of adequate and accurate information, he is likely to be interested in collecting new and relevant facts and opinions (Nunnally, 1961).

Informative presentations of such general topics as child-rearing techniques, family dynamics, anxiety, depression, alcoholism, drug abuse, the characteristics of mental illness, or the varieties of treatment modalities available for the mentally disordered can contribute to the development of a community of well-informed citizens who are able to accurately identify psychological strengths and weaknesses in themselves and in those with whom they live and work.

(b) *Orientation to Human Service Resources.* Some persons do not receive needed and available mental health and related services simply because they do not know that they exist, do not know how to arrange for these services, or do not know how to get to the relevant service centers. Informational segments dealing with the availability, appropriateness and accessibility of human resources can help to stimulate relevant requests and referrals.

Other persons do not receive mental health services because they do not know what will happen to them or what will be required of them once they apply for these services. As Crichton (1970) has observed of hospitals, a person visiting Europe can get better advance information than a person entering the "foreign country" of a mental health center. This lack of accurate knowledge, and the anxiety which frequently accompanies it, can be reduced by providing these persons with an opportunity to vicariously navigate mental-health and related human service systems through viewing the videotaped experiences of another person who has entered such a system. Such videotaped segments could trace the activities of the model as he passes through various phases in the provision of services, viz., entry, intake, disposition, treatment or follow-up. Informational segments dealing with issues such as patients' rights or the financing of mental health care can also facilitate appropriate service requests.

Education for Effective Personal Functioning. Whereas the general informational component of public mental health education is addressed to the wide range of community television subscribers, education for effective personal functioning provides direct factual and experiential information to populations-at-risk and to other specified audience subgroups. This information can be made available through one or both of the following formats.

(a) *Anticipatory Guidance.* Persons in impending crises (Lindemann, 1944; Caplan, 1964; Erikson, 1950, 1959) or role transition (Rapoport, 1964; Tyhurst, 1957) who are presented with factual information regarding the stresses and life changes they will most likely experience, and who are provided with opportunities to rehearse their emotional reactions to these events, can begin to work out strategies in advance for coping with the "blooming, buzzing confusion" of their transitional state. This information can readily be provided via community television to persons in an at-risk category, as well as to their family and friends who can help them in time of crisis. The availability in the audience of members of the kith-and-kin networks which surround persons in an at-risk category is especially important because as Caplan (1963) has noted, "the intellectual knowledge derived from public education is not likely to be remembered during the emotional upset and the confusion involved when a person goes into crisis. It is much easier to help someone else who is upset than to remember what to do when you are yourself off balance."

(b) *Modeling for Personal Growth.* Unidentified segments of the community television audience are likely to experience a series of "hang-ups" or learned prohibitions and obligations which interfere with their ability to enjoy successful interpersonal relationships or to initiate and maintain self-directed activities. Dramatized or filmed sequences of others who function without these role restrictions or requirements can provide an effective technique for stimulating the unlearning or maladaptive behaviors and the learning of the newer, more satisfying behaviors. These program segments might include behavioral sequences such as the sharing of thoughts and feelings between marital partners or other family members, the demonstration of physical expressions of caring between a father and young son, parental limit-setting in response to undesirable behaviors in children, or self-confidence in interviewing for a job

Resource Development

The development of resources which address the mental health needs of community members can be considered under two headings.

Stimulation of Natural and Professional Care-Giving Systems. Where care givers are available as well as where they are scarce there often remains a need for additional natural and professional care-giving resources. The regular opportunity to address a wide local audience via community television makes it possible for the mental health worker (1) to alert community members of pressing service needs, (2) to encourage participation in voluntary mutual-help groups or in public and private care-giving agencies and, when warranted, (3) to raise funds for the operation of needed service programs.

Advocacy for Social Planning and Social Change. Some problems which come to the attention of mental health professionals are more the consequence of malfunctioning social and economic systems than of maladaptive personality systems. The resolution of these problems typically follows more from a social change than from personality change, situational adjustment or the development of new resources. Community television provides the mental health professional with an opportunity to publicly advocate relevant social change.

A MODEL FOR MENTAL HEALTH PROGRAMMING ON COMMUNITY TELEVISION*

The model currently suggested includes several of the above listed service segments combined to address a variety of audiences. The objectives of this model are to achieve increased community awareness of and sensitivity to mental health issues and resources and, when warranted, to provide preventive intervention to at-risk groups, to present strategies for personal growth, to stimulate care-giving systems, and to advocate social change. The tasks to which the mental health professional will have to address himself in order to accomplish these mental health education and community development goals via community television are outlined below.

Contract Negotiation

In the preliminary meetings between representatives of the mental health agency and the community television management two issues should be resolved: (1) the frequency and regularity of mental health programming and (2) the roles of the mental health and television personnel in planning, implementing and evaluating the effectiveness of these programs.

The amount of time made available for televised programming could range from thirty minutes to twenty or more hours a month. One to four hours a month spread over two to four programs would be satisfactory for the application of the present model. Over several years the availability of reusable taped sequences from prior programs and of previously collected information on a variety of issues will result in a decrease in the amount of effort required for the representation of some formerly discussed topics and an increase in the amount of television time which can be effectively utilized.

There are no fixed rules for determining the roles of the mental health and television professionals in planning for, implementing or appearing on the televised programs. There are a range of roles available to the mental health worker including the following: technical consultant, liaison with other professional and nonprofessional spokesmen on mental health issues, guest commentator, or moderator of the program.

While no fixed rules apply, some pitfalls can be avoided. By far the best choice as regular program moderator is an intelligent, confident and skilled interviewer who is attractive and familiar to the audience. Since mass audiences tend to prefer

*The author wishes to acknowledge the contributions of Dr. S. Robert Sheridan, director of the Tri-City Mental Health Center, Malden, Massachusetts, and of Mr. Howard Kaye, Jr. formerly of Cablevision Corporation of America-Malden Cablevision, in the development and implementation of this model.

entertainment to educational programming (Bogart, 1968), the more personable the moderator, the more effective the communication. The choice for moderator among a well-informed professional television interviewer, a well-practiced mental health worker, and even a talented community representative might ultimately depend on issues of personal interest, audience recognition or community trust.

One approach that can be especially effective is the sharing of the role of moderator between a mental health worker and either a television professional or a community representative. Sharing the duties of moderator provides the mental health worker with an opportunity to assume different professional roles (e.g., educator, clinician, advocate, etc.) when discussing different mental health topics.

Program Planning

Once these preliminary negotiations have been completed, the program planning and implementation phases can begin. The planning tasks will tend to be recurring functions and will need to be addressed for each new topic. Figure 1 represents a schematization of the series of tasks which constitute the planning phase of program development, and serves as a partial outline for the following discussion.

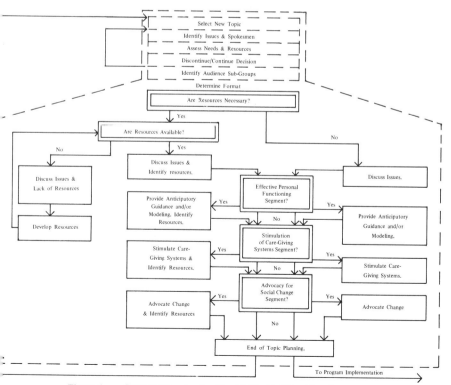

Figure 1   Steps in Planning for Mental Health Television Programs

Selection of Topic. The selection of salient topics which not only address relevant individual and community concerns but also stimulate viewer interest and vicarious participation is the major task of the mental health professional, regardless of his other roles. While a new crop of relevant or "in" issues come to public attention each year, these issues quickly become deleted or depleted, and there remains the task of providing for twelve months of television programming. Where does the mental health professional get more material?

The answer lies within the daily professional and personal contacts of the mental-health worker. Why are individuals being referred to local mental-health and other human service agencies? What issues are discussed in consultation with other professionals? A review of recent agency records will generate a list of problems, complaints and symptoms which might include such potential topics as enuresis, family disharmony, child abuse, acute grief, school phobia, work failure, depression, sexual impotence, etc.

What problems confront or will soon confront the community? The agenda of the meetings of local civic organizations and state human services agencies, as well as media reports of new state and federal policy decisions, are additional sources of potential topics. The issues discussed in these settings might range from the increased incidence of pregnancy among high school girls to the proposed deinstitutionalization of the state mental health system and to changes in the availability of federal or state funds for programs serving high-risk groups.

Many topics are suggested by the predictable developmental crises and critical role transitions chronicled by Erikson (1959) and Rapoport (1964), and by the accidental and situational crises described by Lindemann (1944), Caplan (1964) and others. Another source is the list of life change events compiled by Holmes and Rahe (1967).

The scheduling of topics can be very important in the overall effectiveness of the presentation. When the impact of an identified community concern or individual crisis is predictable, relevant television service segments (e. g., advocacy for change or anticipatory guidance) can be implemented at the time of maximum effectiveness. For example, general information, anticipatory guidance and modeling segments dealing with children's and parents' reactions to school entry are much more relevant and effective when presented in early and mid-September than in early February or mid-July. Likewise, other separation-related topics such as going on vacation, leaving school or getting married are more timely in late May and June than during October or March.

Identification of Issues and Appropriate Spokesman. Once a potential topic has been selected, the mental health professional should begin to gather information concerning the relevant subtopics and points of view associated with this topic, and to identify responsible spokesman for the varying perspectives. Whenever possible, local spokesmen who are familiar to the audience and respected by them should be included.

The systematic accumulation of information relevant to the proposed topic helps the mental health worker to identify the range of salient issues which can effectively be presented to the community television audience, and helps him to determine the number of programs which will be necessary for the successful and complete presentation of this topic.

Assessment of Community Needs and Resources. The presentation of mental health information, and especially the delineation of strategies for effective personal functioning to a large and anonymous audience, frequently results in increased demands for mental health and other human services. To directly or indirectly raise the prospect of assistance with personal problems in the absence of sufficient and appropriate resources can promote personal frustration and community resentment. Therefore, an important phase of program planning is the assessment both of current and anticipated needs for mental health and related human services and of the availability of appropriate resources to satisfy these needs.

Such an assessment also supplies the mental health professional with the major criteria for determining whether the televised programming should emphasize the more efficient use of existing resources, the development of new resources or social change.

Decision: Discontinue or Continue Planning. Up to this point the mental health professional has accumulated a considerable amount of information relating to a specified mental health topic. He has identified a variety of points of view, along with their spokesman, generating a series of judgments concerning the most important issues for presentation and an estimate of the number of program hours that will be required to satisfactorily present this topic. He has also assessed the necessity for and availability of mental-health and related human services, especially those services for which the presentation of this topic might generate an increased demand.

With this information, the team of mental-health and television professionals should decide whether to discontinue or continue planning for a presentation of the topic at hand. This decision will depend primarily on their assessments of the salience and feasibility of presenting this topic on community television and of the availability of necessary follow-up services.

Nonsalient topics should not be presented. Other topics, like sexual perversion, may prove to be salient but, depending upon local mores, might not be feasible topics for investigation and discussion on community television.

Where follow-up services are not necessary, as well as where they are both necessary and available, the decision of whether or not to continue with program planning will depend primarily on the judgments of salience and feasibility. Where suitable resources are required but are not available, the program format should be limited to general information and resource development segments. If this format is judged to be too restrictive, then a new topic should be selected. In all cases the decision to discontinue planning leads to the selection of a new topic. The decision to continue leads to the final planning stages: the identification of relevant audience subgroups and the determination of program format.

Identification of Audience Subgroups. The mass media audience is composed of a variety of culturally and functionally defined subgroups. Since diverse groups have different needs and different interests, target groups to whom the various service segments will be addressed should be identified early so that a relevant format can be developed. Problems of school entry, for example, affect the lives and roles of the students, their parents, their teachers, school officials and, indirectly, the other citizens in the community. But the impact of this problem is rarely felt by all groups with equal interest or intensity. The ultimate format for a series of televised programs on school entry problems would depend partially on the choice of audience subgroups to which the presentation would be addressed.

Determination of Format. The final format of a series of television programs highlighting a specific mental-health or community issue will be determined by the answers to the following set of questions.

(1) *What are the limitations to the presentation of this topic?* For any series of programs the absence of representative spokesmen, talented models or relevant audio-visual materials limits the range of service segments which can be included. The lack of necessary human service follow-up resources limits the program format to a discussion of general issues, a recognition of the unavailability of these services, and strategies for the development of these resources.
ailability of these services, and strategies for the development of these resources.

(2) *What service segments should be included in the presentation?* The goals of the presentation, the range of audience subgroups to be served and the limitations of resources and facilities noted above will determine the types of service segments which can be included in the televised programming. All series should include a general informational segment. Those series that are addressed to at-risk populations can include an anticipatory guidance segment. Modeling segments can be included as an anticipatory guidance technique or to stimulate self-directed activities. Where mental health or human service resources are inadequate, care-giving systems can be encouraged. Social planning and social change can be advocated where oppressive social and economic conditions prevail.

(3) *How shall fiscal, temporal, personnel and audio-visual supplies and resources be utilized?* How shall the following format types be distributed over the several programs scheduled for this topic: lecture, dialogue, group discussion, site-visit, prepared audio-visual materials?

Because of limited funds the format of most programs will be restricted to interviews with and discussions among interested and informed consumers, citizen representatives, government officials, and formal and informal care givers. However, when additional funds are available, many program series can be greatly enhanced by the utilization of existing mental health films. The presentation of ''A Two-Year-Old Goes to Hospital'' (James Robertson, 1952) or ''Children in the Hospital'' (Edward A. Mason, M.D., 1962) would provide an engrossing counterpoint to a discussion of the various aspects of childhood separations, or, more pointedly, of the effects of hospitalization on children. Likewise, "Widows" (Edward A. Mason, M.D., 1972) would be a sensitive and sensible addition to a series of televised programs on the topic of bereavement.

Program Implementation

While the technical aspects of program production are the province of the television professionals, the program moderator should assume three major responsibilities in inplementing the program plans.

First, he should be responsible for safeguarding the privacy of individual citizens. Prior authorization for inclusion of filmed or videotaped sequences should be obtained from all persons who appear in these sequences. When case records are discussed, names and events should be changed to assure the anonymity of the clients.

Secondly, the moderator should inform all guest participants of the scope of the present series of programs as well as of their anticipated contributions. Whenever possible, participants should have an opportunity to view previous programs in the current series.

Finally, the moderator is responsible for maintaining an impressive and informative program which does not exceed audience comprehension or community norms. He should be especially alert to the use of jargon, always translating it into terms familiar to the audience.

Program Evaluation

Unlike a presentation to the local PTA at the school auditorium, the model for television mental health programming presented here can become very expensive. Even when produced as a public service by the community television management, professional planning and implementation time can range in cost from $30 to $100 per hour of televised programming. When not provided as a public service, studio rental and videotape recorder rental costs range from $75 to $200 an hour. But also unlike the school hall talk, community television places the mental health professional in simultaneous contact with several thousand community members.

A service delivery system of this cost and range warrants regular evaluation of its effectiveness. Regular surveys of audience participation should be of mutual interest to both the television and mental health professionals.

Reports of the activities of local mental health and human service agencies will provide information concerning how well the goals of early case finding and more appropriate utilization of existing service resources have been realized. Using a sequential time-sampling technique, the rate of referrals related to topics discussed on television can be recorded for several weeks before and after relevant television presentation. Changes in this rate during and after the programming will provide an indicator of the effectiveness and impact of the presentation of that topic. In a similar manner the effectiveness of the stimulation of care-giving systems segments can be evaluated through reports of increased citizen participation in care-giving agencies and voluntary groups.

Because radio also directs public interest communications, including mental health programs, to groups of persons at home and in other private settings it is also reasonable to evaluate whether the impact of the video component of community television is sufficient to offset the additional effort and expense required to provide audio-visual programming. When community television programs are little more than radio with pictures, the result of such an evaluation will most likely be negative. But when community television is used to familiarize community members with local care-giving agents and agencies, and to provide individuals at risk of ineffective personal functioning or of mental disorder with visual models coping effectively with life's hazards and responsibilities and, when necessary, navigating the network of available human service resources, the additional time and money will hopefully be found to have been well spent. The chance to deliver these kinds of visual as well as verbal messages to individuals in their own homes is the real challenge and opportunity of community television.

BIBLIOGRAPHY

Bogart, L. Social sciences in the mass media. In F. Yu (ed.), *Behavioral sciences and mass media*. New York: Russell Sage, 1968.

Caplan, G. Emotional crises. In A. Deutsch and H. Fishbein (eds.), *The Encyclopedia of Mental Health*. New York: Franklin Watts, Inc., 1963.

Caplan, G. *Principles of Preventive Psychiatry*. New York: Basic Books, 1964.

Coltman, R. TICCIT and beyond. *Mitre Matrix*, 1972, *5*, (No. 6), 23-38.

Crichton, M. *Five Patients*. New York: Knopf, 1970.

Erikson, E. H. *Childhood and Society*. New York: Norton, 1950.

Erikson, E. H. Identity and the Life Cycle. *Psychol. Issues Monogr.*, 1959, *1*, No. 1 New York: International Universities Press.

Holmes, T. H., and Rahe, R. H. The social readjustment rating scale. *J. Psychosom. Res.*, 1967, *11*, 213.

Lindemann, E. Symptomatology and management of acute grief. *Amer. J. Psychiat.*, 1944, *101*, 141-148.

Nunnally, J. C. *Popular Conceptions of Mental Health*. New York: Holt, Rinehart & Winston, 1961.

Rapoport, Rhona V. Transition from engagement to marriage. *Acta Sociol.*, 1964, *8*, 1-2.

Sloan Commission on Cable Communications. *On the Cable: The Television of Abundance*. New York: McGraw-Hill, 1971.

Tyhurst, J. S. The role of transition states—including disasters—in mental illness. In *Symposium on preventive and social psychiatry*. Sponsored jointly by the Walter Reed Army Institute of Research, Walter Reed Army Medical Center, and the National Research Council, April 15-17, 1957, Walter Reed Army Institute of Research, Washington, D. C.: U. S. Government Printing Office, 1958, pp. 149-169.

13

Preventive Programs and Strategies

SANDRA RASMUSSEN

INTRODUCTION

Four of the five essential services required for federal assistance under the Community Mental Health Centers Act of 1963 and its amendments focused on new methods of treatment and care; the fifth service, consultation and education, was concerned with the prevention of mental illness and the promotion of mental health. Yet, according to Goldston and Brown (in press), the current status of preventive efforts is limited when viewed in terms of the resources devoted to consultation and education services. They cited a 1971 National Institute of Mental Health report which indicated that 4.7 percent of all expenditures and 6.6 percent of the total staff time in 205 community mental health centers were devoted to consultation and education services. This proportion of staff time coincided with an approximation given in a study by the Joint Information Service conducted in 1969 that 5 percent of centers' staff time overall was devoted to prevention.

Findings from the most recent NIMH survey were similar. Based on data provided by 325 federally funded Community Mental Health Centers, consultation and education services accounted for 5.5 percent of total staff time and earned .3 percent of total center revenue (about one million dollars). There was considerable variation among centers in the extent to which staff time was invested in consultation activities. The number of hours devoted to consultation and education services during the sample month, *viz.*, February 1973 ranged between 7 and 9752. In comparison with the other mandated services, consultation and education ranked fourth in percent utilization of staff hours, exceeded by all except emergency services. Consultation and education commanded 5.5 percent of total staff hours as compared with inpatient care, 32.2 percent; outpatient care, 20.6 percent; partial care, 13.7; and emergency service, 4.8 percent.

Is prevention of mental illness and promotion of mental health rhetoric or reality? Is prevention fiction or fact? Is it propaganda or program?

DEFINITIONS AND ASSUMPTIONS

The term "prevention" as used in this chapter refers to primary prevention; it means (1) trying to change situations which contribute to the development of mental and emotional illnesses, and (2) working directly with people who are at high risk of developing mental and emotional disorders if nothing is done. This definition is consistent with public health usage of the term. It is consonant with the definition articulated by Caplan and Grunebaum (1972):

> Prevention is aimed at reducing the incidence of mental problems and breakdowns (primary prevention), preventing incipient problems from becoming worse (secondary prevention), and stabilizing people who have had an emotional disorder, received treatment, and are now back in the community (tertiary prevention).

Two assumptions—perhaps biases—influenced the design of this chapter, and they must be acknowledged initially. First, consultation and education services per se are limited as an indicator of the extent and nature of mental health prevention activities. Second, many human service agencies are involved directly and indirectly with the prevention of mental illness and the promotion of mental health.

PREVENTIVE PROGRAMS

In 1973 a questionnaire about primary prevention programs and ideas was developed and circulated to state agencies responsible for the planning and delivery of health care. Because of the preventive aspects of certain social and rehabilitation service programs (e. g., Title XIX, Early and Periodic Screening, Diagnosis, and Treatment—EPSDT), information from SRS agencies was desirable. However, because responsibility for SRS programs varied greatly from state to state, the questionnaire was sent only to the ten regional commissioners of Social and Rehabilitation. It was assumed that many human services agencies are involved directly and indirectly in mental health primary prevention (e.g., education, labor, corrections, vocational rehabilitation); however, the study was limited to the nature of prevention programs and ideas among health agencies per se.

A cover letter explained the purpose of the query, identified the agencies being contacted, and included a definition of primary prevention. Letters and questionnaires were mailed to 243 agencies. Some 119 replies from 46 different states, territories and the District of Columbia were received. A return cover letter accompanied most of the responses; comments on questionnaires were frequent and detailed. Approximately one-third of the respondents included pamphlets, reports and publications.

Primary prevention was reported to be a program objective by 102 of 119 respondents; it was considered to be a program of priority by 96 respondents. A great variety of preventive programs were described. There was a tendency, however, for the programs to cluster around categories of maternal and child health (parenting), prevention of alcoholism and drug abuse, screening of high risk populations, health education, and support of health maintenance organizations.

Some of the preventive programs described by state Departments or Divisions of Mental Health included the following:

> During the past year, a Mental Health Division task force explored models of prevention and made recommendations. During the 1973 legislative session, significant legislation was passed and funds appropriated for primary prevention in alcoholism and drug dependency. It is a priority toward implementation during the 1973-75 biennium. This will consist of primary prevention projects funded with $250,000 appropriated by the legislature. (Oregon)

Vermont described its mental health prevention activities as including:

> —cooperation and participation with infant and pre-school screening
> —treatment, diagnostic, and consultative services to schools
> —pre-marital, pre-natal, couple, parents, etc. education
> —service (crisis intervention) to select groups under stress, i.e. parents at birth of defective child, surviving spouse, retirement, etc.
> —aggressive outreach to families in their homes
> —advocacy for sufficient income, adequate nutrition, prompt legal assistance, decent housing, etc.

South Carolina reported:

> For ten years we have had a special primary prevention program in a school district. It operates from a crisis intervention stance. In 1967 it won the American Psychiatric Gold Award as the best project in the National competition. During the past four years the project has focused on the junior high school/middle school as a life space area.

In Colorado, preventive programs were described as relating to parent effectiveness training, child rearing, classes for expectant parents, premarital counseling, and services made available to school districts by various mental health centers and clinics. Arizona reported:

> About six months ago at Apache County we began a program educating mothers and mothers-to-be in the rudiments of effective parenthood. At another clinic we currently have under way a community survey of needs of the elderly. We hope this will lead us to supportive services which will prevent breakdown of independent living. We plan to emphasize child advocacy programs during the next two years.

Kentucky described an active preventive program:

> We maintain a $150,000 annual program through the Department's Office of Preventive Programs. The Director reports directly to the Commissioner. We generate media compaigns, originate brochures, public displays, etc., and pursue a rigorous public education approach.

Consultation and education, especially to schools and community groups, was reported by many states as a mental health preventive effort. *Pierre the Pelican,* the educational series for new parents, and *Inside Out,* the mental health curriculum for elementary grade children, were reported in use by several states.

Preventive programs identified by Social and Rehabilitation Service included:

—EPSDT (Early and Periodic Screening, Diagnosis and Treatment)
—Family planning
—Home-management services
—Delinquency prevention programs
—Day care for elderly
—HMO development
—Parental capacity building
—Early child development educational services
—Rehabilitation services under the Vocational Rehabilitation Act
—Work incentive services

Several of the regional medical programs reported programs that focused on high-risk populations, e.g., a multiphasic screening project for an urban black population in Memphis and one for rural counties in north Mississippi. (Memphis Regional Medical Program) The Allegany County Mobile Health Unit provided health education and screening services to isolated rural communities in a predominantly rural county of western New York. (Lakes Area Regional Medical Program) In addition, a nurse was supported in their Family Practice Center to work as a team member with physicians making neighborhood contacts with a heavy emphasis on preventive health activities. Intervention with a high-risk population was exemplified by the Nebraska Migrant Health Program. During the eight-week "migrant season," emphasis was placed upon health education for the workers and their families and acquainting them with available health services in Nebraska. Environmental health programs, e.g., minimum housing code enforcement, satisfactory recreational facilities, mobile home safety, institutional health and safety, were described by several health departments as preventive efforts. (Virginia, South Carolina, Kansas, Nebraska) And in a few states, such as Wisconsin, the comment was made: "all of our programs have a primary prevention component." The table of contents of the report *Toward Preventing Social Health Problems: Interim Report* (1972) supported the statement:

Conceptual Scheme and Assumptions
Conceptual scheme—major elements
Conceptual scheme—subsidiary elements
Principles and assumptions
Poverty and prevention
Public Action for Delinquency Prevention
Preventive Action for Older Adults
Preventive Action in Family Services

Preventive Action in Rehabilitation
Preventive Action in Health
Actions to Prevent Mental Retardation
Action to Prevent Alcohol Abuse and Alcoholism
Action to Prevent Mental Illness/Emotional Disturbance
Preventive Action at Department and State Levels
Appendices

The first assumption, that consultation and education services per se are limited as an indicator of the extent and nature of mental health prevention activities, was confirmed by the questionnaire survey; the preventive programs described were far more extensive than that of consultation and education alone. The great majority of respondents indicated that preventive programming was an interagency collaborative effort, thus confirming the second assumption, that many human service agencies are involved directly and indirectly with the prevention of mental illness and the promotion of mental health. Furthermore, in response to the question, "Whose business is primary prevention?" the most frequent answer was "everyone's."

> The individual, his health educator or guide, his health counselor or the organization which treats him or diagnoses his condition, components of the health industry, media which disseminate information, employers who must protect a personnel investment, local governments responsible for municipal services, eduational institutions responsible for teaching about personal health or training health industry workers, and official agencies. In short, everyone's. (New York Department of Public Health)

Many agencies, however, identified the need for a "lead agency, a responsible agency" to coordinate preventive efforts.

The most common problem, as reported by the health agencies surveyed, in the beginning or planning of primary prevention programs, was lack of funds. Other barriers to the development of preventive programs mentioned frequently were lack of qualified staff; resistance toward prevention by health professionals, especially private physicians; reluctance of legislators to fund long-term programs; public ignorance or apathy about primary prevention; and failure to "sell" primary prevention to the community as well as to those in power (top administrators and legislators). It is interesting to note that many respondents assumed personal and/or professional responsibility for failure to advocate effectively for preventive programs.

The three most frequent answers to the question, "What evaluative measures are you using or developing to determine the human and economic effectiveness of primary prevention programs?" were:

—none
—mortality, morbidity statistics; hospital admission rates
—we are developing evaluative measures now

Use of less traditional evaluative measures was reported by several states. For example, the Kentucky Office of Primary Prevention in the Department of Mental Health stated that their Office of Program Analysis is working on follow-up, i.e., pre- and post-campaign attitude surveys, as well as incidence and prevalence rates, vital statistics and public reaction. In Connecticut, evaluation included use of data to assess reduction in morbidity and mortality of certain diseases, reduction in hospitalization for certain diseases, reduction in absenteeism for certain diseases, changes in death rates for certain diseases. Number of work days lost per year from illness or disability was one evaluative measure in use in New Mexico. In Massachusetts, all of the primary prevention demonstration programs developed in conjunction with the Office of Prevention of the Department of Mental Health utilized control and experimental groups in program evaluation. Michigan reported use of "Impact Indicators" to measure the effect of a particular effort on the problem. This also involved the identification of measurable aspects or factors in the intervention situation. Pennsylvania acknowledged use of normal statistical data, yet reported that an application had been submitted for federal funding to plan and develop a state-wide data and information system for program evaluation. One example of evaluation based upon epidemiological surveys was reported by the Lakes Area Regional Medical Program. The Mobile Health Unit Project included a sample survey of the population to be served prior to initiation of the Unit. Subsequent surveys were planned to measure the changes in knowledge and attitudes from the original survey.

Based primarily on findings from the questionnaire survey, conclusions reached about the nature and extent of preventive programs were as follows:
1. Preventive programs were considered an objective and priority by most health agencies.
2. Preventive programs were varied and innovative.
3. Most frequently, preventive programs were interagency collaborative efforts.
4. Lack of funding hampered extension and expansion of preventive programs.
5. Sound evaluation of preventive programs was beginning.
6. Prevention is "everyone's business."

While there was no base line data with which to compare the questionnaire survey findings, it seemed that interest in primary prevention was high and preventive programs were increasing.

PREVENTIVE STRATEGIES

The following section identifies and describes strategies—practical, economic and ideological—that can prove useful in the development, extension, expansion and evaluation of preventive programs. The suggestions are based on the knowledge and experiences of many individuals; however, they are neither exhaustive nor representive of all current thinking about preventive programming.

Obtain sanction for prevention. It is desirable that sanction for preventive programs be legitimate and public, that is, that it come from those speaking for the mental health establishment (both public and private sectors), and that this sanction be overt and open. Lack of such legitimate and public sanction, however, is no reason to abandon or postpone planning for prevention. It only means that alternative, extra-system, covert sponsors and spokesmen for prevention need to be found to ground the effort. Such swimming upstream can be exhilarating, but over a long period of time may prove exhausting. Certainly the emphasis on consultation and education services and the new Section 204 (Grants for Consultation and Education Services) of the Community Mental Health Centers Amendments of 1975 increase federal sanction for prevention.

Plan preventive programs on the basis of identified needs, defined problems. In most communities, "felt needs" are known and common problems can be identified. The demographic make-up of many inner city and rural catchment areas has prompted mental health personnel to address themselves to program development for populations at risk; preventive programs, by necessity, have come to have high human and economic priority. Psychiatric epidemiological identification of needs—more precise descriptions of the populations at risk, delineation of risk factors—is recommended, however, for planning appropriate intervention and especially for evaluating outcome.

Initiate interagency collaborative efforts to implement preventive programs; participate actively in preventive programs spearheaded by other human service agencies. In general, a problem-solving approach to preventive program development requires interagency collaboration. Too frequently, however, mental health practitioners have remained aloof, distant and uninvolved.

Some will argue strongly that prevention ought to develop as a mental health speciality. Granted, on paper, consultation and education is *one of five* essential mental health services. Yet the possibility of consultation and education being on a par with the other four services in terms of expenditures and staff time, let alone being co-equal to therapeutic activities, as Goldston and Brown anticipate, is remote. In addition, I contend that the development of such a prevention empire *within* mental health is undesirable.

Include a rigorous evaluative component in every preventive program. Evaluation of prevention *is* possible. The notion that it is impossible to prove the merits of prevention has been used too often as an excuse to "prevent prevention." The literature on evaluative research in general, as well as the practical use of psychiatric epidemiology for evaluative purposes, has increased markedly in the last decade.

Advocate preventive programs that are politically popular, safe and sound. Prevention of alcoholism and drug dependency, and mental health programs for children, are good for "openers." Several state legislatures have appropriated monies to implement prevention programs to prevent alcoholism and drug dependency; an increasing number of states are using existing federal and state drug monies for prevention. The heavy emphasis on prevention in the report of the Joint Commission on Mental Health of Children underscores the political salience of mental health programs for children. The number one priority of the National Institute of Mental Health is child mental health with two major goals: the development of preventive programs that will reach out to children and their families in their every-day life settings; and the provision of appropriate clinical service to ill and disturbed children. The recent publication of the National Association for Mental Health, Inc., of *Action Guidelines* chose to focus on primary prevention of mental disorders with emphasis on prenatal and perinatal periods.

Support efforts to make prevention profitable. Illness in general, and mental illness in particular, is an extremely profitable commodity. According to Graziano (1972), "In the mental-health industry, illness is our most important product." There is voiced concern about the increasing cost of health care; some people are raising an even more basic question: "What are we getting for our money?" Yet it is doubtful that economic reasons in and of themselves will convince American politicians that preventive programs are desirable as long as diagnostic, treatment and, to some extent, rehabilitative modalities are so profitable to so many. When I questioned a dentist colleague of mine as to why preventive dentistry was so well developed, in contrast to preventive health programs in general and mental health programs in particular, he stated: "First of all, we dentists have more business than we can handle. Second, we can make money from preventive services, for example, dental hygiene, plaque control. Third, we had a few crusaders who really believed in preventive dentistry who became national circuit riders for the cause. And finally, I guess it is good for people." I would suggest that, in the future, prevention of mental illness and promotion of mental health will become a profitable commodity on the American scene. Hopefully, it will become an integral part of group practice health programs and health maintenance organizations. Crass as it may seem, for those of us committed to prevention who happen to live in an economic society, support for efforts to make prevention profitable are legitimate. (Hopefully, they are interim in nature.)

Work toward an ideology that embraces the notion that people are healthy, whole, good and social. The United States is part of a culture, actually a civilization, in which an illness norm rather than a health norm predominates. People are considered broken, alienated, fallen, bad, sinful, evil, etc. In general, individuals have learned to cope with or adapt to these given, accepted negative phenomena of existence. Elaborate social systems have developed to reinforce this norm of illness: the church, the legal system, the military, the state and the health industry itself. Contemporary media feed this sentiment directly. As a strategy, work toward an ideology that embraces the notion that people are healthy, whole, good and social is less specific and more controversial than former recommendations. I believe that it is fundamental, however, if promotion of mental health and the prevention of mental illness is an objective.

SUMMARY

This chapter describes preventive programs and strategies. Prevention is defined as trying to change situations which contribute to the development of mental and emotional illnesses, and working directly with "O.K." people who are at high risk of developing mental and emotional disorders if nothing is done.

Preventive programs are considered an objective and priority by most health agencies; programs are varied and innovative; most frequently, programs are interagency collaborative efforts. Sound evaluation of preventive programs is developing. Although prevention is recognized as "everyone's business, " lack of funding hampers program development.

Suggested strategies to develop preventive programs include:

—Obtain sanction for prevention.

—Plan preventive programs on the basis of identified needs, defined problems.

—Initiate interagency collaborative efforts to implement preventive programs; participate actively in preventive programs spearheaded by other human service agencies.

—Include a rigorous evaluative component in every preventive program.

—Advocate preventive programs that are politically popular, safe and sound.

—Support efforts to make prevention profitable.

—Work toward an ideology that embraces the nation that people are healthy, whole, good and social.

BIBLIOGRAPHY

Action Guidelines: Primary Prevention of Mental Disorders with Emphasis on Prenatal and Perinatal Periods. Arlington: The National Association for Mental Health, Inc., 1974.

Caplan, G., and Grunebaum, H. Perspectives on Primary Prevention: A Review. In Gottesfeld, H. (ed.), *The Critical Issues of Community Mental Health.* New York: Behavioral Publications, 1972.

Community Mental Health Centers Amendments of 1975, Title III, Public Law 94-63. Section-by-Section Summary Highlighted with Extracts from the Legislative History. Morris Associates, Inc.: Washington, D.C., 1975.

Consultation and Education: A Service of the Community Mental Health Center. Public Health Service Publication No. 1478, 1969.

Consultation and Education Services Community Mental Health Health Centers - January 1970. Statistical Note 43, National Institute of Mental Health, Biometry Branch, February 1971.

Consultation and Education Services Federally Funded Community Mental Health Centers 1973. Statistical Note 108, National Institute of Mental Health, Biometry Branch, September 1974.

Consultation in Mental Health and Related Fields: A Reference Guide. Public Health Service Publication No. 1920, 1969.

Consultation Research in Mental Health and Related Fields. Public Health Service Publication No. 2122, 1971.

Expenditures and Sources of Funds - Federally Funded Community Mental Health Centers 1969. Statistical Note 42, National Institute of Mental Health, Biometry Branch, February 1971.

Graziano, A. M. In the mental-health industry, illness is our most important product. *Psychology Today,* 1972, *5,* 12-18.

Goldston, S.T. and Brown, B.S. Prevention Today and Tomorrow in Otto, H.S., and Lewis, A.J. (eds.).*Preventive Programs: The Growing Edge in Mental Health, Vol. I.* La Jolla: The National Center for the exploration of Human Potential (in press).

Joint Commission on the Mental Health of Children. *Crisis in Child Mental Health: Challenge for 1970s.* New York: Harper & Row, 1970.

Rasmussen, S. *Preventive Health Services: Preventive Medicine* (A selected bibliography). Harvard School of Public Health, Department of Behavioral Sciences, 1973.

Rasmussen, S. *Primary Prevention: Programs and Ideas* (A report of a national questionnaire survey). Massachusetts Department of Mental Health, Office of Prevention, 1974.

The Practice of Mental Health Consultation. DHEW Publication No. (ADM) 74-112, 1975.

The Scope of Community Mental Health Consultation and Education. DHEW Publication No. (NIH) 74-650, 1974.

Toward Preventing Social and Health Problems: Interim Report. Wisconsin Department of Public Health, 1972.

Part IV

Themes of the
Mid-Seventies

Our national ideology is changing. With changing values, new expectations are emerging. Buffeted by multiple crises, our citizens are no longer content to accept dependency-reinforcing styles of leadership. Harris polls conducted from 1966 through 1973 have shown remarkable declines in the "level of confidence" in leaders or agencies that have traditionally wielded influence in the society. Confidence has declined in all sectors from political and business leaders to physicians and psychiatrists. Credibility has been challenged, and the ability of human service providers to represent interests other than their own has been called into serious question. The paternalism of leaders and service providers who have expected of themselves—and, often, have been expected—to decide for others what was best for them is being attacked. The expectations of constituents, citizens and service consumers have changed; increasingly they expect—and sometimes demand—involvement in their own fate and destiny, in decisions that concern them. They have raised new definitions of the rights of citizens and of consumers: to everything from information and quality assurance to privacy and confidentiality.

Some consumers of human services have developed or sought "alternatives" to existing modes of professional service. They have resisted the *content* of services, the *presentation* of services and the role *expectations* of service providers. Declining preferred roles as consumers, clients or patients, they have sought help free of existing professional trappings and encumbrances. In consequence, we have witnessed the emergence of alternative agencies and mutual help groups. Some professionals have united with consumers to question the "clinical" assumptions held by mental health practitioners about problems of human distress. They have, in effect, pressed for alternatives to the profession's institutionalized principles and practices.

In this section, we analyze changes in citizen attitudes and consider themes pressing increasingly upon the consciousness of concerned human service professionals. We have distilled four such major themes: mutual help; the rights of privacy, professional confidentiality; citizen participation; and the implications of general systems theory for mental health services.

Silverman's chapter develops themes of amateurism, mutual help and support systems. She discusses self-help groups available to people with widely varied problems. These include smoking, obesity, burn disfigurement and ileostomy. Some groups help people cope with tasks of transition but, unlike those described by Hirschowitz, are led by amateur "veterans" of the transition. However, more typically, the "mutual help" vehicles she describes serve people coping with prolonged or chronic deficit conditions such as alcoholism or mental retardation. She also discusses groups that provide "mutual help" support linkages for the family members of people with disability. In dissecting the "amateur" aspects of mutual help, she warns of the danger of its distortion by professional annexationism. She suggests that mental health professionals provide support and consultation to "self-help" groups without trespassing on amateurs' "ownership" of their self-help structures. Her "widow-to-widow project" illustrates such synergistic collaboration between professionals, successful veterans and the newly widowed. Her chapter makes a compelling point: amateur helpers are little different from professionals in being helped by giving help.

DeMarneffe reminds us of the general public's consistently high expectation that the doctor, like the minister, be relied upon to respect confidentiality. At a time when citizen groups are vigorously asserting rights to privacy, we deem it useful to record the many safeguards built into the protection of confidentiality for mentally ill patients. It is encouraging to note the strong support for privacy provided by both medical tradition and the law. DeMarneffe describes the supportive legislation, advocating that responsible mental health professionals resist attempts by powerful groups (often, law enforcement agencies) to coerce them into the violation of citizen-patient rights. He describes such coercive gambits, and how to combat them.

Warren, in his chapter on citizen participation, raises crucial questions for mental health agencies such as these: who represents whom? who can legitimately claim to advocate on behalf of what consumers? how are the differing perceptions of citizens, users and service providers in the public mental health sector to be reconciled?

He describes the gulf between the concept and intent of "citizen participation" and its translation into action by different groups. In noting the posture of mental health agencies, he contrasts very significant differences between citizen participation as viewed by agencies, on the one hand, and by citizens, especially low-income citizens, on the other. He calls their respective translations of citizen participation "citizen involvement" and "citizen action."

For mental health agencies and professions, *citizen involvement* views citizens as service *users* who can provide some useful consumer input but are not expected to call agency legitimation or expertise into question. Policy and its implementation are held to be professional prerogatives. It is therefore expected that citizen participation be heavily colored by the values of agency professionals. Low-income citizens decline these proferred roles as compliant consumers. They refuse to be "patient" and they actively demand *citizen action*. Citizen participation is negotiated as "power to the people." Citizen *action* is demonstrated by attempts to direct decisions about turf and resources; in effect, they seek citizen *control* over agency behavior. As citizens asserting their rights, they often see agencies as adversaries, not legitimated service "providers."

Clearly, the gulf is wide. Understanding this gulf and the differences between the "appreciative systems" of agency professionals and low-income citizens may make it possible for Warren's plea for the elaboration of crisper citizen participation guidelines to be met.

In our final chapter, we recognize the relevance and application of systems theory to mental health services. *Clark's* concepts serve to anchor and organize our approach to the interaction between organization, organism and environment. The complexity of the interdependent factors operating in a social field to prevent, promote or combat behavioral deviance is captured within an integrative general systems model. This model has practical relevance for the delivery of direct, indirect and preventive services and is applicable to both macrosystems (populations) and microsystems (individuals). In addressing the needs of any single individual, he points to the need for appraisal of the troubled person's social context and network so that leverage is applied at points in the social field where effective results can be achieved at least cost. Clark thus provides conceptual foundations for an applied ecological systems theory.

In addition to emphasizing the influence and potential impact of environmental forces and "significant others" upon patient careers, he emphasizes the interdependence of agencies and political constituencies in the sanctioning and planning of mental health programs.

14

Mutual Help

PHYLLIS R. SILVERMAN

INTRODUCTION

We are currently witnessing the flowering* of mutual help groups. These involve people with common difficulties developing services to meet their own needs. This chapter is about such groups. I will define mutual help, try to describe what conditions give rise to such organizations, and discuss the unique aspects of the help they offer.

All of us participate in helping interactions, helping networks, in which we are recipients as well as helpers. The help provided is often specific, concrete and directed at aiding an individual improve his situation. Human life is not possible without such helping exchanges. However, such help takes on special meaning when the person helping has experienced the difficulty firsthand, and it is this experience that provides the basis for the help he now offers. This is the unique element of a mutual help exchange. In the process of helping, the helper may still be working through some of his own residual difficulties and therefore derives some help from the process of helping another. Such help can take place in a group setting or in a one-to-one encounter. Because there is a mutual exchange between the formal helper and the individual being helped, I prefer the label "mutual help" rather than that of "self-help," as such efforts, when they become formalized, are more popularly known. Self-help is really a first step** as one becomes aware of one's own problems and moves to do something about it. Once there is a move to involve others so as to learn from them, the concept of mutuality, of exchange, comes into play. This indicates that more than one person is involved with a common problem and there is an opportunity for the help to go two ways.

One manner of understanding people and the problems they may develop in a lifetime is to see them as they move through the human life cycle with all the many role changes involved. These changes can be seen as turning points, movements of

---

*It is not clear to me whether this is a new bloom or is simply that the community of professional observers is larger and more likely to become aware of these groupings as legitimate subjects of their research and involvement. Peyser quoted by Katz wrote in *952 ". . . Associations of people with the same handicap or need have been known throughout the ages and all over the world . . ." (Katz, p. 14) What we see is undoubtedly an extension of this process.

**Gunnar and Rosemary Dybwad of the International Association for Retarded Children made this observation in considering parent involvement in programs for their retarded children.

critical transition, when an individual has to learn to behave in a new situation with a new definition of self. In my experience, mutual help groups seem to evolve at such turning points in an individual's life. They develop at a time when people need to learn to behave differently in a different role. (Silverman and Murrow, 1974)

When people come together in some formal way to find or exchange solutions to common problems, they form mutual help groups. These become mutual help organizations when the process of institutionalization creates a formal organizational structure.

A mutual helping grouping tends to become formalized when need extends to individuals beyond a neighborhood so that it is not possible for these people to come together in natural groupings; when the interest is so great that the number of potential members cannot be absorbed by an informal network; when the problem affects so few people that effort has to be made to reach out and bring them together.

DIFFERENCES BETWEEN VOLUNTARY AGENCIES AND MUTUAL HELP ORGANIZATIONS

It is essential to distinguish mutual help organizations from the typical community voluntary agency. These latter are usually service programs developed by others for a client population. Whether public money or private philanthropies support these agencies, the organizational model is the same (Seeley, et al., 1957, pp. 13-38). Over the last century the development of formal human service agencies was accompanied by a professionalization of the helpers involved. (Greenberg, 1969) This professionalization process seems to coincide with the growing application of scientific thinking to understanding human behavior. Helping became regularized and procedures were developed to make the help more consistent with the current scientific thinking about the cause of special and psychological problems. (Greenberg, 1969; Levine, 1970)

At one time, people's psychological and social needs were met in the context of religious institutions, the family, friendships and the neighborhood. Today, many of these needs are met by professional helpers. It is commonly accepted that "professional training has uniquely fitted one for carrying out mental health services and that anyone who does not have the requisite training not only will not be able to perform such services but will in fact do harm." (Levine, p. 5)

It is easy to see where a conflict could occur between the professionally trained, accredited helper and other helpers over his potential client population.* It is

---

*One reason why professionals fail is suggested by the Levines. They note that the focus and nature of service programs change as the thinking and conditions of society change. In a conservative period, the focus is on changing the individual, on psychotherapeutic interventions, while in a more radical period the professions focus on changing the institutions of society. In the former, the source of difficulty is seen in the individual. One result of this is that the professional trained in one ideological school with the appropriate techniques for that approach may not be able to help in situations whose parameters have different definitions.

fallacious, of course, to think that any one group or groups of experts can solve all human problems. Most people do not abdicate responsibility for dealing with or solving their own problems to others participating in their own helping networks. Such networks depend on the community in which people live, and on ideology and life style. People can petition the professional human service system to change, to more effectively meet their needs or, as is most relevant to this chapter, they can develop their own alternative services. Mutual help groups are one direction citizens have taken to help themselves.

Over the years, in the United States, there have been many service programs that began as mutual help groups (Katz 1961). Often, when they became part of the human service establishment, their focus and control were diluted and ultimately lost because of the ensuing development of a typical agency with a client population for whom services were developed and provided by professional helpers. This has been a desirable evolution in some instances; in others it has been regressive (Katz 1961).

As mutual help groups develop, they may turn to the professional community for guidance. To retain the mutual help aspect of the organization, however, the helping program must not only be initiated by people who have experienced the problem, but the helping method must be consistent with their personal experience of what works in the particular problem situation. The service offered by these experts must therefore be on a consultant model. How any professional knowledge is integrated with a program is left to the decision of a mutual help group. (Silverman, et al., 1975)

Mutual help groups can also produce social change. (Theodore, 1973) With the development of new services, new helpers emerge and new divisions of labor change the role of the professional expert. As a result, the next decades may see a gradual change in the very nature of human services.

TYPOLOGY OF MUTUAL HELP GROUPS

It is possible to classify mutual help groups into three broad types based on their primary activities. There are those groups whose primary function is *fund raising.* These raise money for something that they experience in common. The March of Dimes began this way, using polio victims and their families as fund raisers. At this point, mutual help ceases, since the money is then given to professionals who provide needed services and research that may prevent or cure the disease. Second, there are those groups that have as their primary function *political action*, which involves changing laws affecting their situation, and *changing public attitudes* toward the condition they share in common. The gay liberation movement and the women's liberation movement exemplify this category. Finally there are groups that devote themselves primarily to *personal help* for their members. Alcoholics Anonymous and La Leche League for Nursing Mothers typify this group.

There are many mixed models as well. Examples for such models are found in many chapters of the National Association for Retarded Citizens and in the

Foundation for Sudden Infant Death. These groups are involved in raising money for new research and for additional services. They are trying to educate the public about these conditions, and they have mutual help programs in which members offer personal help to each other. Many services in the Association for the Retarded are run by professionals, as is all research in those groups where the parents or veteran retains control and a reasonable division of labor develops so that the talents of all are utilized as needed, such as in teaching children or treating illness.

I am most interested in those groups which offer individual guidance to their members. This service is provided by other members who have become helpers because they have solved a special difficulty and are willing to use their experience to help others. A.A. is one of the best-known examples. Only a former alcoholic who has been dry for two years and who was helped by the A.A. method can become a helper. No donor can give more than a limited amount of time a year to the group, thus ensuring that it remains a voluntary organization dependent upon the members' own talents and resources for continued existence. Helpers are not accredited by professional schools; their expertise comes from their experience of successful coping. Help is personal, often on a one-to-one basis.

THE DEVELOPMENT OF MUTUAL HELP GROUPS

Mutual help organizations develop 1) when the professional care giver fails to deal successfully with a problem; 2) when the professional care giver solves a problem but does not appreciate the additional problems created for the affected indivuduals by these solutions; and 3) at times of rapid social change, when there is a gap between existing services and the needs of new situations.

Professional failure

Former clients may seek other solutions when they are not helped by the methods used by professionals who claim responsibility for treating and/or curing their particular difficulties. Since I have already used A.A. as an example, let me extend this here. A.A. grew out of the meeting of two alcoholics in the mid-1930's who had been in the same treatment program. In an effort to stop drinking, they found that their association enabled them to remain dry. The recent proliferation of self-help drug programs emerged from the same experience; that customary professional therapies were not effective in eliminating the addiction.

Mental retardation was another area where the professional community staked out an exclusive claim. For the most part, retarded children had competent families who took concerted action about their child's special problems. The literature on retardation contains many poignant pleas by parents for understanding of their situation. They protest neglect, misunderstanding or mismanagement by professional helpers, (Boggs, 1969; Patterson, 1959) Part of the problem arose from a professional attitude toward them as people with emotional problems.

Psychotherapy was inappropriately given to help them cope with their problems, and some professionals may have been unable to admit they did not know how to help these children and their parents. Ultimately, a solution arose when parents joined together. (Katz, p. 29) The movement began in 1949 when several families advertised for other families to start a cooperative nursery school for their children.

The mutual help aspects of the mental retardation movement were complex. The parents had to prod the legislature for more money and improved resources. Parents first needed to learn that they were not alone (Lund, 1969), and that they could learn a good deal from each other about how to help their own children and develop more comprehensive programs for all retarded children. It was clear from the beginning that children often required services from trained professionals. Parents collaborated with receptive professionals to understand their difficulties so they could develop appropriate services.

As local groups evolved, they formed the National Association for Retarded Citizens, which has attempted to identify the problems that are the province of the human service institutions of society, and those that must remain the unique province of parents. We see a growing number of new programs for parents which are based on mutual help principles. Most recently, outreach programs have involved parent outreach to parents who have just learned that their child is retarded. In these programs, parents are utilizing their own experience as the basis for counseling others and offering them guidance and information. (Weingold, 1969)

New Problems

A second stimulus for the development of mutual help groups seems to stem from the consequences of improved medical intervention. With modern medical technology, many people are living who previously would have died from their condition. For example, people with cystic fibrosis live into their early twenties and sometimes marry. Victims of extensive burns now survive who formerly would have died from their wounds. But physicians, in developing such medical procedures as ileostomy, did not develop parallel services to assist the patient to live with his disability. With this medical condition, advanced technology solved one problem, and created others that were unanticipated.

The history of the Ostomy society is well documented. (Lenneberg, 1970) Patients met together in 1952 to share their common problem and began to learn from each other what was being done to solve their common problems of odor, leakage and skin irritation. An engineer among them working with the medical staff developed appliances that allowed the individaul enough freedom of movement and independence to pursue his usual activity. Here, a former patient developed a response to new needs and became the proponent of his responsive techniques through a mutual help organization.

However, the mutual help group offers more than the sharing of techniques.

There is usually a more intimate sharing at an emotional level. In such exchanges, participants learn how to cope and sustain hope. By his very presence, a recovered patient is a living model for identification. The new patient does not feel isolated, realizing that he is not the only one in the world who has this problem. A woman with a mastectomy has similar feelings and she, too, must adapt to a changed body image and use of an appliance. Both the Ostomy Society and Reach for Recovery (for women with mastectomies) send people to hospitals, when invited by staff, to talk with patients prior to their surgery.

Another group built on a mutual help principle is emerging. This consists of helpers who have recovered from a given condition and want to help others who are currently trying to deal with it. These individuals do not form organizations or work through them, but instead, choose to become professionals in order to help fellow victims. For example, a blind woman studying counseling in order to help other blind people describes her motivation: "From my own suffering and experience something must come that would be helpful to other newly blinded individuals." (*Boston Globe*, June 1974) A young woman badly burned as a child is studying to be an occupational therapist to work with burn victims. These people feel that they have unique understanding of the problems the new victim faces, and with additional training, will have something very special to offer.

Lenneberg (1970) outlines another course available to individuals who have gone through a mutual help group. They move from the role of helpee to that of amateur helper, and then to that of professional helper. New professional services have emerged, in consequence, such as that of ostomy therapist. Individuals bring to this role the special understanding that only the veteran can have. Mutual help groups thus develop as ancillary services to medical programs, and there seems to be a growing acceptance of their value.

TIMES OF RAPID SOCIAL CHANGE

In the past, the family oriented people, providing them with values and behavior repertoires to deal with the outside world. The son identifying with his father acquired coping skills to deal with his eventual adult role. This no longer works. With rapid social changes, the family cannot keep up with changing needs and is losing its function as an interpreter of society and as an educator to future generations. Role vacuums exist, so that people do not know how to behave as they move from one experience to another. To fill this void, mutual help groups have developed to meet the coping needs of their members.

As we look at how family functions are changing, we ask what changes have taken place in the passage of people through the normal transitions of the life cycle. Births and deaths now occur in the sterile atmosphere of the hospital, thus removing the events from their natural family and community contexts. We have extensive knowledge of parent/child relationships, and our understanding of child rearing is sophisticated and expanding, but we do not have equally sophisticated technologies to put this knowledge into effect. The new mother has no easy access to the latest information on child rearing. Significant life-cycle events were often shared by the family with the clergy, who provided religious supports through such transitions as birth, marriage and death. Battered by twentieth-century rationalism, the ministry is only now recovering to cope with some of these matters in ways that are relevant to present and future generations.

The La Leche League for Nursing Mothers is an example of a totally voluntary mutual help group in which only nursing mothers or those mothers who have nursed successfully can qualify as leaders, educators or as direct helpers. This group developed in the living room of a nursing mother when she and her friends came together to help each other cope with the inadequate support they received from pediatrician, family and friends. (Silverman and Murrow, 1975) The group in its twelve years of life has grown to a centralized national organization with 1,800 chapters and with groups outside of the United States as well (one new group affiliates every day). It flourishes at a time when the family is under attack, when the role of mother is being demeaned, while simultaneously psychological research informs us how important the early mothering experience is to the child's future well-being. L.L.L. provides meetings for both parents, as well as guidance for women who are seeking clarification of their roles as mothers. Here they find positive role models for mothering and a respect for their own child's needs, and they learn responses to these needs as well as to their own, as mothers and as women. Because members of a mutual help group are deeply involved in the issue that brings them to the group, they often have more relevant knowledge about the subject than the professional. In the area of nursing, La Leche League now gives courses for general practitioners on nursing. These courses are not accredited, since the professional organization is not able to accept the idea that a volunteer organization can sustain the quality of information and knowledge which is being displayed at these classes.

In dealing with death, there is an even greater vacuum between knowledge and practice. People live longer, and rarely in the United States are we witness to mass death from disease, famine or war. Patterns of grieving, religious tradition and social support are changing. (Silverman, 1969) To some extent, this is a result of the mixing of cultures in this country. Some Americans emulate the stoic Anglo-saxon who suffers silently during bereavement. (Gorer, 1965) The bereaved feel isolated and cut off from their community, and have no adaptive patterns to allow them to grieve adequately. The younger widowed individual, and the parent who loses a child are in particular need of help. These groups have formed mutual help associations. The Foundation for Sudden Infant Death responds to the needs of parents whose young infants died of "crib death". This group has a parent contact program in which veteran parents reach out to the newly bereaved. The purpose of these contacts is to help these families express their grief, and to learn to deal with the problems that the death has caused for them.

In like fashion we have seen a mushrooming of programs for the widowed over the last decade. The oldest of these is probably NAIM Conference in Chicago. In addition to social activities, its members reach out to the newly bereaved in their community (Silverman, et al., 1975) to share with them the pain of their grief, to give them perspective on what is happening to them and, in time, to help them build new lives. The widow-to-widow program joined the service scene for the widowed in 1967. This service was an attempt to implement the findings of earlier research I did into services available for the widowed. (Silverman, 1966) I learned that the service of another widowed individual was most helpful. I was interested in following a public health model of prevention to reach every member of the population of widows at risk. The widow-to-widow program was an experiment in intervention using widows as primary care givers. Technically this program would not qualify as a mutual help organization, since I was the director and was ultimately responsible for what was being done. The helping mode was, however, that of mutual help. The success of this program legitimated mutual help programs as a way of meeting the needs of the newly widowed, and is changing care-giving patterns throughout the country. As they learn of this work, widowed individuals are supported in initiating programs to help themselves. These, then, are true mutual help organizations. Many groups for the widowed have been influenced to add an outreach service or committee to their already active organization.

The growth of a self-help movement among adolescents and young adults (Dumont, 1974) may have started in response to the drug problem. We now find them focusing on the broad spectrum of needs in adolescence, with young people helping each other. Families are often at a loss to help young people deal with the complexities of their world, so they begin to find direction from each other.

In this country we have very few ways of integrating the experience people gain from living. Traditionally the elderly were respected for the experience they could share with the young, but today they are not valued for this. Mutual help groups fill this experiential vacuum and provide a means of making the knowledge gained from life experiences available to others who may require it. Under-appreciated elders have also banded together in groups such as the Grey Panther Movement to meet their mutual support needs.

Other Issues

There is a need for research into the developmental cycle of mutual help groups. We need to discover how they are influenced by current professional practice and how they, in turn, influence future patterns for organizing services. Other questions that need exploration are the conditions that lead to the development of mutual help associations, the nature of the people who organize mutual help groups, and the duration and conditions of their involvement in such groups. I see certain common qualities in their situations which may be motivating forces. Most people are struggling with problems that are currently central in their lives. Their well-being demands that they find a meaningful solution to their problems. For some, there is no entirely satisfactory resolution. As with the parents of a retarded child, they may form groups that meet lifetime needs. For others, the group serves needs during a transition; as they become capable of dealing with their difficulty, they leave the group.

There are people who are not satisfied by helping themselves only. They are concerned about others, learn from others and help themselves while ensuring that others can learn from their experience. In this way they feel that their past suffering gives their lives a new meaning and purpose. They have a capacity to educate themselves about their problem, so that they are indeed expert in all its aspects, even to the extent of acquiring an exhaustive and critical knowledge of the professional literature on the problem area.

MUTUAL HELPING

In discussing mutual help I am not talking about the sense of achievement that comes from joint legislative activity or a successful fund raising project to support the group; I am talking about the *personal* help that is typically offered in mutual exchange. This help can be given face to face or on the telephone, or in small groups. The most important quality of this help is that it is offered by someone who is or was a *fellow sufferer*. The helper is someone who is willing to relive his own experience many times over, because in so doing he can help someone else. In turn, he is likely to learn some new dimension of the problem from the person he is helping. Both parties are aware of the mutuality of the relationship. It is therefore not necessarily limited by time, or limited in space as a more circumscribed professional helping exchange might be. Out of mutual helping exchanges long-term friendships can and do develop. Lenneberg has likened this helping exchange to that which goes on between siblings.

The person being helped has *easy access* to the helper, often at any time of the day or night. There is a spontaneous quality, since he can call for help when his need is greatest and is not constrained by office hours.

Most often the help is specific advice about how to deal with a problem, or information about what to expect in the situation. This provides *perspective* on the problem. A newly bereaved individual does not know if he will ever abe able to stop crying or ever feel some joy again. In a mutual help exchange the individual is given information about what he is experiencing, about what to expect, and what he can do. In this way his coping repertoire is expanded. Not only does he master what is happening immediately, but he comes to anticipate other problems that will arise and gains ideas on how to meet them. He comes to understand that what he is experiencing is to be expected. This allows him to acknowledge normal feelings and to find hope for his future.

In a mutual help experience the helper or organization becomes a bridge (Silverman, 1970) between the new victim and the larger community. A new widow often complains of being a fifth wheel, a stranger to her old social circle.

She needs to learn to reintegrate herself into the community as a widow, a formerly married woman. The role skills she had as a wife may not serve her now, and she learns new techniques fromfthe widow who has successfully made the transition to widowhood. (Silverman, 1971) This bridging phenomenon may have two outcomes. In one the individual functions in the larger world only by remaining permanently in the mutual help group. By remaining involved with A. A., many former alcoholics remain dry and live normal lives. For others with a variety of problems, mutual help may be only one stage in solving their problems, and effective groups allow people a way of moving on. The next step depends on the nature of the problem. The former alcoholic has needs different from those of the widow. The former's need for his group is likely to be more permanent than the widow's. In either situation, a next step can involve the transition from helpee to that of helper.

A most important function of the mutual help group is in the provision of role models for new members. Mutual help groups develop in situations where role vacuums exist, so that the individual does not know how to be what he has become. How does one's role change as a diabetic, as a widow, as a new mother or father? In consequence, there is a great need to find someone who understands what one is feeling, someone with whom one can identify, a role model.

The helper in a mutual help exchange appreciates and respects the newcomer's suffering. In consequence, his feelings are normalized and legitimated; his problem is typical, not unusual, and the helper can teach him rules for coping. The individual facing these typical transitions often experiences great loneliness. He fears that he is the only one in the world with his problem. Through a mutual help experience he finds a community of like people who give him direction and hope. This is as important to the parent of a retarded child as to the nursing mother.

Communication between participants in a mutual helping exchange involves nonverbal as well as verbal exchanges. It is no longer necessary for the initiate to struggle to find words to describe an experience because it becomes apparent very quickly that the other person understands. As a newcomer fumbles and stutters looking for words, the helper knows what he means and can help him put it into words. Many people talk about keeping feelings suppressed or unspoken for years because there was no one who understood what they experienced. They describe the lifting of a burden when at last they met someone else who could share their experience.

In mutual help situations, we usually encounter people who are psychologically adequate. In their current situation they have no precedent for how to behave. As they learn new patterns of dealing with the world in the light of their changed situation their competence is improved, as is their mental health. In mutual help efforts it may be possible to find ways of developing programs for the prevention of emotional illness or difficulties. (Silverman and Murrow, 1974) This involves changing the concept of prevention from a negative one, in which something is averted, to a positive one, in which someone is taught how to cope, how to solve a problem, how to deal with a critical transition and a new role. Most people do not want to be miserable. They will find a way to learn what they need to know to solve the problem by finding a teacher. If necessary, they will initiate a new program or they will informally find what they need to know, from whatever source is available. When they are involved with another person in this pursuit, this is mutual help.

CONCLUSION

I have been trying to describe a process by which people join together to meet basic human needs. Out of compassion comes cooperation and community. The basic dignity of men is expressed in helpful reciprocation. The quality of life of an individual is enhanced by his participation in helping networks or exchanges.

Mutual help organizations or groups provide help during changes in the human life cycle. The help that is offered is available at the time when need is greatest. Mutual help increases the average individual's self-reliance and his ability to take charge of his own life. It helps him build networks and forge links which maintain his connectedness to his community. Professional helping systems cannot do this linking as naturally and easily. Mutual help organizations have thus emerged independently of most professional human service agencies. They represent an opportunity for helpful collaboration between nonprofessional people—and with the professional community as well.

BIBLIOGRAPHY

The A.A. Way of Life, A Reader by Bill. New York: Alcoholics Anonymous World Service, Inc., 1967.

Alcoholics Anonymous Comes of Age. New York: Alcoholics Anonymous World Service Inc., 1957.

Amir, S., and Laron, Z. Family to family guidance. In *Habilitation and Rehabilitation of Juvenile Diabetics*, ed. Zvi LaRon, M.D. Leiden, H. E. Stenfert Kroese N. V., 1970.

Boggs, Elizabeth M. Pointers for Parents. In Part X.

Dumont, Mathew. Self help treatment modes. *Amer. J. of Psychiatry*, 1974.

Dybwad, Rosemary. Mobilizing for action around the world. In *Challenges in Mental Retardation*, by Gunnar Dybwad. New York: Columbia University Press, 1964.

Gorer, Geoffrey. *Death, Grief and Mourning*. Garden City: Doubleday Co., 1967.

Greenberg, Estelle F. *Pioneers of Professional Social Work: A Case Study in Professionalization*. Unpublished Ph.D. dissertation, New York Univ., 1969.

Hughes, Everett. *The Sociological Eye*. Chicago: Aladine Press.

Katz, Alfred H. *Parents of the Handicapped*. Springfield, Illinois: C. C. Thomas, 1961.

Lenneburg, Edith. Mutual Aide Groups for Ileostomy Patients. In *The Ileostomy Patient*, by E. Lenneburg and J. L. Rowbotham. Illinois: C. Thomas, 1970.

Levine, Murray, and Levine, Adeline. *A Social History of Helping Services*. New York: Appleton-Century Crofts, 1970.

Lund, Alton F. The Role of Parents in Helping Each Other. In Part X.

Weingold, Joseph. *Parents Counselling Other Parents of Retarded Children*. New York State Welfare Conference, November 14, 1960, Mimeo.

Parents helping parents. In *Management of the Family of the Mentally Retarded*. W. Wolfensberger and R. A. Kurtz eds., Follet Educational Corporation, pp. 496-510, 1969.

Patterson, Lethal, The Role of the Parent. In *The Child With a Handicap*, ed. Edgar E. Martmer, M.D. Springfield, Illinois: Charles C. Thomas, 1959.

Peyser, Dora. *The Strong and the Weak*. Sydney, N.SW., Currawong Publishing Co. LTD., 1951, p. 24. Quoted in Katz's *Parents of the Handicapped*.

Seeley, John R., Junker, B.H., and Jones, R.W. *Community Chest*. Toronto: Univ. of Toronto Press, 1957.

Segal, Robert. *The Associations for Retarded Children: A Force for Social Change*. Springfield, Illinois: C.C. Thomas, 197-.

Silverman, P.R., Services for the widowed during period of bereavement. *Social Work Practice*, Columbia University Press, 1966.

Silverman, Phyllis R. The widow to widow program. *Mental Hyg.* 1969, 53-333-337.

Silverman, Phyllis R. The widow as caregiver. *Mental Hyg.* 1970, 55, 540-547.

Silverman, Phyllis R. Widowhood and preventive intervention. *Family Coordinator*.

Silverman, Phyllis R., D. MacKenzie, M. Pettipas, and E. Wilson (eds.). *Helping Each Other in Widowhood*. New York: Health Sciences Publish. Co., 1975.

Theodore, Athena. Social Change and Voluntary Action. In Voluntary Action Research, D. H. Smith, et al. 072, Boston: Lexington Books, 1972.

The Womanly Art of Breast Feeding, Franklin Park, Ill.: LaLeche League.

Management of the Family of the Mentally Retarded. Wolfensberger, W., and R. A. Kurtz (eds.) Follet Educational Corporation, 1969.

15

Confidentiality
Some Practical
Suggestions For Psychiatrists

FRANCIS DE MARNEFFE

INTRODUCTION

Since the days of Hippocrates, physicians have upheld the medical ethic which calls for maintaining the confidentiality of the physician-patient relationship.* Today, however, it is becoming increasingly difficult to maintain this confidential relationship as the health care delivery system becomes more complex and increasingly involves other health professionals, the government, changing organizations, new funding mechanisms, and even the computer.

Among physicians, psychiatrists have always recognized the particular sensitivity of the information which patients communicate to them and have been especially diligent in protecting the confidentiality of patient communication.

In psychiatry, in fact, there has been a twofold basis for the confidentiality ethic. The first, shared with the general medical community, is the fact that confidentiality is essential to protect the the patient's right to privacy. The second, peculiar to psychiatry, is the fact that confidentiality is the sine qua non of effective treatment. The very essence of treatment requires full and open communications, with confidentiality guaranteed to the patient.

The grounds for maintaining the confidentiality ethic obviously have not changed. They are as valid as they always were. What has changed is that far more people are involved in the delivery of care to patients, with each, to some extent, feeling entitled to information which once rested with physician and patient.

The problem for the physician is that everyone who believes he needs confidential information seems to be in favor of confidentiality as a principle, but as a practical matter, feels he must have the information to do his part in the delivery of health care. Hence he claims the principle should not apply to him.

Part of the dilemma for the psychiatrist is that while the arguments in favor of exceptions to confidentiality are often unjustified, in many cases they are plausible, sometimes convincing, and even compelling. Therefore, it is clear that confidentiality is not a black-and-white issue. Rather, the psychiatrist is likely to be in a position day-in and day-out of having to make decisions in many individual

*Hippocratic Oath. ". . . Whatever, in connection with my professional practice, or not in connection with it, I see or hear, in the life of men, which ought not to be spoken of abroad, I will not divulge as reckoning that all such should be kept secret . . . "

cases—decisions which will typically involve a compromise between two extremes: on the one hand, absolute confidentiality, which might deny information needed to help the patient; and on the other hand, total disclosure, which might be illegal as well as harmful to the patient and his family.

Thus, the psychiatrist may expect daily challenges to the principle of confidentiality, and daily will make decisions about whether to release information, how much, to whom and under what circumstances.

LEGAL ISSUES

To make sound decisions, the psychiatrist must be fully aware of the laws governing the release of information. These vary from state to state, and therefore he should familiarize himself with the laws governing the release of information in his particular location. Congress has not yet passed any legislation concerning a general psychotherapist-patient privilege, though one has been proposed.* What federal law exists concerning either a general physician-patient privilege or the confidentiality of the psychotherapist-patient communication deals only with a question of admissibility of such information in federal court proceedings.

In the absence of the federal statutes on these matters, the psychiatrist must familiarize himself with any applicable state laws, court decisions and regulations governing confidentiality and the release of information. The legal basis for the release of information usually comes from four sources:

1. There may be a state law or laws governing the release of medical records of psychiatric institutions as distinct from the release of medical records from general medical facilities. In Massachusetts,** for instance,

---

*The following proposal for a testimonial privilege (under Rule 504) was approved by the Judicial Conference and is under review by Congress pursuant to P.O. 93-12. "A patient has a privilege to refuse to disclose and to prevent any other person from disclosing confidential communications made for the purpose of diagnosis and treatment of his mental or emotional condition, including drug addiction among himself, his psychotherapist or persons who are participating in the diagnosis or treatment under the direction of his psychotherapist, including members of his own family . . . "

**Throughout this paper, applicable Massachusetts laws and regulations are cited in the footnotes as examples of the kinds of statutory boundaries within which the psychiatrist must make decisions.

there are two such laws.*,**

2. Another common legal basis in some states are other laws which deal with the issue of protecting the confidentiality of a communication between the patient and his psychotherapist.†

---

*Massachusetts General Laws, Chapter III, Section 70, as amended by Chapter 614 of the Acts of 1970, states in relevant part ". . . provided that such records and similar records kept by the licensee, except a hospital or clinic under the control of the Department of Mental Health, may be inspected by the patient to whom they relate or by his attorney upon delivery of a written authorization from said patient and a copy shall be furnished upon his request and a payment of a reasonable fee; and provided further than upon proper judicial order, whether in connection with pending judicial proceedings or otherwise, or, except in the case of records of hospitals under the control of the Department of Mental Health, upon order of the head of the state department which issues the license or of the head of the state department having jurisdiction or control of such licensee, and in compliance with the terms of said order, and, in the case of a hospital or clinic under the control of the Department of Mental Health, when the Commissioner of Mental Health determines that a disclosure would be in the best interests of the patient as provided in the Rules and Regulations promulgated by the Commissioner, such records may be inspected and copies furnished on payment of a reasonable fee."

**Chapter 123, Section 36, as added by Chapter 888 of the Acts of 1970, of the Massachusetts General Laws provide in relevant part ". . . Such records shall be private and not open to public inspection except (1) upon proper judicial order whether or not in connection with pending judicial proceedings, (2) that the Commissioner may allow the attorney of a patient or resident to inspect records of said patient or resident if requested to do so by the attorney, and (3) that the Commissioner may permit inspection or disclosure when in the best interest of the patient or resident as provided in the rules and regulations of the department . . . "

†Chapter 233, Section 20B of the Massachusetts General Laws provides in part ". . . Except as hereinafter provided, in any court proceeding and in any proceeding preliminary thereto and in legislative and administrative proceedings, a patient shall have the privilege of refusing to disclose, and of preventing a witness from disclosing, any communication, wherever made, between said patient and a psychotherapist relative to the diagnosis or treatment of the patient's mental or emotional condition." The exceptions relate to an examination for purposes of commitment, an examination pursuant to a court order, child custody cases, if the patient introduces his emotional illness in a court proceeding, if the patient sues the psychotherapist for malpractice, in certain cases after the death of a patient in which his mental or emotional condition is introduced as an element of a claim.

3. A third source of the legal basis for the release or nonrelease of psychiatric information are the regulations and memoranda of state departments of mental health pursuant to the various laws.*

4. A fourth source of information are court decisions interpreting existing statutory and regulatory provisions.

The psychiatrist must familiarize himself with any and all applicable laws, case decisions and regulations in his area, and decide how they apply to a particular situation. Their application is frequently complex, and he may, from time to time, need legal advice as to the applicability to the case at hand of the various statutes and regulations. No attempt is made here to give a comprehensive description of possible exceptions to these laws and regulations because they vary from state to state and, also, because the permutations of individual cases are endless.

It cannot be emphasized too strongly that in order to discharge his responsibility to his patient, the psychiatrist should be aware of these laws, case decisions and regulations, as well as of his responsibility to protect the patient's rights. Furthermore, he should not assume that the particular agency asking him for patient information has the standing to make such a request or is aware of the laws, case decisions and regulations, or is acting in the patient's best interest. This is not a responsibility that he can delegate with equanimity to the agency asking for the information. There is no substitute for his awareness of his rights and responsibilities to protect patients, of the precise legal basis, and for seeking legal advice when any issue is unclear.

---

*Proposed Massachusetts Department of Mental Health Regulation 7.2 (formerly 6.1). "All records relating to any person admitted to or treated by a facility under the supervision and control of or licensed by the department shall be private and not open to public inspection except in the following instances: A. Records of patients or residents shall be open to inspection upon proper judicial order whether or not such order is made in connection with pending judicial proceedings. B. The Commissioner or his designee may permit inspection or disclosure of the records of a patient or resident on the written request of the attorney of such patient or resident provided that the request is accompanied by the written consent of the patient or resident if he is competent; of the guardian of such patient or resident if he has been educated and is competent; or of the parent or legal guardian of such patient or resident if he is a minor. C. The Commissioner or his designee may in his discretion permit inspection or disclosure of the records of a patient or resident, or of departmental records, upon the written request of a third party where the Commissioner or his designee made a determination that such inspection or disclosure would be in the best interests of the patient or resident, etc. Such inspection or disclosure may be made in the patient's or resident's best interest in the following cases: 1. When the record will enable the patient or resident or someone acting on his behalf to pursue a claim, suit, or other legal remedy to endorse a right, or to defend himself against such action; 2. When the treatment of the patient or resident is to be continued by other professional personnel; 3. To insure that the civil rights of the patient or resident are protected; 4. To enable the patient or resident, or someone acting on his behalf, to obtain third party payment for services rendered to such patient or resident; 5. To persons engaged in research approved by the department, etc. . . ."

SOME COMMON SITUATIONS AND SUGGESTIONS

The situations in which the issue of confidentiality arises, and requires a decision on the part of the psyciatrist, are many and varied. Below are several which will occur with varying degrees of frequency, depending upon the psychiatrist's type of practice and/or his role in a given institution. Much depends, for example, on whether he is a private practitioner or a member of the staff of a psychiatric hospital or general hospital; or whether he is the chief administrative officer of a psychiatric facility. Some suggestions for dealing with each situation are also offered.

1. *Forwarding Medical Records to Other Physicians*. The forwarding of medical information to another physician who is assuming responsibility for the patient's treatment, or the forwarding of a consultation report, is probably among the most frequent occurrences involving the issue of confidentiality. It is also probably the most clear-cut and simplest to deal with. Presumably, the patient is seeking the advice of the other physician, and wishes any psychiatric information to be forwarded in order to enhance the quality of treatment. Thus, there should be no problem in obtaining the patient's permission in writing, even if there appears to be no special reason to question the role which the requesting physician is going to play.

There probably is no legal requirement for the forwarding physician to assure himself by affirmative action that the requesting person is a bona fide physician. However, if there is any reason to suspect that the requester is not what he is purporting to be, checking the A.M.A. Directory (or the Handbook of Medical Specialists, or the Board of Registration in Medicine in the State House), may be necessary to assure oneself that the requester is entitled to the medical information. More important, the psychiatrist sending the information should assure himself that it is being sent to a physician who, indeed, needs the information in order to treat the patient. The best way of confirming this is to obtain the patient's permission. Occasionally, a member of the family may enlist the assistance of a physician to obtain information to which he is not entitled, realizing that only a physician may be in a position to request and receive the information. One can avoid this trap by routinely checking directly with the patient. It is embarrassing even to have to raise the questions, but it is nevertheless wise for the psychiatrist to be aware of the various possibilities and of the lengths to which some people will go to obtain information to which they are not entitled.

2. *Third-Party Payers*. Second in frequency only to requests for patient information from other physicians are requests from third-party payers. With the tremendous increase in insurance coverage for psychiatric illness, the funding for appropriate treatment continues to shift more

and more away from payment by the patient and/or family to payment by insurance companies. Each insurance company has its own standards as to the nature and extent of required information. It is essential that the patient's written *specific permission* be obtained before forwarding any data. Preferably the specific request should be shown to the patient.

Frequently, the insurance carrier, in requesting medical information, will forward the physician a photostatic copy of an authorization signed by the *subscriber* for the release of information. Such authorizations, signed at the time subscribers apply for insurance, are inadequate. For one thing, the subscriber may be different from the patient. For instance, in many group plans the subscriber would be the employee of the company taking out the health insurance for its employees. The patient may be the subscriber's spouse or child. It is the patient's permission which is the operative document. Even if the patient is the subscriber, however, the chances are that when the authorization was signed (i.e., when the insurance policy was applied for), the patient had no idea under what circumstances information would be requested, nor what type of information might be transmitted. Therefore, it is also important for this reason to obtain a current authorization from the patient so that the patient can know the kind of information which is going to be transmitted.

Insurance companies have a tendency to request more sensitive information than the psychiatrist or the patient may feel comfortable in sending. Therefore, it is the responsibility of the psychiatrist to protect the patient's privacy to the maximum extent possible, and to send as little sensitive information as he possibly can and still ensure payment by the carrier. This sometimes leads to frequent and difficult communications between the insurance company and the psychiatrist and patient, but the only protection for the patient in these situations is for the patient to be kept fully informed by the psychiatrist, and his permission obtained every step of the way as increased information is requested. Again, preferably this request should be shown to the patient. One reason why it is so important for the psychiatrist, particularly, to be sensitive to the issue of confidentiality is that in psychiatric records there is usually far more than is found in a medical record. Part of the history of a psychiatric patient does not involve merely the personal history of the individual patient and the mental status and progress notes about his behavior and condition, but it also includes a great deal about several generations of the family and of the extended family. Therefore, even though the patient gives permission, he is automatically releasing information concerning many people who have not usually been consulted.

3. *Transfer of Records Throughout Community Mental Health Centers.* One of the requirements for the federal funding of Community Mental Health Centers is an agreement among their various component parts for the automatic transfer of patient records from one component to

another.* The idea is to ensure the continuity of care of the patients who, themselves, are entitled to move freely among the components. It is worth noting that unless specific state laws have been passed to require this, the automatic transfer of medical information, unless supported by the written permission of the patient, may be in violation of other laws in the state of the type described earlier which govern the release of psychiatric information.

4. *Reporting Admissions, Discharges, Diagnoses to State Agencies.* In most states there is probably a department of mental health regulation requiring all psychiatric institutions under the supervision of the department (both state facilities and licensed private psychiatric facilities) to submit monthly reports of admissions, discharges and diagnoses of all patients admitted. The reason for this type of regulation is to give such departments data they feel they need to discharge their responsibility of ensuring the availability of facilities to all the citizens within their respective states. While probably all would agree that forwarding such information is useful for statistical purposes, for study of public health matters and for assessing trends in patient flow, diagnostic categories and the like, it is nevertheless worth pointing out that this information is typically passed on to state agencies without the explicit permission of the patient. How safe this is for the patient may be determined to some extent by how careful particular departments of mental health are in the dissemination of this information. To some extent also, safety will depend upon what is in the reports in the way of identifying data, etc., and the existence of statutory or regulatory rights to request that information.

5. *School and College Admissions.* Increasingly, psychiatrists are being asked by the admissions offices of schools and colleges for information concerning their patients in order to assist them in admissions decisions. This can certainly be done, but again, only with the patient's written permission. It is important in obtaining the patient's permission to share with him the kind of information which the psychiatrist is being asked for and would plan to send. As in many of these situations, informed consent is really not informed unless the patient is aware of the kind of information which is going to be sent. It is worth noting here that many patients are not aware how complete psychiatric records usually are.

6. *Employers.* Most employment application forms contain a question concerning previous illness, including mental illness. Even though

---

*The Federal Register of May 6, 1964, prints the regulations of the Community Mental Health Centers Act of 1963 entitled 2 Public Law 88-164. Under Section 54.212 5C3 states "The clinical information concerning a patient which was obtained within one element be made available to those responsible for their patient's treatment within any other element (of the Community Mental Health Center)".

new labor laws are being passed which limit the kinds of questions which an employer may ask a potential employee, psychiatrists are frequently called upon at the present time to supply information to employers to help them make employment decisions.

Sometimes, it is the prospective employer who makes the request; other times, it may be an independent credit or investigation agency acting for the prospective employer. In either case, care should be taken not to say anything when initially contacted which reveals the candidate is or is not a present or past patient. One way to do this is to inform the requester that as a matter of policy you release no information to prospective employers either on your patients or your employees unless they ask you directly to do so. You can ask the requester to have the person on whom they want the information to contact you and give permission. This will give you an opportunity to secure the written permission of the patient. And again, the patient should fully understand what is going to be said or written.

7. *Request for Information by the Patient.* Increasingly, patients are requesting access to their own medical records. At the present time, this access in psychiatric institutions is still governed by the kinds of laws and regulations mentioned earlier.** In other words, the patient is in the same situation as everyone else in obtaining access to his psychiatric record. Usually a different situation prevails in general hospitals where, at least in some states, patients have a right of access to their own medical records.

---

*Under Massachusetts General Laws, Chapter 151B, Section 4, as amended by Chapter 701 of the Acts of 1973 adding paragraph 9A, there is a prohibition against discrimination in the recruitment and employment of persons who have been discharged from mental health facilities. It makes it unlawful to discriminate in employment because an individual has been admitted to a public or private facility for the care and treatment of mentally ill persons, provided that such persons have been discharged from such facility or to inquire on an application form about such admissions.

**Massachusetts General Laws, Chapter III, Section 70, as amended by Chapter 614 of the Acts of 1970, states in relevant part ". . . provided that such records and similar records kept by the licensee, except a hospital or clinic under the control of the Department of Mental Health, may be inspected by the patient to whom they relate or by his attorney upon delivery of a written authorization from said patient and a copy shall be furnished upon his request and a payment of a reasonable fee; and provided further than upon proper judicial order, whether in connection with pending judicial proceedings or otherwise, or, except in the case of records of hospitals under the control of the Department of Mental Health, upon order of the head of the state department which issues the license or of the head of the state department having jurisdiction or control of such licensee, and in compliance with the terms of said order, and, in the case of a hospital or clinic under the control of the Department of Mental Health, when the Commissioner of Mental Health determines that a disclosure would be in the best interests of the patient as provided in the Rules and Regulations promulgated by the Commissioner, such records may be inspected and copies furnished on payment of a reasonable fee."

Increased concern for civil rights and general issues of consumer protection are eroding the acceptability of a blanket denial of patient's access to psychiatric records. One may anticipate that, in the future, patients will have increased access to their own psychiatric records. This is a matter of concern to many psychiatrists who believe that access to his own psychiatric records by a patient is not always in his best interest. It may be, if access to psychiatric records becomes more prevalent, that this will inevitably change the content of the medical record. Because the psychiatrist will feel it is his responsibility in writing his notes in the record to assume that at some point the patient will see them, he will be more reticent about what he writes. While the psychiatrist may do this in part for his own protection, primarily he will do so out of his belief that the information and comments which he writes may not be beneficial for the patient to read.

8. *Family Requests for Medical Records.* How to respond to families of patients who request medical records would depend on the circumstances. If a former patient's family requests information for the purpose of ensuring that the patient will receive appropriate treatment, then information may be sent with the patient's written permission. If the patient's written permission cannot be obtained, then it may be necessary for the family to take appropriate legal steps to obtain the information. An alternative which the psychiatrist may suggest to the family is that the physician who is currently treating the patient request the information. It is important to note, however, that the psychiatrist should assure himself that the motives of the family are in the best interest of the patient. For instance, members of a family sometimes request medical information not for the purpose of assisting the patient but for the purpose of pursuing some litigation such as in a child custody case or a divorce.

9. *Probation Officers.* With the increasing number of patients in one kind of legal difficulty or another being seen by psychiatrists, the probation officer is more and more another party involved in the life of the patient. Frequently, this involvement is beneficial to the patient and the probation officer's assistance can be furthered by his obtaining appropriate information from the treating psychiatrist. The circumstances governing the release of such information would differ in various situations. For instance, if the hospitalization of a patient has been ordered by a court as a *condition of probation,* then the understanding reached between the court and the institution is that psychiatric information will be forwarded to the probation officer. There would be no point, under these circumstances, for the institution to insist upon a judicial order for the release of this information because the same court which sent the patient to the hospital can readily issue the order. Obviously, however, patients with probation officers may be hospitalized for treatment either prior to, or subsequent to,

any court involvement, and not hospitalized as a specific condition of the probation. In that case, it would be necessary either to obtain the patient's permission in writing to release the information, or if he were unwilling to do so, to ask the probation officer to obtain a judicial order to require the institution to release the information.

10. *Verbal Communications of Physicians and Other Health Professionals.* The above examples have dealt mostly with the release of medical information from the patient's records. This is relatively easy to control by the exercise of the authority of a medical records department in a hospital or by the psychiatrist in his own private office. More difficult to control is the communication, especially in a complex institution, of various members of the staff—particularly where there are many professionals and paraprofessionals with different degrees of training—all involved in the treatment of the patient and all needing to share information with each other in order to treat the patient. It is very important for the issue of confidentiality to be kept constantly before the staff in order to guard against some unwitting breach. For instance, many different staff members may meet patient families or friends on hospital visits, or have telephone contact with them. Questions about the patient are frequently asked. It is essential to keep in mind the issue of confidentiality and to make sure that the patient has given permission for the staff to communicate with the one who requests the information.

11. *Inquiries from News Media.* The news media have the responsibility of collecting information and disseminating it to the public. On the other hand, we, as psychiatrists, have the responsibility of protecting the patient's privacy. If a case comes to the attention of the news media of an individual in the public eye admitted to a psychiatric institution, a news reporter is quite likely to call the institution to find out about the patient. If the institution expects the admission of a prominent individual and that inquiries are going to be made, it would be wise to discuss with him and his family how best to handle inquiries. In the absence of such agreement, however, and generally speaking, the wisest course is to establish as an institutional policy that it neither will confirm nor deny whether a specific individual is or has been hospitalized. This can be stated to the press. It should be clear that newspaper reporters are not happy with this kind of reply, but it is nevertheless an important stand to take in order to protect present and future patients as well as past patients.

12. *Inquiries from Federal, State and Local Law Enforcement Officials.* Psychiatrists familiar with the importance of maintaining confidentiality and the legal protections which underlie it, will be surprised to find law enforcement agencies rather unconcerned about a patient's right to privacy. Many seem to feel that the information which a psychiatrist or psychiatric institution has about a patient should be transmitted to them

somewhat automatically. Some state laws which reflect the same attitudes are being questioned. For example, until fairly recently in Massachusetts, there was a law* requiring physicians and institutions to transmit information to the Public Health Department concerning drug addicts within seventy-two hours of their admission. It was clear from the form to be completed that the information could be forwarded by that department to any federal or state agency which requested it. This law has now been repealed.

However, it is not an infrequent occurrence for an institution to be approached by an officer of the FBI, Secret Service or police department requesting information on a particular individual. Some arrive at the institution, flash their badge or other identification, and make very clear by their demeanor their assumption that they consider themselves entitled to the information requested. They do not take kindly to a refusal on the part of the institution to pass it on. It is therefore particularly important for the institution or the psychiatrist to be very clear about his responsibilities and his rights in this matter because quite often the officers who appear can be somewhat intimidating in their demeanor. To refuse to give the information without proper legal steps is not to assume a posture of being against law enforcement, nor of failing to recognize their legitimate obligations to protect society.

Secret Service Inquiries. Since the assassination of President Kennedy, the United States Secret Service has had the responsibility of inquiring every six months at all psychiatric institutions in their area about the presence of patients who might pose a threat to one of the protectees of the Secret Service.** The inquiries usually take one of two forms. Either there is a specific individual who has come to the attention of the Secret Service, perhaps because of a threatening letter sent to the White House, in which case the Secret Service is interested in knowing the writer's whereabouts and whether he is still a patient; or it can take the form of asking whether in the past six months there has been anybody in the institution who has been heard to threaten the life of one of their protectees. No sane person can possibly want a repetition of a presidential assassination, and certainly no institution wants the burden of one of its patients

---

*Massachusetts General Laws, Chapter 94, Section 210-A, repealed by Chapter 1071, Section 2, of the Acts of 1971.
**Under Section 3056-A of Title 18 of the United States Code Annotated, the United States Secret Service USSS (Department of the Treasury) has the responsibility to protect the person of the President of the United States, the members of his immediate family, the President Elect, the Vice President and other officers next in order of succession to the office of President and the Vice President Elect, and former presidents, vice presidents, certain members of their families and the person of a visiting head of a foreign state or foreign government, etc.

being the assassin. However, inquiries of the Secret Service present a very difficult situation for the institution. With respect to the first type of request, namely, inquiries about *specific* individuals, ways are open for the Secret Service to go through regular channels and apply to a court for a judicial order. With respect to the second type of request, however, there appears to be no legal basis for its engaging in what is in effect a "fishing expedition," i.e., requesting information about the presence in the hospital in the past six months of anyone who may have threatened the life of a Secret Service protectee. To some extent, some difficulty arises due to an apparent conflict between federal and state law. The Secret Service is authorized to investigate the commission of felonies. Such authority, however, does not extend to any compelling degree to the investigation of persons merely considered a *potential* danger. Under these circumstances, the hospital is therefore under no obligation under federal law to furnish the Secret Service with information concerning a patient's propensity for violent behavior. At the same time, however, state statutes and regulations may exist which do impose such obligations on an institution. For example, in Massachusetts,* a hospital has an obligation to notify the appropriate authorities of escapees who present a danger to themselves or others. In other situations, it would also appear that the state law would prevail. In

---

*Proposed Massachusetts Department of Mental Health Regulation, Section 225.25 and 24, formerly 22(2)(a) and (4)(b). "Any patient absent without authorization who is considered a danger to himself or others shall be classified on escape by the superintendent or other head of the facility." Under proposed 225.25 (formerly 22(2)(a) "A. the facility shall take prompt and vigorous measures to secure the patient's return; B. the superintendent shall notify by the quickest possible means of communication the following parties: 1. the patient's legal guardian; 2. the patient's nearest relative or other persons who have indicated on the patient's record to be informed; 3. local and state police. The police shall be provided with the patient's description and such information as the patient's tendencies to be assaultive, homicidal, suicidal or to use weapons; 4. the district attorney of the county in which the facility is located; 5. any person known to be placed at risk because the patient has left the facility; 6. the department and regional offices."

Massachusetts, again as an example, the laws and regulations*on disclosing the contents of mental health records are such that law enforcement agencies may not be given access to such records unless it can be shown that the patient would benefit from the disclosure. It is difficult, if not impossible, to envision the circumstances in which it could be shown to be in a patient's best interests to release personal information about him to the Secret Service, especially if such information was indicative of criminal liability. Therefore, it would appear that under Massachusetts laws and regulations, at any rate, the patient's mental hospital records may be granted to the Secret Service only by proper judicial order.

FBI Inquiries. With respect to inquiries from the FBI, the situation is somewhat simpler, because unlike the Secret Service, they usually

---

*Proposed Massachusetts Department of Mental Health Regulation 7.2 (formerly 6.1). "All records relating to any person admitted to or treated by a facility under the supervision and control of or licensed by the department shall be private and not open to public inspection except in the following instances: A. Records of patients or residents shall be open to inspection upon proper judicial order whether or not such order is made in connection with pending judicial proceedings. B. The Commissioner or his designee may permit inspection or disclosure of the records of a patient or resident on the written request of the attorney of such patient or resident provided that the request is accompanied by the written consent of the patient or resident if he is competent; of the guardian of such patient or resident if he has been educated and is competent; or of the parent or legal guardian of such patient or resident if he is a minor. C. The Commissioner or his designee may in his discretion permit inspection or disclosure of the records of a patient or resident, or of departmental records, upon the written request of a third party where the Commissioner or his designee made a determination that such inspection or disclosure would be in the best interests of the patient or resident, etc. Such inspection or disclosure may be made in the patient's or resident's best interest in the following cases: 1. When the record will enable the patient or resident or someone acting on his behalf to pursue a claim, suit, or other legal remedy to endorse a right, or to defend himself against such action; 2. When the treatment of the patient or resident is to be continued by other professional personnel; 3. To insure that the civil rights of the patient or resident are protected; 4. To enable the patient or resident, or someone acting on his behalf, to obtain third party payment for services rendered to such patient or resident; 5. To persons engaged in research approved by the department, etc. . ."

make inquiries on a specific individual and do not engage in the kind of "fishing expedition" described earlier. Here, too, it is not infrequent that an FBI agent will appear at an institution, usually without an appointment and without advance notice, to request access to a patient's record. There are times when a request from the FBI about a patient would serve the patient's best interest. For example, occasionally the FBI will investigate a prospective employee for the government, and, certainly, if an ex-patient, for example, is seeking such employment, it would help him to comply with the request. In such cases, the request should be handled as a request from any other employer. If the FBI agent objects to the normal procedure, he should be informed that the record can otherwise be made available to him only by presentation of a judicial order.

Local Police Inquiries. Local police departments will also approach psychiatric institutions for information. Sometimes when a police officer has been admitted to a hospital and then discharged, the police department may request that if he is readmitted, the chief of police be notified automatically. The position which I believe the institution must take in these instances is to notify the chief of police that the hospital cannot pass on this information without the specific written permission of the patient. However, I would assume it to be entirely within his prerogative to make a regulation for his department requiring officers to ensure he is notified in the event any of them is admitted to a psychiatric hospital.

13. *Research.* From time to time, various research projects involve following patients over many years during which the patient may have been admitted to a number of institutions. I believe that in former times such research inquiries—if limited to the patient's record—were routinely answered after the institution assured itself that the research team was providing adequate safeguards on maintaining confidentiality. Nowadays, however, the situation is changing. In Massachusetts, for example, approval of the Department of Mental Health is required prior to obtaining

access to patient records for research purposes.* Federal regulations are also in the process of being tightened up with regard to the release of patient information.** This has, without a doubt, made retroactive research very much more difficult, since the whereabouts of the former patient may not be known. Also, even if it were and he could be contacted, it would be considered to be detrimental to the patient to ask belatedly for his permission to review his record.

---

*Proposed Massachusetts Department of Mental Health Regulation 7.2 (formerly 6.1). "All records relating to any person admitted to or treated by a facility under the supervision and control of or licensed by the department shall be private and not open to public inspection except in the following instances: A. Records of patients or residents shall be open to inspection upon proper judicial order whether or not such order is made in connection with pending judicial proceedings. B. The Commissioner or his designee may permit inspection or disclosure of the records of a patient or resident on the written request of the attorney of such patient or resident provided that the request is accompanied by the written consent of the patient or resident if he is competent; of the guardian of such patient or resident if he has been educated and is competent; or of the parent or legal guardian of such patient or resident if he is a minor. C. The Commissioner or his designee may in his discretion permit inspection or disclosure of the records of a patient or resident, or of departmental records, upon the written request of a third party where the Commissioner or his designee made a determination that such inspection or disclosure would be in the best interests of the patient or resident, etc. Such inspection or disclosure may be made in the patient's or resident's best interest in the following cases: 1. When the record will enable the patient or resident or someone acting on his behalf to pursue a claim, suit, or other legal remedy to endorse a right, or to defend himself against such action; 2. When the treatment of the patient or resident is to be continued by other professional personnel; 3. To insure that the civil rights of the patient or resident are protected; 4. To enable the patient or resident, or someone acting on his behalf, to obtain third party payment for services rendered to such patient or resident; 5. To persons engaged in research approved by the department, etc. . ."

**Informed consent of the patient or guardian will be required under proposed federal regulations. Federal Register, Volume 38, No. 221 of November 16, 1973, page 31748, Section 46.54 - Limitations on Activities Involving the Institutionalized Mentally Infirm.

14. *Biography*. From time to time, a psychiatrist or institution may be contacted by a writer who is preparing a biography of an eminent author, scientist or politician known to have been hospitalized at some point in a psychiatric institution. Often, it involves an individual long since dead. While providing the information might make an important contribution to history, it is my belief that the institution should not do so. Presumably, even if the patient was admitted in the nineteenth century, there was an assumption then on his part and his family's that information gained in the course of his diagnosis and treatment would be kept confidential. I personally recognize no statute of limitations on such commitments. Nor do I believe that permission from a living descendant, which might be obtained by the biographer, constitutes appropriate authority for releasing the information.

This type of request obviously places the psychiatrist in a position of having to recognize and weigh competing social goods. While it is important to think each through separately, it is essential for him to remain clear in his own mind about where his primary obligation is. In my view, that obligation is to focus on his ethical responsibility to protect confidentiality. I would also add that even when the psychiatrist feels that legally he can release information but has reservations about doing it from an ethical standpoint, he should be guided by the latter.

With respect to the biographer, presumably nothing would prevent his trying to demonstrate to a court of law or department of mental health the imperative social good to be obtained by releasing the information and to seek a judicial order. I am not aware that any such judicial order has ever been issued for such a purpose.

15. *Patient Suing a Psychiatrist or Hospital*. Since the number of local suits being brought against doctors and hospitals is increasing, psychiatrists will want to explore state laws and regulations in their localities with respect to the confidentiality issue. That is, they should explore whether they have any right to use information divulged to them by a patient in the event that that patient at a later date brings suit against him. The same question should be raised with respect to psychiatric institutions if they should be sued. The statutes or regulations may apply differently. In Massachusetts, for example, under the law referred to earlier regarding the

---

*Chapter 233, Section 20B of the Massachusetts General Laws provides in part ". . . Except as hereinafter provided, in any court proceeding and in any proceeding preliminary thereto and in legislative and administrative proceedings, a patient shall have the privilege of refusing to disclose, and of preventing a witness from disclosing, any communication, wherever made, between said patient and a psychotherapist relative to the diagnosis or treatment of the patient's mental or emotional condition." The exceptions relate to an examination for purposes of commitment, an examination pursuant to a court order, child custody cases, if the patient introduces his emotional illness in a court proceeding, if the patient sues the psychotherapist for malpractice, in certain cases after the death of a patient in which his mental or emotional condition is introduced as an element of a claim.

protection of the confidentiality of a communication between the patient and his therapist, the psychiatrist is free to use the information he has received in the course of his professional contacts with the patient to defend himself in any suit brought by that patient.

With respect to medical records of psychiatric facilities, however, which may be covered by other local statutes, such waivers may not exist. For example, in Massachusetts it would appear that this is the case, and therefore if a hospital is sued by a patient, the hospital would be wise to follow applicable legal procedures for releasing such information even to the hospital's own attorney.

16. *Photographs, Films and Tours.* For various public information and promotional purposes, psychiatric facilities often need to prepare brochures which are markedly enhanced by the inclusion of pictures depicting various programs and activities in the institution. It is also true that to do so in the most realistic way involves including human beings in the pictures. It is extremely important, in my view, that the institution maintain the privacy of the individual patients and also keep confidential the identification of the patients in treatment. This often has to be done, despite the patient's willingness to be depicted. From a purely legal standpoint, I suppose that if the patient were to be both competent and willing to give a signed release authorizing the use of his picture, the institution would be legally protected. However, again, it seems to me that the institution has a higher responsibility than merely what is legally technically correct. Therefore, it is my position that no recognizable individuals in photographs should be patients and, furthermore, if models or nonpatients appear in pictures, that a disclaimer be included in the script indicating that they are not patients. This way, there is no chance of outsiders' misinterpretation. I might add that when any members of the staff, volunteers or other principals appear in such pictures, it is important to obtain from them a signed release authorizing the use of the photographs in order to protect the institution. Tours of psychiatric facilities also can pose invasion of privacy and confidentiality issues. Again, one faces competing goods: educating the public about mental illness and treatment, as against preserving patient privacy and identity. The policy at our institution is that we do not routinely take community groups through patient living quarters. These are shown by film, and walking tours are limited to areas thought not to intrude on the patient activities.

With respect to films, I believe that the same considerations with respect to competing social needs and social goods should apply. Some years ago in Massachusetts, a film was made called *Titicut Follies* about Bridgewater State Hospital, an institution for the "criminally insane." Mr. Fred Wiseman, an enterprising film maker, along with many other people, was appalled by the conditions there and believed that making and distributing a film depicting the conditions there would facilitate bringing about change. One can agree with that social objective, one can support it in many ways. But the permission of the patients was not routinely obtained (though even if it had been, questions about the competence of individual patients to give permission might have remained). In any event, this film was banned for public showing in Massachusetts, although it was shown in New York. There are still a number of suits pending in connection with it.

One can comfortably debate, to some extent, on either side of the question. There is no doubt that disseminating the film would have provoked horror on the part of spectators and that this might have started some pressure on the legislature and the executive branch of the state government to bring necessary changes at Bridgewater. Yet, at the same time, the film depicted recognizable individuals in very embarrassing and offensive conditions displaying their pathology and their illness; and also an alleged interview between a psychiatrist and a new admission. The patients were obviously all from Massachusetts and, therefore, could easily have been recognized in their neighborhoods by friends, families, etc. I believe the state government and the courts took the correct position in deciding the film had invaded the patients' privacy.

My personal position is that, as psychiatrists, we must stand firm in protecting the principle of privacy and confidentiality which has existed through the ages and which has determined the doctor-patient relationship. I also believe that we do not have to forgo films and documentaries with a social purpose. They can, I believe, be made without breaching the confidentiality and privacy of patients. True, it poses a great artistic challenge to the producer, but it can be done.

NEWER ISSUES ON THE HORIZON

The situations in the examples discussed so far have been with us for some time. They have had to be dealt with by psychiatrist and/or psychiatric institutions with varying degrees of frequency depending on the type of practice, facility, etc. Other issues are newer and are likely to be of increasing concern in the future. A couple of those which quickly come to mind follow:

1. *Increasing Use of Computers*. The advantages of the computer, and the contributions it can make to more efficient health delivery systems, are obvious and will not be discussed here. But what is currently receiving a good deal of public attention is the threat they pose to the confidentiality of the patient data they can hold. While this problem will no doubt be of increasing concern as the years go by, it would seem not to be insoluble. It should be possible for an institution to make use even of a computer jointly owned by a number of different institutions (for regional planning

purposes or simply for economic use of a single computer) without danger to confidentiality. For quick and effective retrieval, information on the patients could be fed into the computer using a special code system which would identify the patient not by name or by address, but by a code. The code would be kept confidential within the institution itself so that neither outside computer personnel feeding information into the computer nor unauthorized persons with access to computer printouts could identify any individuals. As with so many of these situations, what is needed is the foresight to structure safeguards into a system or procedure so that the means do not become insuperable obstacles to good ends.

2. *Peer Reviews and PSRO's.* With the development under federal law* of professional standard review organizations, the number of patient records which are going to be reviewed for cost control and treatment purposes is going to increase tremendously. These records are going to be reviewed by individuals outside of the treating institution—and perhaps not even by medical personnel, since it is expected that certain types of technicians will be specially trained for these reviews. At the present time, I believe that these laws and the regulations governing PSRO's and peer reviews do not adequately provide for the protection of the confidentiality of the information. As psychiatrists, we should carefully watch this development and be continuously alert to the potential for abuse.

3. *New Commission on Human Research.* I began this chapter by saying that everybody seems to agree in principal on the need for confidentiality, but those who wish the information seem simultaneously to assert the principle and the reasons why it should not apply to them. This is illustrated in HEW rules and regulations pursuant to a new law establishing a national commission and Institutional Review Boards for protecting human research subjects. The regulations stipulate that institutional records will be retained by the institution and that information which can be identified with a particular subject may not be disclosed except with the consent of the subject or his legally authorized representative or as the Secretary of HEW may need the information to discharge his responsibility. Thus, exceptions to confidentiality are built into the same provisions which seek to protect it.

CONCLUSION

The delivery of health and specifically psychiatric services has changed a great deal over the past decade. This has made much more difficult the

*HR.1, 92nd Congress.
*P.O. 93-348 amending the Public Service Act (42 USC 204) and pursuant regulations published in the Federal Register Vol. 40, No. 50, March 13, 1975.

maintenance of absolute confidentiality of information exchanged between patients and psychiatrists. While one may bemoan this fact, it is inevitable and irreversible. It must be recognized that there are many competing forces at work and many competing legitimate requirements to satisfy the various agencies and people who are involved in patient care. It will become increasingly important as the years go on to develop new and better methods for determining which competing need must take precedence. It is essential that psychiatrists, whether in private practice or in an institutional practice, familiarize themselves with the laws and regulations governing the release.of medical information. It is also essential that the psychiatrist familiarize himself with the legal basis on which his rights and responsibilities to protect confidentiality is based. And finally, the psychiatrist should not assume that those requesting information are either aware of what the laws and regulations are, or, indeed, that they do not consider their requirements for information to override whatever laws and regulations there may be. There is no way in which the psychiatrist or physician can delegate this responsibility. While he may occasionally need legal advice in specific cases, he himself must be the first line of defense of patient confidentiality.

Acknowledgement

I wish to acknowledge the invaluable help of Arthur Rosenberg, J.D., civil rights officer and legal consultant at McLean Hospital, for much of the legal information contained in this paper. Particularly, I am indebted to him for an in-depth study of the legal grounds on which the United States Secret Service requests information from psychiatric hospitals.

Note

This chapter was adapted from a presentation at the annual meeting of the Massachusetts Psychiatric Society held in Boston on April 24, 1974.

16

Citizen Participation

ROLAND L. WARREN

Anyone who has read Clifford Beers' dramatic personal account of a mind that lost itself and *A Mind that Found Itself* knows that citizen participation in the mental health movement began not in the 1960's but over half a century ago, with the founding of the first nation-wide citizens' organization concerned with mental illness and its treatment. His purpose, and that of the citizens and professonal people who allied themselves with him, was to bring about more humane treatment of the mentally deranged.

Since that time, much has been added and elaborated in the activities of citizens in connection with mental health. Part of the reason we continue to be perplexed about citizen participation is our lack of clarity as to what we mean by the term, and consequently a lack of clarity as to what should be done, and how. At the same time, citizen participation has been proposed or advocated for a wide variety of purposes. When we think about citizen participation in any given context we are not always clear as to what purposes we hope it will serve, and consequently we do not gain clarity as to what form it should take.

At the outset, let me simply enumerate some of the different reasons given here or there for the desirability of citizen participation:

1. It gives local people a sense of sharing in the agency— that the agency is not imposed from without but in part belongs to them.

2. It conforms to democratic principles in that people have a part in forming the institutions which surround them.

3. Since service agencies are not subject to consumer preference through usual market behavior such as in the profit sector, it provides a different way of relating the agency's actions to "consumer demand."

4. It provides a useful input to help guide agency programs in closer accordance with local cultures, needs and wishes, thus making for more effective programs.

5. Citizen participation reduces threats of various kinds of protest behavior, since it provides a more acceptable channel through which citizen concerns can be expressed.

6. Through citizen participants, the policies and programs of the agency are interpreted to others in the local population, so that there is an

increase in general knowledge and understanding of what the agency is doing, and why, and what kinds of services it can offer to potential clients.

7. It provides a means through which the agency can be accountable not only to funding sources or to higher echelons of authority, but also to potential clients in particular and the general citizenry as well.

8. The citizen understanding of programs and policies gained through citizen participation creates the basis for support of the agency by those citizens when hard budgetary or domain considerations have to be decided.

9. The input from citizens can constitute an important source of program innovation.

10. It is generally believed that participation in important activities helps prevent alienation in individuals and groups, gives them a stake in the institutions which surround them, and encourages them to take responsibility. It thus has a therapeutic effect on individuals and groups.

11. It helps distribute power more equitably, so that not only professionals and elite citizens have a voice in shaping local organizations, but also "the man in the street." It thus helps make our system of "democratic pluralism" work.

12. It provides a channel through which individuals may acquire skills and experience which will help them move up the vocational ladder as well as the voluntary ladder of citizen responsibility.

13. It develops a core of leadership particularly where it is most needed—in disadvantaged neighborhoods, which for various reasons are often not well organized and skillfully led.

This is a rather extensive list. Let us note a few things about these purposes or reasons for citizen participation. Some of them have to do with strengthening the agency and enhancing its *viability*, thus assuring its continuation and possible expansion. Some of them, on the other hand, deal more specifically with increasing the effectiveness of the agency's *program*. Some of them, of course, do both.

Again, many of the presumed advantages have a reverse side. The input from the citizens may not be what the agency staff wants. The innovations suggested may lead in a direction which various agency personnel feel rightly or wrongly is unwise. Citizens participating may provide a platform for opponents of existing policies and programs to generate strong pressures against the existing agency staff and program. Complaints by knowledgeable, involved citizen participants may be more harmful to existing staff and programs than complaints by less knowledgeable outsiders. Indeed, the position which the agency gives the citizen participant lends support to that citizen's voice, both when he supports the agency and when he opposes it. The leadership which is developed in the process may be turned against the agency, and will be all the stronger for the experience it has gained in citizen participation.

But again, the most important reason for supporting citizen participation may not be any of its alleged advantages, but it may simply be that there is pressure for such participation, pressure on the local community mental health center either from NIMH or some other funding source, or pressure from the people of the area which the center serves. Like equal opportunity programs, citizen participation programs are more or less a part of the mandate of the times, and each agency feels pressures toward presenting at least the appearance, if not the reality, of a lively participation.

Much of the mythology which circulates among people in the social services field and in the field of social planning is centered around an implicit assumption of similarity or compatibility of interests on the part of different groups affected by any given agency or policy. To put this another way, an informed and responsible group of citizen representatives would in the final analysis come to agreement with the programs and policies of an informed and responsible professional staff. If they do not, one begins to question whether the staff is actually as well informed and responsible as it presumes itself to be, or whether the citizens are not taking their antagonistic position because they themselves are not sufficiently informed or responsible, or are involving themselves in community and organizational politics instead of sticking to the professional issues of service delivery. Thus, a CMHC director balefully observes:

> I am becoming increasingly more distressed and disturbed and unhappy, about what is going on. My job is to plan and deliver mental health care to patients in the entire catchment area. In order to do this and to to it well, I need an advisory board that is going to be able to advise me and the staff. I find to my dismay that the advisory board is being caught up in the politics of the district . . . I can't go on with the political in-fighting. I do not know the solution. Our obligation is to service patients; we saw over 30,000 patients the last fiscal year. I am frustrated by all members of the Board. Cannot we somehow or other try to see the CMHC as a service agency apolitical, trying to do a job in servicing the patients of the community?*

One is reminded of the farmer who prayed for rain during a drought. Soon after came a downpour which lasted for days and days and threatened cattle, crops and countryside with inundation. The distraught farmer finally strode out of his house, fists clenched, face contorted. He looked up at the sky and shouted, "Dear God, I prayed for rain. But this is ridiculous!" The corresponding complaint would be: "Dear God, I asked for citizen participation, but this is *irresponsible!*"

From the professional staff standpoint, citizen participation which does not agree with the staff on the main points of professional practice is irresponsible. From the citizen standpoint, agency actions and programs which do not conform to the expressed needs and wishes of the citizen participants is irresponsible. Such mutual recriminations are more likely to occur in disadvantaged areas and with poverty area representatives than with elite citizen boards. Why is this so?

---

*Cited in "Evaluation of Community Involvement in Community Mental Health Centers," Health Policy Advisory Center, Inc., New York, no date, page IIB 37.

The answer seems to lie in the circumstance that social services are largely based upon methods and processes which are compatible with middle-class culture and values. This is no coincidence, since both professional and administrative personnel are largely middle-class in orientation. Further, the older, more conventional modes of citizen participation are based on advisory or administrative boards which themselves are largely middle-class or even upper-class. Numerous studies have shown that health and mental health services are strongly biased toward middle-class patients in their distribution, in their diagnoses and in their treatment. Much the same has been found to be the case with other social services of various types. Since they are largely compatible with middle-class values and under middle-class control, there is a large basis of support for these services, their distribution and their professional rationale by citizen representatives of the middle class. Hence, the older elite citizen representation by leading laymen—clergymen, professionals, well-to-do-businessmen—could well be based on a strategy of collaboration, since little basic disagreement is involved. A recent contract study of citizen participation made for NIMH found this to be the case with elitist governing boards. On the other hand, it found the community control pattern, where policy prerogatives were turned over to representatives of the poor, to be fraught with controversy. These participants were not so willing to accept the presumed scientific basis for professional decisions, and they were more likely to place greater stress on community programs to change the institutional structure of the environment, as compared with emphasizing individual therapy, than were the elitist boards.

But such emphasis, of course, leads into political issues of control and power and wealth distribution and institutional change which not only carry the mental health professional away from his professional base of competence, but challenge his desired professional autonomy and also place him in conflict with other agencies in the community.*

In a recent study of the behavior of six types of community decision organizations in nine cities across the country, my colleagues and I gathered extensive data on citizen participation by low-income people and derived a model which differentiated two aspects of citizen participation whose confusion often leads to ambiguity. We were studying not only mental health planning organizations, but also community action agencies, model cities agencies, health and welfare councils, boards of education and urban renewal agencies in these nine cities.

As a result, we see such participation as comprised of two juxtaposed forces, *citizen involvement* and *citizen action*. Citizen involvement is the orderly, channeled input into agency decision making by low-income people through

---

*Wilfred E. Holton, "Citizen-Participation and Interagency Relations: Issues and Program Implications for Community Mental Health Centers," Final Report, NIMH Contract Number HSM-42-70-99, Department of Community Health and Social Medicine, Tufts University School of Medicine, Boston, January, 1972.

appropriate structures set up for this purpose. Decisions arrived at through such structured participation or through negotiating with independent organizations of low-income citizens are constrained by the maintenance needs of the agency and by the nature of its technical rationale—its own sphere of professional competence. Agencies may be more or less enthusiastic about such citizen input, and it can often be burdensome in time and effort and what seems to be needless delay. But it results by definition in decisions the agency can ''live with,'' for any other outcome would be labeled as ''irresponsible.'' Thus, citizen involvement provides for citizen input but input that is always subject to the prior claim of the agency's viability. Within that constraint, citizen input may be accommodated, and even positively welcomed, in view of the advantages listed earlier.

Citizen action is the juxtaposed force to citizen involvement. *Citizen action* is the effort of low-income people to influence organizations to act in ways which give first priority to the needs and wishes of low-income people—as defined by low-income people—and to consider as secondary such constraints as organizational maintenance, survival or convenience.

Citizen participation, with all its vicissitudes and misunderstandings and, sometimes, modest accomplishments is the resultant of the interplay of these two contrary forces. Let us distinguish them analytically from each other.

Citizen involvement is the process viewed from the standpoint of the agency's initiatives and priorities.

The *status of citizen participants* is that of clients (consumers), whose opinions are solicited as a means of considering changes to make the organization more effective in treating them and people like them.

The *source of legitimation* of the citizen participation is the formal provision for it within the structure of the organization, or of a group outside the organization as an appropriately interested and qualified group, and the continued recognition of it as ''acceptable'' and ''responsible'' by the organization.

The *resources available* are the organization's position within the interorganizational structure, its professional expertise, its command of a paid staff, and its accessibility to funds and support from various sources.

The *tactics employed* by the agency are the assertion and interpretation of the organization's professional expertise and its organizational requirements, backed up by the implicit threat to terminate the citizen participation if these are not respected, i.e., if the participation becomes ''irresponsible.''

The *orientation toward professionals and technology* is favorable. Technological solutions are seen as the remedy for technological and other problems.

''Successful'' citizen participation consists in ''responsible'' suggestions from low-income people which help make services more effective in meeting the needs and wishes of low-income people insofar as this can be accomplished without major inconvenience and without jeopardizing the maintenance needs of the organization.

Citizen action, on the other hand, has a quite different set of characteristics:

Citizen action is the process viewed from the standpoint of the needs and wishes of low-income people—as defined by low-income people.

The *status of citizen participants* is that of adversaries, of citizens demanding their rights.

The *source of legitimation* of the participation is the claim to represent validly the needs and wishes of low-income people, as defined by low-income people. It is external to the agency.

The *resources available* are potential external funds (usually federal) which can be blocked or delayed by citizen action, and the power—such as it is—which comes through organization.

The *tactics employed* are requests, demands, threats and acts of disruption, attacks on the target organization's legitimation, appeals to third parties (usually federal), and development of competing organizations.

The *orientation toward professionals and technology* is hostile. They are considered part of the problem.

"Successful" citizen participation consists in citizen control which "turns the agency around" by subordinating its maintenance, comfort and viability to the priorities of responding to the needs and wishes of low-income people.

Since issues arise in which these different approaches are in conflict with each other, there is a constant confrontation of the two sets of dynamics involved in citizen participation in which the agencies attempt to control the participating citizens and to channel their inputs into acceptable form, and the citizens attempt to control the agencies so that their activities more adequately meet citizen needs and wishes as they see them. The tension caused by these two sets of dynamics is always present in citizen participation, but in some cases it is minimal, while at other times it breaks out as an overriding and dramatic confrontation.*

It is quite understandable that a CMHC director usually looks at citizen participation as citizen involvement. Rightly or wrongly, he believes that he should not give over control of basic policy to a group of citizens, especially if they are not from the more well-to-do and professional circles which "understand" his agency's problems from the agency's point of view.

In considering the question of input from citizens, it is interesting to contrast the different ways in which citizen participants may be perceived.

First, they may be perceived as *clients or patients,* as the direct recipients of services. As one thinks of them in this way, attention is directed to the desirability of feedback about what it is like to be a client of this particular agency, and to suggestions as to how this experience may be made more acceptable and more effective in bringing about the desired treatment and the desired response to treatment.

---

*The above paragraphs contrasting citizen involvement and citizen action are taken, with minor adaptations, from Roland L. Warren, Stephen M. Rose, and Ann F. Burgunder, *The Structure of Urban Reform: Community Decision Organizations in Stability and Change* (Lexington, Mass.: Heath-Lexington, 1974), Chapter 6.

This is a rather different perception from that of citizen participants as representatives of a constituency to which the agency is responsible, and through whom it exercises a degree of accountability to this constituency—not only for reporting what it is doing, but for help in formulating what it will do in the future.

In this connection, the use of the word "consumers" to designate the citizen participants is indicative. For if they participate as consumers, they are participating in the patient role, to whom the most accustomed response is treatment. If, on the other hand, they are thought of as representatives of a constituency of accountability, then their participation is more likely to be seen in terms of self-sufficient citizens who are not primarily to be treated by the agency but rather to judge its activities and to help give it direction.

It seems to me that the use of the term "consumers" rather than the term "citizen leaders," or something similar, tends to diminish the concept to one of feedback from patients, thus not only demeaning the relationship but, of course, casting it in a manner which keeps control firmly in the hands of the agency administrator.

I would like to raise the question whether citizen participation can be meaningful if complete control is kept in the hands of the administrator, staff and superior officers, say, in the state department of mental health. Where this prevails, citizen participation must become little more than an animated "suggestion box" where the citizens may be heard from but where they have virtually no voice in determining whether their wishes and suggestions will be implemented. I suspect that many CMHC advisory boards actually function in this way, and some of the contract research reports on citizen participation in CMHC's tend to bear this out.

What I am suggesting is that meaningful citizen participation must imply the loss of some measure of control. I do not by any means suggest that it means loss of all control over policy decisions. Much of the confused rhetoric about citizen control in the decade of the sixties and early seventies was misleading because people were led to believe that citizen control involved total loss of control by constituted authorities. Few if any citizens groups ever advocated such a takeover. Most of them, although they were using the misleading term "citizen control," or "black control," or "neighborhood control," were struggling not for exclusive control over the organizations involved but simply for a meaningful voice which did imply a measure of control, a measure which was not afforded them if their wishes could be totally ignored by the organization.

For the CMHCs, the difference is rendered somewhat imprecisely by the distinction between advisory boards and policy or administrative boards. Presumably, policy boards do imply at least partial control—a definite constraint on the administrator—whereas advisory boards have no authority, no formal control prerogatives. Yet we all know that the distinction is not that easy. For some advisory boards actually do exercise a good deal of influence over policy, even though they have no formal authority to do so; and on the contrary, many policy or administrative boards exercise little if any influence on policy, even though they have authority to do so. The genuine test is whether situations regularly arise in which the executive modifies his decisions in accordance with the views of citizen participants, regardless of which type of formal board mechanism is operating.

Power, according to a classic definition, is the ability to impose one's will even over opposition. The ability of citizen representatives to have their way in situations where the executive agrees with their suggestions is no measure of power. Rather, the valid test is the extent to which they get their way when the director does not favor their position.

From this distinction, one other important aspect of the form of citizen participation should be clear. Citizen participation may take place through channels other than the formal provision for citizen boards in the organizational structure. It may be exercised from outside the organization, in a bargaining or negotiating situation in which mutual concessions are made between independent groups. Service agencies are used to this type of negotiating with various official and voluntary agencies. But the same often occurs with citizens groups who thus influence agency programs or policies even though they have no formal authorization to do so. In our nine-city study, we found many situations where the organizations were influenced by citizens groups not through representation and attendance at formal board meetings, but through the negotiating of various requests or demands made upon the organization from organizations of citizens which were quite independent of the agency itself. Thus, for example, the citizens officially representing the model neighborhood in a model cities program may have more direct impact—through negotiations—on the policy of a community mental health center than does the community mental health center's own citizen board.

In this study, we were interested in the responsiveness of the various organizations under investigation. We defined responsiveness in relation to low-income people, as follows: responsiveness is the acknowledgment by an organization of a legitimate role played by low-income people in the determining of its policies and programs. Under this definition, the responsiveness of an organization may be extremely superficial or it may be somewhat more meaningful. The more superficial type of responsiveness involved the citizens but gave them little power over decision making. It included the following:

—Formal arrangements within the structure of the organization which provide residents of poverty areas an avenue to influence the organization's policies and programs (positions on the board of directors and other decision-making bodies).

—Informal processes which are *regularly* practiced by the organization to give residents of poverty areas some form of policy and/or program review.

—Employment of poverty area residents by the organization, as a matter of deliberate policy.

—Formal relationships of the organization with organized groups of poverty area residents.

As distinguished from these relatively superficial indications of responsiveness, the more substantive types were categorized as follows:

—Contracts are delegated by the agency to low-income resident organizations.

—Poverty area residents of the policy-making board of the organization act as a block to accept or reject plans of the organization.

—Neighborhood residents are involved in changing the organization's hiring practices to employ residents in nonclerical, noncustodial kinds of jobs.

—The organization acts as advocate for neighborhood residents vis-à-vis another organization, or acts in concert with a neighborhood residents group vis-à-vis another organization.

—The organization increases the number of neighborhood residents on its decision-making board or on decision-making boards of its delegate agencies.

—The organization makes additional resources available to neighborhood groups (e.g., in kind donations of space and/or equipment).

—Neighborhood residents effect change in the organization's approach to problems.

—Neighborhood residents initiate new programs.

—Neighborhood residents effect or initiate changes in types of programs administered by the organization.

Roughly, it can be seen that this second list involved participation which "makes a difference," as distinguished from participation which may be merely nominal. It indicates a degree of power exercised by citizen representatives, but it hardly indicates a total take-over.

An aspect of study of the responsiveness of these fifty-four organizations to the needs and wishes of poverty area citizens which impressed us was the safeguards which agency staffs have against the use of power by citizen representatives.

In the first place, despite their sometimes strong language, most of these citizens had only minimal demands to make on the organizations, and most of these demands were ones which the organizations could accede to with neither discomfort nor any threat to the presumed professional standards of the programs and services they offered. Although often the citizens were not satisfied with the agencies' programs, they had neither the specialized competence nor the creativity to offer very drastic alternatives.

Where demands were made which would be inconvenient to the agencies or in their eyes threatened to lower standards of service, there were numerous ways these demands could be pared down to rather insipid changes which were perfectly acceptable. The organization could show how professional standards did not permit the change, or civil service regulations made it unacceptable, or how state law or federal regulations would be violated, or how funding agencies might withdraw support, etc. They could likewise usually obtain the support of the city council or the state department or the feds or the mayor's office in resisting the citizens' demands. Often, they only had to postpone action and wait until the fervor that had been whipped up among citizens had subsided. At specific meetings they could control the agenda and could control access of citizens to important bits of knowledge; they could "train" the citizens so that their participation would be "responsible," thus extracting the potential teeth from the citizen bite; they could offer jobs and vertical mobility to citizens who could touch the organization with the wand of responsiveness but not so forcefully as to make an impact on it.

At the same time, for these and other reasons, citizens groups found it difficult to organize, to keep their constituencies interested and active, to plan systematically to advance their own group's interests, to develop considered policy positions and to defend and advance them forcefully.

For both the citizens and the agencies, one of the greatest problems was the question of representation. It is an abiding problem—so much so, that it is difficult to see any completely adequate solution for it as regards citizen representation on CMHC boards. How do you represent the opinions of people who have no opinion? I do not mean to be facetious and I certainly do not mean to be derogatory in speaking of large masses of citizens with "no opinion." Most people have little interest in the structure and operation of mental health facilities, and have little contact with them. Ask them what they think about them, or how they think they could be improved, and they will give an answer which may approximate in ridiculousness the question itself. Adding up such answers doesn't do much good. Various studies show that public opinion on important issues is developed through various processes of group discussion. Without group discussion, there is little public opinion. How then can ordinary citizens, particularly residents of disadvantaged areas, be expected to have formulated a considered position with respect to the policies and programs of mental health agencies? And under these circumstances, who can speak for them—and with what mandate?

The traditional answer has been to assume that more well-to-do people with leisure time to devote to civic participation can take an unselfish viewpoint and represent the needs and wishes of the disadvantaged. That point of view has been pretty severely battered in the past decade's turmoil.

Choice of representatives through a regular election seems, on the face of it, simple and democratically defensible proposal, but the problem is that there is little inducement for individual citizens to bother with the problems of an election campaign simply in order to win a seat on a CMHC board, and less inducement for the electorate to bother to walk across the street to vote for or against them.

Another alternative is to seek representation from organized groups, from already existing citizens organizations which are more likely to have developed a leadership structure, a means of choosing representatives, and a position on various issues involving health and social services. This is not by any means a perfect solution, yet it would seem to make more sense in terms of the validity of the representation than either elections at large or the alternative of the CMHC staff selecting the board membership, or its appointment exclusively from the ranks of professional and well-to-do people.

Hence, I would strongly support the Health PAC study's recommendation that "Board membership come from representatives of potential patient community organizations, rather than from unaffiliated individuals."*

My one demurrer would be that, as indicated earlier, they not be thought of as representatives of patients but rather as representatives of the citizenry of the community, to which the CMHC has a responsibility as its constituency.

Once selected by whatever process—and let us hope that it is a process which is independent of the control of the CMHC itself—most citizen representatives would need to learn a good deal about the CMHC and its problems and the kinds of issues it faces as well as about how they can use themselves most effectively to represent citizen interests. I would make two observations.

First, it would be wise, unless the idea is to keep them completely under the thumb of the agency administration, that their training be conducted by some party other than the agency itself. Otherwise there is the danger that their training will consist of their being taught to share the present views of the administration and staff, and their learning from them that what the agency is now doing represents the "best of all possible worlds," and hence that they will be captured before they begin to exercise their mandate. I would add the hope that training would include their increasing knowledgeability about substantive issues and also their increasing knowledgeability and competence in the processes of interaction with staff and other board members, on the one hand, and the citizens they represent, on the other.

Second, I would propose that administration and staff need training just as much as citizen participants do. They need training in how to relate to citizen boards, to fear them less and to interact with them more openly and productively.

In this connection, much has been learned about citizen participation in the past decade or so. There has been a wealth of experience with various types of structures and procedures. We do not yet really understand all the nuances. But even on the basis of our present level of understanding, it is strange that several hundred community mental health centers are now in operation under provisions which call for citizen participation but offer no explicit guidelines along which such participation may be developed and utilized. This circumstance, plus the haziness involved—not only in such terms as mental health, community and continuity of care, but also in terms of citizen participation, consumer participation, community accountability and the rest—is both effect and cause of the

---

Op. cit., "Conclusions," p. 6.

notable lack of implementation of effective, forward-looking citizen participation policies in the community mental health field. I understand that the beginnings of the formulation of a guideline document are already under way. I would emphatically hope that in the process of developing these guidelines, NIMH would make appropriate use of the small number of local administrators with useful firsthand experience in innovative community participation projects, and of the small but growing number of social scientists who have been studying citizen participation processes both inside and outside of the Institute. There is considerable knowledge among such persons. But one thing is certain. We all still have a lot to learn.

NOTE

This chapter was presented as a paper at an Interagency Liaison Branch, OPC, NIMH-sponsored Interagency Technical Workshop on "Citizen Participation" on December 14, 1973, in Rockville, Md.

17

A Systems Approach To The Therapeutic Community And The Delivery Of Mental Health Services

ALFRED W. CLARK

INTRODUCTION

This paper outlines the theory and practice of the therapeutic community, emphasizing the approach's dependence on sociotherapy rather than psychotherapy. It goes on to discuss both the forces that push practice back to psychotherapy as well as those forces, such as social and community psychiatry, that encourage the diffusion of the concepts to other settings. On the basis of this analysis it is argued that the delivery of mental health services requires a theoretical model of connected regions, bringing together, in a systems framework, work, education, family, comunity and specialist mental health agencies. Finally, it discusses some of the elements that such a model should include, identifying those formal institutions that lie outside the usual case-work approach.

THEORY AND PRACTICE OF THE THERAPEUTIC COMMUNITY

The theory and practice of the therapeutic community developed in the latter part of the Second World War (Jones, 1968). They were based on an increasing appreciation that social forces could be pathogenic and that the reversal of their consequences depended on the manipulation of reparative social forces. Pioneers of the movement were also aware of the connectedness of service, family and work life. Underlying the move toward social psychiatry was the increasing realization that the traditional mental hospital often acted destructively by institutionalizing both patients and staff. Another strand in the development was the loss of faith in the medical model of psychopathology. As the sociological model of illness became more prominent, the expert role of the medically trained psychiatrist was less easy to justify and sustain.

Specially devised social systems were created to embody these various influences. They were characterized by a flattened hierarchical structure which reduced the power of experts and assigned the therapeutic role to all members of the community, including patients, as well as those staff members who were traditionally excluded from this function.

Group processes in large and small formal group meetings and informal relations were used to explore and reverse pathogenic social forces. The therapeutic community offered the patient a supportive social environment that supplanted his destructive social setting. From the security of this base he collaborated with patients and staff to change the character of his social network and to try out new behaviors. The overcontrolled patient was encouraged to be more outgoing and impulsive; and the undercontrolled patient was encouraged to be more inward-looking and careful. To further these changes, significant members of his network were also included in the therapeutic program. For this thrust to be successful, all participants had to engage in open communication, rather than being party to the collusions, evasions and inconsistencies that characterized the pathogenic network.

The approach assumed that patients were responsible people caught in painful conflict situations that forced them to behave in apparently irrational ways. Once the balance of forces was tipped, it was assumed that the healthy part of the patient and his network would take over. He would then be able to help himself as well as others and to move into full role performance in his family and work settings. For these reasons, the therapeutic community was kept open to the patient's family and work life and he was encouraged to participate as much as possible in these activities during his stay.

The assumption of responsibility also led to the emphasis on self-government, the patient being expected to help evolve the policy of the unit and to implement it through his participation in a variety of committees. Staff participated in these committees, but their views did not automatically carry more weight than those of patients. The opinions of both patients and staff were weighed according to a recognition of their respective roles and the quality of their contributions.

FORCES ACTING TO CONTAIN OR DIFFUSE THE APPROACH

The ideology of the therapeutic community threatened the established professional prerogatives of the various staff groups. At the same time, it offered doctors release from the attribution of omnipotence, and it offered both doctors and nurses release from the frustrations of working in settings that they could see were often pathogenic rather than therapeutic. Nurses were also offered a significant increase in status by the enlargement of their role to include therapy.

The establishment and continuation of the early therapeutic communities depended on a sufficient core of staff adopting a positive attitude toward the ideology. They were then able to act as culture carriers toward new permanent staff and staff who came for a limited period before moving on to other positions. Increasingly, however, it became apparent that staff who adopted this ideology could not move readily into other settings. Staff who valued career mobility exerted continuous pressure on therapeutic communities to value psychotherapy of a more traditional kind above the more radical sociotherapy. This behavior was influenced by the overall culture of the psychiatric and paramedical professions, particularly as most therapeutic communities were part of a larger and more traditional service or setting (Rapoport, 1960; Manning, 1974).

With the introduction of the 1959 Mental Health Act in the United Kingdom, and the 1963 Community Mental Health Center Act in the United States, strong pressures were set up to contain mental illness in the community rather than in the mental hospital. Traditional mental hospitals were closed, and the responsibility was placed squarely on local agencies. Lip service was paid to the notion that families should not be asked to carry undue burdens because of this legislation. Unfortunately, theoretical developments were not sufficient to cope fully with the implementation of the legislation. One of the consequences was the rather frantic borrowing from a variety of fields. Psychiatric wards were opened in general hospitals and some of the trappings of the therapeutic community were introduced. Half-way houses were established, once again with some resemblance to therapeutic community organization. Group therapy sessions were developed in outpatient clinics also claiming kinship with the therapeutic community. Few of these developments, however, amounted to a specially devised social system with the complete character of a therapeutic community. More positively, they may be viewed as quasi-applications or composites that often did valuable work despite the practical and theoretical constraints under which they operated. At least they allowed and continue to allow a break to be made with the rigidities of the past (Whiteley, 1973).

In addition to borrowing from the theory and practice of the therapeutic community, administrators and practitioners also came to borrow from other developments in social psychiatry. Perhaps the most popular model was that of stretching limited expertise by using highly trained people as consultants to other helpers. Caplan's (1970) approach exemplifies this development. The direction has now been extended to include lay people as well as the usual paramedicals and associated professional groups (Williams and Ozarin, 1967; Griffiths and Libo, 1968).

A SYSTEMS APPROACH TO SERVICE DELIVERY

The rather *ad hoc* developments in community approaches to mental illness, as illustrated by the above account, highlight the need for a theoretical model of connected regions. The developments in the therapeutic community approach provide some guidelines about theoretical underpinnings, therapeutic tasks, the mapping of actors and the design principles required to build hierarchical and nonhierarchical organizations that will have a preventive therapeutic or rehabilitative impact. The first step in developing such a model is to get quite clear what theoretical underpinnings are being used to understand mental illness. If these stress biological or intrapsychic processes, they cannot be understood or reversed by social means. It is suggested that the appropriate level of analysis is that of cross-pressures exerted on the patient by other people both as individuals and as members of groups. These are reflected as intrapsychic processes, but their origins are external to the person (Clark and Yeomans, 1969). On the basis of this

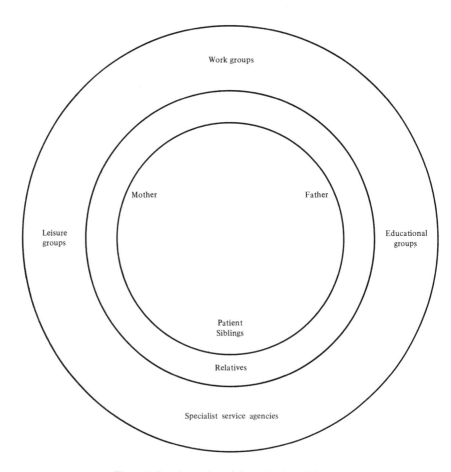

Figure 1. Broad mapping of the patient's social network

analysis, as shown in Figure 1, we can map the actors involved in the particular patient's real life sociodrama. The diagram can then be extended by mapping the work and leisure groups to which each of the parties is affiliated. Next it would be necessary to map the extended groups to which these immediate groups are associated. On this basis it would be possible to evaluate what leverage would be necessary to unsettle the constellation of relationships. This would lead to the identification of those social agencies whose cooperation would have to be sought to effect this unsettling and to introduce new elements to supplant or to replace existing pathological ones.

This is the minimum set of requirements necessary to specify the therapeutic tasks and the means by which they may be achieved. Finally, it would be necessary to coordinate the various agencies that must become implicated and to decide on the actions that each would have to take.

Experienced caseworkers telescope this whole process into an implicit selection of helping agencies, and assume that society has developed the appropriate institutional arrangements to help people who are in trouble. This approach makes no explicit or systematic analysis that is subject to correction by experience or by the opinions of other people, nor is there any way of pointing to gaps in information or facilities. What is needed is some set of design principles that allow us consciously to work toward the type of existing or projected, formal or informal, social organizations that are required to tackle the problem of mental health. The systems may range from loosely knit living communities to more closely knit family and work systems; together these make up the macro-organization in which the patient is embedded. We need to understand the interdependence between these structures; otherwise we cannot rationally approach the prevention, treatment and rehabilitation of mental illness.

In systems theory terms, we want to develop equipotentiality. This means that whatever path of treatment a patient is set on, there is flexibility to change paths, yet achieve similar outcomes. At present, if a child is designated as disturbed he goes into the pathway of the child guidance clinics and his prognosis includes a strong possibility of his becoming a law-abiding citizen with a reasonable adjustment. If he is designated as delinquent he goes into the Children's Court, and, possibly, the correctional stream, with a high likelihood of his coming out as a criminal and with a reduced likelihood of being well-adjusted (Higgins, 1963). The various social agencies have a tendency to deal with a particular type of client and to consider each aspect of life as separate. For instance, there is very little connection between agencies specializing in psychotherapy and agencies specializing in work placement. At best, a client will be passed from one agency to another for treatment of particular parts of himself or of his life space.

We require a theoretical framework that will stimulate a more coherent treatment of the person and his setting. This contextual approach draws on three assumptions central to general systems theory (Emery, 1969; Sutherland, 1973). First, that most human and social systems have a tendency to emphasize differentiation, so that the parts are different from the whole. This means that we may commit errors of synthesis if we try to understand the whole by analyzing the parts. Second, that we should attempt to gain some appreciation of the whole before attempting to understand the workings of the parts. As Lewin (1952) said, "Observation of social behaviour is usually of little value if it doesn't include an adequate description of the character of the social atmosphere or the *larger unit of activity* within which the specific social act occurs." Third, that we should move to a higher level of analysis when entities or systems are too complex to be analyzed in detail or to be made internally deterministic. They may well turn out to be deterministic at the macro-level.

The assumption of differentiation, the holistic approach and the phenomenon of macro-determinancy all direct our analytic, design and intervention strategies to higher level contextual systems. The question then arises of how to use system theory in planning the organizations to deliver services, including their relations to one another, the intercorporate dimension, as Friend and his colleagues describe it (Friend, Power, and Yewlett, 1974). The question also arises about the process of bringing existing organizations into the plan in their original or modified form and of creating new, adaptive organizations.

These questions may well be tackled by bringing together the perspectives of planning and action research (Trist, 1974). Modern planning is increasingly moving away from the notion that comprehensive plans can be developed by the relevant experts, imposed on a passive public and expected to serve the intended function unaltered through time. The first departure was toward an incremental model. This tried to approach the conditions of organic growth in which changed conditions are met by appropriate developments. It also gave more chance for a cast including others besides experts to play a part in the process. But it lacked a value base to give consistency in direction, and it simply reacted passively to changing conditions rather than actively influencing the future.

The latest planning model is based on a normative base that gives priority to the quality of human life as against profit or growth or any other value. In addition, it is proactive, attempting to shape the future rather than reacting to changes as they develop independently. Further, it encourages all parties who will be influenced by the plan to participate directly in its development and implementation. The whole endeavor is to be permeated by the action research mentality. This depends on the scientific attitude that no theory or solution is permanent and that all implemented plans and changes are viewed as experimental manipulations. Their consequences, both intended and unintended, must be evaluated and fed back into a new cycle of appreciation, theory building, change and evaluation (Clark, 1975).

The combination of normative, proactive planning and action research implies decentralized activity and maximum room for local experimentation. At the same time, central bodies may well set the stage for this activity, as well as helping to diffuse learning from one setting to another. At a national level, also, they may well be the appropriate body to initiate such planning activities. For example, when the existing organizations are dealing with only some selected fragments of a problem, when the overlaps and interdependencies are being neglected, or when vested interests and conflicts are acting against problem-solving and effective planning. A complementary relationship must be maintained between central and local bodies.

At the moment, a mental health problem may fall between various agencies or be wrongly monopolized by one or other of them. Once a specialist agency has been created to handle a defined problem, it is easy to forget that other social agencies may already exist that would do a similar job without some of the associated stigma. This was the history of special schools for physically and mentally handicapped children. The fashion was to send them to these schools even when this isolated them from their peers and created an additional difficulty in reintegrating them into the broader society at a later stage. It also prevented their peers from learning how to cope with handicapped people without misplaced solicitude. Present thinking assumes that the child should be kept in the normal school framework and special facilities provided, if necessary, within that setting.

This analysis suggests that we need a classification of organizations that does not depend on splitting them into those that handle normals and those that handle deviants. We should look at their generic function in society rather than the phenotypical characteristics of the prospective clients. Katz and Kahn (1966) provide us with a functional analysis that leads to the following classification of organizations: productive organizations to provide goods and services; maintenance organizations to inculcate shared values and socialize people for societal roles; political systems to allocate human and physical resources and to adjudicate among competing groups; and adaptive organizations to create new knowledge. Maintenance organizations either perform a direct function, as in education, or a restorative function, as in health, welfare, reform and rehabilitation.

While the maintenance organizations may seem to be those that most concern us here, the other types of organizations should not be neglected. They are important not only as potential preventive and therapeutic levers but also in their own right. All citizens must take up roles in them to perform the major tasks of society and they usually perform subsidiary tasks in relation to their primary tasks. For instance, an industrial company may supplement external organizations by having its own induction and training program and a health and welfare service. This points up the isomorphic relationship between the tasks that are basic to the survival of a society and to a single organization: each must produce, maintain itself, manage resources and adapt to its environment.

Despite difficulties with some criminal patients, the therapeutic community was sufficiently robust in function to treat people classified either as criminals or mentally ill. This acted to break down the distinction between services for normals and deviants. Prisons cannot fulfill the incompatible functions of therapy and rehabilitation on the one hand and retribution and incarceration on the other. Therapy and rehabilitation should be the function of a maintenance organization; retribution and incarceration, in rare and specific cases, should be those of a political organization. The distinction is made not in terms of the characteristics of the people concerned but in terms of the function that society requires the organization to perform.

The right-hand side of Figure 2 shows the outcome toward which mental health workers direct their activities. The desired outcome is that clients should be made psychologically comfortable and able to participate effectively in their family, work and associational roles. The lower middle part of the figure shows the set of maintenance organizations that they habitually look toward in achieving this outcome. They cluster in the maintenance classification and have differentiated themselves as specialist services for deviant people. Sheltered workshops and art and leisure pursuits are the only ones that are outside the maintenance classification. There is little overlap between the maintenance organizations for deviants in the bottom middle of the figure and the maintenance organizations for normals in the top left-hand side of the figures. This split increases the difficulty of achieving the rehabilitative outcome. The absence of productive and political organizations in the deviant set also reduces the chance of success in rehabilitation. It means that major levers for therapeutic change are being artificially excluded from the armamentarium of the traditional caseworker. These workers and community psychiatrists must develop theories and means of using these largely untapped resources. This requires a shift from the medical to the sociological model of mental illness. It is largely, as Weakland (1969) puts it, the cross currents within and between the relatively closed systems of the individuals, families and localized pathogenic social networks and the demands of the broader society, at school, at work and in new associations, that must be made more congruent. This cannot be achieved by side-stepping the confrontation completely. It may be timed and strengths fostered to cope with it, but eventually the individual must be helped to confront the schism between his family and the social system. To do this the helping professions must work directly with the major functional organizations of society (cf. Duhl and Leopold, 1968).

Many members of the helping professions appear to have little contact with the productive or the political organizations shown in the top left-hand side of Figure 2. To the extent that their understanding of these organizations is limited, so too is their capacity to use them to help clients. Hirschowitz (1971) analyzes the role strain involved in moving from clinician to that of administrator, integrator and promoter. The dilemma revolves about the choice of a preferred identity between the sensitive, nondirective and professionally pure clinician and the more robust, directive and sullied politician and businessman. To be effective, the community mental health leader must avoid clinging to his earlier role and choose flexibly from a role repertoire that enables him to penetrate communities, and to enter into a collaborative process of promotion, negotiation, planning, implementation and evaluation of programs. These skills overlap precisely with those required of the planner and the action researcher. As vested interests are threatened in both cases, it helps to expect hostility, crisis and disruption as an inevitable part of the process of change, the result, as Schon called it, of dynamic conservatism (Schon, 1971).

Although Hirschowitz's analysis focuses on the role of the formal leader of community mental health programs, the same dilemma faces all professionals caught up in these activities. While the training of social workers, unlike psychiatrists, has included a sociological perspective, they have also been taught and rewarded for individual casework, usually resting on a nondirective value system. Social workers settle readily into the patterns of interviewing clients in the office, even when demands of community work require active penetration of political, work, family and associational domains. Psychologists, too, revert to earlier models of diagnostic testers and psychotherapists rather than taking on the threatening tasks of community involvement.

Psychiatric nurses come from more practical classes in society, with origins and

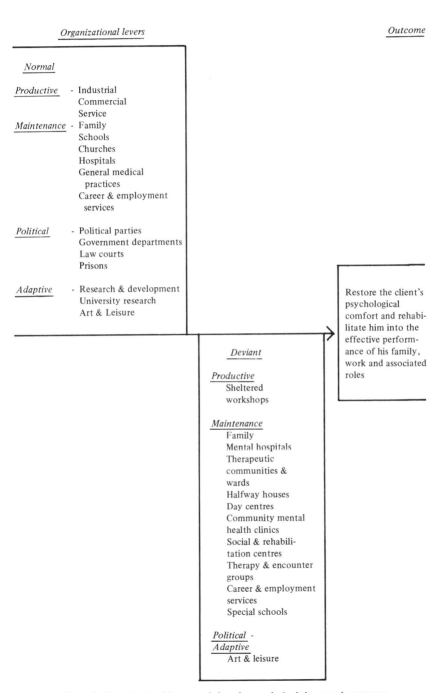

Figure 2. Organizational levers to bring about a desired therapeutic outcome

educational attainments closer to the average of the patient population. Their professional training is less prolonged and conceptual than psychiatrists' for instance. Consequently, a practical bent often characterizes their approach to patients and their problems. In the therapeutic community, when they were released from some of the limitations of their traditional role as custodians and doctors' subordinates, they initiated active help for patients by making direct contact with the workaday world of the community.

It may be that the effectiveness of lay helpers is the result of not being bound by hang-ups of what is professionally appropriate and what is not. They may be able to see most clearly what is needed to help a particular client or ''at risk'' population and how this may be done, for instance, by a commonsense move that gave actual help with a problem by intervening with people who control resources, rather than one that aimed at the development of insight. From observation, a large number of the responses of other patients in the therapeutic community were concrete rather than conceptual. The more highly trained professionals seemed to avoid the concrete and focus on the conceptual. They both see and respond to the pathological side of the patient, whereas people of lesser specialist training see less pathology and respond to the healthy side (Angyal, 1965; Clark and Yeomans, 1969). As estimates of the incidence of psychiatric symptoms implicate about a quarter of the population in the cities of industrialized countries, this approach is functional for the focal individual and for society (Susser, 1968).

People caught in pathogenic family relations may use work as an anchor to prevent them from slipping into more severe pathology. It may also act as a pathogenic force, increasing alienation on the one hand or undue stress on the other. From either point of view it demands serious attention. The most active manifestation of this interest is the industrial democracy movement in Europe (Emery and Thorsrud, 1969) and the job design movement in the United States (Herzberg, 1968; Davis and Taylor, 1972; Work in America Report, 1973). The proceedings of an international conference held in New York in 1972 brought these two traditions together under the rubric of the quality of working life (Davis and Cherns, 1974).

Mental health workers should learn about these developments and evaluate their potential for preventing pathology or for providing a therapeutic input. In addition, as industry provides a leading edge in advanced societies, the character of these developments will shape maintenance and political organizations. The modal character that society required families and schools to mold for assembly lines and highly bureacratic structures will not fit autonomous work groups and matrix organizations (Herbst, 1974; Kingdon, 1973). The criteria of mental health will shift as changes in the productive organizations lead to adaptations in the maintenance organizations. Further, as workers are given more decision-making responsibilities at work, they will come to expect a more direct say in local and national affairs. Thus political organizations will be under pressure to adapt to this new force. In addition, the rate of change is higher in the industrial sector than in the service sector. We may expect, therefore, an increasing wave of work-induced pathologies as many white-collar workers see that their jobs are relatively less satisfying than those of blue-collar workers—what we might label "white-collar blues," to vary Gooding's (1970) *Fortune* title of "Blue-Collar Blues on the Assembly Lines."

There are striking parallels between the characteristics of the industrial democracy and job design movement, and the theory and practice of the therapeutic community. Each rests on a normative base that values the individual as a responsible member of the group, entitled to participate in decisions that affect its activities, receive recognition for his contributions, and give and receive social support as a counter to the stresses involved in achieving its goals. Moreover, each designs situations and tasks that promote well-being, freedom and growth, rather than boring, repetitive behavior, restriction and stagnation. Emery and Emery (1974) summarize the design principles to be used in the shift from bureaucratic organization to team organization based on semiautonomous groups. They also spell out the strategy used in democratization programs and the practical steps required in the implementation process. At the center of the method is the participative design seminar. This lasts from one and a half to three days and allows the various people with the most immediate knowledge of the situation to work together in arriving at a new design. The approach has been effective not only in industrial, commercial, public service and professional settings, including education, but also in regional, urban and community planning. Kepner and her colleagues (1970) have developed a new training model for mental health workers based on a similar philosophy of participation. It achieved change within institutions from which participants were drawn and furthered collaboration and coordination between agencies. Developments based on similar values are apparent in family organizations, as well as in the largely unorganized groundswells of the countercultures of the young, women's and gay liberation movements, and ecological concern (Thompson, 1972; Bateson, 1973).

Evaluation studies of the moves to postindustrial organizations (Davis and Cherns, 1974), therapeutic communities (Sanders, Smith and Weinman, 1967; Hall, 1973; D.H. Clark, 1974), and community psychiatry (Susser, 1968; Wing and Hafner, 1972; Wing and Hailey, 1972) are sufficiently encouraging for them to be accepted as desirable directions toward which to commit physical and psychological investments. This paper has suggested that this investment will lead to greater payoffs if general system theory is used to bring the connected regions into one analytic framework. Not only will their interdependence be more fully apparent but the appreciation of the need for an interdisciplinary approach will also be inescapable.

BIBLIOGRAPHY

Angyal, A. *Neurosis and Treatment: A Holistic Theory.* New York: Wiley, 1965.

Bateson, G. *Steps to an Ecology of Mind.* St. Albans, Herts: Paladin, 1973.

Caplan, G. *The Theory and Practice of Mental Health Consultation.* London: Tavistock, 1970.

Clark, A.W., and Yeomans, N.T. *Fraser House: Theory, Practice and Evaluation of a Therapeutic Community*. New York: Springer, 1969.

Clark, A. W., and Association. *Experimenting with Organizational Life: The Action Research Approach*. New York: Plenum, 1975.

Clark, D.H. *Social Therapy in Psychiatry*. Harmondsworth, Middx: Penguin, 1974

Davis, L.E., and Cherns, A. (eds.). *Quality of Working Life: Problems, Prospects and State of the Art*. Vol. 1. New York: Free Press, 1974 (In press).

Davis, L.E., and Taylor, J.C. (eds.). *Design of Jobs*. Harmondsworth, Middx: Penguin, 1972.

Duhl, L.J., and Leopold, R.L. (eds.). *Mental Health and Urban Social Policy*. San Francisco: Jossey-Bass, 1968.

Emery, F.E. *Systems Thinking*. Harmondsworth, Middx: Penguin, 1969.

Emery, F.E., and Emery, M. *Participative Design: Work and Community Life*. Occasional Papers in Continuing Education No. 4, Centre for Continuing Education, The Australian National University, 1974.

Emery, F.E., and Thorsrud, E. *Form and Content in Industrial Democracy*. London: Tavistock, 1969.

Friend, J.K., Power, J.M., and Yewlett, C.J.L. *Public Planning: The Intercorporate Dimension*. London: Tavistock, 1974.

Gooding, J. Blue collar blues on the assembly line. *Fortune*, July 1970, 68-71.

Griffiths, C.R., and Libo, L.M. *Mental Health Consultants: Agents of Community Change*. San Francisco: Jossey-Bass, 1968.

Hall, J.R. Structural characteristics of the psychiatric patient community and the therapeutic milieu. *Human Relations*, 1973, *26*, 787-809.

Herbst, P.G. *Socio-technical Theory and Design*. London: Tavistock, 1974.

Herzberger, F. One more time: how do you motivate employees? *Harvard Business Review*, 1968, *46*, 53-62.

Higgins, R. The concept of maladjustment: its social consequences. *Human Relations*, 1963, *16*, 61-73.

Hirschowitz, R.G. Dilemmas of leadership in community mental health. *Psychiatric Quarterly*, 1971, *45*, 1-15.

Jones, M. *Social Psychiatry in Practice*. Harmondsworth, Middx: Penguin, 1968.

Katz, D., and Kahn, R.L. *Social Psychology of Organizattions*. New York: Wiley, 1966.

Kepner, E., Harris, C., and Handlon, J.H. *Community Creativity Collaboration: A New Training Model in Mental Health*. Cleveland: Case Western Reserve University, 1970.

Kingdon, D.K. *Matrix Organizations*. London: Tavistock, 1973.

Lewin, K. *Field Theory in Social Science*. London: Tavistock, 1952.

Manning, N. *Values and Practice in the Therapeutic Community*. Unpublished manuscript. London: Henderson Hospital, 1974.

Rapoport, R.N. *Community as doctor*. London: Tavistock, 1960.

Sanders, Smith, R.S., and Weinman, B.S. *Chronic Psychosis and Recovery: An Experiment in Socio-Environmental Treatment*. San Francisco: Jossey-Bass, 1967.

Schon, D.A. *Beyond the Stable State*. London: Temple Smith, 1971.

Susser, M. *Community Psychiatry*. New York: Random House, 1968.

Sutherland, J.W. *A General Systems Philosophy for the Social and Behavioral Sciences*. New York: Braziller, 1973.

Thompson, W.I. *At the Edge of History*. New York: Harper Colophon, 1972.

Trist, E.L. Adaptive planning and action research. In Clark, A.W. (ed.), *Experiences in Action Research*. London: Malaby, 1974. (In Press.)

Weakland, J.H. Schizophrenia: basic problems in sociocultural investigation. In Plog, S.C., and Edgerton, R.B. (eds.), *Changing Perspectives in Mental Illness*. New York: Holt, Rinehart and Winston, 1969.

Whiteley, J.S. *Dealing with Deviants*. London: Hogarth Press, 1973.

Williams, R.H., and Ozarin, L.D. (eds.). *Community Mental Health: An International Perspective*. San Francisco: Jossey-Bass, 1967.

Wing, J.K., and Hafner, H. (eds.). *Roots of Evaluation*. London: Oxford University Press, 1972.

Wing, J.K., and Hailey, A.M. *Evaluating a Community Psychiatric Service*. London: Oxford University Press, 1972.

Work in America Report. Boston: Massachusetts Institute of Technology Press, 1973.

Part V

Leadership Strategies
and Dilemmas

Our final section was conceived in the "think tank" atmosphere generated by a national seminar on "the human service leader as agent of change." Leaders who participated in the seminar occupied administrative seats in mental health and human service organizations. Their positions, while heavy with responsibilities, often critically lacked commensurate authority and resources. The multiple demands of their complex roles generated some nostalgia for the stable simplicity of their earlier roles as clinicians. Their personal reports of the clinician-administrator role shift were similar to Pattison's recent study of psychiatrist administrators. "The emergent role of the clinician-executive poses significant problems in the synthesis of function and identity. There is a disjunction between professional acculturation and this emergent administrative role."*

In sharing information about role overload and inter-role strains, the seminar faculty and participants found the sharing of their *subjective* experiences helpful and supportive. They knew that many colleagues had "burned out" in administrative positions and wanted to prevent this from happening to themselves. Much discussion therefore centered on mastery of the critical transitions en route from the role of "clinician" to the more complex one of administrator or "executive." They deplored the "sink or swim" passage into the role that veterans of the transition had endured. They emphasized the need for training, guidance and support structures for mental health administrators.

In discussion, the ambivalence of "pure" clinicians toward business, politics and planning, exemplified in the "myth of professional cleanliness," was explored. Since mental health administrators were often the target for the negative side of this ambivalence, they felt strong needs for reference groups in which to strengthen and consolidate their identities, and from which to influence the attitudes and training of clinicians.

Participants also sought mentors and role models from whom they could learn and with whom they could identify. Needs for better understanding of the clinician-executive's dilemmas were loudly voiced. In this section, we address these needs through contributions from seasoned administrators whose experience

---

*E.M. Pattison, Young psychiatrist administrators, *Am. J. Psychiatry*, 131:2, 154-158, 1974.

and conceptual approaches can illuminate the clinician-executive route for those newly embarked upon it. These contributions bring the complexity of the mental health "executive" role into sharp relief and chart the milestones likely to be encountered through the clinician-executive transition.

Klerman has been a seminal contributor to our knowledge of the processes that unfold through the critical transition experienced by the mental health professional as he moves from the pure clinician role to that of administrator. He elucidates seven primary role tasks that the clinician-executive must master. His discussion is enriched by examples drawn from personal experience of the joys and vicissitudes to be anticipated throughout the transition. He shares with the reader his personal discomfort with some aspects of the clinician-executive role and emphasizes that the transition involves the experience of loss and dysequilibrium. In his role shift, the clinician-executive experiences critical role transition and an identity crisis which is punctuated by emergency emotions and value struggles.

In her chapter, *Christmas* describes the "personal saga" of an ascent up a career ladder, each successive rung of which placed increasing administrative demands upon her and multiplied the number of community groups and agencies with which she had to interface. In accepting roles increasingly freighted with indirect consultant, supervisory, administrative and political tasks, she had gradually to surrender the satisfactions of direct clinical involvement.

She discusses her pioneering contributions to the development of "new career" paraprofessionals—and some consequences, anticipated and unanticipated. She describes how she came to terms with the language and demands of programming, planning, budgeting, grantsmanship and politicking. From her present position, directing New York City's mental health program, she discusses all the forces, psychological, social and political, to be considered in deciding where to exercise leverage in action for mental health. She addresses in forthright fashion the issue of sociopolitical involvement and social change advocacy. The Christmas saga is a "living-learning" illustration of the working through of dilemmas of the clinician-executive transition.

De Marneffe focuses upon the clinician-executive's role in the changing funding and political environment. His approach demonstrates the depth and breadth of environmental scanning that are required to function effectively in the clinician-executive role. In analyzing mental health's sociopolitical environments, he stresses the building of relationships with the representatives of the many constituencies that influence the course of mental health legislation. He compels us to appreciate the interplay between multiple, sometimes contending, groups and agencies in dealing with such salient issues as affirmative action, privacy-confidentiality, regulation and consumer advocacy. He notes the national crisis of confidence in institutions and leaders and emphasizes the necessity for visibility in the public trenches so that stereotypes associated with these negative attitudes are combated. He discusses the rise of consumerism and suggests collaborative interaction with consumer groups and citizen advisory groups. His acceptance of an interactive "Hellzapoppin' " role compares favorably with the inactive "Hamlet" posture criticized by Warren.

The chapter by *Vanderpol* analyzes the problems confronting the clinician as he attempts to become a community consultant. Vanderpol offers personal vignettes of the shift from the circumscribed role of psychoanalyst in office and hospital practice to the more fuzzily bounded role of mental health consultant in the schools. In doing so, he sheds light on the phenomenon Caplan has described as "role shift discomfort."

He describes the difficulties encountered by placing himself in the shoes of consultees like the youthful volunteers in "hot line" programs or teachers with different levels of psychological sophistication in the schools. He particularly stresses the need to communicate with consultees in their own language and within their particular frame of reference. He discusses changes in the basic assumptions, stance and modus operandi of the clinician as he defines himself in the life space of the schools. While highlighting problems and pitfalls in the transition, he balances his comments with discussion of satisfactions to be derived from the extended role. The effective consultant witnesses growth in his consultees and has impact on primary prevention.

Warren discusses the behavior of mental health agencies and their leaders in the community problem-solving arena. His chapter is a sociopsychological autopsy on mental health agency behavior during the growth heyday of the federal model-cities program. The behavior of most of the mental health leaders studied was reflective, reactive and distancing. He contrasts this "Hamlet" posture with the more energetic, interactive engagement of those agency leaders who immersed themselves in the "Hellzapoppin' " scene, built relationships with agencies and community representatives and participated in the design of umbrella service delivery vehicles in which their own roles were actively negotiated.

Warren's case effectively documents the behavior of clinician-executives who are clinging to the "clinician" role while failing adequately to comprehend the adaptive demands upon them as "executives." The "Hamlet" behavior he describes is not inconsistent with the role of the psychiatric clinician who is accustomed to analyze and interpret without exercising any action initiatives. In the hurly-burly of community negotiation, such clinicians may unwittingly cling to this familiar mode. Clinicians who have shifted more securely into the executive role know the hazards of reflecting too intensively and too long; they vigorously seize opportunities to "talk business" with other interest groups. Our chapters by Christmas, Klerman and De Marneffe show that the administrator who disabuses himself of the clinician's elitist assumptions and myths can successfully master the "Hellzapoppin" role appropriate to the turbulence of the mental health scene.

Our final chapter is a personal account by *Jones* of the development of his theories and practice through many decades as a clinician-executive. He describes his evolution from an early role in research on the biochemistry of schizophrenia to multiple roles in service, training and research. His present approach involves the application of systems theories to the practice of psychiatry. He describes how his perspective expanded through the years to encompass a systems view of the biopsychosociocultural factors that influence deviant behavior and can be harnessed for its management and prevention. He describes this evolving theoretical position and the steps by which he arrived at it. His personal account of innovative adaption to successive mental health challenges is a legacy and role model for young administrators embarking upon the road that Jones, always a forerunner, has mapped for them.

18

The Joys and Vicissitudes of Life As A Clinician-Executive

GERALD L. KLERMAN

This chapter elaborates certain ideas that have proven useful to me in the evolution of my career as a clinician-executive. These ideas derive in large part from a fruitful collaboration with Daniel Levinson, a social psychologist, over a number of years. We published three papers in which we developed the concepts of the clinician-executive and its attendant role transitions. These ideas have proved useful to me in mastering my personal role transitions—as I struggled with the issues of identity and role—when I became the director of Clinical Services and, subsequently, the director of the Connecticut Mental Health Center.

During those transition experiences, as I went through periods of doubt, guilt, anger, frustration, pressure and anxiety, I was greatly helped by having a personal consultant-confidant with whom to review issues. As a result, I urge other clinician executives to seek out a consultant-confidant. He should be outside the organizational chain of authority. He should be more than a sounding board, preferably skilled in a relevant behavioral or social science field, such as management, economics or sociology. With the help of such a consultant, the clinician-executive can place his subjective experience into a more objective context.

THE CONCEPT OF THE CLINICIAN-EXECUTIVE

In the course of my collaboration with Levinson, we developed the concept of clinician-executive. This concept has helped us to understand the subjective experience and career dilemmas of those mental health professionals, trained initially as clinicians, who undertake administrative or executive careers. One important feature of this role is that they are not explicitly trained for executive careers. This transition in professional careers is not unique to the mental health field. In higher education for example, the historian, psychologist or physicist may become a department chairman, dean or university president. An engineer may become the head of a corporation. Lawyers often shift from the practice of law to head government agencies or serve as public officials. Thus it is not an uncommon phenomenon for professionals to move into administrative, managerial, or executive responsibilities for which they were not initially trained.

A second important feature of the clinician-executive career is that it occurs in the context of formal organizations such as a university, corporation, government agency, hospital or veterans administration. Professional careers in modern society increasingly take place in formal complex organizations. The movement from solo practice to positions in complex organizations is rapidly occurring in medicine. This poses specific conflicts for the health professional in this second career because he assumes roles for which he has had little or no direct training or experience. A consequent issue for discussion is: Should we train residents for the executive role during their clinical training or should we, as most of us have done, be retreaded in our mature years?

THE CONCEPTS OF ROLE AND SELF

I have found two concepts from social psychology very useful. One is the concept of role; the other is the concept of self. A *role* is the socially prescribed behavior for a position in a social system. The *self* is the internal representation of this experience.

The process of clinician-executive role transition is paralleled by an intrapsychic change in self-definition and identity. The assumption of the new role initiates a change in identity and is an intrapsychic process that is fraught with conflict as are all role transitions. While there is a rich literature in social psychology on roles, there is little written about the intrapsychic shifts that occur as the clinician becomes an executive. While there are memoirs and anecdotes, little formal attention has been given to the processes by which the clinician broadens his identity to become a clinician-executive. In my experience and that of my colleagues, changes occur in the process of taking on the new role that are akin to an identity crisis punctuated by attendant emotional fluctuations such as guilt, depression, anger and doubt.

THE ROLE-TASKS OF THE CLINICAN-EXECUTIVE

What are role tasks? Why is their achievement problematical? The answers reside in the complexity of the tasks that constitute the clinician-executive role. Levinson and I identified seven role tasks. Individuals struggle with all or some of these role tasks. The ease with which they are mastered depends upon many factors, such as the structure of the organization, the orienting cues from the members of his role set, the availability of support, generic coping skills and personal experience.

The most intellectually demanding task is mapping, developing a conception of the organization. Appreciation of the organization as the social macrosystem is often very difficult for mental health professionals because they have been trained to view the individual microsystem as the main unit of social behavior. An organization is a social structure with its own unique processes and dynamics.

These cannot be sufficiently grasped by clinicians who have the common tendency to reduce organizational problems to psychological or interpersonal phenomena. It is very hard for those of us trained as clinicians to see the organization as a social organism with its own structure and dynamics. An example is the experience of a young physician, not a psychiatrist, I know who is subject to recurrent depressions. He has recently become the administrator of an inpatient unit in a general hospital that has many problems. When confronted with this complexity, this physician's pattern of response was to label the head nurse a "hysterical bitch" and to blame the hospital administrator for not knowing what he was doing. On more sober reflection, the *organizational* diagnosis was that the floor was being shared by two services with no agreement about authority, responsibility or the division of labor. It requires considerable effort for a professional in the health organization to develop a conception of the organization as a functioning social system and to appreciate the uniqueness of the health system as distinguished from other human service or product organization systems. A health organization, be it hospital, mental health center, state department of mental hygiene, or the National Institute of Alcoholism, is different from General Motors or I.T.T. One of the main differences in health organizations is that the physicians have much more power and autonomy than do professionals in other organizations.

The decision as to when to approach a problem in terms of the dynamics of the individual and when to see it in terms of the dynamics of the organization guides one in organizational diagnosis. For example, in the diagnosis of disturbed behavior on a ward, the clinician-executive may approach a problem in terms of the personality of one of the patients, when in fact there is also an unresolved policy conflict at the staff level generating so-called Stanton-Schwartz phenomena in the war milieu. A multifocal systems perspective is required for accurate diagnosis.

The second role task that we identified is that of translating knowledge into action while learning organizational interventions. The first task is *cognitive* mastery—learning to think of the organization as a system; the second task is *tactical* mastery. As clinicians, most of us have been trained to think of treatment as interventions in the lives of individuals. Some of us have learned to intervene in families. What the executive does in an organization is to intervene in the complex social system. He functions in the role described by Greenblatt as "social systems clinician." In his corrective intervention, he exercises administrative, not merely sapiential, authority. He fires, hires, unites, delegates, closes a ward, opens a day hospital, reassigns responsibilities or introduces new operating committee procedures. His interventions may, however, become empty exercises. This is particularly likely when social systems diagnosis is deficient and/or planning is ineffective. On the other hand, dramatic changes have been realized by creative hospital administrators introducing such structural changes as the open door policy in Scotland or the delegation of therapeutic tasks to indigenous nonprofessionals. At the level of state service delivery systems, clinician administrators have used their authority and skill to close down obsolete hospitals, open day hospitals, support community mental health centers and stimulate community residences. In all of these cases the object of the clinician-executive's intervention is not an individual or a family but a social system.

The third problem-fraught aspect of role and identity is the administrator-executive's acceptance of responsibility for authority in a *social* system. This role task involves other staff members and the exercise of authority over them. Most of us trained in the psychotherapeutic role have learned to suspect the exercise of authority. Power becomes tainted by its many possibilities for abuse; this distaste for power or its exercise may eventuate as obsessive substituting for decisive action; this can be supported or rationalized by psychiatric interpretations of unresolved anal conflicts or identification with feared Oedipal figures or exercising power to defend against impotence. A mystique has thus developed. A serious dilemma is created for the clinician-executive as he exercises his authority and makes decisions which are not always popular with his professional peers or subordinates. Occasionally he must make such painful decisions as firing some person. Another dilemma in the exercise of authority stems from the very severe constraints that are often placed upon it. State and federal bureaucracies have so many built-in checks against the illegitimate or arbitrary use of authority that its legitimate exercise becomes impeded. Because of grievance procedures, labor unions and political pressure, it becomes as difficult to fire an irresponsible employee as to discharge a tenured professor.

Eventually each clinician-executive develops a style for dealing with the issue of authority. An interesting style is that of purposeful ambiguity, practiced by some very famous administrators. For example, A. Schlesinger, Jr., in his biography of Franklin D. Roosevelt, describes how F.D.R. would call in three Cabinet members, one after another, and tell them of an important problem that only each of them could solve. He would offer each his full support in dealing with it. He would then wait and see what happened. The consequences of such a style, in terms of distrust, conflict and competition seem to me to outweigh any possible advantage. However, purposeful ambiguity, like other forms of manipulation, is by no means rare. In present organizational climates, styles that are more open, honest and direct appear to be more adaptive than Machiavellian, expedient, manipulative ones.

The fourth task of the clinician-executive is to relate to the mental health profession and the interfaces between its professional groups and training, research and service subsystems. The task is akin to that of labor management in industry. The task of intergroup integration with professionals is unusually delicate because of the considerable autonomy, power and influence with which they have become accustomed to operate. In consequence, they are protective of turf and domain and highly resistant to efforts at creating supraordinate integration. Most efforts to deal with them by direct exercise of authority, however legitimate, are therefore usually doomed to eventual failure. The skill, therefore, is to promote coalitions among professional groups and functionally related divisions in the organization. As Sherif's studies demonstrate, groups will acknowledge their interdependence and coalesce in pursuit of supraordinate goals and shared purposes when unity is required for their realization.

However, mental health organizations are uniquely differentiated: by profession, by function (e.g., out-care, part-care, in-care), and in unitized systems, by community affiliation. The balance to be struck by the leader between subsystem differentiation and supraordinate integration is always delicate and difficult. Supraordinate commitment is also rendered tenuous by the strong affiliation of the mental health professional to his professional group, *not* to the employing organization. This problem, described by Gouldner as the "cosmopolitan-local dilemma" is vexing.

Most of the functions discussed up to now are components of the clinician-executive role in the *internal* integration of his organization, its material and human resource components. I now address the problem-ridden role tasks associated with external integration, collaborative exchange with persons, groups and institutions with which the leader's organization interfaces. In approaching this crucial task, a general systems theoretical frame is helpful: the concept of boundary maintenance helps to define the boundaries of the organization within its relevant environments. For example, as director of an urban mental health center, I must maintain my relationship with such suprasystems as the State Department of Mental Health and its state sib-system, the Department of Administration and Finance, and the Massachusetts General Hospital, itself complexly related to Harvard Medical School. There is also an Area Board of citizens as well as numerous community agencies, institutions and constituencies. The larger the organization, the more complex are the boundary-regulating functions. With a systems view, every unit component of the organization is seen to interface with related suprasystems, sib-systems and subsystems. For example, the director of an adult day hospital program is involved in maintenance functions at the boundary between his program and the inpatient units. This often requires suprasystematic regulation in the form of policy, since the two groups of boundary migrators who most commonly have the requisite information are patients (who have no authority) and suprasystem administrative staff (who do have authority). Most clinical subsystems reflect the preferred patterns of the professionals within them: they strain toward autonomy and fight against dependency, interdependency—or any form of external regulation. Left to themselves, most clinical units attempt to recruit patient populations whom they can serve with satisfying competence. They attempt to develop multiple exclusion criteria, often declining, for example, to accept alcoholics, psychotics, poor people, disruptive people, and people who live outside the catchment area.

The cardinal competence involved in boundary maintenance is that of *negotiation*, often in a psychological climate of high tension and conflict. While negotiating talent is crucial to the clinician-executive career, there is, again, little in the training of clinicians to teach this skill. Lawyers, by contrast, acquire this distinctive competence because so much of the practice of law is the negotiation of contractual relations between parties. We are not used to thinking of ourselves as negotiators, and the concept has become freighted with negative identity connotations.

For me, this is currently the most difficult adaptive demand confronting me as a clinician-executive. Earlier in my career, the exercise of authority was the most painful task for me. More recently, my negotiating skills have been overtaxed by the multiplying demands that emanate from the vying, contending, ideologically diverse human service agencies in the complex urban catchment area we serve. Complex treaty negotiations—interagency agreements and continuity corridors—are required. Quid pro quo resource exchanges must be negotiated whenever service domains overlap. Agreements often break down, requiring the mediation of a highly regarded, acceptable leader who can maintain objectivity, break win-lose stalemates and suggest acceptable compromises. The director often plays the role of a Kissinger in regulating the territorial conflicts within his domain.

The sixth task of the clinician-executive is to ensure organizational adaptation, promoting organizational growth and renewal. Recognition of this task runs counter to the stereotype of the administrator as a paper shuffler and nay-saying obstacle to innovation. Incidentally, this stereotype is consistent with high investment in stability maintenance, and was therefore true of administrators in large organizations like some V.A. or state departments. However, the executive or professional administrator of today is concerned with growth, perpetuation and adaptation with systems tasks: he is challenged to innovate and keep himself and his organization adaptively aligned.

The seventh and last task component of the clinician-executive role is the most difficult for the self-system: achieving and claiming a new identity. Personal experience, supplemented by that of other clinician executives, indicates that the first year of executive responsibility is usually punctuated, like the adolescent's identity crisis, by considerable personal turmoil. One becomes depressed, frustrated, irritable, has trouble sleeping, loses or gains weight—in fact, betrays all the signs of emotional disruption associated with critical role transition. Changes in role behavior are thus accompanied by symptom formation, change in self-identity and self-concept—and fluctuating self-esteem. It is important to recognize that this experience is not unique; in fact, it is an inevitable concomitant of role shift. Role extension or change is a period of transition, like the move from latency to adolescence, from late adolescence to adulthood or from occupational activity to retirement. Developmental transitions are periods of personal crisis attended by intrapsychic conflict and emotional fluctuations. This critical role transition behavior is similarly apparent when people migrate from one country to another. Change, as has been cogently argued in a recent book by Marris, involves inevitable loss. In becoming an executive, one weakens one's membership in the reference group of clinicians while one is still unable to claim full membership in an executives' reference group. Shifts in role and reference group are often further compounded by geographic relocations and attendant multiple life-change events. For example, a promotion with relocation involves selling a familiar nest, buying a new house, moving children into a new school, making new friends and losing old ones. These transitions are accompanied by emotions of grief and uncertainty. This is a painful personal experience. Unsure of his present or future role and identity, the young administrator, lacking support through this transition, may throw in the towel, retreating to lick his wounds in more familiar clinical practice. Most administrators do, however, weather the turmoil of transition. They are then able to look back upon the period of shift not as transient psychopathology, but as a phase of personal growth and identity extension. With the passage of time, this new identity becomes incorporated into an enhanced vision of the self and a stable image as clinician-executive from which to derive strength and support. When this point is reached, the challenge of the seven component tasks of the clinician-executive's role will have been successfully surmounted.

CONCLUSION: THE SATISFACTION OF THE CLINICIAN-EXECUTIVE

I have found great satisfaction in discharging my clinician-executive role. I have been able to influence public policy in the mental health area and have been able to participate in social movements to humanize the fabric of our society. I have been able to "bear witness."

19

Survival as a Program Administrator: A Personal Saga

JUNE JACKSON CHRISTMAS

There is a mixed pleasure in looking back at the changes that one has experienced in moving from a role as a clinician in private practice to that of director of an innovative program in a psychiatric department of an inner city hospital, and then to a role as administrator of the largest mental health service of any city in the world. Certainly, there is a sense of relief in viewing old errors of judgment and of action across a span of time and seeing that they have become minor blots on the pages of one's own personal history—errors that seem even less significant to others. On the other hand, successes and satisfactions are somewhat dimmed by the fact that the progress which seemed so great pales in the wider social context, in which so many problems remain unsolved.

Clinician, program director, administrator—each of these has had its place in my own personal development and in the shaping of my professional career. As all clinicians must, I had experienced the empathy of reaching out to another, touching that person as change came slowly, dramatically, or almost imperceptibly. I had known the sustaining force of having been in communication with another mind, soul, human being; I had been affected by and had affected that other person. There was always the difficult journey toward understanding the complexities of conscious behavior, of unconscious motives, of unknown aspects of that inner person. At the same time, there was the knowledge that over a period of years I might be able to help thirty or fifty persons at the most, and share this growth experience with them. But there were others—family, friends, neighbors —who might also have been of help to that person or who themselves might have been in need of such an experience of self-understanding.

The goals we shared were sometimes clearly expressed in order to relieve that discomfort and dis-ease bared before me which caused much suffering and distress, or to restore a human being to a higher level of personality integration, of health or social functioning. But over the years these limited goals and the more extensive ones of understanding those deeper wells of experience, inner conflict and emotions soon gave way to joint efforts to help that man or woman cope more effectively, more adaptively, and develop alternative ways of behaving. As we looked together at behaviors that took place outside the clinical office or the therapy groups that I had begun, there seemed to be even more present that wider world to which, somehow or other, neither of us was fully relating in the therapeutic process. Thus, I found myself increasingly working with couples, families and groups. I found myself also revealing a little more of myself, hopefully not in a way that intruded or limited the ability of those who came as patients, but in a way that led to a more honest interaction. This change from the narrow psychoanalytic concentration on the individual—from the deeply intense involvement in therapy day in, day out, for three, five, seven or more years, contributed, I believe in retrospect, to my own growth and to the development of skills applied to a larger arena.

At the same time, I found myself asking questions concerning the effectiveness of my work, examining the sudden or gradual change that each patient and I were both aware of, and to query its causes. Did it result from life and interpersonal circumstances unrelated to our task, a change over time, or did it come in part or at all from our search for understanding? I could no longer ignore the fact that there were many other aspects of that individual's life which were strong influences, perhaps even stronger than the unraveling of the complexities of conflicts, the release of material that was once repressed, the lifting of veils.

As I moved to a more open style as a therapist, I became mindful of the greater strengths that lay in people and of the need to look beyond the dyad, important as it was.

When the opportunity came some twelve years ago to teach residents and staff psychiatrists at Harlem Hospital Center, in its newly opened Department of Psychiatry, I decided that some of the skills that I had begun to acquire as I added group techniques to my psychoanalytic armamentarium, would be a complementary experience to my clinical practice. I began to supervise residents and staff psychiatrists in group therapy, helping them move from their initial suspiciousness of this new technique to a point where each felt comfortable being not only a group leader, but a participant in a group process.

What began as a supervisory and training experience soon became an experience in the initiation of programs as traditional therapy groups gave way to innovation. How do you work with a group of black high school girls who have been expelled from a regular school and given their next to final chance at a special school for near-dropouts? This taxed the ingenuity of social worker, psychiatrist and educator as the school hesitated to share information, as guidance counselors sent the students to a therapist as a last resort, or as punishment, or with the hope that the magic of psychotherapy would do what education, parental punishment and the streets had never accomplished.

The cohesion of the group was frequently upset by the sudden plucking out of a youngster, who had finally begun to make progress, because her family was forced to send her South to a grandmother, or because the school boundaries were redrawn and no longer conformed to hospital boundaries, or because there were other extraneous factors beyond our power to control. One of the most difficult of these was the aura of suspicion between the teachers and the mental hygiene clinic.

There was often a long lag between events in the school which might have required our intervention and the girl's ability to share this information. Our successful or, more often, unsuccessful efforts to help group members cope with the difficult situation varied. At one point, in one of the groups, I recollect with a smile and a sense of relief, a mother who had come complaining and concerned about her daughter revealed that she had gone to the school on a number of occasions, and finally, through her own perseverance and talents, had been able to obtain information from a guidance counselor who had refused to return the calls of the social worker or psychiatrist. This mother was a fighter, a strong woman, asserting her rights, sophisticated in the survival techniques of the inner city. We decided to tap these skills and bring her into the helping system, first as a parent volunteer and later as a staff person, in the role that was later to be called aide, assistant, mental health paraprofessional.

Fortunately, the combination of untapped leadership and therapeutic desperation led to a new role. By now, mental health workers are generally accepted. In those days, however, efforts to hire local people from the Harlem community became matters of policy discussions and of ingenious ways to bring people on staff while still conforming to the hiring practices of a rigid municipal hospital system.

What had initially grown out of the need to deal more effectively with outside social and educational agencies and to gain greater numbers of varied staff soon became the development of the New Careerist role, adding a new therapeutic dimension in the human service field. Paraprofessional staff, male and female—not family members of identified patients, but others—sought work for their own special reasons, and embarked on new careers for their own satisfactions as helpers. A few represented the traditional middle-class volunteers, but more often they were working-class and lower-class people, from the patients' own socioeconomic groups.

There were many stresses in this situation. There was the reluctance on the part of the hospital and department administration to recognize these new staff as other than nurses' aides, without uniforms. Some professionals hesitated to open their deliberations to them in staff and case conference or, to consider their notes as valuable material for records.

Thus, moving from supervisor to program developer, I found myself facing deep-seated attitudes that deified the trinity of psychiatrist, social worker and psychologist but looked down upon other professions; for me, there had been a geometric progression in complexities and variables as I became program director, advocate for new careers, neophyte grantswoman.

But times were changing in the field of community mental health. New demands were made upon mental health as patients were discharged from state hospitals in greater numbers, unready for community life, suffering from the effects of illness and institutionalization. There they were, no longer in isolation, but living in single rooms, sitting in welfare centers, crowding the waiting rooms of the clinics.

The community mental health movement was not for them—after-care consisted only of medication. Rehabilitation was unheard of. Lest they inundate the planned community mental health center in such numbers that we would be unable to serve the "true patients," I was challenged by the department director to develop some way of preventing what was viewed as potential interference with the CMHC which would revolutionize mental health care.

We looked first at services being provided. An informal review of current operations and the extent to which they were meeting needs was itself subject to a good deal of suspicion. Impressionistic observations included agreement by staff and administration that there was a definite need to increase the quality of psychiatric service. Community caretakers, patients currently in treatment and their families, and those few patients able to be contacted after long absences all identified a need for both psychiatric and social services. The implicit assumption was held by psychiatrists and social workers that psychotherapy would probably be ineffective with such socially deprived patients, and particularly with chronic schizophrenic persons. Discouragement about the usefulness of any therapeutic intervention with the chronically mentally ill was apparent, along with overt or latent lack of interest by most of the younger and more dynamically oriented psychiatrists.

The organization and staffing of the clinic favored the conduct of traditional psychiatric services, while at the same time allowing relative freedom for the conduct of newer adaptations in social service. There was an openness on the part of the departmental director to potential efforts at program modification, with the implicit reservation that they remain innovations. The proposed social rehabilitation program which we developed was viewed as a deviant appendage of the main agency, trusted to have little permanent effect on the institution toward the solution of whose service problems it was originally conceived. As the process of institutional change set in motion by innovation began to strike at some of the vested interests or practices of the traditional agency, the value of the innovative program as an expression of agency commitment to progress was soon in question. I entered that situation, not as a change agent with a preconceived program which I advocated or, on the other hand, as an opportunist responsive to and relating to the environment in a pragmatic way, but as one who was expected to bring available resources under control. We soon saw that social rehabilitation meant more than coffee and bingo, that rehabilitation meant more than after-care.

In those early days, broadening our concerns to include the social, medical and prevocational aspects of patients' lives resulted in the polarization of some staff in other clinic programs. They had less limited vistas and less vocal staff than our first group of four mental health workers who served as expediters, group leaders, social service assistants and health workers. The program by now had attracted attention for its intensive paraprofessional training program, its willingness to hire welfare mothers and ex-offenders, its collaborative activities with civil-rights and community groups. By the time the program had reached its fourth and final home, a renovated loft near the hospital, it was serving seventy-five patients in a daily social rehabilitation service under an NIMH demonstration grant to evaluate the effectiveness of community-based group approaches with paraprofessional mental health workers as the primary therapeutic agents. The population served was later expanded through Rehabilitation Services Administration and OVR grants to evaluate group methods in prevocational and vocational rehabilitation. The mental health worker staff grew to thirty men and women, at various grades on a career ladder.

The approaches that evolved have by now, twelve years later, become standard community mental health techniques: the use of indigenous mental health workers; the development of coordinated services of an interdisciplinary nature; peer groups; socialization; medication groups, graduated stress; the New Careers concept, whereby people who might otherwise be unemployed or underemployed were hired first and trained later. Yet, even in an atmosphere fostering experimentation and a blending of the old and the new, the stresses were many.

Perhaps one of the most difficult approaches to innovate in those early days was that of the home psychiatric interview. The traditional role of the social worker had been to make an occasional home visit. In this innovation, the psychiatrist and one or another staff member, but always including a paraprofessional, met with the family in one or a series of home interviews. The interviews served as a diagnostic tool for the study of patterns of family interaction, as an enabling technique to increase the involvement of the hard-to-reach family, as a part of the ongoing therapeutic processes, for crisis intervention, as follow-up for the patient who missed a day or two, or as a useful view of the patient's social world, which was then generally unknown to the middle-class psychiatrist. The difficulties of home visits included not only the hesitancy of the psychiatrist but also, occasionally, the reluctance of the mental health worker, who came from a similar social and economic situation, to have a professional see what life was really like in the inner city.

The new roles were not easy to play. For example, professional staff were to serve primarily as supervisors and as co-therapists, in groups. Some asserted that the mental health workers had the only *real* therapeutic role. As program director, I missed the satisfaction of ongoing group therapy, frequently finding that my emergencies were no longer clinical but administrative. For others, the stress was the routine extolling of the virtues of paraprofessional life experience as opposed to professional book learning, as if either could suffice on its own in this setting.

But all of these difficulties proved to be minor. The use of group methods to rehabilitate increasing numbers of chronically disabled schizophrenic people led to the development of demonstration projects and of pilot programs. Ultimately, the Harlem Rehabilitation Center, on its establishment in 1965, became the first full-range social and vocational rehabilitation program in the borough, one of the few in the city.

There were many times when the satisfaction of a work product was there before me, a visible result of staff and patient efforts. There was an activities room, painted and decorated by members, a new machine moved up to the vocational program without the benefit of an elevator, a new kiln or computer key punch—all tangible elements of a positive endeavor but which, at the same time, tended to make me wonder if I were not more of a a contractor, a saleswoman or interior decorator than a psychiatrist. Lack of role clarity was there, as I moved from co-therapist to supervisor, to substitute clinician, to second cook at a Thanksgiving dinner, to proposal writer and budget specialist. We each attempted to identify that which was distinctive about our own discipline in the generic human services. We dealt, more or less successfully, with problems of authority, ambivalence, independence-dependence; with the need to play the sick role; with regression and anxiety presented by the patients in the course of their recoveries; with the bitter disappointments of job failures or failures to find work, as well as with successes.

Yes, there was excitement and joy in being able to be very close to the human beings—staff and members—who were fellow participants in this process. The Center developed its own life, its own spirit, its own identity. At times, its activist role set it in near-open opposition to the mother department. For example, if there was a housing problem experienced by some of the clients, then the community worker and clients would mount a rent strike. If the personnel lines of the pilot project were in danger of not being picked up by the City Department of Mental Health or the hospital, then picketing and petitions were the tools which patients, staff and community used. There was no place for the professional staff members to sit back or to limit their relationship to the struggle to discussing its pros and cons in the therapeutic community meeting. No, professionals must be beside the paraprofessionals and the members and clients in this struggle, and that meant on the line. At times this led to some staff automatically planning the involvement of members against the clinical better judgement of other staff. When the clinical recommendation prevailed—as it did—the supervisor or program director was seen as the bad parent for forbidding client participation for what must be reactionary motives.

There were victories, the greatest of which was the establishment, as a permanent part of the Department of Psychiatry, of what had been viewed as an avant garde pilot project which might well die upon completion of the grant. This resulted from a campaign mounted by the local community, the Center, and joined in by such varied groups as local and borough politicians, the City Council, civil rights organizations, the super-agency Health Services Administrator and, eventually, the Department of Mental Health.

As we developed these programs of sociopsychiatric rehabilitation, implicit in the value system we held was the responsibility to be not only in, but of, the black community. We attempted to contribute to constructive individual and social change by implementing services and activities that might lead to alternatives to the continuing waste of human resources we saw in those who became members/clients and staff. But the path toward change was far from easy; it did not depend on simplistic solutions or follow the forward path this brief description might indicate.

Staff experienced stresses related to their changing work roles and to the social and political context of those years. They were poor black men and women, community residents, coming from lives like those of the patients, of severe deprivation. They were black middle-class professional staff "coming back" (some for the first time) to be a part of the struggle for freedom from racism. They were white staff contributing to their own growth and to the struggle for civil rights. They knew satisfaction and disappointment, success and failure.

The vicissitudes which the program went through were many. Some were a direct result of the problems inherent in any new program that is innovative, lacking in precedent, and beset by under-budgeting, lack of basic supportive maintenance and clerical staff (which had been pared down beyond a minimum because of the grant limits and the lack of support by the medical school affiliate). Some were the pangs of growth and development. For most new programs, such struggles and growing pains are inevitable. Energy was expended in moving from role diffusion to role definition, on all levels. Energy was spent on helping supervisory staff couple their rightful demand for responsibility and authority with their own follow-through and accountability and of linking both of these to the mental health workers' equal right to participate in making important decisions. As program director, I was often torn between my roles as inspirational leader, manager, neophyte administrator, authority figure. Nothing in my own experience had prepared me for the intricacies of budget, cost accounting or indirect cost allowances. Eager as I was to participate in the training program for the mental health workers, I also wanted to be one of the participants in the therapeutic community meetings. I wanted to continue as a co-leader in the medication group counseling meetings we had developed, in which members evaluated themselves and each other. Group discussions led to recommendations for program participation and for medication. Even the writing of the prescriptions by the psychiatrist was used as part of the group process. I was finally forced to admit that my schedule did not allow consistent participation.

We sometimes had to develop program modifications which should have been carefully thought out but were often hurriedly made. They needed to be planned, but were frequently expedient measures. Hopefully, learning did take place, so that past mistakes were repeated less often. But this required not only identification of the error—people were usually quite willing to do that; it also required an equal willingness to find solutions and to participate in order to make them workable.

The increasing gap that separates the planners of programs from those actually providing services places program planners and directors either in the position of benevolence incarnate (as providers of all good things) or evil incarnate (thwarters of all constructive plans). The errors I made as director were more likely to be abstract, related to policy, and more difficult to criticize than the operational errors of staff, which could be readily identified and pointed out by patient and client/members as well as by other personnel. For the staff psychiatrist in such a setting—open discussion and questioning by other staff, from professions that have been taught to be three steps back—was novel; that errors should continue even after he admits them was unthinkable. The medical model had made his position invulnerable, his authority unquestioned. Yet, in programs such as this, multidisciplinary in respect as well as in structure, such openness was absolutely required for effective action. This meant that the program director also was subject to scrutiny as well as solicitude, to reproach as well as recognition. Hopefully, we used these reactions for self-understanding and greater competence in the task.

Life beyond the Center was not organized, not within one's ability to plan, execute or control according to a program plan or need, even when this need was consistent with the common good. It may be useful to determine whether there is anything that emerges from settings using this struggle toward growth to modify behavior which can be applied on a wider context. Can observations, for example, on the transactions that take place between this social system of a Center and the informal groups and street corner societies of the neighborhood contribute to knowledge of group process, of attitude change, and of their relationship to behavior change? Unfortunately, it is all too easy to transpose what goes on within small groups to larger social institutions and to extrapolate sociological phenomena from individual psychology. On the other hand, many of the issues with which staff and members of this program were grappling are similar to issues confronting local community groups and larger social groups. I can think of leadership and authority; the control of the decision-making process; the usefulness of various personality approaches; power and powerlessness; the difference between titular power and true power; the question of whether to concentrate on the provision of services or on social change.

I had hoped that the service model might possibly evolve into the social change model; I had been concerned, too, that greater attention be given to creative use of the community as part of the rehabilitative field. In this approach, immediate life situations were handled as part of the rehabilitative process; participation in social groups in which one had prior membership was tapped; new alliances and coalition with community groups and other subsystems of nonpatients were integrated into the care system. Here was one approach to linking the rehabilitative change system with social change in its wider sense.

As a program director working in a black inner city and confronted with the extreme manifestations of racism, poverty and an externally devalued social position, I was painfully aware of the need to work with other behavioral scientists to use our knowledge purposefully to aid individuals and groups to develop techniques of mastery, to strengthen effective coping mechanisms and social learning, and to alter the systems in which we participate.

The stresses of the wider subsystem of the community did provide an opportunity for individuals and small groups to learn to deal with life situations as individual and group tasks. Thus, the harsh realities of the disadvantaged lives of our patients were not viewed as interferences to be eliminated so that orthodox therapy could then take place. Rather, they were seen as significant aspects of the lives of many individuals and groups, aspects to be understood as forces for growth—or disturbance. The generalization must be open to question that those who have suffered from stresses such as severe poverty, racial discrimination and chronic deprivation are therefore so ill or so deprived that they are not responsive to psychiatric treatment or rehabilitation. I had seen both staff and patients act as co-participants in setting for themselves the goals of greater integration into their own families and community life. We had, together, developed a variety of rehabilitative approaches: therapeutic, social, actional, educational. We had seen hundreds of men and women returned to family and social life, remaining out of psychiatric hospitals, and living in communities where they were more active participants and citizens. But there were many others who did not reach our doors. There were others whom we could not engage, and there were others with whom we failed, even more obviously.

And so I left—with questions as to how we might adapt the skills we did have toward decreasing the waste of human resources that we see not only in our inner cities but in society at large. I gave up, with a great deal of difficulty, my identification with a growing idea, with a place, with a people, with a spirit. These were identifications which were not to be found easily in my next role. But the problems and challenges were there, magnified and more complex. There was still the need to search in our social values, using our limited knowledge, our talents and competence, for ways in which we might better apply our understanding of human behavior and broaden the realm of our mental health concerns to include other human problems. I had become painfully aware that there must be thousands of people in my city who are chronically disabled—without hope and help. In my own community, through a deep knowledge of several hundred whose hope had grown, whose potentials had been tapped, and who had helped themselves even as they were helped, I had seen men and women flourish as they assisted others and, in turn, become strengthened, skilled and productive. What I had only a glimmer of was the thousands to whose needs we in the mental health profession have just begun to attend.

Thus, after ten years in the Department of Psychiatry, I moved to another scene—becoming city-wide policy-maker and administrator in the Department of Mental Health and Mental Retardation Services. This is indeed another theater, whose actors play other roles, where the stakes seem higher because the focus is shifted from individual suffering to group deprivation.

URBAN LIVING, STRESS AND CHANGE

In a heightened and intensified fashion, the large cities of this nation demonstrate some of the characteristics of the wider society: the unequal distribution of goods; an imbalance in the allocation, availability and quality of human services; materialism as a motive force; struggles for power and its misuse; social disorganization, coupled with dispersion of social responsibility.

At its most intense, the urban experience too often consists of a multiplicity of superficial relationships of a segmented and transitory nature. Feelings of anomie, alienation and impersonality result from a continuous impact of stress overload. The pace of life leaves little time for unplanned leisure, reflection or meaningful contact with nature or man.

Contrasts in the mega-cities between extremes of poverty and plenty and the competition for scarce resources lead to an atmosphere of distrust and distance. As cities become the homes for the wealthy, who spend a few months there, insulated and fearful, they become also the homes for those poor who are too powerless to escape to the suburbs, which beckon with unequal hospitality to both the working class and the middle class. Men and women, coming to the cities from other cultures, other milieus, and other life styles, bring with them a wide range of experience and expectation, but often find themselves unable to cope with the daily stresses of urban living. The impersonality of the city, unresponsive service agencies, overcrowding, the multiple barriers erected by economic inequities and deprivation, all intensify these people's feelings of frustration and powerlessness.

Large segments of urban populations have been neglected by mental health: the elderly, facing old age and nonproductivity in a youth- and action-oriented society; the addicted and drug-dependent, seeking the way out of stress; children, youth and their families, not only those severely troubled but those going through crises of daily living and periods of adjustment to stress, struggling with learning, experiencing adaptational difficulties; the retarded and developmentally disabled, each denied the opportunity of habilitation to his potential, too often considered, if at all, only after the higher-priority mentally ill are planned for; ethnic minorities, with their own culture, impinging on the wider society; racial minorities, coping with discrimination and prejudice; the chronically mentally ill and those considered expendable, socially deviant or undesirable; the offender, on a merry-go-round of punishment without rehabilitation. The technologies needed to meet their needs are still to be improved upon; far greater emphasis is needed on prevention and rehabilitation than has been placed heretofore.

The critical issues can only be touched upon: decentralization versus centralization of planning; the varying roles and responsibilities of community members, citizens, consumers; strategies for allocation of scarce resources; territorialities, turf and fiefdoms; the changing role of the state hospital system in a city with both a strong municipal department and a myriad of other providers of care, public and voluntary; needed adaptation to externalities, political, social and economic. All of these arouse in me the urgent wish for new survival techniques, geared to deferred satisfactions, longer range projections, and budgets in the millions (nearly $200) instead of the hundreds of thousands.

The low visibility and priority of mental health has necessitated planning not only *for* but *with* local neighborhood participation. This has required a structure and process which include other human service agencies, the public and voluntary sectors of city and state, and with citizens and community. This process itself is one of creative tension. The satisfactions and stresses are thus of their own nature, as are the challenges. But that tale will be told another day.

The changing nature of mental health services and the expanded purview implied by this orientation require consideration. The broadened realm of mental health concern and less restrictive definitions place demands upon mental health personnel—professional, paraprofessional, administrator and practitioner—to reexamine the nature of their roles and responsibilities not only in regard to those called, not too aptly, consumers of service, but to each other, to community and citizens and, increasingly, to those who make social policy. The context in which these changes are taking place is characterized by external factors which influence the service, the providers, and those served. Fiscal abundance or constraints, financing mechanisms, social revolutions or struggle, and political priorities and expediencies are but a few of the factors that have to be considered. Yet, the apprehension that concentration on these seeming externalities may prove too great a burden may not be easily cast aside. This implies, further, the need to learn new information, a new vocabulary in which task analysis, management by objectives, key factor analysis, PPBS and the like have a real, not a mysterious, relationship to mental health.

Medical school education, psychiatric residencies and even community psychiatry programs do not as yet adequately prepare the psychiatrist for the variety of roles he or she is called upon to play in community mental health. Duties as practitioner, supervisor, trainer of more traditional professionals, consultant, administrator—these may be easier to fulfill. Yet, increasingly, it is necessary to conduct program development, planning and evaluation; to develop and implement relationships with other human service agencies; to relate to a variety of managerial, fiscal and analytic staff as peers; to contribute to social policy. Demands for advocacy, public information and legislative education are seriously considered. Psychiatrists in private practice and in public service are asked to combine their skills. Frequently, persons who, ten years ago, could have spent the major part of their efforts in solo practice combine both areas of service.

This imposes a necessity on educational and training institutions to use the field of work as part of the learning experience and to utilize the talents of persons of all backgrounds as teachers and supervisors.

This involves not only acquiring substantive and technical knowledge but also improving role relationships through experiential training, role definition and ongoing task analysis. For example, the traditionally educated mental health professional, used to a triangular team on which the psychiatrist was always on top (whether openly or not) is now called upon to recognize as collaborators others who were in the arena all along—such as nurses; or whose skills are only now being tapped by mental health—such as vocational rehabilitation counselors; or whose recognized skills have generally been assigned to another system—such as educators. To develop such collaboration may be easier for those educated since community mental health became a byword. Yet, even the more avant garde professional may have difficulty determining what is unique about his or her professional expertise, or, having identified this, what determines who should practice which generic activity.

When, in the midst of this role confusion, problems of status, power and authority emerge, they are frequently neither faced nor resolved. Yet, for creative interagency funding to lead the way to interagency, multifocused programs, these problems require solutions. Interagency boundaries need to be removed and fiscal and jurisdictional barriers done away with.

Another source of identity confusion has been the development of the New Careers movement, as exemplified by paraprofessional mental health workers playing a variety of helping, service and advocacy roles, either as primary agents or as assistants to more formally educated staff. In New Careers, underemployed or unemployed men and women are recruited and hired first, then trained on the job for careers which would provide upward and horizontal mobility, and which would contribute to an improved quality of human service.

The confusion in the identity of these new mental health professionals is marked, relating often to the underlying purposes for which they were recruited. The bandwagon of paraprofessionalism did not have as its wares satisfactory training of the trainers or trainees, continuing task analyses, or improved utilization of "old" professionals. Many mental health workers found access to a ladder lacking both steps and a career; many are stuck in dead-end positions; the communication or linkage role has diminished now that it is no longer fashionable to favor racial minorities or the economically disadvantaged; lateral mobility was never accomplished; restrictive civil service and labor or professional guild practices have combined, in some instances, to put a new title on an old job.

Not only are New Careerists confused about their identity, but they may also wonder whatever became of the generic human service workers they were to become, whatever became of the relevant in-service training and education they hoped for. Why not abandon it all for a job, rather than a career; or, if a career still beckons, let it be a traditional one, with accreditation still possible. Indeed, this retreat may contribute to the security of the credentialed professionals who now no longer need fear a "dilution of standards," a decrease in the quality of care, or competitors without diplomas on the job market. The goals of New Careers have been diminished, its aims diluted, and its high hopes as a force for improvement in service delivery all but abandoned. Yet, it still holds the potential for contributing to a modification in community mental health service.

Among the participants in this changing process are others whose identity is in flux, those who, as "consumers" or partners in service, are the patients, clients and their families, as well as their neighbors and fellow community members.

Certain activities by consumers and consumer advocates have proved stressful and challenging to mental health professionals. Accustomed in the past to relating to more passive patients and clients who saw themselves as recipients of services, these professionals are now experiencing the therapeutic community, social rehabilitation activities in which boundaries between staff and patients are blurred and confrontation or collaboration on issues of consumer and client interests.

Through Community Mental Health Center legislation, new concepts requiring community involvement, consultation and education have been introduced and they have been developed extensively in innovative programs. Even in more traditional centers, initial hesitant steps toward community involvement and community advisory boards and consultation—outreach and education services, both new to mental health—have now been accepted as almost usual rather than exceptional, not only in CMHC's, but in other programs as well. True, the role of the community remains to be defined; the partnership is still an unsteady one, but the advances have been made in the direction of greater accountability and greater responsiveness.

Certainly, consideration of the members of a community should be high in priority from three points of view: as consumers of services; as participants in planning, advice, decision-making and control; and as providers of services. However, the definition of the appropriate role of the community and of the reality of power as opposed to its role as recipient of information and as adviser should be examined. This requires role clarity and an assignment of responsibility and authority. But, too often, consumer and citizen involvement has been perfunctory tokenism. Few programs go beyond the advisory board model to sponsorship by community corporations, by councils of community-based programs linking networks of service, accountable to and controlled by the local community. Yet to be grappled with is the issue of arousing and maintaining the interest of consumers, many of whom are struggling for economic necessities, in what has been for too long a field they sought only when seriously troubled, whose relevance to the social factors in their lives was often neither apparent nor real. How can interest and participation be generated without creating an elite corps of professional community participants?

A number of other issues have arisen. Should the differing roles of consumer, consumer advocate, community "grass rooter," and varied citizenry be made specific; what are their differing responsibilities and contributions? What can be said of the mental health worker drawn from a local community, regarding his own role as citizen? What is the appropriate mix between community resident and expert in the planning and decision-making process? Can a local community do more than cite needs without having its expectations of greater authority and control come to naught? All of these unresolved issues have caused some to retrench on a professed commitment; yet, if we truly believe that there should be shared responsibility and decision-making, these problems must be faced.

ISSUES OF EFFECTIVENESS, EFFICIENCY AND EQUITY

It is not enough, however, to describe what may be an overly optimistic view of the extended realm of community mental health or to point out the program applications of a sociopsychological approach. There is another task to be accomplished which will in itself contribute to the problems of improved community mental health care. It is necessary to begin to look at effectiveness, and at what the costs are in dollars and cents, as well as in human measures, to question whether needs are being met equitably. This requires a greater openness to evaluation and monitoring than the field has shown previously. Far too many assumptions have gone untested. It would be unfortunate to label all mental health interventions as incapable of evaluation, as only to be felt and experienced, not measured. Yet, there is a certain "softness" in the field in an age when there is a press to quantify and justify with "hard" data. Demands for information, for statistical reporting, and for specification of outcomes may leave the clinical professional with the impression that he is being asked to be a statistician. Indeed, information systems should be so structured that they do not intrude upon the service system. Further, it may well be helpful to consider case management by objectives. Unless measures of effectiveness can be developed, the influence on policy makers and program planners may not be realized. Ill men are a relatively powerless constituency. The result of preventive programs are difficult to measure, particularly in areas of psychosocial disability. Yet, the philosophical belief that there should be efforts to restore the health of the sick and maintain the health of the well exerts little pressure on legislators who dole out relatively few funds for health care. As new directions are pursued under the rubric of crisis intervention and emergency stabilization, as well as advocacy and environmental manipulation, greater demands for proof of effectiveness will be necessary.

IMPLICATIONS

This discussion leads to other questions which relate not only to program development and evaluation but to more basic policy issues. How should scarce resources be allocated—to the many, by way of supportive, symptomatic help, or to a few, lucky enough to have intensive care? What should the balance be between services with an immediate pay-off and those whose effects may not be evident or, at least, measurable? Should efforts be made to move closer to the health systems, to human services as an umbrella, or to another yet undefined position? How does one develop evaluative criteria in a field of human services where hard data are difficult to come by, while demands are made for the justification of further funding? How can certain people who have been tracked out of the mental health non-system receive its services—children in the care of public agencies and the courts, drug abusers, the poor elderly, the chronically unemployed? Should a mental health and mental retardation service thrust for children be mediated through the educational or the mental hygiene system?

Beyond these questions there remains an equally serious task—the challenge of broadening the realm of mental health concern to include the social problems which confront us today. That enough of the skills of the various mental health professionals have not been turned toward pressing social issues is apparent. We might well—indeed we must—search for what there may be in our talents and competence, in our social values and knowledge, that can enable us to join the behavioral scientist and others concerned with improving the relationships between man and man and man and society. It will be in the contributions that we can make toward the solution of human problems that we will not only contribute to greater productivity and applicability of our knowledge but also to the constructive change that is so needed today.

Note

Presented at the National Seminar on the Human Service Leader as Agent of Change: Strategies and Dilemmas, sponsored by the Human Resource Institute of Boston, March 25, 1974, Boston, Massachusetts.

20

The Psychiatrist-Executive In The Changing Funding And Political Environment

FRANCIS DE MARNEFFE

INTRODUCTION

Change is not new to psychiatric institutions. All institutions change as a result of internal and external pressures. But for a long time change was slow, and relatively small. More recently the tempo and the forces both from within and without to which psychiatric institutions must respond have increased tremendously. The result has been that they have changed drastically over the last decade and are still changing to meet the challenges of today and tomorrow. The role and modus operandi of the psychiatric executive has changed and must change also.

HISTORICAL OVERVIEW

The changes in the internal environment were heralded first mainly in a clinical context: the traditional isolation of patients in a psychiatric hospital was examined, its clinical implications finally understood and condemned, and steps were taken to avoid it. The wall which literally or figuratively set the mental hospital apart from the larger world began to crumble. Admissions and discharges of patients were made easier; day-care, night-care, outpatient, and halfway-house programs were created; families were deliberately involved in the evaluation and treatment of patients; visitors were encouraged; communication by letter, by phone and in person with people outside were stimulated and expected; volunteers were recruited; auxiliaries were formed; work programs in and out of the hospital were created; recreation outside the hospital was fostered; outside therapists were encouraged to continue the treatment of their patients during hospitalization; college courses were developed for young patients in affiliation with universities—to mention but a few significant steps.

The changes from a closed to a more open society also affected the staff. The number of employees, from the superintendent on down, who once lived and worked on the hospital grounds breathing the hospital atmosphere day in and day out, decreased to the probable benefit of hospitals, employees and patients. Thus the staff as well as patients were affected by the same powerful currents, social and political, which affected the wider community.

What began as a change in the internal environment of the institution, as a result of understanding better the effects of isolating patients, has continued in response to other, largely external forces. Reflecting changing attitudes toward authority in society in general, patients today are no longer passive recipients of the treatment meted out by doctors and other mental health professionals. They have become more active and vocal participants in their own treatment and in the life of the therapeutic community in which they live temporarily. This shift has forced psychiatrists to become more accountable than ever before to patients and their families. Their wisdom and knowledge are no longer either assumed or automatically accepted. Our patients now want to know why we do what we do, and why we don't prescribe other treatments they have heard or read about. Questions about treatment which formerly were never asked are now posed repeatedly; and we have to answer. The patients approach professionals more as equals than formerly, and this has changed the relationship of patients and psychiatrists in the hospital setting.

These changes have received powerful stimulus from changes in the mental health codes of many states which in turn have altered the conditions under which patients may be voluntarily and involuntarily admitted to hospitals. As greater emphasis has been placed on patients' civil rights, and more options made available to them, they now have the legal power to be assured they will be heard. In contrast, the ability of the staff to operate unchallenged from its autocratic pedestal has been markedly diminished. It must now negotiate with the patients. If a patient who is ill and still in need of treatment wishes to leave the hospital, the option is not open to the psychiatrist to recommend commitment unless the patient specifically fits the very strict criteria of involuntary commitment under the law. The only recourse for the psychiatrist is to negotiate with a patient and to convince him of the validity and need for continued hospitalization.

Other changes are challenging the therapeutic armanentarium of psychiatrists. The inpatient population has changed; often half may be adolescent. More patients have drug-related problems. Many being admitted are violent and destructive. Because of greater psychiatric awareness on the part of the courts, and perhaps a growing skepticism that the penal system is the answer for all who break the law, more individuals are admitted to psychiatric institutions because their illegal behavior is thought to be related to a psychiatric illness. How effective psychiatric treatment is for drug addicts and for antisocial character remains to be seen, but in the meantime they pose special problems for the institution. Lastly, at a time when patients are more aware of their civil rights, even a minor restriction on a patient may result in the patient calling his attorney to the hospital to be his advocate. These are but a few of the challenges to which the institution must respond.

In this climate, the psychiatrist-executive must work toward the most effective treatment of the patients in the institution, treading the line carefully between granting patients their full civil rights guaranteed by the law and, at the same time, providing them, the institution and society at large the protection and security needed. This is perhaps not so very different from some kinds of decisions psychiatrists have traditionally made; for example, in weighing the potential benefits to a suicidal patient of a trip home against a potential risk of suicide. But what has changed is, if you will, the relative balance of power. Nowadays the psychiatrist no longer has the ability he formerly had to impose his will over the patient, and the patient, in fact, has greater opportunities for discarding the psychiatrist's advice.

But beyond these kinds of day-to-day management issues, the psychiatrist-executive must also ponder whether the external pressures, which have contributed to these changes in the internal environment, are, in the long run, beneficial to the treatment of patients. Much of what has been happening—that is, much of the foregoing—has, indeed, contributed powerfully to an improvement in patient treatment. But other forces mentioned above may have tipped the balance in the opposite direction and made the effective treatment of certain groups of patients far more difficult than in the past. To the extent that the psychiatrist-executive believes the latter is true, he has a new and important responsibility to play a more active role in political and legislative arenas from which some of these forces are emanating—a role which will be discussed later in this chapter.

The internal environment has also changed from the point of view of the staff. The boundaries between various professional disciplines have become blurred. It is no longer clear what *only* a doctor, a nurse, a social worker, a psychologist, a mental health worker, even a volunteer, can do. The question must be posed over and over again. What is this professional *uniquely* qualitied by training and experience to perform? What activities are generic to all mental health professionals? The pressures for such questions are partly financial and partly the result of shortages in the most highly trained and, therefore, expensive professionals. The expectations of a good staff are that the institution will give them opportunities for full exercise of their talents with less emphasis on their traditional role. With this has come more insistence on participation at all levels in the decision-making process. Just as patients are now more insistent on having a voice in their treatment and in their lives in the institution, so is the staff more insistent on having a voice in their work in the institution and how they are treated there.

The past decade has seen many changes in the relationship between the staff and the institution. For a long time, hospital employees were underpaid as compared to others of comparable training and education in the fields of business and commerce. The dedication and loyalty of employees, and their knowledge that they were helping others, seemed to be their main rewards. Some years ago, this began to change and for several years hospital employees have been catching up financially with their colleagues in other fields. This, of course, has been responsible for the tremendous increase in the cost of medical care—just as it should have been—since health professionals were, in a sense, through their self-sacrifice, subsidizing the cost of treating patients. In many respects, health workers have now caught up with the rest of the labor force, and most of the laws which govern labor now apply to hospitals. This has meant an additional role for the psychiatrist-executive, a role more akin to that of a labor lawyer than his initial role of psychiatrist.

Employees, too, just as patients, have become more militant and vocal, actively wondering at times whether their working conditions and status (if not their pocketbooks) would be enhanced by joining a labor union. While some have unionized, most hospital employees have not, perhaps out of recognition of the fact that direct negotiation with the administration is more effective and beneficial for everyone concerned—the employee, the patient and the hospital.

As one sits back and looks at some of the changes—in patient population mix, in problems they bring in, in the role of staff, and in the aspirations of rank-and-file employees—it is clear that it is impossible to separate the internal from the external forces that play on the psychiatric institution. The institution is part of a changing society from which patients, staff and employees come and to which, increasingly, patients are more quickly returning. Inevitably, the psychiatric institution is tremendously influenced by changes in society as a whole.

MAJOR NEW FACTORS TO RECKON WITH

1. Changing Attidudes toward Institutions

Perhaps one of the most significant changes in society in the last decade is in attitudes toward institutions. There is an almost relentless questioning of the foundations, knowledge, usefulness, ethics and objectives of all professions and all institutions. This has affected social, political, legal, educational and health institutions. It has affected many professionals—politicians, lawyers and doctors particularly. People no longer accept on faith and trust the knowledge, ethics or goodwill of the professionals, including health professionals, and this has significantly changed the context in which mental institutions and the psychiatrist-executive operate. Some of these attitudes have jelled into serious new stereotypes in the past decade and are summarized as follows:

Stereotype #1

Physicians withhold information for their own protection or that of other M.D.'s, rather than the patient's. Therefore, one must force patient information out, sue M.D.'s, and applaud when courts award big damages.

Stereotype #2

Physicians in mental hospitals do not sufficiently protect the civil rights of patients. Therefore, lawyers must be involved in the treatment of patients. Civil rights officers must be appointed to institutions to ensure the protection of civil rights.

Stereotype #3

Inpatient facilities are bad for psychiatric patients and should be abolished. Community services must be developed, not in addition to but instead of inpatient psychiatric facilities (witness trends in New York, California, Massachusetts).

Stereotype #4
Research is being conducted irresponsibly to the patient's detriment in hospitals (witness recent publicity on the Tuskegee study, psychosurgery, research on fetuses, research on prisoners).

Stereotype #5
Physicians are dishonest and make a killing on naïve patients and third-party payers (witness Medicare, Medicaid and publicity on unnecessary operations). Therefore, careful professional auditing and financial auditing must be established.

Stereotype #6
Institutions are self-serving and not sufficiently concerned about the community and holding down costs. They continue to be interested in aggrandizing themselves by new construction, new services, etc., without regard to the public good. Therefore, federal cost control is required, including regional planning, certificate-of-need legislation and citizen groups.

While some of these criticisms may be true, the total indictment of many institutions of different varieties is not justified. Justified or not, however, these attitudes prevail and affect the psychiatrist-executive's role. First, he must be sure, that to the extent that they may be true about the institution which he operates, that they are corrected. But his responsibility does not end there. This changing attitude has meant that the executive must assume a more important role as an educator and communicator and be more involved in public relations. Difficult and time-consuming though the effort may be, it is essential that the executive seize every opportunity he can—through the public media and other means—to educate increasing numbers of groups to the true state of affairs and to explain the reasons why certain things have come under criticism that are done in institutions.

Employees and families of patients should not be overlooked as groups where this kind of communications effort can begin. Open meetings in which the psychiatrist-executive gives a brief report on the institution as a whole and its plans, and then opens the meeting to questions from the floor, are an effective way of helping these groups understand the institutions, its problems and goals. Let me assure you, though as one who has handled both kinds of meetings, that the psychiatrist-executive can expect searching and often belligerent questions on almost any subject during these meetings—particularly from families of patients whose anxieties and frustrations over their relative's illness can be great. He must be willing to take these in stride and use them as opportunities to correct mis-understandings, and to educate the meeting participants about the issues involved. In general, however, we have found that families and employees have reacted most favorably to the opportunity they have biannually (in separate meetings) to have an open dialogue with the director and psychiatrist-in-chief of the hospital. We, in turn, continue to hear from them reports of feelings and issues we should take into account in managing the institution.

2. Rise of Consumerism

The widespread distrust of institutions has resulted in the age of consumerism and a greater voice in the affairs of institutions on the part of people who can be considered consumers only in the very broad sense of the word. Increasingly, institutions are not only answerable to their direct consumers, such as their patients and families, or to state and professional organizations, but also to groups in which some or a majority of participants are indirectly involved citizen representatives.

An example of this is in terms of research. Over the past ten years (either on their own initiative or stimulated by HEW regulations on human studies), health institutions have developed human studies committees to review research projects, not in terms of scientific merit but primarily in terms of the civil rights of the patient participants—that is, to ensure the civil rights of patients in the research and, especially, their informed consent with respect to weighing potential risks against potential gains. But judging by a recent law (P.L. 93-348) amending the Public Health Service Act and pursuant HEW regulations, it is clear that efforts made to date have not been sufficient to meet the criticism. Rather, there is a trend toward broadening the Human Studies Committees, referred to in the new legislation as "Institutional Review Boards," to include some members who are not associated with the institution. Furthermore, such boards may not consist entirely of members of a single professional group and must include persons with concern for "community attitudes."

Another example of this increased citizen participation may be seen in the development under Comprehensive Health Planning legislation (federal and state) of health councils established as voluntary corporations. These health-planning councils require a preponderance of consumers (in many cases, two-thirds consumers versus one-third providers). They have a broad responsibility to review and make recommendations on the delivery of services, changes in services, increases in the number of beds, new construction over prescribed dollar maximums, etc. Established initially out of concern with rising medical care costs and duplication of construction in urban areas, they now have the expanded role of being watchdog over the whole range of comprehensive services for a given geographic location. Nowadays, institutions must justify not only to the government but also to these state citizen groups the validity of their plans before they can change or expand or construct new services.

This state of affairs means that the psychiatrist-executive must do more than recognize these changes and passively accept them. Rather, he should actively involve himself in these various groups in order to educate, in order to communicate, and in order to enlarge the concepts of individuals who are not primarily trained in his particular profession. He must become an advocate not only for his own institution but also for the range of services which he represents and for the objectives for which he strives.

3. Changing Funding Picture

Changes in the funding of institutions and psychiatric services differ to some extent according to whether the institution is a state institution, a community mental health center or a private institution. But changes there have been, and psychiatrist-executives in all of these situations have had to respond. Institutions dependent on federal funding have found long-range plans almost impossible to make in view of the on-again, off-again, on-again shifts in federal funds. Some institutions have had to dismantle certain programs as a result of sudden cutbacks, or have had to use initiative and ingenuity either to convince state authorities to fund them from state funds or to develop potentials for better coverage by third-party payers.

State institutions have found themselves in an increasingly difficult situation. Legislatures and executives in state governments, reacting to the taxpayers' revolt at rising taxes, have not expanded state budgets for mental health services. What this has meant in recent inflationary times is that the amount budgeted in many states for mental health services is now lower in terms of real dollars. Another problem that executives in state institutions have had to deal with is the shift, sometimes suddenly and arbitrarily determined by centralized departments of mental health, to change direction toward the development of community services. This has often resulted in cutbacks in existing services provided by state institutions without a commensurate decrease in the number of patients whom they must serve. While these changes in funding have taxed the imagination and initiative needed on the part of state institutions, they have also raised the possibility of an expanded role for private psychiatric institutions, where, at least, there is less dependency on the vagaries of state funding. These changes, as well as those which will eventually come about from National Health Insurance, will mean a changing role for the psychiatrist-executive in both state and private institutions. Neither has had, as a general rule, much experience in relating to the other. But this they will have to do because to serve the needs of all the people— both in the state and private sectors—they will have to work hand in hand under a variety of funding mechanisms.

Perhaps the most significant change in private psychiatric institutions has been the tremendous increase in third-party payments. A decade ago, almost 100 percent of the patients admitted were self-payers. Now, often over 90 percent of the patients are covered by third-party payment, which might cover as much as 50 percent of the total annual patient billings. Typically, insurance coverage is limited to a 60- or 90-day maximum.

The effects of this have been many. The patient population of private institutions comes from a wider socioeconomic base than ever before and now frequently represents the whole range of citizens. Hospital stays have shortened and the treatment that patients receive is now more often geared to the financial situation and the length of insurance coverage than to the optimal clinical objective. This has meant faster turnover and more patients admitted per year than ever before. The documentation of treatment has increased tremendously in order to meet the accounting and reporting requirements of third-party payers. On the plus side, shorter hospitalizations have placed pressure on institutions to improve short-term treatment modalities in their inpatient services, and also to develop less costly alternatives to hospitalization. One result is a proliferation of partial-care programs; outpatient clinics, day-care programs, halfway houses and evening, night and weekend programs. The problem, however, with so much of patient care being covered by third-party payers is the gaps in coverage. When the patients themselves were paying for their treatment, they could move from an inpatient facility to day care, to outpatient or to halfway houses, and benefit both therapeutically and financially because of the lower costs of partial care. Today, since so many insurance policies still favor inpatient treatment and have not yet developed adequate coverage for partial care, this often presents a financial problem for the patient and also tends to militate against adequate continuity of care.

Until such time as these gaps are covered by insurers, fund raising—always an important element in obtaining capital funds for the development of new programs and buildings in private institutions—will continue to be relied on to help fund patient care.

Private philanthropy has played an important role in our society in the development of institutions and programs, and universities and hospitals could not have achieved what they have without very large sums of money being contributed by private foundations and individuals for construction of buildings and program support. The psychiatrist-executive should be aware, however, that raising funds for a mental health facility presents certain specific problems. Although it is fashionable to say that the attitude of society has changed toward the mentally ill, I believe this is more apparent than real. Mentally ill patients do not arouse in others the same degree of compassion as the physically ill, and as psychiatrists we should not be terribly surprised. Mentally ill people are unhappy people, and unhappiness usually breeds anger, and anger arouses not compassion but usually the opposite. The antagonism of society toward the mentally ill often spills over onto the institutions which treat them.

Compared to general hospitals, institutions which treat the mentally ill are at a disadvantage in matters of fund raising. Because of the complexities of figuring out the workings of the human mind, as well as the limited research which has been carried out in psychiatry, this specialty has developed at a slower rate than the rest of medicine. There are few dramatic cures which can be widely publicized in the daily press and popular magazines. There are no equivalents in psychiatry for open heart surgery, kidney transplantation or the sewing on of a severed limb. Psychiatric treatment as interpreted to the general public lacks dramatic appeal. A further handicap is that psychiatric treatment must be conducted in private. Medical treatments are often publicized in the form of human interest stories which describe the benefits received by an individual as a result of a medical or surgical "miracle." Because the mentally ill already feel very vulnerable and exposed, we as psychiatrists take particular care to assure the patient as much confidentiality and privacy as possible. Therefore, institutions which treat the mentally ill are further deprived of publishing their successes widely and dramatically. The fact that these handicaps exist only increases the responsibility of the psychiatrist-executive to educate the public to the needs, opportunities and performance of mental health institutions.

The above-mentioned problems create a need for the psychiatrist-executive to play a vigorous role in educating insurance companies and seizing every opportunity to advocate extending maximum-coverage periods and filling gaps. This can be done on a direct basis with various insurance carriers and also through professional organizations.

Also, since in all probability, at some point in the next few years, we shall have national health insurance mandated by the Congress, it is important for psychiatrists to involve themselves now in the developing legislation and insist upon equal coverage for both psychiatric illness and for physical illness. Ways of doing this are discussed later in this chapter.

Perhaps the most important reason why there is reluctance on the part of the government to insure mental health services on an equal basis with other forms of medicine is the belief that it will cost too much and will break the back of funding mechanisms. Use must be made of all existing studies showing the insurability of mental illness on the same basis as physical illness, and plans set for constantly updating these. It is undoubtedly true that if mental services were covered fully in the same way as physical illness, it would increase the total cost of medical care. At the same time, however, it would not cost as much as many people think. Furthermore, a telling argument is that if mental health services are provided adequately, it decreases the use of other medical services; that is, a cost offset is effected. It has been found, for instance, in prepaid insurance programs such as Kaiser-Permanente, that if mental health services are provided, it decreases the utilization of other medical services. The reason for this, not surprising to a psychiatrist, is that many people who are in difficulty will seek treatment from their general practitioner or a medical specialist. It is the experience of most general practitioners that for at least half the patients they see, the problems they describe are actually due to emotional problems. Therefore, providing a financial mechanism whereby these patients can seek the proper medical care, i.e., mental health services, will reduce the demand placed upon other sections of the health delivery system.

4. Expanding Applications of Labor Laws

Still another force that has been reshaping the role of the psychiatrist-executive stems from changes in labor laws and regulations. For a long time, hospital employees were affected by a very limited number of fundamental rules governing employee-employer relations. But in recent years, labor laws have been more broadly applied and now extend to employees in health institutions, including hospitals. To give you an idea of their proliferation, a recent review of labor laws applicable to private nonprofit hospitals in Massachusetts revealed that there were fifteen such federal and twenty-three such state laws. It is not my purpose to describe these laws in detail, but to point out how they significantly changed the role and knowledge required by psychiatrist-executives today.

Foremost among his aims to fulfill the basic objective of the institution—providing patient care—is to have the required number of employees with appropriate training to deliver services. Proper selection and maintenance of highly qualified employees is particularly critical in the treatment of mental disease where the attitudes of employees are essential in providing an optimum environment in which to treat patients. Many of these laws restrict options institutions once had in selecting and maintaining employees. For example, unemployment compensation laws in some states are such that it is virtually impossible to discharge an unsatisfactory employee, even for cause, without the hospital ultimately sustaining a financial loss should he not find employment elsewhere.

Another constraint which has been placed on the selection and hiring of employees results from the Executive Order requiring institutions to establish an Affirmative Action Program. It is no longer sufficient for organizations to implement a hiring program of nondiscrimination on the basis of race. What institutions must now do is to take extraordinary steps to recruit women and minority employees in all segments of the institution. This program must be carefully monitored with objectives set ahead with target dates improving the percentages of women and minority employees in the various departments. Both the objectives and performance must be approved and reported quarterly to the federal government. Designed to fulfill most laudable social objectives, the Affirmative Action requirements inevitably pose special problems for the psychiatrist-executive in charge of a psychiatric institution. The required numbers of well-trained professionals are often very difficult to find among minority groups, and when they are found and asked to join the staff, they often feel that the objectives of the institution are at variance with their social and professional objectives. Although the increase in insurance coverage for psychiatric illness has resulted in a broader representation of the general population among the patients of a private psychiatric institution, minority patients still form a small percentage of the total patient population, and well-trained professionals who themselves belong to minority groups often feel that their professional dedication and expertise should be applied directly in the community in the deprived large urban centers of population.

Affirmative Action Programs affect recruitment in other ways. Frequently professionals are recruited by word of mouth; someone applies for a particular professional job at a specific institution rather than the institution itself embarking on a broad recruitment effort to fill the position. If the person is hired, it is because the institution needs the particular skills and experience of that specific individual.

It is at that juncture that Affirmative Action requirements tend to impose a constraint which may result in no approved person being hired. Whether successful or not, the financial cost of implementing an affirmative action program is high and is inevitably passed on to the patients.

More recently, there has been increasing emphasis on the quality control of patient care. This trend has been emerging simultaneously from several sources. The federal government has been setting more standards for delivering care as it has become a larger health-care payer through Medicare and Medicaid. State governments have also developed standards for the operation of institutions as they have become more involved in the delivery of service. And finally, professional organizations have, on a voluntary basis, also developed standards for the practice of their members. Twice in the last five years the American Psychiatric Association has revised its standards for psychiatric facilities. It has also written standards for psychiatric facilities for children. While these particular regulations are not binding on the psychiatric institutions, they are nevertheless an indication of the tremendous importance placed by professional organizations on providing guidelines for the development of services.

More significant, perhaps, have been trends and changes apparent in the work of the Joint Commission on Accreditation of Hospitals. While a voluntary organization, its accreditation is eagerly sought by institutions throughout the country because very frequently payment by third parties depends on it. Five years ago, in association with five, and more recently seven, national professional organizations, the Joint Commission developed councils for special categories of institution. One of these, the Accreditation Council for Psychiatric Facilities, has developed standards specifically applicable to psychiatric facilities and more recently to children's facilities. It is also in the process of developing standards for community mental health centers, psychiatric services of general hospitals, alcohol programs and drug treatment programs. These new standards are the basis on which psychiatric facilities applying for accreditation are evaluated by accreditation council surveyors. These standards are more stringent and more pertinent to psychiatric facilities than formerly. It is terribly important for the psychiatrist-executive to familiarize himself with these new guidelines which psychiatric facilities must follow and to ensure that all sections of his institution comply with the standards. But the role of the psychiatrist-executive should not be limited merely to being a passive recipient of such data on standards and an overseer of their application. We need not be the passive victims, if you will, of new rules written by others. We can and should take an active part in forming the rules and feeding in information and comments to the Council. Also, I believe that it is important for the psychiatrist-executive, to the extent that he can and to the extent that he is invited to do so, to participate in the actual activities of the Joint Commission on Accreditation of Hospitals, on the Accreditation Council for Psychiatric Facilities, and in his professional organizations and the committees that are developing standards for his practice.

5. Health Planning Councils

Other forces restricting the options and initiative of psychiatrist-executives today stem from state laws and regulations designed to achieve comprehensive health planning under federal enabling legislation. The effect of these has been that the states now control in large measure the services which an institution may develop and the amount of money it may commit to capital improvements. In the past, if an institution saw a need for additional beds, or for changing services, or for new construction, outside of obtaining a building permit in advance and the approval of the Public Health Department after the facility was built, the institution could go ahead provided it had the money. It was, in a sense, master of its own destiny and master in its own house. This is no longer true. Today a first step the institution must take is to apply to the state for a Certificate of Need. It must justify the need for the particular facility, and typically go through a very complicated set of steps before the state is willing to agree to the need and issue a certificate. Pending its issuance, the institution is not even permitted to begin its fund-raising efforts to collect funds for construction. There is no question that this has hamstrung many institutions. The objectives of comprehensive health planning are valid, but, unfortunately, the implementing procedures to date are not operating sufficiently smoothly to convince health institutions that it is an improvement over the past situation. There is no doubt that the role of the psychiatrist-executive has been significantly affected by this new legislation, but here again he can choose to be more than a passive object of external forces. He can decide to participate in very active ways in the improvement of the regulations and the implementation of the law. Throughout the country, health planning councils have been developed, as described earlier, with ·both consumer and provider representation. They provide the psychiatrist-executive with chances to participate at the area planning committee level, at the regional council level or at the level of the Board of Directors and its various committees. Their recommendations are passed on to those official state bodies which are ultimately empowered to license new health care building. In addition to their impact on licensing, health planning councils have another function: reviewing what services are being provided in a particular area, identifying any gaps in services, and taking the initiative in conjunction with providers in that area for filling the gaps. These are matters the psychiatrist-executive cannot afford to leave only to others to decide.

6. Commitment Laws

State commitment laws governing the involuntary admission of patients to psychiatric hospitals—alluded to earlier—must be counted as another force for changing institution policies and procedures, as well as the role of the psychiatrist-executive. Not only have these laws restricted the options of the psychiatrist on how to treat the patient and the hospital's power to retain patients who need treatment, but the commitment procedure, in some states, has become very much of an adversary proceeding. Often the patient is now represented by counsel, forcing the psychiatrist-executive applying for the commitment also to be represented by counsel. In fact, the civil rights lawyer has become an essential right arm of the chief executive, not only to ensure that the rules and regulations governing the treatment of patients are being obeyed within his institution, but also to represent him at commitment hearings. This advice is necessary for the chief executive, who almost daily must decide on how to reach the best compromise between optimal treatment for the patients and compliance with a maze of regulations governing their civil rights.

7. Cost Control

For a two-and-a-half-year period through April 1974, the federal government controlled prices and wages. Initially, health institutions welcomed this step because it seemed to promise a slowing down of the rate of inflation of the whole economy, including the rising cost of medical care. As time went on, however, and controls became less popular, gradually various industries were decontrolled until in the final few months one of the few industries controlled was the health industry. This placed tremendous additional burdens on health institutions because they found the prices of virtually everything they need to operate escalating and yet they were not permitted to pass the additional costs on to their clients.

The reason for this appears to be that the cost of medical care had been rising for years at a faster rate than the rate of the economy. I believe that the health industry has not been very successful at educating the public, the legislators and the government to a full understanding of the reasons. There is a tendency in our society to blame the hospitals and the physicians for the rising costs. What is not sufficiently understood are two things: that because for many years those who worked in institutions were grossly underpaid (alluded to earlier), there has been a process of catching up which inevitably increased the cost of medical care; and the tremendous increase in cost of medical technology. The American people are constantly asking for better medical care and more of it. There is also the expectation that one level of quality of care shall prevail for both the rich and the poor. Add to these factors the many recent major discoveries resulting in far more expensive procedures than formerly. For instance, the number of intensive care units for a whole range of medical emergencies has increased tremendously in recent years. Also, new techniques of open heart surgery and others have been developed. All of this is pushing toward increased medical care costs. Yet the taxpayers, the legislators and the government are most distressed that there is a price tag associated with these improvements, and thus we can expect that as the years go on, there will probably be renewed pressures for some kind of control over the health industry.

These trends and attitudes dictate that both psychiatric and medical administrators must do whatever they can to educate the public, legislators and the government, as well as their own consumers, to a better understanding of the issues and the choices. Ultimately, society must decide how much it is willing to pay for medical care. In large measure, the hospital and the doctors do not in fact control what the cost of medical care is going to be. Salaries—the biggest single expense factor in hospital care—are really outside the control of hospitals. It is the pressures in society as a whole, the labor unions and the settlements they get that ultimately determine how much people who work in all fields of labor are going to be paid. Hospitals are in the business of treating patients, and they will try to treat patients to the best of their ability within the means available, but controls or not, the public will have to understand that hospitals cannot provide service without adequate funds. Society must choose between paying the cost of medical care or reducing the quality of its medical care.

MOVING INTO THE LEGISLATIVE-POLITICAL ARENA

Throughout this chapter I have been postulating that the psychiatrist-executive lives in a "future shock" kind of world in which he has two options. He can actively try to influence changes affecting him and his institution, or he can sit by on the sidelines and react to changes after the fact.

Many of the major changes with which he must reckon today can be influenced in the legislative-political arena: funding and insurance mechanisms, commitment laws, certificate-of-need legislation, federal and state standards affecting patient treatment, etc.

There is much the psychiatrist-executive can do to influence the legislative-political environment positively. Professional organizations like the American Medical Association and American Psychiatric Association have recognized the necessity of advocacy and the importance of bringing to the attention of legislators issues they should consider in drafting legislation. Too often, professionals have remained completely uninvolved, and then only when a law has been passed and they suddenly realize how it is going to affect them, their practice and their patients, have they complained. On the whole, professionals have underestimated the political impact which they might have. They tend to see politics as outside their ken. In fact, some have felt that somehow to involve themselves in the political process is to surrender some of their professional dignity and ethics.

This traditional stance of lack of involvement in the political process must change. There could not be a more suitable time for it to do so. We live in an age of consumerism and in an age of advocacy, which presents many opportunities for professionals to become involved in the legislative mill and to ensure that their views are heard and understood *before* legislation is passed.

What must be recognized is that legislators are, on the whole, generalists. They know a little about a great number of things but probably not much about any single one, with the possible exception of one or two particular interests which they have. Yet, as legislators, they are called upon, year in and year out, to cast a vote for or against a very large number of legislative proposals. They cannot possibly have the knowledge to understand the issues on which they must vote unless they receive a great deal of information from many people, and they know this. The truth is that, for the most part, they are dedicated public servants interested in doing what is best for the people and receptive to hearing different viewpoints. Therefore, it is up to us as professionals to convey to them our special viewpoint in order to ensure that the interests of our patients and institutions are taken into account in the legislative process. Despite the almost dirty connotation the word "lobbyist" has, the fact is that lobbyists are absolutely essential in our form of government. We need to be among them, given the increasing pieces of legislation that are being passed that affect us. We are in a unique position to convey to legislators what given issues are, why what we do is important, what difference it makes, and how much it will cost. We can help the legislator make better decisions—to cast his vote in directions more likely to fill the objectives of our profession. But to have influence on him, we must know him, we must communicate with him, we must keep in touch with him on some ongoing basis rather than calling him cold out of the blue only when a critical piece of legislation is up for action. One way of doing this is to work through our professional organizations. We must develop a relationship on a continuing basis with important legislators, communicating to them the important issues of the day as they affect mental health treatment. (For the past two years, the American Psychiatric Association through its district branches has developed a network of legislative representatives and committees throughout the country. In addition to district work, each of the district branch legislative representatives has met periodically in Washington to attend institutes on government operations.) In turn, we can also offer to be resource people for them to call upon whenever they have questions. Most legislators, before they act on a particular piece of legislation, contact a number of people to inform themselves. Thus it is important that on mental health legislation, the legislator knows at least one person in the mental health field who can give him sound advice.

It is essential for this mission to be accomplished. Psychiatrists and other mental health workers must involve themselves either directly as private citizens or through their professional associations. A grass-roots effort is needed because the officers of the organizations cannot possibly do alone the work that needs to be done. It requires a tremendous amount of manpower. It is best if a psychiatrist who is a constituent contact his legislator, because in the last analysis, legislators listen best to their constituents—or at least have to pay some attention to their opinions if they wish to be reelected.

Certainly, if the psychiatrist-executive wishes to assume an active role in changing the environment, he cannot eschew the many ways in which he can involve himself in the legislative-political arena.

CONCLUSION

In this chapter I have tried to trace the history of the internal changes in mental health institutions and some of the external forces—social, legal, political, professional and financial—that are impinging on them. I have tried to show how these have affected the role and function of the psychiatrist-executive. In one sense, his basic mission remains what it has always been: he is still an administrator charged with directing and guiding the multiple resources of the institution toward its basic objective—the delivery of psychiatric services. Whereas once, however, he had relative freedom and flexibility in performing this function, today a confluence of disparate forces threaten to limit, restrict and dictate what shall be done. Whether the threats will become irreversible realities will depend largely on him—on whether he chooses to be a passive victim of change or an active participant in it, seizing opportunities to direct it into positive channels where he can.

The thesis of this chapter is that the psychiatrist-executive must be actively involved in the process of change in order to fulfill his job. He must look beyond the internal hospital environment. He must do more than simply balance resources with needs within the institution itself, and be intimately aware of outside political, governmental, social and financial forces impacting upon his institution. He must understand the origin and the process by which decisions are made and implemented in those outside spheres, and he must identify the pressure points at which his activity, advocacy or lobbying can and should make a difference. Simultaneously, he should identify those organizations in his area which may have some influence in making these decisions—health planning councils, legislative committees of district A.P.A. branches, and so on. He should involve himself in their activities, volunteering his services at all levels in order to try to alter, suggest and channel forces in directions which will help our patients and our institutions. He should recognize himself as an expert. He has probably always recognized himself as an expert in psychiatry or in administration, but the new role calls for additional interests and activities. He must become much more of a public man than he ever was before. He must recognize that he has something specific to offer to the deliberations of others—consumers, legislators and others—which they need as they struggle toward developing new laws and regulations that are going to affect health care.

If the psychiatrist-executive chooses to rise to these new responsibilities, he will no doubt experience some frustration. His activity will not always achieve results immediately. The satisfaction that comes from one's contributions making a real difference may often have to be deferred. But over time, as he sees his influence having an effect the personal satisfaction and sense of reward can be great.

We live in an exciting era of kaleidoscopic change. It is a time when we can discover new combinations of opportunities and open up new corridors of understanding which will help our institutions and patients.

21

Mental Health Consultation in Schools: The Clinician-Consultant Transition

MAURICE VANDERPOL

When a traditional psychiatrist changes his customary role from clinician in a private office or hospital to ''consultant'' in community schools, he has reason to feel uncertain. His goal is better mental health for the *schoolchild*, but he works through the school, or the school system staff. He has, at first, no role model, no defined task and no client whose pain he must still. Because of this built-in uncertainty he is perpetually in danger of clinging to some aspect of his traditional role and of seriously limiting his potential as a consultant. But those who struggle through uncertainties and inevitable failures have opportunities to shape an environment which enhances children's growth and education. As a shaping influence, the school, like the family, is where efforts to prevent emotional or mental crippling can be optimally effective.

The purpose of this chapter is to help colleagues who are making the same shift in role from clinician to mental health consultant by sharing my experiences, defining some issues and suggesting ways of dealing with these; and to emphasize the enormous potential for primary prevention in schools.

Part I will explain some personal issues involved in the shift. Part II will show some progressions in the process and content of consultation using illustrations. In Part III, I shall attempt to define a direction for school consultation by considering its history, main emphases and future.

PART I: UNEXPECTED PARTNERSHIP

The schools and I might seem on the surface to be unlikely partners. My training in psychiatry was a classical one, consisting of dynamic psychiatry, one-to-one psychotherapy, chemotherapy, group therapy and somatotherapy. After my residency, I became a practicing psychoanalyst. More recently I developed an interest in building a bridge between mental health and education. The dynamic force of three experiences emerged to guide me toward the schools.

The first was that when I was a child going to public school, the teachers who were so important to me did not have the depth of understanding so essential to a student's future direction in his life. I paid dearly for this lack, and the need to diminish this risk for other children may have stimulated me in choosing my present work with teachers.

The second experience was the exhilaration and freedom I felt during my fourth year in medical school when I was finally allowed outside the confines of the hospital to do community medicine. On call in a poor, multi-racial urban district, I could go on my own as a doctor to see patients in their homes. It was exciting, it was rough, and it was human and real. I could make a much better judgment about the practicability of a prescription for treatment knowing the possibilities and limitations of the patient's environment. Prescribing absolute bedrest was not feasible, for example, for a mother without help and a one-year-old infant in a crib at the foot of her bed.

The third experience was my training exposure to the teachings of Stanton regarding the importance of the milieu in the hospital treatment of the mentally ill. With Schwartz, he maintained that intrapsychic dynamic processes necessarily related to the quality of the milieu. (30) The outcome of this interest was a symposium in 1965, in which the synergic or conflictual dynamics between individual therapy and the hospital milieu for schizophrenic patients were discussed by Winnicott, Searles and others.(12)

My first contact with public school teachers came when a small group of them requested advice on the "educational" management of some junior high school students. The students they taught in their "transitional" class turned out to include a catatonic, mute, schizophrenic girl and other similarly disturbed adolescents in no way less sick than our inpatients at the psychiatric hospital. What especially impressed me, the sheltered psychiatrist, was that these teachers and counselors were in many ways successful in their efforts to help these students by using only their own intuitive ingenuity and sensitivity in the confines of the educational setting. My help consisted of expressing genuine admiration and respect for their efforts, providing a better theoretical framework with which to observe the children's behavior, teaching them how to elicit needed information, how to plan an intervention, and giving them a realistic time schedule for anticipated improvements.

A case-seminar format promoted the teachers' ability to develop problem-solving skills, and encourage them to devise realistic management plans and evaluate their outcome. My role was still close to the traditional one in many ways; although I learned a lot about teachers' management, it was mostly I, the expert, who gave support and information to them.

Although I had already decided on a move from the hospital setting to that of the public school, a profound change in my professional orientation occurred through a critical inauguration into the adolescent drug culture. Through work with schools and with adolescents in my practice, I had become increasingly concerned about the alcohol and drug culture among teenagers. Along with other professionals, I joined a group of recent high school graduates in forming a hot line to help those in trouble through emergency counseling. Each professional, in the initial plan, was to be a back-up to the young counselors in his own professional line. I knew nothing, however, about the "lingo" of bad trips, O.D.-ing, purple pills, and the general condition of kids who never see the medical establishment. I found myself outside my professional environment, and besides I was an "old" man and a "shrink" to boot. Yet there was a need for help, so I *had* to stick it out. I had to take some time to readjust and find ways to be useful. Even though the young counselors were open in their skepticism, they seemed to support the expectation that as a professional back-up, I would turn out to be useful, even essential—but on grounds yet to be defined and yet to be determined. They needed a *stable person*, nonjudgmental, not afraid of crises. While the counselors were searching for their own identity (many of them had been on drugs), they needed *adult models*; they needed support and certain medical information, firm guidelines for acceptable behavior and a basic ethical code. They, in turn, showed a willingness to help, and a skill in informal, sensitive and nondefensive interaction with clients who might be reluctant to state their need for assistance in the first telephone call or first visit. Young counselors who had successfully mastered their own problems turned out to be very effective with troubled adolescent clients.

The Process of Role Transition

In making the transition from clinician to school consultant, I found that many basic personal issues—some obvious, some subtle—had to be dealt with. Many of my habitual assumptions about work-life had to be changed.

Setting: First I had to move from a familiar private office decorated to my personal taste or from a very structured and predictable hospital environment to the unfamiliar school building or hot-line cubicle. My first office in a school was the women's lounge. I was then faced with the decision whether to structure my office along traditional lines or have an open door with no shingle, no rigid office hours and ready availability. I discovered that the *quality* of availability meant everything—any setting that could convey an inviting, low-key attitude saying, "Come and visit when I am around; I respect your decision as to when you are ready to tell me what you really want to talk about," was appropriate.

Focus of Service: I had to move from giving *direct* service to a client (patient) to giving *indirect* service through a consultee. This immediately put me in a difficult spot: a suffering patient comes to be healed by a doctor, but why does a consultee see a consultant? Is the consultee hurting? If so, it has nothing to do with an illness that needs healing; the contract has a different motivation and the roles are different. That meant I had to work much harder to clarify for myself and for the potential consultee how collaboration could help. The consultee had no background for such an alliance either. There is no tradition in schools for a practicing educator to work with a psychiatrist.

Alliance with Consultee: A consultant works with professionals of other disciplines, with paraprofessionals, or with volunteer lay persons. The goal of this alliance has to be determined and clarified repeatedly as the relationship unfolds. As a therapist, I had become familiar with the fact that a patient's presenting complaint is usually just an "entrance ticket" and that my job was to find the underlying cause for the patient's seeking help at a particular time. This offered a clue to what the patient was basically looking for. I found in the new setting that all my clinical skills of observation and of eliciting pertinent information and probing were needed to answer similar crucial questions regarding the reason and timing for the consultation request. I had to work out a basic working contract with the consultee; we had to answer the questions, How shall we work together? What shall we expect as a result?

Because two different professional disciplines were involved, I had to continuously clarify what in my own expertise would be useful and relevant to the consultee while at the same time supporting and enhancing the consultee's expertise.

Yet, moving from a one-to-one therapeutic relationship to a one-to-many working relationship in an institution creates special problems. There can arise a personal urgency to make a contract too quickly in order to feel one is "doing" something. There is a maze of invisible forces sabotaging the best intentions of any consultant. Obviously, I had to clarify the meaning of the contract to me, to the consultee and to the rest of the school system. Groundwork is essential for a contract to have good possibilities of success. For instance, when a team of three fourth-grade teachers asked me to consult with them about an innovative and exciting classroom approach, we dutifully went to the principal for his sanction. Only later did I find out how angry the principal and other competing staff members were because they had been "excluded" from the consultation. As a result, my consultees had extra troubles; the rift between them and their colleagues widened. Although our target work proceeded well, we had to make special efforts to resolve the polarized staff relationships that I had helped to aggravate without premeditation or malice. This brought me face to face with issues regarding *social system dynamics*, a dimension I knew little about, but one that was clearly of basic importance to the success or failure of the consultation process.

Language: Every profession preserves its self-esteem by using language and codes unintelligible to those in other professions. In a multiprofessional setting, the use of idiosyncratic language is counterproductive. "Tonight" in teachers' communications means the time after school is out (e.g., after 3 P.M.); to nonteachers, it may mean after 6 P.M. *Discipline, articulation, Iowa, California, Minnesota, enrichment, L.D., E.D., M.R.*, and many other words have special meanings to educators. *Borderline, E.S.T., E.E.G., functional, organic, acting-out, defenses* and *dependency* are mental health terms requiring special definition for others. In hot-line language terms like *O.D.-ing (overdosing), bad trip, stoned, laced, spaced out* are common parlance.

Target Group: As a clinician, I dealt with people who had gone through a long process of assuming the identity of a patient who was ill. They had suffered or made others suffer, and had decided to enter a relationship with a medical practitioner for diagnosis and treatment. Often doctors are not aware how much has happened in a person prior to his contact with the medical establishment. In the community I had many opportunities to see potential candidates in need of help, who were engaged in the difficult process of facing the fact that something had gone wrong. I noticed how they carefully selected nonthreatening people to talk with in a setting that would encourage them to find out whether something was wrong and whether they could do something about it. More preventive work could be done by reaching people in this earlier stage if we as professionals create the proper milieu with more flexibility and sensitivity to the needs of the potential help-seeker. We often turn them off and scare them away with our professional procedures, which to us seem so reasonable and so efficient.

Financial Arrangements: In community work I was obliged to negotiate fees for my consultant services with practical school administrators. Representing a mental hospital and being a psychiatrist, I could not negotiate the specific program budgets that could be explained easily to a school committee. Although financial support was gained slowly, our programs were slowed down by diminishing federal funds. Such a worrisome financial situation makes a consultant more vulnerable to resistance in the consultee's system as well as in himself and therefore makes the work possibly less effective.

PART II: SCHOOL CONSULTATION: A PROGRESSION

Consultation in schools develops at two parallel levels: a progression in process and a progression in content. The *process* aspect refers to the working alliance between consultant and consultee(s); the formulation of the explicit contract as well as the implied psychological contract, the development of trust, of communication, etc. The second aspect is *content*, more closely related to *in-service training*, opening up dimensions regarding problems, issues and final goals. These dimensions are closely related, and we see successful school consultation evolving along both in very definite ways. The process develops from case-oriented, direct services to more indirect services, from a consultant-consultee ratio of one-to-one to one-to-many; and it also leads to an increasing integration of two or more professional disciplines resulting in a flexible shift in the roles of consultant and consultee. Related to this is a frequent change in the consultee's involvement in the consultation from requesting consultation for a specific problem to seeing it as necessary for professional growth and development.

Along the *content* line, we see progression from *remedial* to more *preventive* measures, similar to Caplan's definition of tertiary, secondary and primary prevention. This brings with it a better understanding of salient factors relating to the child's development and new techniques or approaches to more effective intervention or prevention. These progressions are illustrated with case vignettes showing how these appear in the school setting.

The Courageous Junior High School Teacher
One woman teacher presented her case in a seminar called "The Hard to

Manage Child.'' She was very concerned about a ninth-grade boy who, according to school rules, could not be promoted to high school unless he handed in his English term paper at the end of the year. He refused to do so. However, the teacher had found out from the boy's mother that the paper was ready but was kept in his locker. An interesting discussion ensued about the boy's clear decision *not* to hand in his paper. We could have dealt exclusively with the child's ''dynamics,'' but the interest of the teacher and support of her seminar group allowed me to venture into the issue of the teacher's conflict and feelings of helplessness to promote the student to the tenth grade. All other seminar members could identify with this issue. As a result of the discussion in the trusting and problem-solving climate of the seminar, the teacher began to understand the student,* and to question her own exaggerated and rigid stance on this ''rule,'' which turned out not to be so iron-clad as she had assumed. This case illustrates the progression from the teacher looking at the problem as identified *in* the ''hard to manage'' child to the teacher looking at her own reactions and her relationship to her department's rules. The seminar setting also allowed other teachers to identify with the presentor. As a result of this experience the teacher in a subsequent year asked my help with her ninth-grade class of ''dum-dums,'' a group of bright, turned-off, acting-out students who had assumed a strong and persistent negative group-identity in the school, a group familiar to anyone working in junior high schools. She had been courageous in candidly but dramatically acknowledging to the class the utter failure of the educational and personal contract between these students and the school system. This indicated to these students that she took this contract seriously and was indeed proposing to renegotiate it in a relevant and realistic way. She succeeded in doing so during that school year and the results were spectacular in two ways: first, the students *learned* (English reading, verbalizing, writing and spelling); second, the classroom formed a model working group, drawing (in a most efficient way) on all personal resources available in its membership, and giving support and feedback to each other.

My role as consultant in this seminar instance was to support, raise new questions and clarify as well as give information. I spent a year in the classroom, being present approximately one period a week. I observed and sometimes participated at the teacher's request in role play or in a co-leadership role with the teacher. Then the teacher and I would discuss what had happened and evaluate progress. In this supportive alliance, she used all her educational inventiveness and expertise, and I did the same with my mental health expertise, as illustrated by the following account.

In May of that school year the teacher came to me looking depressed and desperate, saying that all was lost because the class seemed to have reverted to its early chaos. It occurred to me that this well-functioning group would be disband-

---

*The boy's favorite grandfather had died after a long illness and the information had been withheld by his parents.

ing in a few weeks when the students would leave for high school. I explained loss and separation, a process especially painful for adolescents. When she asked me what she could do about it, I suggested she use any English literature she could find dealing with loss. When I came in, she had written on the blackboard the following quote from Ernest Kroll's "Drag Race":

> Recklessly
> (Morituri)
> They roar to
> the Town's
> (Te)
> Edge, blaring
> their
> (Salutamus)
> Horns

The class began exploring death, their own game of Russian Roulette, and whether other people really cared if a friend left or died or got killed. The discussion helped these young people to deal with their anxious and sad feelings and to grow in an important way through incorporating and identifying with what they had shared with each other and, especially, with the teacher.

This vignette shows first the teacher's reason for asking help was ostensibly for an educational problem: intelligent students were not learning English. However, the teacher had become more knowingly alert to psychological and system issues. In our work we stayed away from any "pathology" issues, but focused mainly on motivational factors, adolescent developmental issues and the issue of loss and separation. The primary task was to help the students to abandon their negative group-identity. This required an intrapsychic shift as well as a resistance to the school's need, as a system, to use these "dum-dums" as a contrast to the "spes patriae"—the fair-haired achievers. The teacher, through carefully planned educational techniques, had brought them around, encouraging the students to express in nonverbal and verbal ways anything relating to their own identity: feelings, fantasies, dreams, hopes, relationships. The crunch came with the separation problem, so poignant in the adolescent phase. I had learned how an able teacher can lead a class skillfully from a long-standing negative relationship with a system to a more positive direction; she made herself available for these adolescents to test out their fantasies and eventually come to a more realistic conclusion about their own and their teacher's identity. This gave me the courage to advise the teacher to work on the separation issue in full force. It seemed a natural next step for all of them to come to grips with the loss of closeness, the moving on to "bigger" things, and to incorporate what they had "learned."

As a result of her experience, this teacher, as the head of her department, carefully planned with the consulting psychiatrist a special remedial program to be implemented the following year. This involved motivating the school system to provide finances, personnel, as well as the necessary space (a hard commodity): it involved some specialized staff training in a mental hospital school, the home base of the consultant. The plan included team formation with time to criticize and evaluate the results. The program was quite successful in a number of ways: as a model program it helped several teachers to develop a profound change in their approach to students with behavior problems. This had a ripple effect among other staff members. The teachers no longer felt so helpless about students who had been turned off for years by the system. However, as is seen frequently, as parts of the program were gradually adopted by the school staff, the program became less innovative, less necessary, and over a three-year period, lost much of its raison d'être.

As we move from consulting with one teacher to consulting with a social system, we encounter dimensions that as mental health professionals, we are usually not trained for. These include the dynamics of power, institutional structure, group functioning and the process of change. Clinicians venturing into consultation are sometimes made uncomfortable by these elements and react as if these phenomena have no business being there. But they *are* there, and must be coped with even if they cause frustration, anguish and anger. Pejorative diagnostic labeling of "culprits" who are creating obstacles is a clear sign that a consultant's own feelings are in the way of his work.

The Reluctant Principal

Let us take some examples of system issues that figure prominently in the consultation relationship. In the aforementioned elementary school, it turned out that two important issues influenced the consultation process. The principals of most schools are in a key position to set the climate for the school: in this case, the principal was a man whose main philosophy was to keep things operating smoothly and treat problems at their manifest level or deny their existence—in other words: "Don't rock the boat." For a group of his teachers to invite a consultant implied that a problem had been identified; asking the help of an outsider was tantamount to washing dirty linen in public. The second major factor in this school was a polarization which exists in many elementary schools between factions: here they were the progressive "young Turks" in opposition to the "establishment." The content of such polarization varies from one school to another—open vs. traditional classroom, types of discipline, etc.—but often the content issues are thoroughly confused and ill-defined in the heat of battle. In this case, the consultant invited by one faction made the other faction furious and envious. As a result, the consultant had to renegotiate a contract with the school staff as a whole and in this way show that he intended to be of use in a nondivisive way. Factions often have identified leaders with charisma and power, and unless these leaders cooperate in setting up the contract for consultation the results will be negative.

Progression with this school as a social system thus began by a seminar member planning to present the case of a depressed child, inviting her two teammates to attend (it was an explicit policy of the seminar to invite to that session the other staff member involved with the presentation). In this way a relationship started between the team and the consultant; the content was ostensibly how to handle the depressed student, but in reality, as the process moved, it began to help the team of three teachers to work more effectively with each other and, subsequently, to resolve the bigger conflict between them and the principal as well as the other school faction. The consultant proceeded to work with the team on planning the management of the depressed girl and other problem students, which then led to planning techniques of classroom management (progression from one student to more students, and then to the classroom which included troubled and *untroubled* students). Simultaneously, the consultant clarified his role with the principal by clearly defining what the consultant would and would *not* do (would not be a decision-maker, nor assume an administrative role). The consultant then offered to work with lower-grade teachers (kindergarten, first and second grade); this cut across faction lines and also filled an expressed need for help. Our consultation process had now involved more teachers and enlisted the cooperation of the principal, indirectly reaching more children. The teachers raised issues rather than cases so that a preventive rather than intervention orientation prevailed. (Issues, for example, were the handling of serious losses, such as a student's death, or dealing with parents in an ongoing relationship.) A next step occurred when a parents' night was being planned. To the consultant, it appeared that the whole faculty followed the principal's example of ritualizing the program so that the least amount of useful contact would occur. The consultant, who had been invited to be on a panel, raised the question whether professionals, as we all were, should seriously plan to underutilize a night in this fashion? The faculty began to discuss a different approach while reassuring the principal that they could manage an innovative program. The parents' night program was a complete departure from the traditional one; there was an overflow crowd, and the teachers and the organizing parents felt they had something vital to invest in. The meeting allowed for open discussion and disagreement, but all people attending were, each in his or her own way, interested in understanding problems and issues and in finding solutions. A strong preventive potential of this episode was the realization of the school's need to encourage parents to be clearer in their own role, rather than to let schools act in the place of parents. From a process point of view, the school staff and parents, were able, with the principal's sanction, to generate their own momentum and direction. The consultant advised parent organizers and teachers on issues regarding whom to involve in planning and when, what the proper sequence was for obtaining approval—in a sense, how to tackle the system knowledgeably in order to get results.

Who is the Host? Where Are the Fathers?

Another important component of this interdependent system is the *students*. Their active confrontation of an issue was illustrated when the school planned another parents' night. The question arose: "Who is really the host? the superintendent? or the school board or the principal? who did the school belong to? Often the covert assumption is that the school board and administration dictate, hence the passive compliance by staff and children. Raising the above questions permitted the staff to generate the alternative that the school served the children, who therefore merited roles as hosts for the parents' night. This led to a complex planning process, which was anything but perfunctory. A basic mental health issue arose: Would the children, being hosts, be successful in getting their fathers to come, particularly the reluctant fathers who considered child rearing and education the mother's department? The children were quite eager to have their fathers come to *their* turf and take a look at *their* world, where they live a large part of each day in their own setting and with a different identity and different relationships than at home.

Some Special Considerations

From a process point of view, the basic guideline for the consultant is to mobilize as much initiative from within the system as it is capable of producing. Particularly in short-term consultation arrangements, to prevent it from being just an interesting session without any lasting results, the school staff and its leaders need to take a more active role in the preplanning and follow-up stages of the consultation. This requires a well-functioning and assertive group with whom the consultant can involve himself in a clear way regarding his role and the staff's expectations.

It is clear that the consultant conveys an attitude of mastering issues through a nonjudgmental questioning approach; he conveys that it makes sense to observe and reflect before suggesting answers. Behavior modification is often used indiscriminately because it is a behavioral technique that does not ask "Why?" and gives one the feeling one is "doing" something to help. The attitude of open questioning sometimes cuts through prejudicial stereotyping of roles. For example, to pay serious attention to the relationship between students on one hand and custodians, kitchen personnel, secretaries and librarians on the other is often considered of little value. Yet to anyone who wants to look, the enormous psychological significance of these members of a school staff is obvious, and everyone knows it at some level of awareness. These people have some important common denominators: they are *not* tightly scheduled, and one does not need appointments to join them; they deal with basic and concrete matters such as providing food, cleaning, making repairs and (for secretaries in elementary schools) attending to students who are hurt. Librarians in the secondary schools are often bartender-type therapists; the library also may offer some privacy. The students are clear about the roles of these members of a school staff and use them to the fullest, unscrutinized by the powers-that-be because members of this service staff are not seen as "professionals." Yet they are the invisible but important gatekeepers who create a hidden system of maintenance crucial to the climate of the school. As an outsider, a consultant can relate to this and recognize it more easily.

Our discussion would not be complete without saying a word about the consultant's role in a system in crisis. A not unusual occurrence is that a staff member becomes mentally ill in a very evident way, raising anxiety levels to a contagiously high pitch, often resulting in isolation of the afflicted person. Another crisis situation may occur when a school principal gives up his post under unclear and ambiguous circumstances, leaving the school in a state of uncertainty and chaos. The role of the consultant is not to relate primarily to the troubled person as a patient but to relate to the school as a totality. This means to clearly establish the reality issues as to the cause and effect of events, to promote communications among members of the system, to delineate and define the problem and the responsibilities people have toward each other, as well as the limits of what people can do to help. The emphasis is on the consultant encouraging the members of the staff to deal with the crisis using their own styles. The consultant also ensures, when the immediate crisis is relieved, that continuing work is done to deal with personal issues of guilt, loss and anger, as well as system issues of shifts in power and allegiance. This may also be used as a general learning experience in emphasizing how people deal with upsetting feelings and events, stumbling in defensive maneuvers of avoidance, scapegoating and denial, or seeking creative solutions when reality issues are clearly established.

PART III: SOME CONCEPTUAL CONSIDERATIONS REGARDING CONSULTATION IN SCHOOLS

Here I intend to connect the historical development of school consultation to a viable future.

Many directions have been defined regarding consultation in mental health. Golann and Eisdorfer (14) state: ". . . for each phase of mental health ideology there has existed a system of classification (which tells us much about the interests, beliefs and values of the persons who developed it), a preferred theory of causation and a sanctioned structure and form of intervention" (and prevention). The development in the roles the consultant has played in the last twenty-five years reflects an emergence of new and essential vantage points. As in the personal developmental scheme, each new dimension incorporated the previous one and extended it with a new body of knowledge. These range from individual to group consultation (Caplan and Berlin), to group functioning, to social system dynamics (Sarason) and sociocultural (Hirschowitz, Pavenstedt) and societal dimensions (Bower).

History
The initial contributors in the field of mental health consultation in the last decades have had a psychoanalytic orientation. This is clearly discernible in their conceptual approach to consultation. Caplan (9) defines a consultant not primarily as an information-giving expert who advises a consultee on how to solve problems, but instead as a facilitator who through the systematic consulta-

tion process helps the consultee to define and overcome his own obstacles in ways relevant to his present life space in the working situation. Caplan (10) emphasizes certain differences in the role of consultant, as compared to that of supervisor, teacher or therapist; the responsibility for action outcomes is the consultee's. Caplan indicates that learning through the consultation process involves intrapsychic, often unconscious, mechanisms.

Berlin (1,2) focuses particularly on the *alliance.* He emphasizes the consultant's initial lack of knowledge about the consultee in his work setting as well as the vagueness of the psychological contract. Since the consultant is being asked for help, the dynamic meaning of the consultee's having failed after having tried everything and of needing help and feeling inadequate are major issues. They give rise to specific resistances, such as challenging the consultant to prove that he can do better than the consultee "who has tried everything," yet at the same time wanting to preserve the image of the onmiscient and omnipotent consultant who will have a ready solution for everything. Berlin (3) notes that these aspects of transference and countertransference are particularly relevant to school consultation. The common transference phenomena are ascribing omnipotence and omniscience to the consultant, followed by disappointment, anger (and relief) when reality prevails. Or the consultant might be seen as an intruder who will psychoanalyze everyone, or who will upset the established order and, through his permissiveness, create chaos. Berlin also mentions dependency and the transference cure. The countertransference phenomena he notes are the desire to be wise, nice and helpful or the inability to recognize the point when services are no longer needed. He regards as the consultant's defensive stance against his own helpless feelings the dehumanizing of groups such as parents or administrators or custodians by stereotyping them.

However, transference is a ubiquitous phenomenon, a *natural* part of human relations, a definite motivational factor in the functioning of a social system. In the school it combines with certain cultural and economic factors to support a hierarchical authoritarian structure which results in a tendency to underestimate the intelligence and understanding of those low in the hierachy (teachers and children) and to overestimate upwards (administrators). The mental health consultant, especially the psychiatrist, tends to be put in a high place, accompanied by stereotypes about his magical powers to solve everything, along with fear of his permissiveness and tendencies towards extensive reflection without action. Although a certain amount of positive transference can be useful in starting consultation, hard proof of the consultant's usefulness must develop if the relationship is to hold.

Caplan has recently begun to emphasize the use of group consultation for peer learning. Sarason (26) emphasizes the need to know the culture of the institution within which everyone is operating. He traces, for example, the following important dynamic of communication: "Although the principal and the teacher are acutely aware that their relationship takes place in the context of power and evaluation, neither of them knows how to minimize the negative consequences of such a concept except by minimizing contact.'' Hirschowitz (16) and Pavenstedt (23) emphasize socioeconomic factors as an essential dimension for a consultant's overview; these affect development, possibly in irreversible ways, and often create self-fulfilling negative prophecies for many youngsters.

Future: Primary Prevention

Inevitably the consultation method and the philosophical bias of primary prevention flow together in our work in schools. We have moved into the field of *public* mental health and need a societal framework to clarify our direction, as well as sources of help or assistance.

Bower (6) has conceptualized a useful schema of Humanizing Institutions and their functions: a primary group of KISS (Key Integrative Social Systems) institutions that serve and are served by all members of a society providing ''values, goals, means and rules by which existence is to be gratified, endured and suffered.'' Examples are family, neighborhood and peer groups, school, church, health-enhancing agencies, etc. Bower postulates that each of the first four institutions has an epigenetic integrating quality. He addresses himself to the basic question of whether any subsequent institution can undo or remedy defects created by a previous one, referring particularly to the family and the school. The school succeeds earlier socializing institutions and Bower points up the popular assumption that therefore the school *must* be successful with each child.* The secondary group is the AID (Ailing-In-Difficulty) institutions—physician, hospital, jail, court of law—that temporarily help those not able or allowed to live in society. The tertiary group is the ICE (Illness Correctional Endeavors) institutions—prisons, state mental hospitals—that aid the more severe cases. If the KISS group is successful, it will *prevent* the need for AID or ICE institutions.

It is within this framework that some recent legislation such as Massachusetts public law 766 stands out in its support and strengthening of the KISS institutions: school and family. It is an example of political-social influence of great magnitude profoundly affecting the operation of public schools by mandating (1) the fullest integration possible for every special-need child into the regular classroom, and (2) an active and equal role of parents in deciding on the proper educational and remedial plan to be instituted for their child. This is for many school systems a drastic change that will take some years to show the expected results. Our roles as consultants are clearly to do the following: to *facilitate the change*; to perform *crisis intervention* with teachers threatened by very difficult children in their classrooms; to help specialists enter the classroom to collaborate with teachers; to help families and school staff collaborate; to help *evaluation teams* to function well in these critical cases, using the sequence of description, analysis of data, causation, intervention and evaluation with flexibility and effectiveness; and to

---

*Although this is an unrealistic expectation, the school's potential ability to have an important remedial effect on children whose family is destructive is generally underestimated.

facilitate the collaboration between school staff, families and community resources.

In order for a school system to adopt the basic philosophy of this law, the consultant needs to approach the system on different levels, he must ask superintendents to allow the school staff enough time to meet and learn about the change, and urge principals to see to it that the team meetings are well organized, allowing teachers, parents and students an important place in decision making. Also, he must ensure that the child's needs are adequately represented.

In summary, this law demands the collaboration of the key adults in a child's life—parents and school staff—in planning, problem-solving, resource enrichment and mutual support. It has the potential to enhance early detection of problems and normalization, as well as tolerance for minor deviance. (17) This is not an easy task, particularly since the most available and effective resources are the ones *within the school* and *the family* where the child spends his life. The consultant's task is to promote and facilitate this process in any way he can: as diagnostician, teacher, co-leader of groups, social system expert, change agent, crisis-intervenor, advocate, political and social activist, researcher and learner. This may seem an awesome array of roles, but a clinician already has the basic training which is a solid foundation for developing these extended functions. Although the transition from clinician to school consultant requires changes in attitude and behavior, it is achievable. Once achieved, the role can be deeply fulfilling in an arena which holds great promise for primary prevention.

REFERENCES

1. Berlin, Irving N. Some implications of ego psychology for the supervisory process. *Am. J. of Psychotherapy*, Vol. 14, 1960, pp. 536-544.
2. Berlin, Irving N. Learning mental health consultation: history and problems. *Mental Hygiene*, Vol. 48, 1964, pp. 257-66.
3. Berlin, Irving N. Transference and Counter-transference in Community Psychiatry. *Archives of General Psychiatry*, Vol. 15, Aug 1966, pp. 165-72.
4. Bloch, H. Spence. Experiences in Establishing School Consultation. *Am. J. of Psychiatry*, Vol. 129, #1, July 1972, pp. 63-68.
5. Bower, Eli M., Hollister, William G. *Behavioral Science Frontiers in Education*. John Wiley and Sons, 1967.
6. Bower, Eli M. Education as a Humanizing Process and Its Relationship to Other Humanizing Processes. In Golann and Eisdorfer, *Handbook of Community Mental Health*.
7. Bower, Eli M. Primary Prevention in a School Setting. In Caplan, Gerald, *Prevention of Mental Disorders in Children* Chapter XVI. New York: Basic Books, 1961.
8. Brown, Roger. Social Psychology. Chapter X in *The Authoritarian Personality and the Organization of Attitudes* New York: Free Press, 1967.
9. Caplan, Gerald. *Prevention of Mental Disorders in Children* New York: Basic Books, 1961.

10. Caplan, Gerald. Types of Mental Health Consultation. *Am. J. of Orthopsychiatry*, Vol. 33, 1963. pp. 470-481.
11. Chapter 766. Commonwealth of Massachusetts Public Law. State Department of Education, Boston.
12. Eldred, Stanley H., and Vanderpol, Maurice. *Psychotherapy in the designed therapeutic milieu*. International Psychiatric Clinics, Vol 5, #1. Boston: Little-Brown, 1968.
13. Frey, Louise. Organization and social change. *Psychiatric Annals*, March 1973, pp. 17-41.
14. Golann, Stuart E. and Eisdorfer, Carl. *Handbook of Community Mental Health*. New York: Appleton-Century Crofts.
15. Goldman, Ruth k., and Cowan, Philip A. Teacher cognitive characteristics, social systems variables, and the use of consultation. *Am. J. of Community Psychology*, 1975 (in press)
16. Hirschowitz, Ralph G. Psychiatric consultation in schools: sociocultural perspectives. *Mental Hygiene*, Vol. 50, #2, April 1966, p. 218.
17. Kessler, Jane W. Chapter 17: Prevention in *Psychopathology of Childhood*, Englewood, N.J.: Prentice-Hall, 1966.
18. Levinson, Harry. *Organizational Diagnosis*, Part I, Introduction. Harvard University Press, 1972.
19. Lindemann, Erich, and Dawes, Lydia G. The use of psychoanalytic constructs in preventive psychiatry. *Psychoanalytic Study of the Child*, Vol. VII, 1952, p. 429.
20. Murphy, Lois Barclay. Preventive implications of development in the preschool years. Chapter X in Caplan, Gerald, *Prevention of Mental Disorders in Children*. New York: Basic Books, 1961.
21. National Institute of Mental Health. Mental health consultation to programs for children Chapter II, DHEW Publication No. (HSM) 72-9088, revised 1972, Washington, D.C.
22. Newman, Ruth G. *Psychological Consultation in the Schools: A Catalyst for Learning*, Introduction. New York: Basic Books, 1967.
23. Pavenstedt, Eleanor. *The Drifters*. Boston: Little, Brown, 1967.
24. Redl, Fritz. The Concept of a "Therapeutic Milieu" *When We Deal with Children*, New York; Free Press, 1968, p. 68-94.
25. Santostefano, Sebastiano. Beyond Nosology: Diagnosis from the Viewpoint of Development. In Rie, H.E. *Perspectives in Child Psychopathology*. New York: Aldine-Atherton Co., 1971, p. 130.
26. Sarason, Seymour B. *The Culture of the School and the Problem of Change*. Chapter 13. Boston. Allyn & Bacon, Inc., 1973.
27. Shore, Miles F. The five principles of change. *Psychiatric Annals*, March 1973, p. 8-15.
28. Signell, Karen A., and Scott, Patrician A. Training in consultation: a crisis of role transition. *Community Mental Health J.*, Vol. 8 (2), 1972, pp. 149-60.
29. Silberman, Charles E. *Crisis in he Classroom*. New York: Random House, 1970.
30. Stanton, Alfred H., and Schwartz, Morris S. *The Mental Hospital*. Section V, Informalities. New York: Basic Books, 1954.
31. Vanderpol, Maurice. The Designed Milieu as an Extension of the Psychotherapeutic Process. In Eldred, Stanley H., and Vanderpol, Maurice, *Psychotherapy in the Designed Therapeutic Milieu*. International Psychiatric Clinics, Vol. 5 No. 1, 1968, pp. 33-43.
32. Vanderpol, Maurice, and Waxman, Harvey. Beyond pathology: some basic ideas for effective school consultation. *Psychiatric Opinion*, August 1974, pp. 18-24.
33. Zetzel, Elizabeth R. The Capacity for Emotional Growth. Chapter 16 in *Psychoanalysis and Psychic Health*. New York: International University Press, 170.

22

Mental Health Agency Participation in Community Decision Making

ROLLAND L. WARREN

The development of the community mental health movement has inexorably thrown the mental health agencies into the arena of community decision making. The change in major focus from mental hospital to community mental health center has engendered a series of administrative strains within state mental health departments and between mental hospital officials and community mental health center administrators. The two types of facility represent, symbolically, an emphasis on two different approaches: one emphasizing illness, the other health; one seeing mental health as an essentially medical problem, the other seeing it as having broader implications; one emphasizing custody and treatment, the other emphasizing prevention; one taking the patient from his day-to-day environment, the other bringing services to him so that he may remain in his customary environment.

The community mental health movement has had two other ramifications, partly anticipated, partly not. One is that community mental health centers cannot operate in a sociopolitical vacuum. They need support for budgets, and they must also develop a set of linkages with related service agencies and with political decision-makers enabling them to survive in the crowded interagency environment. To assure their continued access to resources, they need linkages over and above the types of interagency relationship necessary to assure "continuity of care" for their patients. Further, the very nature of mental health and mental illness, as viewed by community mental health advocates, implies a larger area of services of mental health relevance, connections with schools, churches, general hospitals, housing facilities and similar institutions.

The second is recognition of the need for "citizen participation" in community mental health policy-making. Unless mental health facilities are to be enclaves of professionalism walled off from citizen decision-making processes, they must develop linkages not only with groupings within the general citizenry, but also with their own service clientele—linkages which constitute two-way channels of communication and thus have their impact on the policies and programs of the centers themselves.

THE MODEL CITIES LEGISLATION AND PROGRAM

Title I of the Demonstration Cities and Metropolitan Development Act of 1966 had as its overall objective the improvement of the quality of living in American cities. Its scope was indicated by the following specific legislated objectives: rebuilding or revitalizing large slum areas; expanding housing, job and income opportunities; reducing dependence on welfare payments; improving educational facilities and programs; combating disease and ill health; reducing crime and delinquency; enhancing recreational and cultural opportunities, and establishing better access between homes and jobs.

Cities participating in the Model Cities program were required to engage in a broad process of social planning involving the agencies appropriate for the objectives listed above and engaging the residents of the Model Neighborhood in the planning process. It was envisaged that sufficient efforts would be concentrated in the Model Neighborhood so that a tangible impact could reasonably be expected. Creative new programs were to be developed along a broad spectrum of social concerns. The entire program was coordinated within a City Demonstration Agency with final authority resting in the municipal government.

The program was limited to a specific number of cities which were to be selected more or less competitively. After an appropriate period of preliminary planning, cities submitted an application for a planning grant. One hundred and ninety-three cities applied in time for the first year's deadline of May 1, 1967, of which seventy-five were eventually awarded a planning grant, permitting a year's time for the development of an overall problem diagnosis five-year plan, and first-year detailed plan, and providing funds for this purpose. On the basis of the plans submitted after the planning year, the major Model Cities grants were to be awarded. A similar number of planning grants were awarded in the second year of the program's operation.

All appropriate parties—municipal government with its various departments and agencies, voluntary agencies and Model Neighborhood residents—were to plan a concentrated, coordinated, innovative program designed to improve living conditions in the Model Neighborhood, and, incidentally, have a favorable impact on the entire city. There was an assumption that if the problems of America's cities were to be adequately addressed, their governments must be strengthened and must acquire knowledge and experience in broad social planning. Hence, one of the Model Cities goals was a strengthened City Hall, with skill and power to provide the necessary leadership and coordination to meet the social problems of the city.

PERTINENCE OF MODEL CITIES TO MENTAL HEALTH AGENCIES

The general field of health was mentioned among the many fields of direct involvement in the original Model Cities legislation, but mental health as such was not. Later, however, when the detailed guidelines for the development of the program were released by the Model Cities Administration, mental health was mentioned explicitly under the general health rubric. The legislation did not specifically make mental health programs mandatory for acceptance of Model Cities plans, but most cities "got the message" that there had better be something about mental health in the planning grant application and in the subsequent plans. The situation regarding mental health was not at all clear, and in some cities the mental health agencies were almost totally oblivious to the plans being made for the Model Cities programs. This occurred in spite of the many aspects of relevance for mental health programs such as the following:

1. Many community mental health leaders contend that the institutions affecting mental health are numerous, and often unnoticed. If mental health agencies are to do anything effective about primary prevention, they must have a voice in the shaping of institutional structures. Hence, decisions involving housing, education, urban renewal, police administration, employment, social services, and so on, all have their mental health aspects and, consequently, mental health personnel should have an active voice in shaping these policies. In fact, few aspects of social planning in American cities can be considered entirely extraneous to mental health.

2. The specific mental health agencies such as clinics and community mental health centers are located within a broader network of services within which the patient's continuity of care must be considered. Model Cities provided an opportunity for joint planning among human service agencies.

3. Like other organizations, mental health agencies are concerned with preserving and enhancing their service domains and organizational viability. Agency officials might view the Model Cities program as an avenue to expanded funding and expanded service domains.

4. A further consideration was that if mental health agencies did not perform vigorously in their presumed area of competence and legitimation, other agencies would exploit their domain.

As is widely known, a highly varied situation exists in the types of mental health services and agencies which are present in different cities in the United States. Services available in local communities may be provided by a branch of a state department, a county department or a municipal department, or they may in some cases involve special boards with relationship to one or more counties or municipalities. In addition, many hospital and other clinical facilities are under nongovernmental auspices.

Likewise, the diverse programs are financed out of various combinations of voluntary donations, fees and tax monies, and through grant-in-aid programs principally of state governments or of the National Institute of Mental Health. NIMH, through its program of support of community mental health centers (CMHCs) and specifically through its grants-in-aid for construction costs and staffing costs of such centers, has been a prime mover in the development of

CMHCs across the country. As of July 1969, NIMH had funded 91 CMHCs serving all or part of 73 Model Neighborhood Areas in the 150 Model Cities. Some cities—those which had Model Cities programs and those which did not—had mental health centers which approximated part or all of the requirements for NIMH funding (which were, chiefly, providing at least the following five essential services: inpatient care, outpatient care, partial hospitalization, 24-hour emergency care and consultation and education), but were funded from other sources. NIMH-funded CMHCs are generally required to have a "catchment area" which includes between 75,000 and 200,000 people. Cities over that size therefore must be divided into a plurality of catchment areas, which has constituted a problem in Model Cities planning efforts (as will be described later).

It is against this highly varied background of community mental health centers and individual facilities and service agencies that the planning and programming for Model Cities was to take place.

A SCENARIO OF VIGOROUS MENTAL HEALTH AGENCY PARTICIPATION

As a preface to examining the response of mental health agencies to the Model Cities challenge, it might be well to construct a "scenario" of what vigorous participation in the Model Cities planning process would look like—hence the following fictitious account.

Dr. Horace Streben, the director of the Delco City Community Mental Health Center, first learned about the pending Model Cities legislation in the fall of 1966 at a conference on the social problems of the inner city, at which he had given a paper on the interrelation of poverty and mental illness and its implications for social planning. He drafted a memo for the mayor, after speaking personally to the mayor's development coordinator, whom he knew from numerous previous contacts in connection with the Center's activities with urban renewal relocation projects and with his membership on the mayor's Task Force on Poverty and Housing. He also began to propose the idea to various other officials of governmental and voluntary agencies, including the police commissioner (whom he knew well in connection with the Center's consulting relationship with the Police Department), the director of the health and welfare council, the director of the community action program, and the superintendent of schools.

The mayor took the matter under advisement and decided that it would be wise for the city to make a vigorous effort to be designated as one of the country's Model Cities. He set up a special task force on Model Cities, under the chairmanship of his development coordinator. All of the above-mentioned officials were named as members of this task force, including, of course, Dr. Streben, as well as other officials of various municipal departments and voluntary organizations.

Dr. Streben had several meetings with his own professional staff and with the Center's advisory committee on the social implications of the Model Cities program and the appropriate services which might be developed for it, as well as what the mental health implications of other aspects of the program might be, such as education, housing, employment and welfare. He took a vigorous part in the task force deliberations, constantly reminding the other task force members that they should be establishing a relationship with citizens groups within the section of the city which would probably be designated as the Model Neighborhood.

The application for a Model Cities planning grant, completed just before the May 1, 1967, deadline, incorporated a number of projected program areas, including mental health services.

At about this time, citizens groups in the designated Model Neighborhood began to demand and obtain a more active role in the Model Cities planning. After a period of months, word was received that Delco City had been awarded a Model Cities planning grant. An official City Demonstration Agency was set up by the mayor, which was linked to a Model Neighborhood Board of citizens who were elected. Much of the ensuing action revolved around the respective rights and prerogatives and budgets of these two organizations, and for a while the substantive program issues were eclipsed. Gradually, task forces were set up in each of several program fields.

Although no special task force was set up for mental health, the foundation had been laid in the health task force for a vigorous representation of mental health considerations, and members of other task forces were also aware of the pertinence of mental health to the issues they were addressing. This process was aided by the fact that some of the members of the Community Mental Health Center's advisory committee were Model Neighborhood residents active in the health task force and other parts of the planning structure.

The plans which emerged from this complex process—which included consultations with regional and federal offices of HUD and the National Institute of Mental Health, as well as the other pertinent agencies of the state and federal government—contained a number of mental health components such as the following:

> Mental health programs based in a number of neighborhood health centers
> An extensive consultation program with teachers, police and health personnel
> An extensive drug addiction program, oriented toward medical and psychological and social aspects of the problem
> Programs for mentally retarded children and adults both within and outside the formal educational system
> Collaboration on a program of intergroup relations among various ethnic groups in the neighborhood
> An alcoholics rehabilitation program
> A special program operating out of the recreation centers dealing with teenage youth

The establishment of two additional community mental health centers, which had been under consideration for a number of years, was incorporated into the

Model Cities planning, although separate applications for their funding were being developed in connection with the construction and staffing grants programs of NIMH. Early consideration was given to how the catchment areas of the three mental health centers would overlap with the Model Neighborhood boundaries, and a satisfactory working solution to this problem was reached by extending the catchment area of one of the centers to include the entire Model Neighborhood.

The strong support by citizens groups within and outside the planning task forces for mental health programs was a result of many months of intensive effort on the part of Dr. Streben and his staff to participate in the joint planning undertaking. While some of the programs listed above were to be funded through various grant-in-aid sources outside the Model Cities program, a number of them were paid for directly out of Model Cities supplemental grants. In addition, Dr. Streben, though not satisfied, felt that the mental health aspects of a variety of program and problem areas had been given explicit consideration in the Model Cities planning process. He was especially proud of the extent to which the Police Department, the Housing Authority, and the Public Welfare Department had set up programs to avail themselves of the extensive consultation and education efforts of the Center. He was also gratified that the obvious need for a city-level decision-making mechanism for the allocation of mental health resources had been recognized, and that steps were under way to set up such a body.

ISSUES RAISED BY MODEL CITIES FOR MENTAL HEALTH AGENCIES

The Model Cities program confronted mental health agencies with a series of questions which, while not new to the mental health field, had never been completely resolved:

1. Could mental health agencies now win for themselves a greater voice in community-level planning? What competencies could they offer for such planning? In addition, to what extent would these competencies be recognized by other, better-established parties to the community planning arena?

2. Need community mental health balance its concern for individual mental illness with work toward creating a social environment more positively conducive to mental health? If so, how?

3. If mental health personnel confined themselves to influencing community-level decisions in health, education and welfare services, could they do so while maintaining a stance of scientific impartiality?

4. Mental health leaders prided themselves that laymen played an important role in the mental health movement, but such laymen had usually been fairly well-to-do civic leaders in the community, and input was strongly circumscribed by the firm hold of the psychiatric profession on substantive decisions. In what sense, other than mere "public relations," could Model Neighborhood residents be encouraged to take an active part in policy-making and program formulation?

5. Finally, there was the issue of the severe constraints operating on anyone seeking to expand the mental health role much beyond the most conventional clinical services. Granted the will to play an active role in Model Cities planning, how could these constraints be overcome?

The fictional scenario depicted above indicates how these issues might be resolved in an active orientation toward Model Cities. A study that was conducted in nine first-round cities active in the Model Cities program affords systematic data on the *actual* participation of mental health agencies and the relation of this participation to the issues listed above.

The Nine-City Study

A research effort entitled the *Interorganizational Study Project* was developed at the Florence Heller Graduate School for Advanced Studies in Social Welfare at Brandeis University for the purpose of studying the interaction of a number of community decision organizations in nine different cities.[1] By "community decision organizations (or CDOs)" is meant organizations which are legitimated at the community level to engage in planning and/or programming on behalf of the community in a particular sector of community interests. A number of such organizations were chosen for the study, including the board of education, the urban renewal agency, the health and welfare council, the anti-poverty agency and the mental health planning agency, where there was one. In addition, as the City Demonstration Agency (or Model Cities agency) emerged in each city in connection with the Model Cities planning, it was likewise included in the group of agencies under systematic study. Seven cities of approximately the same size were selected so as to secure a broad distribution regionally and also on thirteen different variables thought pertinent to the study, such as "percent non-white" and "per capita income." In addition, a larger city (Detroit) and a smaller city (Manchester, N.H.) were chosen to give some indication of the importance of differences in scale to the variables under study. All of these cities were in the "first round" having submitted their planning grant applications by May 1, 1967.

The study was based on the assumption that community decision organizations, such as those in the sample, play an important role in efforts to guide the course of events at the community level, since purposive efforts at change in their respective sectors take place in or around just such agencies. Since they operate in overlapping sectors of interest, they come in contact with each other in many different ways, and since there is usually no overall planning or coordinating body under which their respective plans and programs would be brought into systematic relationship to each other, the aggregate of social planning in the city emerges from the interaction—sometimes cooperative, sometimes competitive—of these organizations. There are few systematic studies which investigate their overlapping relationship to each other, the circumstances in which different types of interaction take place, and the manner in which this affects plans and programs.

The inclusion of mental health CDOs in the sample was a bold venture, since they were marginal in two senses. First, it was apparent that in most cities there was no mental health CDO which could compare in strength to the board of education or urban renewal agency; and second, mental health itself, as mentioned earlier, was marginal to the Model Cities program. Hence, it constituted a fruitful sector for studying the difference between those cities in which mental health agencies participated strongly and those in which they did not.

Field research associates were employed in each of the nine cities for a period of slightly over two years to gather data, both in the form of narrative reports and in the form of a series of more systematic schedules. In connection with this broader study, an intensive study of the participation of mental health agencies in the Model Cities program was carried out. It is from this study that the following findings are taken.[2]

PLANNING, POLITICS AND PARTICIPATION

Of the many major stages in the Model Cities process, only three are considered here. The first may be called the "pre-planning" stage, and consists of the activities engaged in with respect to Model Cities up to the submission deadline for the first-round Model Cities planning grant applications May 1, 1967. The second consists of the "planning" stage, from May 1, 1967, until roughly July 1, 1969, by which time most of the plans were submitted. The third consists of the implementation stage. These time periods should be considered highly approximate, since there was considerable variation among cities.

It is interesting to present the assumptions of the Interorganizational Project staff as to what was expected to take place in the various cities. They assumed that Model Cities would offer to the existing interorganizational network both a threat and an opportunity. The threat would be the uncertainty posed by the participation of Model Neighborhood residents and the possible encroachment on well-established organizational domains by other organizations. The potentiality was not only the existence of new funds which might become available to any particular agency, but also the possibility that in the fluid give-and-take opened up by Model Cities planning, the agency might be able to expand its domain. To oversimplify, it was expected that the community decision organizations would cooperate in bringing the funded program to their city, but would compete for the funds available through the program.

Actually, the events took a somewhat different turn. In most of the cities, the preplanning stage occurred as expected. Characteristically, the mayor's office called together a planning task force made up of officials of pertinent departments and agencies of the municipal government as well as other agencies. Uniformly, the process in these nine cities engaged City Hall and the agencies, with virtually no resident participation in the planning process, although in a number of cities some contact was made with residents of the Model Neighborhood at the very end of the initial planning period.

During the second, "planning" stage, the focus of interaction changed from the City Hall-CDO axis to the City Hall-Model Neighborhood resident axis. In most cities, a contest for power over the program took place as the residents attempted to gain as great a measure of power as possible, usually against the resistance of City Hall and the City Demonstration Agency. The same thing happened in Oakland during this period, although Oakland did not yet have its planning grant, having been delayed by this very struggle between the neighborhood residents and the city manager's office.

The participation of the CDOs was less with City Hall than through a number of task forces set up to establish priorities and develop plans in various program areas such as education, health, manpower, urban renewal and social services. These task forces were likewise largely engulfed by the struggle of residents for power, both internally as well as against City Hall and individual agencies. Because of these factors, as well as numerous delays at the regional and federal level, most cities were not able to do the detailed, careful, coordinated planning envisaged in the Model Cities program, and as a result the detailed planning, even for the first implementation year, had to be carried over into the implementation period itself.

PARTICIPATION OF MENTAL HEALTH AGENCIES IN NINE CITIES

Participation by mental health agencies in the preplanning stage of Model Cities was virtually nil in eight of the nine cities of the Interorganizational Study. The modal behavior at the preplanning stage was nonparticipation, and this extended in most cases far into the planning stage itself.

The lack of interest was two-sided. Reports from each of the nine cities emphasized the low priority given to mental health either by the neighborhood residents or by the task forces or both. Richard H. Uhlig[3] compared the responses of CDO personnel at different levels—policy-making, administration and professional operation—to a series of questions regarding the complex Model Cities goals. In a list of ten goals, of which one was improved mental health services, he found that mental health was third from the bottom in priority, being exceeded only by transportation and recreation. In these cities, employment, education and housing headed the list. Most mental health administrators were either unaware of the possibility of participating actively in the preplanning stage or, if they were aware of the program, considered it peripheral to their own interest. In view of the fact that the Model Cities guidelines had specifically mentioned the relevance of mental health services to a Model Cities program, one gets the impression from reading the planning grant applications that most such mentions of mental health were merely a minimal response to what was thought to be expected by the funding agency.

There was a noticeable difference between the vague mentions of mental health in the planning grant applications and the somewhat more specific mental health programs which began to be formulated during the subsequent planning stage.

Task forces were formed to plan for component programs in each of a number of different subject matter areas, including health. With some exceptions, the final plan documents were made up of the contributions of these individual task forces, with or without major editing and even substantive changes by the City Demonstration Agency.

The Model Cities legislation called for resident participation in planning for the various programs. In regard to the mental health programs, such participation took place characteristically through resident participation on the health task force. But often this was *not* where decisions in mental health planning were being made at the time, for in many cases they were being made at the community mental health center level, usually by a county-level planning body, with little coordination with the Model Cities planning. Altogether, modest resident participation in mental health planning pertinent to Model Cities can be said to have taken place in the planning stage in only two or three of the nine cities.

THE RELATION BETWEEN PARTICIPATION
AND PROGRAM COMPONENTS

In the light of the foregoing findings, it is interesting to speculate about the extent to which active participation by these mental health agencies in the Model Cities planning process affected whether or not there were strong mental health components in the plans resulting from this process. Of the seven cities for which a reasonably confident judgment can be made, six indicated a strong association between participation in planning and substantive mental health components in the plan itself. It is interesting that there was no case where high participation of mental health agencies was followed by a Model Cities plan with low mental health components. Intimate knowledge of the sequence of events in these cities leads the author to conclude that the relationship is more than coincidental. The data from these cities supported our early hypothesis that degree of participation in Model Cities planning would be positively associated with strength of mental health components in the plan itself.

MENTAL HEALTH AND THREE MAJOR OBJECTIVES
OF THE MODEL CITIES PROGRAM

Three major objectives of the Model Cities program were: coordination of organization efforts; increased responsiveness of service agencies to the wishes and needs of Model Neighborhood residents—(largely through resident participation in the program); and the development of innovative programs suited to the special situations of the Model Neighborhoods. While it is still too early to assess the final outcome, experience in these nine cities affords the basis for some observations

Coordination. Fragmentation of service programs is widely acknowledged to exist in all the problem areas which the 1966 legislation envisaged. It results not only from the local organization of different service structures, but also from the narrowly confining nature of several hundred grant-in-aid programs of various federal agencies as well as an array of similarly fragmented programs of various state agencies. An important goal of Model Cities was to develop a decision-making apparatus for bringing such fragmented programs into a coordinated relationship with each other at the local level. This involves both functional and geographic aspects.

Functional coordination refers to the manner in which the specific services mental health agencies offer are related to the services of other agencies, such as the probation department, the various services of the school system (e.g., visiting teacher, counseling), the hospitals, the court system, the police, the welfare department and other health services. Geographic coordination refers to the manner in which functionally different but related services can be organized with respect to each other within a specific geographic unit—in this case, the Model Neighborhood.

It is difficult to bring about functional coordination of agencies even when their service area has been the characteristic geographic unit for the organization and distribution of mental health services in relation to the local population. But in none of these nine cities has a CMHC catchment area coincided with the Model Neighborhood area. Both types of geographic demarcation are highly arbitrary, and quite different types of consideration went into the establishing of their respective borders. No catchment area typically is restricted to the Model Neighborhood, but at the same time the Model Neighborhood typically contains parts of more than one catchment area. Coordination thus constitutes a problem of geographic distribution of services, as well as one of their functional interrelation.

Hence, the usual difficulties of functional coordination among relatively autonomous agencies have been compounded by the boundary discrepancies between CMHC catchment areas and Model Neighborhoods.

Despite these difficulties, there has recently been the beginning of an exercise of influence by the Model Cities Agency over the development of mental health services, and a reciprocal process of entrance of mental health agencies into the Model Cities planning and implementation process. Five of the nine cities studied had community mental health centers financed in part by staffing grants from the National Institute of Mental Health.

Responsiveness. A goal of the Model Cities program was to make various agencies, governmental and nongovernmental, more sensitive and responsive to the needs and wishes of the resident population. Like other general goals of Model Cities, what seems simple in reality is highly complex both conceptually and empirically. Resident participation as a prod has been guided more by the legitimating and support function of prominent citizens, who could be recruited to endorse mental health legislation and programs, than by any sense of direct accountability to a service clientele. Yet, in the Model Cities situation, two categories of "citizens" are relevant to the question of resident participation and responsiveness, but in different ways which are poorly defined not only in the mental health field but in other fields as well.

It is one thing to relate to the residents of the Model Neighborhood as essentially a service clientele to whom the agency acknowledges a responsibility to give ever better service. But it is quite a different thing to consider these residents as a citizen constituency, to whom the agency is accountable in its policy-making. It is perhaps not an exaggeration to say that in mental health planning in these cities, Model Neighborhood residents have been seen by the community mental health centers as clients, while within the rubric of the Model Neighborhood Boards (a generic name for the formally recognized organizations through which the participation of Model Neighborhood residents in Model Cities decision-making is channeled), the residents are seen as citizen constituents.

Although the results are far from breathtaking, there is substantial indication that in a number of these cities, a type of relationship to Model Neighborhood resident groups as constituents is beginning to be acknowledged by the mental health agencies, whether deliberately or unwittingly, willingly or unwillingly. In addition, there is the kind of responsiveness which arises through confrontation. In one of the cities, for example, an open meeting was held to brief local residents on the projected location of a mental health center at a particular location in the Model Neighborhood. The residents were not pleased with the decision, and stated that if the center was located there, they would burn it down. The center was not located there.

A larger question, of course, is the extent to which the "trappings" of participation are really meaningful in terms of impact. It is too early for a final assessment on this question, particularly since the participation in mental health decisions has been so modest, and since mental health has up to this time received such relatively little attention compared with other concerns such as education, housing and jobs. But regardless of how much actual difference it makes, the idea of resident participation in policy and program development has been strengthened, even though minimally, through the Model Cities experience thus far.

Innovation. "New and imaginative proposals" is the wording employed in the introductory paragraphs of the 1966 Model Cities legislation. But what is new, what is "innovative"? Often the allegedly innovative program turns out to be merely the particular development which happens to be "stylish" at the time. For example, "store-front service delivery centers" is just such a fashionable idea, as is the "crisis-intervention team." The Interorganizational Project staff at Brandeis University has gone through a series of experiences in coming to different conceptualizations of the term "innovation," and has not yet found a completely satisfactory conceptualization, but it leans toward defining "innovation" in terms of a basic change in the way problems are defined, with corresponding changes in agency policy and program. Thus, on one level, the shift in emphasis on legal-punitive aspects to an emphasis on medical-therapeutic aspects constitutes such a basic change in definition.

The program descriptions and supporting rationale in the various Model Cities plans are generally so vague and ill-defined that it is difficult to use them for an assessment of innovativeness, whether one uses this more rigorous conceptualization or a broader one. In service distribution patterns, perhaps the most notable change is the emergence of the notion of the geographically decentralized functions of the mental health center, the "store-front" delivery unit, if only for screening and referral.

A further observation: in the Project's narrative reports from field research associates in the nine cities, there are numerous instances where a program proposal, whether originated by neighborhood residents or by agencies or by some combination of both, was sloughed off in the review process by a funding agency, either at the regional level or at the federal level. In some cases, proposals by residents are modified on the advice or insistence of professionals in the local planning process. One gets the impression from reviewing these nine cities that there are severe built-in constraints operating against innovation. These can perhaps be summarized in a proposition: In stimulating innovation, it is necessary to be willing to risk a number of failures for every innovation which proves viable, and to be open to proposals which do not fit neatly within existing norms of professional acceptability. Such conditions are seldom met in the Model Cities planning experience, whether in mental health or other fields. In the mental health field, the funding agency review and consultation process apparently has the effect of modifying all original proposals toward conformity with the accepted pattern for community mental health centers.

MAJOR DETERMINANTS OF PARTICIPATION

In the experience of mental health agencies in the nine first-round Model Cities of this study, two issues appear to have played a crucial role in determining the extent, direction and effectiveness of mental health agency planning. One is commitment; the other the relation of catchment areas to Model Neighborhood areas and to city-level planning activities.

1. *Commitment.* To what extent did mental health agency officials really want to become involved in the Model Cities planning? How relevant to the program goals of Model Cities did they consider mental health to be? How did they feel about citizen participation? Examination of the individual narrative reports leaves one with the impression that different conceptions of mental health and its role in the community were of importance in the actions which mental health agencies took or did not take.

As is widely known, there is great divergence among mental health agency administrators as well as other professionals in the mental health field regarding their attitudes toward community mental health. As a part of the Interorganizational Study Project, Robert A. Porter, at the time a doctoral candidate at the Florence Heller Graduate School at Brandeis, did a study in ten cities, including the nine of the study project, on *Community Mental Health Planning Ideology of Organiza-*

tional Participants in the Model Cities Program.[4] He administered a community mental health planning ideology scale to mental health professionals at four different levels in the mental health CDOs (or the nearest thing to them) in these ten cities, as well as to top-level administrators from the other CDOs of the Interorganizational Study. His scale had a number of dimensions pertinent to the questions raised about commitment. One, for example, had to do with the relative emphasis on bringing about change within the individual patient or bringing about change in the social system. Mental health administrators were more inclined toward the individual-change approach than were most administrators of these other CDOs. With the exception of the board of education administrators, all the others—the urban renewal, health and welfare council, and antipoverty agency administrators—stressed social change in mental health more than did the mental health administrators.

Other dimensions of the scale included degree of politicalization of the planning process, citizen participation, bureaucratic vs. collegial administrative orientation and interdisciplinary management of mental health centers, all of which were given appropriate weighting. In the responses to this total scale, *the same pattern applied*, with mental health agency administrators being on the conservative side, exceeded only by the boards of education.

One item which was not used in the final scale is nevertheless important in its direct bearing on the commitment of mental health agency officials to participation in a program like Model Cities. Agree or disagree: "Community mental health programs should give first priority to broad programs of social intervention and reserve individual treatment for particular instances where these larger approaches fail." Porter reports that "The mental health group [was] on the disagreement side of this issue, while all other agency groups [were] on the agreement side."[5] Likewise, he reports that mental health administrators were exceeded by all agency administrators except boards of education in their relative confidence in the ability of mental health professionals to contribute to Model Cities planning.[6] Porter also found that the other agency administrators attributed to mental health agencies a wider purview than did the mental health agency administrators themselves. The data indicate a general lack of strong commitment to the importance of mental health participation in Model Cities planning and programming, although there was much variation among these administrators.

2. *The catchment area.* Quite understandably, the community mental health centers were interested primarily in their own catchment areas and in their own continued viability within those areas, and only secondarily in being of service to the Model Neighborhood as an area. As mentioned earlier, even when the will to participate was there, the overlapping nature of Model Neighborhoods and catchment areas made it difficult to set aside part of one's catchment area for special treatment. When more than one CMHC catchment area overlapped with the Model Neighborhood, the problem became double-ended.

Model Cities involved two decision-making levels, neither of which was well suited for catchment area participation. The one was the Model Neighborhood level, just discussed. The other, equally important, was the city level—this is the level at which city policy was determined, and it was the level on which other service fields such as those in this study were represented by relatively strong CDOs—the board of education, the poverty program community action agency, the urban renewal agency, and the health and welfare council.

The problem of the lack of a strong, viable CDO for mental health became apparent early in the study, as field research associates found little difficulty in identifying and making contact with CDOs in other fields, but reported that "There is no CDO in mental health. How shall I proceed?" or "There are three agencies, each with possible claim to being the mental health CDO. Which one shall I take?" The lack of a strong CDO meant that in cases where there was more than one CMHC catchment area overlapping with the Model Neighborhood, there was needless confusion and conflict. In other cases, where a single CMHC catchment area contained the entire Model Neighborhood, it was not "plugged in" to city-level decision-making.

It is apparent that however useful the catchment area concept is for focusing comprehensive mental health service programs and planning, it is not helpful at the city level, where in large cities it results in a fragmentation of planning capacity; nor, in the special case of Model Cities, was it helpful at the Model Neighborhood level, but rather constituted an obstacle to be overcome. It would seem that if strong focus is to be given to catchment area planning, a strong mental health CDO is necessary if mental health agencies are to participate effectively in the fast-moving, coalitional, ad hoc programs which have heavily involved city-level planning in recent years.

CONSTRAINTS AND OPPORTUNITIES SUGGESTED
BY THE MODEL CITIES EXPERIENCE

The Model Cities program was not entirely unique, nor was it expected to last forever. It was only one in a series of efforts to engage communities in broad social planning efforts which exceed the purview of any one type of agency or of any single federal or state agency.

An active participation, such as depicted in the fictional scenario presented earlier, is at least theoretically possible. Nevertheless, the nine cities of the Interorganizational Study Project showed a tremendous gap between theoretical possibility and actual performance. The constraints which reduce mental health agency participation can be divided into those having to do with mental health ideology, those having to do with mental health agency organization, and those having to do with the mental health "image."

It is obvious that willingness on the part of agency executives to participate in Model Cities is of a piece with their conception of what the mental health field is, of how mental illness and mental health can be most effectively addressed, of the extent to which competence in the mental health field equips a professional person for participating in broad-gauge social planning, of the extent to which mental health planning is seen not only as a rational-bureaucratic but also as a political process, of the extent to which laymen are to form a constituency of accountability for mental health agencies.

It is possible to take a relatively negative side on all of these issues, and as Porter found, to take a negative side on one of them increases the likelihood that an individual will take a negative side on the others. These issues constitute the substance of an ideological division running through the psychiatric and other professions related to mental health. For those who take the negative side on these issues, Model Cities is likely to be perceived not as a potential opportunity, but as a trap, a source of deflection from more important endeavors by scarce professional personnel, an extension into fields which stretches the professional beyond his capacity, a confusion of illness with social problems, a politicalization of scientific therapy, and an abdication—by professionals to laymen—of responsibility which only professionals should carry. Looked at from this standpoint, the term "constraints on participation" appears misleading. For from this standpoint, anything more than a minimal amount of participation is not desirable. But from the standpoint of community mental health advocates, the constraints are real and formidable.

A second order of constraints concerns the extent to which the organization of mental health services hampers the ready and fluid entry into such a planning-politics-participation venture as Model Cities.

A third type of constraint concerns the "image" of mental health, and mental health agencies, which is held by various groups. In this part of the Model Cities Study, Porter found that:

> The majority of respondents in all five agency groups are foremost in their agreement that the underprivileged residents of urban slum areas perceive little relevance in traditional mental health services to their needs, and that major decision makers in the community do not acknowledge or support a very active role for mental health professionals in community social planning. The majority in all (CDO administrator) groups also are in agreement that there is an appreciable relationship between the social problems of the urban ghetto and the incidence of mental illness; and that the planning of community programs aimed at the prevention of social stress is fundamentally the same task as the planning of programs for the prevention of mental illness.[8]

This paradoxical finding is worth pondering. For, as indicated earlier, most of the CDO administrators were more confident than the mental health administrators of the importance of mental health agencies to Model Cities; yet at the same time, mental health agencies were faced with the fact that mental health services were given a low priority.

It would appear that the most powerful constraint is that of the indecisiveness of the mental health profession as to what role in the affairs of the inner city it considers suitable for the mental health agencies. Beyond that, if the goals of the community mental health movement are to be achieved through active participation, lies the question as to whether the model of community mental health centers with five "essential" and another five "desirable" services, and an urban terrain divided into a number of mutually exclusive catchment areas, will not need continuous rethinking as mental health agencies gain experience and knowledge in confronting urban social problems.

Note

The author's work was supported by a research scientist award from NIMH. The research on which this chapter, written in 1970, is based was supported by NIMH Grant No. 15082.

[1] An elaboration of the concept of community decision organizations, as well as part of the theoretical rationale for the study, is given in two articles by the author: "The Interorganization Field as a Focus of Investigation," *Administrative Science' Quarterly,* Vol. 12, No. 3, December 1967, and "The Interaction of Community Decision Organizations: Some Basic Concepts and Needed Research," *Social Service Review,* Vol. 41, No. 3, September 1967.

Preliminary reports from the study are given in the following two articles by the author: "Model Cities First Round: Politics, Planning, and Participation," *Journal of the American [2] Institute of Planners,* Vol. 35, No. 4, July 1969, and "Mental Health Planning and Model Cities: Hamlet or Hellzapoppin?" *Community Mental Health Journal,* Vol 7, No. 1, 1971, pp. 39-49. The final report is given in Roland L. Warren, Stephen M. Rose and Ann F. Burgunder, *The Structure of Urban Reform: Community Decision Organizations in Stability and Change* (Lexington: D.C. Heath, 1974).

[3] Richard H. Uhlig, *Goal Conception in the Planning Phase of the Model Cities Program,* Doctoral Dissertation, Florence Heller Graduate School for Advanced Studies in Social Welfare, Brandeis University, Waltham, Mass., 1969

[4] Robert A. Porter, *Community Mental Health Planning Ideology of Organizational Participants in the Model Cities Program,* Doctoral Dissertation, Florence Heller Graduate School for Advanced Studies in Social Welfare, Brandeis University, Waltham, Mass., 1969.

[5] *Ibid.,* p. 143.

[6] *Ibid.,* p. 150.

[7] This assumes that issues raised in the paper previously cited—"Mental Health Planning and Model Cities: Hamlet or Hellzapoppin?"—are affirmed in the direction of greater agency intervention and a less "professional" definition of treatment.

[8] *Op. cit.,* pp. 160-161.

23

Why Open Systems?
A Personal Account

MAXWELL JONES

When I was asked to write a chapter for this book telling in the first person my experiences in developing the therapeutic community (open system) concept, I was somewhat hesitant. It is a ''we'' rather than an ''I'' concept, and I feel the presence of a host of my former colleagues, several of whom were far more courageous and imaginative than I was.

I was no brash innovator at school or college; quite the contrary. I was a strict conformist in a tradition-ridden Scottish day school. It never occurred to me to question the rigid authority structure of my Edinburgh school. A mediocre student, my only flair was for literature and writing. But nature was kind, and by the age of fifteen I was relatively strongly built, and success in competitive sport (rugby, cricket, tennis, golf, and swimming) led to new aspirations. I was never *the* outstanding player, but I sensed a qualitative difference from my peers; I liked watching and coaching promising youngsters and got a warm response from them. I think I realized that if I couldn't be outstanding, I could at least be useful. This quality contributed to my being made captain of all the first school game teams.

In this context a bit of individuality became manifest even at this age. Edinburgh has many well-known schools, and there is intense rivalry in the athletic field. In my final school year as captain of rugby I did something which at the time seemed completely out of character. We played against all the schools, but one, on equal terms; but Watsons College (twice the size of our school—Stewarts College) traditionally sent their second team to play us. Without consulting anyone, I went alone to Watsons College and asked to see their games master (coach). I told him that I was certain that we were capable of defeating their first team, and that the ignominy of playing their second team had a bad effect on our morale. Luckily, he seemed to like my ''cheek'' and agreed to give us a trial game with their first team. Both the headmaster (principal) of our school and the games master (coach) were furious with me, and feared a disastrous defeat. But my team members were thrilled, and when the great day came, we never looked as if we could be defeated. From that day on, I've been aware of the power of internal commitment by a group of people toward a common goal.

This combination of a team and leadership function had no opportunity for further growth in medical school. I felt keenly a loss of individuality in the large impersonal world of the university. Nothing mattered, it seemed to me, but one's capacity to memorize subject matter and achieve high grades. I hated the intellectual hierarchy which put me nowhere—an "also-ran." In any case, "success" would have terrified me and meant a responsible clinical role. Surgery and the "violent" side of our training were both frightening and distasteful to me; my goal was psychiatry—born of a deep interest in literature, particularly those books which achieved a deep portrayal. This blossomed into ideas of "change" when, as a medical student, I read William James' *Varieties of Religious Experience.*

Graduation brought no relief, and the demands of orthodoxy were paramount. Delivering babies, emergency room duties, etc., still horrified me—I never really felt I was a doctor. Training in psychiatry brought gradual relief but, also, new problems of self-fulfillment. Did patients with schizophrenia really change as a result of our efforts, and even if they did, what was the process of change? I worked hard and, at the age of twenty-eight, became the youngest lecturer at the University of Edinburgh. The need to understand more about change, if any, in psychiatric patients led to increasing involvement in research in biochemistry and biology. This work and several publications helped me to obtain a Commonwealth Fund Fellowship first to work with William Stadie in enzyme chemistry at the University of Pennsylvania for a year, and then a further year with Philip Smith at Columbia University in New York, doing biological research.

I returned to the United Kingdom and worked at the Maudsley Hospital as assistant to Professor Aubrey Lewis for five years. This period finally convinced me that I had little investment in traditional psychiatry, which at the Maudsley was largely organically orientated.

The war years helped me to "find" myself. Heading a psychosomatic unit studying cardiac neurosis in soldiers, we came to realize that the peer group of one hundred men could develop a therapeutic culture which changed their perception of their symptoms. This experience with a neurocirculatory asthenia (Effort Syndrome) unit at Mill Hill near London has been described elsewhere.[1] What I want to stress is that our physiological and research findings in relation to N.C.A. were shared in daily groups of one hundred young soldiers, who were able to realize that their supposed heart disease could be understood mechanistically. Their left chest pain resulted from muscle tension in the intercostal muscles, which disappeared if Novocaine was injected into the intercostal muscles in the region of the heart, or by root block. The rapid shallow breathing was related to tension of the diaphragmatic muscles easily demonstrated on the X-ray screen. These two factors contributed to the muscle pain inevitably resulting from continued spasm, and was recognized on the *left* side of the chest "over the heart" as a consequence of their own subjective expectation. We were able to explain mechanistically their postural giddiness and fainting, as well as their poor exercise tolerance.

This process of objectifying and externalizing their internalized symptoms entirely changed their attitudes toward their symptoms—they no longer feared sudden death or permanent incapacity. We helped them to share their new knowledge with new referrals who almost invariably believed that they were victims of heart disease. Many had seen cardiologists, who, finding no organic disease, had told them they had nothing wrong with them, which made no sense in view of their symptomatology. The peer group of patients was able to explain the meaning of their symptoms to the newcomers, and we learned for the first time the important therapeutic potential of a patient peer group and the development of a therapeutic culture. This period (1940 to 1945), which can be described as the physiology of change, was followed by an equally important experience in the sociology of change.

In May 1945 I was asked to head a unit staffed from the Maudsley Hospital to rehabilitate the most disturbed of the hundred thousand British prisoners of war, returned from Europe and the Far East. This unit of three hundred beds existed for a year and gave us a wonderful opportunity to develop the concept of helping patients to help themselves. We were divided into six cottages, each housing fifty men. Daily cottage community meetings of all patients and staff helped them to work through their fears of impotence, inefficiency and paranoid feelings in relation to their wives, former workmates, etc., resulting from up to five years of incarceration in prisoner-of-war camps. The patients were bussed daily to the forty-seven outside employments that they could choose from, ranging from farms to factories. This early example of a program based on reality confrontation effected significant changes in the men. Follow-up figures after return to civilian life for the six-month period July to December 1945 showed that of 687 discharged during this period 610 (90 percent) were in jobs or in training, 31 not yet at work, and 8 unfit for work.[2]

This promising experiment in rehabilitation resulted in the decision of the Ministries of Health and Labor to initiate a unit for the rehabilitation of the hard-core unemployed in London. This unit of one hundred beds for both sexes was opened in April 1947. Originally known as the Social Rehabilitation Unit at Belmont Hospital, near London, the name was changed to Henderson Hospital shortly before I left in 1959. During these twelve years my colleagues and I developed what can properly be called a therapeutic community. In common with the medical profession as a whole, we had little idea of how to help these social casualties who, in most cases, demonstrated symptoms of psychopathy. Our very impotence helped us to develop the idea that much potential help lay in the patients' own peer group. And we were not to be disappointed, as others have demonstrated with alcoholics (A.A.) and drug addicts (Synanon, Phoenix Houses, etc.).

Communication and information sharing were attempted by daily community meetings of the total population of patients and staff. This meant a daily meeting of approximately one hundred people, sitting in concentric circles, in a relatively small room. To have a concentration of about ninety character disorders of both sexes in such a setting probably sounds crazy to most people, but the community soon established ground rules, such as one person talking at a time, identifying problems and then setting priorities, controlling irrelevant inputs and, by implication, listening to each other. Slowly the concept of social change, through interaction regarding current concrete situations, began to take form. The staff's skill in psychotherapy helped the patients to become aware of the part which ego defenses, such as displacement, projection, repression, etc., play in our ordinary lives.

More specifically, psychotherapeutic skills were shared in the small groups of approximately ten patients which always followed the daily community meetings. After both large and small group meetings, the staff reviewed the process in the groups and attempted to analyze retrospectively what they had done in terms of group dynamics and team work, with particular reference to the role of the patient.

Our experience with the ex-prisoners of war had taught us the value of a realistic work program, which had significance for patients' future "work in the community." We developed a "home group" which did general housekeeping chores alongside staff participants, a carpentry group which made lockers and did repair work, a tailor's shop which made overalls and other utility garments, and a painting and decorating group. Patients clocked in as they would have in real life, and the work groups ended with a discussion of the interaction within the work situation, with the instructor acting as group leader. We found that many of our patients with character disorders could learn more about themselves as viewed by their peers and the staff in such a setting than they could in the more abstract small and large therapy groups. Responsible roles like foreman and timekeeper were held in rotation, so that patients came to realize the difficulties inherent in responsible roles.[3]

Activities during leisure time were also seen as important, and often reflected the growing sense of responsibility in the peer group which handled crisis situations that were frequent, especially at night, or dealt with acting-out behavior by early confrontation. Indeed, the night staff consisted of one R.N. and one assistant nurse, and support from the patients was taken for granted.

Along with our expectation of positive and often skilled support from the patients, we developed patient roles which implied status and responsibility. To be chairman of the patient committee became a very responsible post, and the committee came to assume most of the responsibility for patient discipline.

We came to see treatment more in terms of growth than of psychopathology and psychotherapy. Our patients came, in the main, from broken homes, and their social maturation had suffered from the absence of positive role models in their parents (if any). Many of the patients seemed incapable of empathy, and one of our goals was to try to compensate for this lack of social maturity even at their late age. Their intelligence as measured by I.Q. tests was in the normal range, but Social Maturity Scales[4] showed their personality integration to be well below that of the normal population. We felt that this growth coincided with the patients' lack of capacity to form a group identification and, indeed, to correct this became the cornerstone of our treatment approach.

After twelve years of the hurly-burly of such a therapeutic community I felt both emotionally drained and in need of a change. The exciting work going on in the California Department of Corrections, mainly the work of Douglas Grant,[5] made me more than ready to accept the offer of a visiting professorship at Stanford University in Palo Alto in 1959. The work at Henderson Hospital had achieved international recognition, and I was awarded the Isaac Ray Award of the American Psychiatric Association in 1960.

More important, our work effected the Mental Health Act of 1959. In this liberal and imaginative piece of legislation, psychopathic disorder was defined as "a persistent disorder or disability of mind . . . which results in abnormally aggressive or seriously irresponsible conduct on the part of the patient, and requires, or is susceptible to, medical treatment." In other words, psychopathy was seen as a manifestation of sickness rather than sin. Despite government encouragement to set up more psychopathic treatment units like Henderson in psychiatric facilities, there has been no definite response, but Henderson itself continues to this day.

My year at Stanford in 1959 was unsatisfying largely because psychiatry there seemed to focus almost exclusively on psychopathology. Residents would listen patiently to an account of therapeutic community principles and at the end ask, "But what about treatment?" Luckily for me, San Mateo Community Hospital ran its psychiatric ward as a therapeutic community, and it was possible to demonstrate to the Stanford psychiatric residents and others the meaning of this approach to treatment.

I was reluctant to return to Henderson in 1960 mainly because my colleagues and I had become associated with the treatment of psychopaths, and therapeutic communities were seen by many psychiatrists as appropriate for this specialized area but not for psychiatry in general. We knew this to be a misconception of the whole idea of social organizations which could develop a dynamic of their own, which complemented rather than excluded other treatment approaches based on psychopathology or organic factors. It must be remembered that systems theory and organizational development were still in an embryonic state, and as yet relatively little direct support was available from the behavioral sciences. We knew we belonged more in this field than in traditional psychiatry, as taught in the medical schools or practiced in the state hospitals. We were deeply indebted to Bob Rapoport[6] and a team of seven behavioral scientists who worked with us at Henderson for three or four years and widened enormously our perspectives in relation to health and social change.

The Department of Corrections had been extremely receptive to our ideas, and Richard McGee, Administrator of Youth and Adult Corrections in California, made it possible for me to work as a consultant to this agency for four years. My main area of operation was at Chino, the reception guidance center for Southern California. I learned a great deal from my collaboration with many fine workers at Chino. An inspiring account, covering a period of four years describing one of the therapeutic communities for sixty first offenders, has been written by Dennie Briggs.[7]

But I wanted to get back into an active psychiatric setting and test the importance of social organization and therapeutic community principles, generally, in effecting positive change in social casualties. Luckily for me, a young psychiatric resident at Oregon State Hospital, Dr. Stu Hollingsworth, was alert to the growing possibilities of social psychiatry and came to see me in Palo Alto. I decided to visit Salem, and met the superintendent of Oregon State Hospital, Dr. Dean Brooks. He is a remarkable man who really loves his work, and has the capacity to make a state hospital what it is meant to be—a friendly asylum for people whose mental distress calls for a (temporary) supportive and understanding environment. I spent four happy years in Salem (1959 to 1962), where the social organizational development of the hospital flourished, greatly helped by sanctions from above. Even the four admission wards, with a relatively rapid turnover of patients, benefited by the application of therapeutic community principles.

I was back in general psychiatry and satisfied that the social organizational approach had relevance for any social system in psychiatry or in corrections.

Inevitably, therapeutic communities had relevance for the community outside hospitals and we began to envisage more involvement in the counties which referred cases to us. We began to plan county treatment teams staffed in the first instance from the State Hospital. I was doing consulting work on therapeutic communities in various parts of the United States, and on one of these trips met Leonardo B. Garcia, the originator of the Clarinda Plan.[8] Like that of many pioneers, his work has, in my opinion, never enjoyed the acclaim it deserved. His development of communal links paved the way for much of present-day community psychiatry. Certainly, he helped us to develop some excellent county units in Oregon, which had close links with the State Hospital.

It was at about this time that our therapeutic community work had aroused sufficient interest to produce a two-day conference in Salem, sponsored by W.I.C.H.E. (Western Interstate Conference on Higher Education). Here I met Dr. Alan Kraft for the first time. He was collecting ideas for the newly formed Fort Logan Mental Health Center in Denver, Colorado. This center was to become a new model for change in state hospital practice.[9,10] From the start (1961), it was planned as a therapeutic community, but its emphasis was on community involvement and minimal use of hospitalization—only three hundred beds for the Denver population of a million people. Ahead of its time, Fort Logan has had a tremendous impact on American psychiatry. Its team approach has from the start favored the development of multiple leadership in a multidisciplinary setting. M.D.'s may work under a nurse, social worker, psychologist or mental health worker as team leader. The therapeutic community principles of open communication, shared decision making and learning as a social process have been carried on for thirteen years (1961 to 1974), and have helped to attract some of the finest professionals in psychiatry to work in such a liberal environment. The evolution of social psychiatry and the passage of the Community Mental Health Act in 1963 have robbed Fort Logan of some of its innovative functions as a state hospital, such as doing home visits or crisis intervention work. But the community mental health centers owe much to Fort Logan's early community work. It has been my pleasure and privilege to consult at Fort Logan from its inception and ultimately to spend five fruitful years there as a staff member (1969 to 1974).

To return to my autobiographical theme, I left Oregon State Hospital in 1962 much impressed by the work being done by my colleagues Joy Tuxford and Stu Hollingsworth in the Marion Polk County Unit, which epitomized the wider concept of a therapeutic community with a balanced intra- and extra-mural social organization.

I was eager to try the use of power to sanction change in a traditional mental hospital in the direction of a therapeutic community, both intra- and extra-murally. Fate was kind to me and I succeeded in being made the physician superintendent of Dingleton Hospital in Melrose, Scotland. The setting was perfect for what I had in mind. Already known internationally as the first open hospital in the United Kingdom or the United States—the work of my precedessor, Dr. George Bell—it served a population of 100,000 in the south of Scotland. It had the familiar hierarchical authority structure, but Dr. Ken Morrice and other staff members were eager to develop a therapeutic community. The board of management was a group of local citizens, who proved to be wonderfully supportive and understanding. Their representative to our staff was the hospital secretary, Jimmy Millar, a wonderful administrator who smoothed the way for administrative change in a way which at times was quite heroic. Between us we had an internal commitment to change, which on numerous occasions might have cost us our jobs. The seven years I spent at Dingleton were probably the most constructive of my life. From the start, I kept a weekly record of the process of change, and hope to publish my findings in book form.* Two books published during this period[11, 12] reflect my growing awareness of the wider application of therapeutic community principles to social change in general.

We spent two to three years in developing a therapeutic community in the 350-bed hospital itself. This involved a long process of change in opening up communications between all patients and staff, and establishing a shared decision-making process at all levels of the social organization. Our treatment philosophy came to center around the concept of social learning. By this we meant a process of social interaction around any significant problem, with a view to modifying attitudes and beliefs held by the parties concerned. We realized the importance of timing, so that feelings could be mobilized to enhance learning as a social process. Our social structure was made as flexible as possible so that crisis confrontation could occur within an hour of the event. Dr. Paul Polak and I[13] published our

---

*"The Process of Change: From a Closed to an Open System in a Mental Hospital." I would have thought that the present dilemma regarding the future of mental hospitals would make this a relevant work, but publishers appear to disagree!

findings in this area, and he went on to develop the beginnings of a crisis intervention service in the community surrounding Dingleton, a concept which he developed further after his return to Fort Logan Mental Health Center in Denver, Colorado, in 1966.

Having developed a reasonably effective therapeutic community in the hospital, we began to slowly infiltrate into the surrounding community. This process was made relatively easy because of the presence of 68 family doctors who, under the National Health Service, looked after the health problems of the 100,000 people in our catchment area. We set up traveling units comprising a psychiatrist, social worker and nurse in the three-county areas we served. Clinics were developed in the three major towns, and home visits became the preferred method of evaluation of prospective patients. These visits were always preceded by a planning meeting in the referring doctor's office, and he acted as our sponsor and adviser when the family contact was made. We achieved what to me represented the most balanced coordination between the intra- and extra-mural dimensions of a therapeutic community I have seen anywhere. The value of this model was seen by the various mental health services in Edinburgh, and Professor Morris Carstairs and Professor Henry Walton were always glad to integrate our respective resources in the interests of teaching. A BBC documentary film of Dingleton aroused much interest, and Swedish TV made another documentary, which questioned the reasons for the relatively rigid structure of the mental hospitals in their country.

But I was beginning to get restless and needed the stimulation of the behavioral science scene in the United States. In particular, our developments in community psychiatry in Scotland had led me into the local schools with a view to exploring the possibilities of positive health programs (and preventive mental health) in the school educational system.

I saw the possibility of an educational revolution as being much brighter in the United States than in the United Kingdom. So I was glad to accept an appointment in the Staff Development Department at my old favorite, Fort Logan Mental Health Center, at Denver, Colorado.

But the process of leaving Dingleton after seven years seemed to me to necessitate my becoming largely redundant. This objective met, I think, with a fair degree of success. Multiple leadership in a multidisciplinary setting had become a way of life, by a continuous process of delegation of responsibility and authority throughout the system, and it would have been unthinkable (and untenable) for me to make a unilateral decision. One example of this distribution of power was my discharge from the post of psychiatrist to the Berwickshire county team. I was trying to be clinically involved both intra- and extra-murally while at the same time fulfilling the duties of physician superintendent, and making consultant trips to the United States and Europe. My frequent absences from the Berwickshire team irked them, and they fired me! They had the responsibility and authority to provide a good service to their county, and there was nothing left for me but to make way for a more acceptable and available psychiatrist.

During my final weeks at Dingleton we reached consensus on two important issues: (1) I would withdraw from my previous responsibilities and attempt to chronicle the process of change during the past seven years at Dingleton; (2) multiple leadership would become a reality so that the post of physician superintendent would be abolished. It was formally agreed that the responsibility for the running of the hospital would be shared by six people, including the three senior psychiatrists, the heads of the social work and nursing services, and the hospital administrator.

During the past five years at Fort Logan Mental Health Center in Denver, Colorado, I have had the opportunity to explore the role of a change agent in psychiatric hospitals, community mental health centers, schools (elementary, junior high and high schools) and with groups of industrialists and ministers.[14] I have had the privilege of acting as a consultant (facilitator), to help the process of developing an open system, for periods of time varying from a few days to two months.

It seems to me that if psychiatry is to extend its functions beyond what is commonly called treatment and become involved in many of the social problems of our time, then new skills and new perspectives are called for. In my experience, the present training given to young psychiatrists, and other mental health workers, leaves them with a deep feeling of dissatisfaction. To "treat" drug addicts is to bypass the deeper underlying social problems. To witness the effect of racial tension on individuals as a passive observer is to experience a feeling of impotence. But how many mental health workers feel equipped to enter such problem areas as change agents?

I feel a need for psychiatry to concern itself more extensively with the promotion of health, and not just with prevention and treatment of mental illness. Such changes are already advocated by some individuals, particularly in the behavioral sciences.

The enormous potential of the peer group in school classes to go beyond the mere accumulation of facts and knowledge, and become involved in problem-solving, critical examination of social values and learning as a social process, is just beginning to be appreciated. When children and young adults have been educated to understand the dynamics of behavior, or social, economic and cultural factors in determining one's self-image, they will have the skills to help in developing social systems and values which will enhance personality growth and mental health.

My hope is that the development of open systems in schools will prepare children for the adult world so that responsibility for one's peers' peace of mind is not seen as a burden, but as a natural part of one's social role, holding the same position in our future culture as material success and social status do today; only then can we expect the general population to understand and carry out some of the present-day expectations related to community psychiatry.

It may be that in this growth process, psychiatry will lose much of its present-day importance. My hope is that mental health professionals will change with the times and find a valued place as facilitators in such an educational system, helping people to help themselves, and largely eliminating the artifact called "illness."

REFERENCES

1. Jones, Maxwell. *Social Psychiatry*, Tavistock Publications, 1952. Published in the United States as *The Therapeutic Community*, Basic Books, 1953.
2. Jones, Maxwell, and Tanner, J.M. *Jour. Neurol. Neurosurg. and Psychiat.* II, 53, 1948.
3. Jones, Maxwell. Social rehabilitation with emphasis on work therapy as a form of group therapy. *Brit. J. Med. Psychol.*, 33, 67-71, 1960.
4. Sullivan C. Grant, M.D., and Grant, J.D. The development of interpersonal maturity. Applications to Delinquency, *Psychiatry. 20*; 373-85, 1957.
5. Sullivan C. Grant, M.D., and Grant, J.D. The development of interpersonal maturity. Applications to Delinquency, *Psychiatry, 20*; 373-85, 1957.
6. Rapoport, Robert N. *Community as Doctor*, Tavistock Publications, 1960.
7. Whiteley S.; Briggs D.; and Turner M., *Dealing with Deviants*, New York: Schocken, 1973.
8. Garcia, Leonardo B. The Clarinda Plan: an ecological approach to hospital organization. *Ment. Hosp.* 30-1, Nov. 1960.
9. Schiff, S.B. A therapeutic community in an open state hopsital. *Hospital and Community Psychiatry*, 20, 259-268, 1969.
10. Jones, Maxwell, and Bonn, Ethel M. From therapeutic community to self-sufficient community. *Ibid.* 24, 675-681, 1973.
11. Jones, Maxwell. *Beyond the Therapeutic Community*, Yale Univ. Press, 1968.
12. Jones, Maxwell. *Social Psychiatry in Practice*, Penguin Books, 1968.
13. Jones, Maxwell, and Polak, Paul. Crisis and confrontation. *Brit. Jour. Psychiat.*, 114, 169-174, 1968.
14. Jones, Maxwell. Psychiatry, Systems Theory, Education and Change, *Brit. Jour. Psychiat.*, 124, 75-80, 1974.

SUBJECT INDEX

Accountability, 193-4
ACTION FOR MENTAL HEALTH, 3
Adaptation, 93, 133
Affirmative Action, 328-30
Aftercare, 29
Attachments, 94
Authority, 310
Behavior Modification,
  techniques, 201
Belmont-Henderson Hospital, 369-72
Caregivers, 68
  clergy, 75, 77
Civil Rights, 253, 320
Citizen participation, 4, 84, 265-76, 313,
  324, 351
  and community decision organizations,
  268-9
  and power, 266, 272
  representation, 274
  and social class, 268
  training for, 275
Clinician-executive role, 295-301, 319-34
  integral integration, 299
  legislation, 322-3
Community alternatives, 20
  foster homes, 58
Community decision making, 341
  mental health agency participation, 351-67
  organizations, 357
Community mental health, 87, 130, 192
  209-18, 351
Community Mental Health Centers Act, 3,
  27, 279, 319
Community television, 209-18

Confidentiality, 245-64
  and law enforcement agencies, 254
  legal basis for release of records, 246-62
  and the media, 254
  and privilege, 246
  research on, 258
  and the Secret Service, 255
Consultation, 67, 86
  school, 335-48
Consumer protection, 253, 324
Continuity, 17, 69
Coping, 109
Cost effectiveness, 45-7
Crisis, 99, 171, 211
  and attachments, 100
  attention in, 100
  distress signalling in, 104
  identity in, 101
  intervention, 78, 105, 110
  memory in, 103
Double bind, 118
Education, public, 48
Ethology, 116
Evaluation, 53, 316
Fort Logan Mental Health Center, 374
Goal Attainment Scale, 21, 53
Group for Advancement of Psychiatry, 2
Groups,
  consciousness raising, 160
  encounter, 155-70
  mutual help, 144, 156-8, 233
    Alcoholics Anonymous, 235, 367
    La Leche League, 235, 239
    Ostomy society, 237

380

AUTHOR INDEX